OTHER BOOKS BY EDGAR O'BALLANCE

The Arab-Israeli War, 1948–49
The Sinai Campaign, 1956
The Third Arab-Israeli War, 1967
Arab Guerrilla Power
The Electronic War in the Middle East, 1968–70
War in the Yemen
The Kurdish Revolt, 1961–72
Korea, 1950–53
The Algerian Insurrection, 1954–62
Malaya; The Communist Insurgent War, 1948–60
The Greek Civil War, 1944–49
The Indo-China War, 1945–54; Study in Guerrilla Warfare
The Red Army of China
The Story of the French Foreign Legion
The Red Army (of Russia)
The Wars in Vietnam
No Victor, No Vanquished

Language of Violence

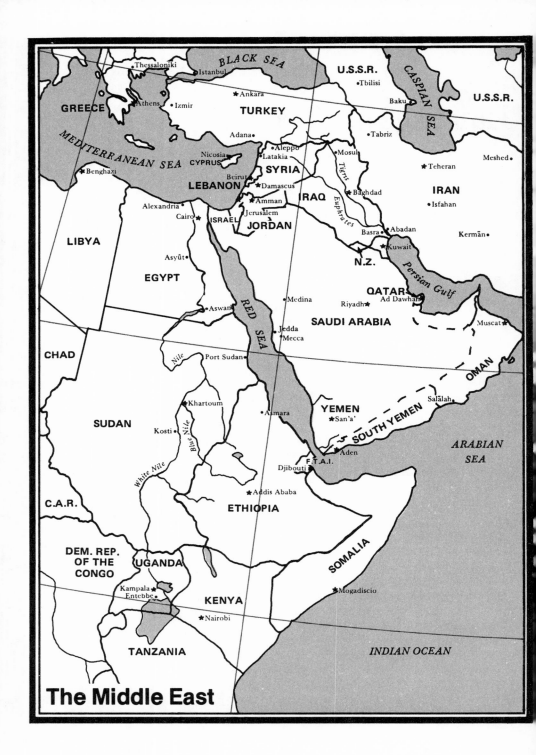

The Middle East

Language of Violence

The Blood Politics of Terrorism

Edgar O'Ballance

PRESIDIO PRESS
SAN RAFAEL • CALIFORNIA

Published by Presidio Press,
San Rafael, California

Library of Congress Cataloging in Publication Data

O'Ballance, Edgar.
  Language of violence.

  Bibliography: p.
  Includes index.
  1. Terrorism. 2. Terrorism—Near East.
3. Fedayeen. 4. Jewish - Arab relations. I. Title.
HV6431.022   904',7   79-15974
ISBN 0-89141-020-1

Book design by Hal Lockwood

Map by Vicki Martinez

Cover design by Don Fujimoto

Printed in the United States of America

Contents

1   The Weapon of Terror   1

2   Zionist Terrorism   15

3   The Israeli Mossad   29

4   The Fedayeen   45

5   Hijacking Begins   67

6   The Black September Organization   93

7   International Terrorist Contacts   129

8   The Japanese Red Army   147

9   Terror by Post   163

10 Twilight Terror   171

11 A Year of Hijacking and Horror   187

12 Carlos the Jackal   205

13 Fedayeen Sacrifice and Failure   221

14 The Entebbe Legend   239

15 The Volume of Terrorism   259

16 Fedayeen Infighting   285

17 The Terrorist Profile   299

18 The Nuclear Question   309

19 Thoughts on Countermeasures   317

    Bibliography   339

    Abbreviations   341

    Appendix   343

    Index   349

Language of Violence

1 The Weapon of Terror

Saul has slain his thousands, and David his tens of thousands.
1 Samuel 21:11

IN ITS CONTEMPORARY context the expression *terrorism* is derived from the terms "Reign of Terror," or "Red Terror," applied to the period of vindictive and deadly atrocities, committed during the French Revolution, which lasted from March 1793 until July 1794. The ruling faction ruthlessly executed people of all ages and both sexes, including the king and queen of France. During the last six weeks of the Reign of Terror, 1,366 people were guillotined in Paris alone.

French terrorist excess went to the ridiculous. In their zeal the revolutionaries even knocked the heads from statues of the kings of Judea in the Notre Dame Cathedral in Paris, thinking they were statues of the kings of France. The stone heads have recently been recovered.

The word *terror* comes from the Latin word *terrere*, which means simply "to frighten." It was well known to the ancient Romans who, for pleasure and relaxation, watched gladiators fight each other to the death, and Christians being thrown to the lions. Nowadays, psychiatry recognizes several degrees, or stages, of fright, varying from vague uneasiness to an acute state of anxiety, and from mild apprehension to abject terror. Everyone does not have the same fears, and indeed one man's fear may often be another man's thrill. While one person may suffer from vertigo, another may find enjoyment in parachuting, mountaineering, and even hang-gliding. But most of us fear death, or at least the manner of dying, and we all dread the thought of pain, injury, or mutilation. It is upon these fears that the weapon of terror plays.

Terrorism predated the French Revolution by milleniums. From time immemorial terrorist acts have included assassination, execution, arbitrary imprisonment, mutilation, seizing hostages and slaves, and a wide variety of atrocities that only fiendish minds

1

could devise. In ancient times captains freely used the weapon of terror to help them win battles, while kings unashamedly harnessed it to govern their countries, hold peoples in subjection, or simply to collect taxes. A fearsome reputation was often deliberately sought, or manufactured, by leaders, as demonstrated in the biblical song: "Saul has slain his thousands, and David his tens of thousands." Barbarities and sudden, violent deaths were commonplace throughout the Middle Ages, but they certainly did not cease then, nor did human nature change for the better.

Turning to the Middle East, the most frequent terrorist act over the centuries has been that of political killing. Perhaps the spiritual ancestor of the present day Middle Eastern terrorist is Hassan Ben Sabbah, the original Old Man of the Mountains. Unlike Sinbad the Sailor, who was a somewhat mythical character, Hassan Ben Sabbah was a real person who left an indelible imprint on the world: He bequeathed us the dreaded word *assassin,* now in universal usage.

Hassan Ben Sabbah was an Iranian (Persian) and a dedicated member of the Ishmaili sect, which venerated the Imams, religious leaders descended from Ali, the Prophet Mohammed's son-in-law. The Ishmailis had broken away from the larger Muslim Shia sect owing to differences over the accession of an Imam. One branch, known as the Carmathians, or Qarmites, organized themselves into an independent state in the Persian Gulf, which expanded until it threatened to encroach upon the domain of the all-powerful Caliph of Baghdad, but it soon declined.

Another branch moved, or was moved, southwards to establish an Ishmaili state in what is now Yemen. In A.D. 950 its army marched northwards against the Holy City of Mecca—the very font of Islam. At odds with the city's inhabitants over interpretation of the teachings of the Prophet, the Ishmailis sacked the city and removed the sacred Black Stone, which was built into the southeast corner of the Kaaba, the building housing it. This triumph was short-lived, and the Ishmailis were dispersed into scattered groups across the Middle East, persecuted by other Islamic sects for alleged religious backsliding.

The tenth century was one of heresy and religious schismatic struggles in Muslim parts of the Middle East. Of the two major rival sects, the Shia, having captured Cairo in A.D. 969, became dominant in Egypt. Three years later this sect founded the now famous Al Akzar University there to propagate its own particular version of the Prophet's teaching. The other sect, the Sunni, was embraced by the Seljuk Turks, who swept down from the north to occupy Baghdad. However, by the end of the eleventh century the Baghdad Sunni power center had fragmented into several petty but autonomous emirates. The groups of Ishmailis scattered across northern Iraq and parts of Syria lived uneasily under the domination of unsympathetic Sunnis, against whom they frequently rebelled.

Onto this scene of religious strife came both Hassan Ben Sabbah and the Christian Crusaders. The Crusaders later came into contact with Ben Sabbah's governors, and from both the Crusader Chronicles and contemporary Muslim accounts we know a great deal about Hassan Ben Sabbah.

Born in Iran in the year 1007, Hassan Ben Sabbah became well versed in the high standards of esoteric scholarship maintained in the Ishmaili sect. An indefatigable traveller, he was also a zealous missionary, propagating the Ishmaili brand of Islam. In turn he visited Cairo (the center of Shia power), Baghdad (the center of Sunni power), and other major Muslim cities in the Middle East in an effort to persuade them to forsake their own interpretation of the Koran and accept the Ishmaili version in its place—but without success.

At the age of forty, while on one of his missionary journeys in Iran, he visited the Alamut Valley in the northern mountains, some fifty miles from the Caspian Sea, which had been one of the early strongholds of the Persian Kings. He was immediately impressed by its remoteness and defensive potential. Ten years later, after more fruitless missionary wanderings, Ben Sabbah returned to Alamut, and by means that history does not exactly make clear, took possession of the whole sparsely populated valley.

Establishing himself as an Ishmaili political leader, he began a campaign of terrorism against the Sunni overlords, and was so successful that by the time of his death in 1091 his terrifying influence extended from the Persian Gulf to the Mediterranean Sea. Emirs, governors of cities, commanders of fortresses, and even religious dignitaries all took to wearing a coat of chain mail at all times, so fearful were they of death from the dagger of one of Ben Sabbah's killers.

Having firmly settled himself in the Alamut Valley, which he never left again, the Old Man of the Mountains sent out his indoctrinated murderers and waited for them to return to report to him the equivalent of "mission accomplished." By selective killing, Ben

Sabbah gained control over about fifty fortresses and fortified towns in northern Iran, and then extended his empire to take in other Ishmaili groups in Syria. The Christian Order of the Knights Templars, who came into contact with some of Ben Sabbah's commanders during the Crusades a few years after his death, were reputed to have adopted Ben Sabbah's system of military organization.

Hassan Ben Sabbah conditioned and organized a band of fearless political killers such as had never been seen before—or since. His method of indoctrination was unique. He constructed a secret garden and furnished it with all the delights promised in the Koran to the faithful when they reached paradise. The chosen were drugged, one or two at a time, and taken to this garden by night. When they woke up in the morning they were surrounded by beautiful and scantily clad houris who would minister to their every need and desire. After being allowed to savor this false—but pleasant and sensual—paradise for a day or so, they were again drugged before being taken back to awaken in their own squalid hovel or cave dwelling. To them it was as if it had been a vivid dream. Ben Sabbah then sent for them, told them that Allah had given them a preview of paradise, and surprised them by telling them exactly what each had been up to while in the secret garden. So successful was he in this method of conditioning and indoctrination that it was said he once astounded a visiting emir whom he wanted to impress with his power by sending for one of his men and ordering him to kill himself—which he immediately did.

As these political killers had been drugged with hashish to be taken to the secret garden, and also to sustain them on their missions, they became known as *hashishim* or *assassins*—a word that has since become universally synonymous with political murder. To Ben Sabbah, who selected individuals with lower than normal intelligence, they were his faithful *fedai*, or Fedayeen, "Men of Sacrifice," whom he sent out on specific murder missions in the name of Allah—usually suicidal ones. His Fedayeen would accomplish their task at all costs, even though they knew that the very moment after one of them thrust his dagger into the body of a victim the victim's bodyguards would immediately cut him down with their scimitars. Convinced their reward lay in paradise, the indoctrinated Fedayeen welcomed death. Ben Sabbah often paid his Fedayeen in advance so they could give the money to their families.

One of his first political murders was that of Nizam al-Mulk, the Persian Vizier to the Seljuk Caliph of Baghdad. He had founded the first Muslim university of the Sunni persuasion in Baghdad in 1066 as a counterblast to the religious teaching emanating from the Shia Al Azar University in Cairo. It is not known exactly how many political murders Hassan Ben Sabbah's assassins committed, but most authorities agree that it must have been several hundred during his thirty-year reign of terror. He has been dubbed the First Grand Master of the Order of Assassins — a title justly bestowed.

After his death the assassins remained as a political organization based in the Alamut Valley, but successive Ishmaili Grand Masters did not have the same flair for the special form of indoctrination and wielded a much less effective weapon of terrorism for the next century and a half. In 1256 the Mongol invasion of northern Iran, led by Hulagu, the grandson of Genghis Khan, successively seized Ishmaili forts and towns. The Ishmaili bloc that survived under the umbrella of assassination was forcibly fragmented and scattered as far afield as India and Zanzibar. Two years later Hulagu captured Baghdad and, after killing all its inhabitants, erected 120 towers built with their skulls — a terrorist symbol extraordinary. Hulagu was later decisively defeated by the Egyptians in northern Palestine. However, the cult of the assassins left a deep imprint on the peoples of the Middle East. Over the years numerous secret societies with political aims appeared and attempted to emulate Ben Sabbah's Fedayeen to further their own devious purposes. Few lasted long or were very successful, most becoming involved in factional feuds, but they murdered many people.

An Ishmaili tailpiece of interest occurred in 1866, when the claim of the Aga Khan for recognition by the British, who then ruled India, as the spiritual leader of the scattered Ishmaili sect was investigated and confirmed in a Bombay court. The Ishmaili tithe, instituted by Hassan Ben Sabbah, is now officially paid to the Aga Khan, and on certain anniversaries, amongst other dues and gifts, he is entitled to receive from his faithful followers the equivalent of his own weight in silver, gold, or precious stones. Today this custom is more symbolic than real.

Shifting for a moment to the twentieth century, the inherent tendency of secret political groups to resort to assassination manifested itself again in Egypt with the al-Ikhwan al-Muslimin, or "Muslim Brotherhood," formed in 1928 by Hassan Banna, a teacher. Its aim was to establish a theocratic society in Egypt and eventually to spread this idea throughout the Muslim world. The slogan of the Muslim Brotherhood was "Allah is our aim, the Prophet our Leader, the Koran our institution, the Holy War our way, and death in Allah's service our supreme desire." Its immediate political objective was to remove the British presence from Egypt. Although Egypt had been formally granted independence in 1922, the British army had remained as a virtual army of occupation. In the 1930s the Muslim Brotherhood began to work for the overthrow of the Wafd government, led by Mustafa Nahas, who was alleged to have compromised with the British government. He had made a treaty with the British in 1936, which allowed them to station troops in Egypt and gave them other strategic advantages in return for a British nomination for Egypt to become a member of the League of Nations. This made Premier Nahas unpopular with the Muslim Brotherhood, which by this time had taken to using the weapon of assassination. Its special method of killing was known as "garrote and hang," which meant the victims were quietly strangled at night and their bodies hung in some prominent place to be seen as a macabre symbol of terror by large crowds of people when the sun rose.

Being basically hostile to communism and parliamentary democracy, and having pro-Nazi and pro-Fascist sympathies, Hassan Banna developed the terrorist element within his organization with German help in 1940. During World War II, when Egypt was heavily occupied by huge British and Allied armies, the Muslim Brotherhood carried out a spate of killings of Egyptian politicians and officials. Under British pressure Hassan Banna was arrested in 1941, but was released a few weeks later. Anticipating that once the war was over the British and other foreign troops would quickly withdraw, he intended to take over control of Egypt by force. In case that aim was not immediately achievable, the intention was to wage urban guerrilla warfare until it was accomplished. However, British troops remained in Egypt in the Suez Canal Zone.

In 1945 the Brotherhood was responsible for the assassination of Premier Ahmed Mahir just after his government had declared war on Germany. This act began a campaign of assassination and bomb exploits that lasted for three years until the Muslim Brotherhood was proscribed in December 1948 by Premier Nokrashy Pasha. He was assassinated by the Muslim Brotherhood three weeks later. By this time, Egypt, with other Arab states, was involved in the first Arab-Israeli War with disastrous results.* Hassan Banna was himself shot dead in 1949, in unexplained circumstances, his death being attributed by the Muslim Brotherhood to Egyptian government agents.

The ban on the Muslim Brotherhood was lifted in April 1951, providing that it did not engage in political activities, a condition that was not adhered to. By this time it was at the height of its power and influence, with a membership of over half a million and a strong following amongst the conservative *fellahin*, the agricultural peasant class. In 1952 the Egyptian monarchy was toppled by the Young Officers organization, which formed the Revolutionary Council. Gamal Abdul Nasser eventually emerged as the new leader of Egypt. Nasser, who worked on developing his theme of turning Egypt into a socialist state, soon clashed with the Muslim Brotherhood, which wanted the country governed by the precepts laid down in the Koran. At first they had briefly supported the Revolution, but soon turned against it.

On 26 October 1954 an attempt was made on the life of Nasser in Alexandria, and about 18,000 people were arrested. One of them, Mohammed Nosseiry, admitted he had been instructed by the Muslim Brotherhood leadership to kill the president. A series of trials followed in which fifteen death sentences were passed, although all except six were later commuted to imprisonment. Over 300 other people were sent to prison. Once again proscribed, the Muslim Brotherhood was compelled to go underground, but it remained alive, although its activities were stifled. In 1964 an amnesty was granted to the Muslim Brotherhood by President Nasser, and members in prison were released. This was to counterbalance the Egyptian communists, a number of whom were also released from detention at the same time.

The following year a Muslim Brotherhood plot was unearthed in which a triple attempt was to be made on Nasser's life in July during the celebrations marking the anniversary of the Revolution. One group was to attempt to bomb Nasser's motorcade, and if that failed another was to blow up the train in which Nasser was riding. If this also failed, yet another group was to shoot him down on his way home. This time about 6,000 people were arrested on suspicion of being involved in this conspiracy or for belonging to an illegal organization, since the Muslim Brotherhood was again

*See Edgar O'Ballance, *The Arab-Israeli War, 1948–49*.

instantly banned. Seven persons were sentenced to death, and over eighty to terms of imprisonment.

In recent decades political murder has occurred in most Middle Eastern countries, and a number of prominent personalities have fallen to the assassin's gun or bomb. For example, the Premier of Iran, General Ali Razmara, was assassinated in Teheran on 7 March 1951 by a member of the Fedayeen Islam, the "Islamic Self-Sacrifice Fighters," a fanatical organization dedicated to opposing Western influence in the country. On the 25th of that month Abdul Hamid Zanganeh, president of Teheran University, was also killed by a member of the same organization. Zanganeh had been responsible for banning communist and left-wing propaganda in academic institutions, but he was pro-Western in outlook and thus had incurred the enmity of the religious fanatics. The Fedayeen Islam was not proscribed until November 1955. In January 1956 four of its leaders were executed and others were imprisoned. Later, on 21 January 1965, yet another Premier, Hassan Ali Mansur, was assassinated in Teheran by the same group.

In August 1949 General Hinnawi effected a military coup in Syria and executed President Marshal Husni Zaim and Premier Mohsin Berazi. Hinnawi was himself ousted in December that year, being first imprisoned and later released to live in exile in Lebanon. On 30 October 1950 he too was assassinated in a Beirut street. In the days before popular television, probably the largest audience on record to watch an actual assassination was attending a football match in Damascus. On 22 April 1955 Colonel Adnan Malki, the Deputy Chief of Staff, was killed in full view of over 10,000 spectators by an army sergeant who was a member of the Parti Populaire Syrienne, a right-wing organization working for union between Syria and Iraq. The sergeant committed suicide immediately afterwards.

On 16 July 1951, while on a visit to King Abdullah of Jordan, Riad es-Solh, twice premier of Lebanon, was killed in Amman. His murder was attributed to the proscribed Syrian National Party. A few days later, on 20 July, King Abdullah himself was assassinated in Jerusalem while leaving the al-Aksar Mosque. The assassin, Mustafa Shukri, a Jerusalem tailor, was shot and killed by Abdullah's bodyguard. A grenade and ammunition were found in his home. He was a member of the Holy War Organization, an extremist group founded in 1948 by the ex-Mufti of Jerusalem. It was suspected that King Abdullah, who had held secret meetings with the

Israelis, was about to make a peace agreement with them. In Amman, on 18 August 1951, eighteen Palestinian Arabs were put on trial for this murder. Four of them were executed on 4 September. Two were acquitted and the remainder were sentenced to terms of imprisonment.

On 17 February 1948 the ruler of remote and backward Yemen, Imam Yahya, was machine-gunned to death by a rival family, which thought it had a better right to the throne. His successor, Imam Ahmed, was one of the world's great survivors. Many assassination attempts were made on his life—at least seven in his last year. He died peacefully in bed on 18 September 1962.

An assassin's bullet found its mark in Libya on 5 October 1954, when Said Ibrahim Shalhi, minister of palace affairs and a nephew of King Idris, was killed for "personal reasons." Several members of the royal family were deported to a desert oasis. In Iraq, on 14 July 1958, King Feisal II, Prince Abdullah, the Prince Regent (his uncle), and Premier Nuri Said were killed in a military coup. Their bodies were mutilated and then exhibited in the streets for all to see. The leader of the coup, Colonel Abdul Karim Kassem, was himself assassinated on 8 February 1963.

More recently, Qadi Abdullah Ahmed al-Haji, who fought on the Royalist side in the Yemeni Civil War (1962–1969), changed sides when it ended.* He became premier of Yemen in 1972, but only remained in office for four months. During that short time he imprisoned thousands of political opponents and held many public executions. He too was assassinated while visiting London on 10 April 1977, with two other Yemeni diplomats, by a terrorist later identified as Zuhair Akache. In Saudi Arabia, on 25 March 1975, King Feisal was assassinated by one of his many nephews, Prince Feisal Ibn Massaed, who fired shots at him at a reception on the Prophet's birthday in Riyadh, the capital.

The Ben Sabbah heritage also reached out to touch the United States when Senator Robert Kennedy was shot dead in Los Angeles on 6 June 1968 by an Arab. He was Sirhan Bishara Sirhan, a Jordanian who was born in a village near Jerusalem in 1944 but had lived in the United States since 1957. He fired eight shots, of which two hit Kennedy; the others wounded five people. When arrested he said, "I did it for my people."

The foregoing comprise just a few selected examples of assassi-

*See Edgar O'Ballance, *War in the Yemen.*

nation as a terrorist technique in the Middle East; many more could be cited.

Apart from political assassination, terror in other forms has been freely used over the centuries by kings and governments to persuade their subjects not to transgress the civil code of their country. Capital punishment, now fast falling out of favor in civilized and advanced nations, has been the age-old ultimate penalty for a number of offenses ranging from murder to simple theft. Throughout history serious crimes such as treason usually merited a ghastly or painful death, such as being "hung, drawn, and quartered." This meant that the unfortunate individual was hung by his neck on a gallows until he was unconscious, and sometimes not as long as that, and then taken down, his stomach slit open, his intestines torn out, and his body hacked into four parts. Other punishments included cutting off hands for theft, branding, and disfigurement by slitting the nose. For committing what may then have been regarded as lesser crimes, punishment was by the scourge, the stocks, the pillory, the ducking-stool, and the scold, the latter being affixed to the tongues of shrewish women. Punishments were meant to be harsh and salutary, and since they were inflicted in public they attracted morbid crowds. They were deliberately designed as an object lesson to cause apprehension in the minds of all watching, in case any should be tempted to break the civil code.

In case one thinks that such barbaric practices have thankfully been relegated to the pages of history books, it may be of interest to know that Prince Ibn Massaed, the assassin of King Feisal of Saudi Arabia, was executed on 18 June 1975 by being decapitated in public with a sword. Since he was a royal prince, it had to be a golden one. At El Hasa, also in Saudi Arabia, four men were convicted of rape on 28 March 1977. Three of them, being married, were stoned to death, while the fourth, a bachelor, was decapitated with a sword. There was a public execution in November 1977 in the main square at Jeddah, in the same country, when a young commoner was beheaded. It took six strokes of the executioner's sword to sever the head. His crime was a liaison with a royal princess, who was reported to have been stoned to death. In 1978 public floggings of individuals for a variety of criminal and political offenses were instituted.

Punishments for contravention of the Koranic Law in some Middle Eastern states can still be harsh. For example, on 3 August 1977 a Lebanese man was awarded one hundred lashes in public for rape in Dubai, one of the United Arab Emirates, where earlier in the same year the civil code had been discarded and the Koranic one adopted in its place. A few days previously an Arab had been flogged for kissing a girl in public, and on 4 November 1977 a Pakistani in Dubai had his forearm judicially amputated for stealing from the home of a British pilot.

Religious authorities have not scorned to use the weapon of terror to win converts and to ensure that the faithful obey their canons. Punishments have ranged from stoning a culprit to death for infractions of the Mosaic Law in biblical times to the tortures of the Spanish Inquisition. Right up to the late Middle Ages heretics were frequently burnt alive at the stake, as were those convicted or even suspected of sorcery. The rack, the wheel, and the thumbscrew were readily applied by both church and state to obtain confessions. While such torture was not made into a public spectacle, knowledge of it was widespread enough to generate fear.

Terror also includes intimidation. The threat or indication that a person may be killed or injured or his family harmed if he either does or does not do something specified creates fear. Terrorist threats have to be taken seriously, especially from organizations that have been known to commit acts of terrorism. On 2 July 1977 it was announced in Tokyo that the Israeli Karate Team had been banned from participating in the world championships then being held in Japan, owing to Arab pressure and telephoned death threats.

Two of the most vivid instances of modern intimidation can still frequently be found in Northern Ireland and Italy. In Northern Ireland the Provisional Irish Republican Army shoots traitors or those suspected of working against it in the kneecap, both as a punishment and as a warning to others. The wound is most painful and difficult to heal. "Kneecapping" is another expression we are taking into our working vocabulary.

A similar practice is occurring in Italy, where since 1974 there has been a campaign of intimidation by terrorist organizations to defeat justice and bring the daily life of the country to a halt. Many people have been killed in shootings and bombings, including judicial officers, officials, and police. Others have been deliberately wounded rather than killed. In June 1977 fourteen medium-grade executives at large commercial concerns were deliberately shot in the leg. This practice is known as *azzoppanento,* or "laming." Responsibility for these lamings has usually been claimed by the extreme Red Brigade, whose declared objective is to "break up the components of the capitalist machine." In 1978, during the long-drawn-out trial of fourteen of the Red Brigade leaders in Italy, there was a spate of lamings in an effort to intimidate authority. Kneecapping and laming have the advantage of producing living examples of terrorist capability and intention. When death occurs, memories tend to fade with the passage of time, and with them the terrorists' object lessons.

Terror can also be induced by a fearsome appearance. Tribal warriors painted their faces and bodies with vivid colors to over-awe their enemies, and wore grotesque masks, lions' manes, tiger skins, or tigers' heads. Today the blackened face and leopard-patterned combat uniform of a commando are partly designed for the same purpose—to cause apprehension. The large, high bearskin headdresses and shakoes of the tallest soldiers in Napoleon's armies were deliberately designed to make them look like giants on the battlefield when advancing upon their enemies, and military beards and mustaches have been traditionally trimmed and twirled to give the devilish, fearsome look. George Washington's opinion of the green uniforms of the British riflemen during the War of Independence was that "it is a dress which is justly supposed to carry no small terror to the enemy, who thinks every such person is a complete marksman."

Terrorism loses its effectiveness if overdone. A surfeit tends to bring about a reaction of either revolt or suicidal resignation. Over-applied, terror may simply incite whole groups or classes of people to rise in rebellion. On the other hand, people can become used to living under almost any conditions, no matter how terrifying, as evidenced in parts of Northern Ireland.

An historical example of terrorism backfiring occurred at the Siege of Jerusalem in A.D. 70 by the Romans under the Emperor Titus. Jewish defenders who deserted or were caught foraging outside the city walls were taken, tortured, and then crucified in full view of the defenders. Josephus the Historian tells us that sometimes as many as five hundred a day were dealt with in this manner. Since crucifixion was supposed to have been the most painful form of execution known to man, the sight of their comrades dying slowly and painfully only made the defenders all the more determined to resist, if only to avoid a similar fate. In other words, they were over-terrorized. Would the famous defenders of Masada, who killed themselves and their families in A.D. 73, rather than fall into the hands of the besieging Romans, have done so if they had known they would have been given a fair trial?

The taking of hostages is another terrorist tactic which has been commonplace in history. One startling example of hostage technique was revealed in Yemen in 1948. When Imam Yahya was assassinated, it was discovered that he held about four thousand hostages in his several fortress prisons, some living in reasonable comfort, but others in abject misery. The hostages were the sons of his princes, governors, tribal chiefs, and others beyond his physical reach. Any suspicion of plotting against him or disloyalty would result in the relevant hostage being executed, and perhaps tortured as well. Imam Yahya kept two of his own sons chained in a dungeon as an object lesson in terror to his other relatives and those who might be tempted to try to wrest power from him. Nowadays, terrorists play on the modern regard for the sanctity of human life, and when hostages are taken by them, the purpose is either to obtain a safe-conduct for themselves, the release of terrorists held in prisons, or the payment of ransom.

2 Zionist Terrorism

By the rivers of Babylon, there we sat down. Yea, we wept when we remembered Zion.
Psalms 137:1

THE TERM *ZIONISM*, in its present sense, was first coined in 1886 by Ben Acher, a Jewish European journalist. Mount Zion, one of the hills upon which the ancient city of Jerusalem was built, epitomized the yearning of Jews to return to the land from which their ancestors had been evicted so many centuries previously, where they could found a Jewish state and so be secure from the persecution that had always plagued them wherever they lived. Theodore Hertzl, founder of the Zionist movement, wrote a pamphlet in 1896 entitled *Judenstaat* in which he advocated the formation of a Jewish state in Palestine, with its capital at Jerusalem. This aim was approved by the First Zionist Congress held in Basle, Switzerland in 1897.

Herodotus was the first to use the term *Palestine*. The name comes from the Hebrew word *Pelescheth,* meaning "land of the Philistines," which was possessed by the Jews in the twelfth and eleventh centuries B.C. after their biblical Exodus from Egypt. About the year 1000 B.C. King David established his capital at Jerusalem, where a few years later King Solomon built the First Temple. In 586 B.C. the Babylonians sacked Jerusalem, destroyed the Temple, and carried off large numbers of Jews, but not all, into exile. Many of these exiles or their descendants returned to Jerusalem some seventy years later to build, or rather rebuild, what became known as the Second Temple, which in turn was destroyed by the Romans in A.D. 70 when the Jews in Palestine, then part of a Roman province, rose in rebellion. Other Jewish revolts followed, which caused the Romans to banish the majority of Jews (again, not all) from Palestine, an enforced depopulation that was known as the Diaspora. The expression "Third Temple" is sometimes used by Jews to denote the present era, dating from the establishment of the State of Israel in 1948.

15

In A.D. 636 the Arabs won the Battle of Yarmuk in northern Jordan and then moved on to occupy and hold Jerusalem in one of the campaigns by the Prophet Mohammed's followers to spread forcibly the new religion of Islam. Apart from a short period from 1099 until 1291, when the Christian Crusaders ruled Palestine, or parts of it, Islam remained the dominant religion in that country. In 1517 Palestine fell to the Osmanli Turks and so became part of the Ottoman Empire for exactly 400 years, until they were driven out by Allied troops in 1917 under the British General Allenby. The Muslims had a legend that Jerusalem would only fall to the Christians when a white bull walked through the Damascus Gate of the walled city. General Allenby, who was nicknamed the Bull because of his squat build, dismounted from his horse and walked through the Gate on foot to receive formally the surrender of the city. A few years previously, Kaiser Wilhelm of Germany had not been so humble, and on his visit to Palestine he rode through the Damascus Gate on his horse.

Although the Turkish government was Muslim, as were most of the inhabitants of Palestine, there was a fairly large degree of religious freedom for non-Muslims. But there were restrictions. For example, Jews and other non-Muslims were not allowed to enter the confines of the Al-Aksa Mosque, which had been built on the site of the ancient Jewish temples. The nearest they were allowed to approach what they considered to be their Holy of Holies was the Western Wall, a remnant of the original Second Temple outer wall more familiarly known in the West as the Wailing Wall. The walled Old City of Jerusalem was a veritable rabbit warren of a slum. It was full of narrow, winding streets and alleyways, deliberately made crooked so that each door or window was out of arrow-shot from that of a neighboring one. While not exactly given equal treatment as citizens within the Ottoman Empire, Jews, and indeed members of other religious minorities such as the Armenians, could and occasionally did rise to occupy high positions of state, responsibility, and importance, or to become rich merchants. The majority of them, however, remained at the poverty level, concentrating upon survival.

To the Christians, Bethlehem and Jerusalem were the scene of the birth, sufferings, and death of Jesus Christ, and thus were sacred. The Muslims also regarded Jerusalem as a holy city, considering it third in order of sacred precedence — that is, after Mecca and Medina. Islamic tradition held that the Prophet Mohammed ascended to paradise from Haram al-Sharif, or "the Noble Sanctuary," which was the site of the beautiful Al-Aksa Mosque and the ancient Jewish temples. It was known also as Kubbat al-Sakhrah, "the Dome of the Rock." The famous golden dome is placed over a slab of flattish rock, traditionally the original Jebusite threshing floor on which King David built his altar, and which King Solomon enclosed within his Temple.

In the nineteenth century conditions of life for Jews in Turkish-governed Palestine were hard, inhospitable and hostile. Although Theodore Hertzl was gaining the confidence and support of the powerful Rothschild banking family, Sir Moses Montefiori, and other influential European Jews for his idea of a Judenstaat, the response from powerful gentiles, who were the only ones in a position to help this ideal to become a fact, was indifferent or negative. Hertzl drew a blank with the unsympathetic German Kaiser, the Russian premier, and the Turkish sultan.

However, some sympathy was shown by the British, who then controlled about one-quarter of the land surface of the world. During World War I the British government tried to persuade various Arab tribes, or groups of tribes, states, and leaders to rise in revolt against the Ottoman government in support of the Allies. It had two distinct, but opposing, successes, which were largely the cause of the present Palestine problem. Conflicting promises were made to both Arabs and Jews. When Germany and Turkey were defeated, the Ottoman Empire was dismantled and a new map of the Middle East was drawn—mainly by Winston Churchill in 1922 when he was the British colonial secretary. Arabs who had helped the British were rewarded, particularly the Hussein family. Emir Abdullah was confirmed as king of an independent Hajez, and his sons were also given kingdoms. One son, Abdullah, became the Emir of Trans-Jordan.

Palestine was given to Britain under a League of Nations Mandate, while Syria was similarly given to France. Both nations were extremely pro-Arab at this stage. Palestine was to be prepared for self-government, and no Arab doubted that it would eventually become an independent Arab state. However, the British government also wanted the support of the Jews, who had money and commercial influence, but many of them were already in sympathy with Hertzl's idea of a Judenstaat. This led to the Balfour Declaration, which was a private letter written on 2 November 1917 by Arthur Balfour, then British foreign secretary, to Lord Rothschild, the chairman of the British Zionist Federation, which stated: "His Majesty's Government view with favor the establishment in Palestine of a national home for the Jewish people," but qualified this statement in the next paragraph: "It being clearly understood that nothing should be done which might prejudice the civil and religious rights of existing non-Jewish communities in Palestine." This indecisive and vaguely worded letter proved to be most divisive.

Encouraged by the Balfour Declaration, which was given wide publicity by the Jews and was written into the 1920 League of Nations Mandate, European Jews began to flock to Palestine in ever-increasing volume. The census of 1922 showed them to number 83,000, and the census of 1931, about 174,000.

After the Armistice in November 1918, Palestine was placed under military government until it was superseded by a civil administration headed by Sir Herbert Samuel, a sophisticated British Jew who was appointed high commissioner. One of his first acts was to appoint Haj Amin al-Husseini to be Mufti of Jerusalem, an appointment of immense influence and importance to Arab Muslims, since he became their religious leader. There were two powerful, but rival, Arab families in Palestine, the Hesseinis and the Nashashibis, and as a Nashashibi had been appointed mayor of Jerusalem, another prestigious and influential position, the Mufti's appointment was a sort of political counterbalance. Seeing the rate of Jewish immigration, the Mufti began to work actively against British policy, which allowed Jews to enter Palestine in moderate numbers. In 1921 anti-Jewish riots broke out in protest against the Balfour Declaration.

After Adolf Hitler came to power, in 1934 and 1935, a total of over 100,000 Jews fled Germany and arrived in Palestine. This, of course, alarmed the Arab Palestinians.

In April 1935 riots in Jaffa developed into the country-wide Arab Revolt by the following year, instigated and organized by the Mufti. Overnight a benevolent British bureaucracy turned into a police state. For example, forty fortresses manned by armed police were constructed at strategic points to control the countryside. The rival families, the Husseini and the Nashashibi, each had their own armed private militias, which clashed violently with the British security forces and also on occasions with each other. British security forces were hastily reinforced. Arab groups, some only partly politically motivated, bent on killing, destruction, and loot, attacked isolated Jewish settlements.

In 1936 the Arab Higher Committee was formed under the chairmanship of the Mufti of Jerusalem to unite the existing Arab political parties into one group and negotiate with the Mandate government. They included Nashashibi's National Defense Party and another faction called the Palestine Arab Party. The committee told the British High Commissioner that Jewish immigration and land purchase must cease. When this demand was rejected, the Mufti gave his full support to a general strike.

In 1937 the British Commissioner was murdered by Arab terrorists in Nazareth. The British High Commissioner dissolved the Arab Higher Committee, and the Mufti fled the country. The Arab Revolt was reaching the height of its ferocity. During 1938 there were some 5,700 major acts of terrorism recorded, resulting in the death of 69 British personnel, 486 Arab civilians, and 1,138 Arab rebels. Approximately one hundred Arab terrorists were convicted and hanged. By 1939 the sting had been taken out of the Revolt.

Meanwhile, exposed and vulnerable in their isolated agricultural settlements and harassed by armed Arab gangs that roamed the countryside, the Jewish settlers developed a defense organization. In Turkish days, the Jewish settlements appointed their own guards against Arab depredations. After the Russian pogrom of 1905 a number of Jewish refugees who had undergone some form of military training arrived in Palestine. This experience enabled the Hashomer ("Watchmen") organization to develop. After World War I the Hashomer expanded into a larger body known as the Haganah ("Defense Organization"), which had a small permanent staff. The Haganah had a police, rather than military, character. The Jewish Agency which controlled it was not in favor of producing a purely military arm.

After the riots of 1929, in which 133 Jews were killed and six of their settlements wiped out, the Haganah expanded, acquired firearms, and commenced training. By 1936 it was able to give a degree of protection to Jewish settlements against raiding Arab gangs, many settlements having acquired secret stores of arms and ammunition. During the Arab Revolt the Haganah was recognized by the British authorities as the Jewish Settlement Police, and some arms, training, and other support was provided. One of several British officers working with the Haganah was Major Orde Wingate, later of Burma Chindit fame.

In 1939, when the Arab Revolt was all but quelled, the British authorities insisted that the Haganah be disarmed and disbanded, but the Jewish Agency had by this time realized the value of having a military arm. The Haganah remained in existence, handed in the absolute minimum of arms and ammunition it had been issued by the British, and went underground to continue training.

During the Arab Revolt the policy of the Jewish Agency was one of defense and restraint, and it did not really approve of the aggressive raids made by the Jewish Settlement Police under the urging of such British officers as Wingate and the more aggressive Jewish leaders. A small number of Haganah personnel, favoring the harder and more offensive action against the Arab gangs, broke away from the Haganah to form their own militant organization. Most were members of the Revisionist Party, so called because it wanted a revision of the Mandate "in favor of the Jews."

Under the leadership of David Raziel and Abraham Stern, this breakaway group was known as the Irgun Zvai Leumi Be Eretz Israel ("National Military Organization of Israel," the IZL), sometimes referred to as the "Etzel" from its initial letters. It was in effect the military arm of the Revisionist Party, and it adopted as its symbol a raised hand grasping a rifle and bayonet, with the motto "Only Thus." In 1939 the IZL retained its arms and went underground, never having been officially recognized by the British. The IZL adopted the aggressive military doctrines of Captain Vladimir Jabotinsky (1880–1940). A former leader of the Revisionist Party, he had organized and led the Zion Mule Corps in 1915, which fought with the British in the Dardanelles campaign. Afterwards, he was involved in organizing the Jewish Legion, a British infantry formation in which David Ben Gurion served as a lance corporal.

In 1941, when British military fortunes were at a low ebb in the Middle East and it was feared that Palestine might have to be evacuated in the face of the strong German threat, it was proposed to leave a sabotage fifth column behind. The Haganah volunteered for this role, and elements of it were again given arms and some military training. One member was Moshe Dayan. The Jewish Agency in Palestine offered to raise a Jewish brigade to fight with the British, and while this offer was accepted in principle in 1941, no immediate action was taken for fear of arousing Arab suspicions.

On the other hand the Palestinian Arabs were slow to volunteer to fight with the British against Hitler. Arab hostility towards the British had been roused by the four-year Arab Revolt. The Arabs were disillusioned by the fact that the British authorities had allowed Jewish immigration at such a rate. Also, their religious leader, the Mufti of Jerusalem, was anti-British and pro-German, and he urged them not to cooperate with the Mandate authorities. The Mufti spent some of the war years in Nazi Germany, making anti-British broadcasts relating to the Middle East on behalf of the Nazis. In all, only about 9,000 Arabs were enlisted into Palestinian units, the majority of them from neighboring Syria and Trans-Jordan.

In contrast, Jewish recruiting soared and the Jewish Agency eventually registered over 300,000 volunteers. At first the enlistment rate of the Jews was deliberately slowed down to equal that of the Arabs to try to avoid suspicions of favoritism, but this policy soon had to be abandoned, and eventually over 27,000 were enrolled. In 1944 the Jewish Brigade was formed and saw active service in Italy, distinguishing itself at the Battle of Rimini.

In the early days of World War II the Nazis encouraged a certain amount of illegal Jewish immigration into Palestine to embarrass the British authorities in their relations with the Arabs. This was a sad saga, since the British intercepted ships carrying Jewish immigrants, who were not allowed to land in Palestine, but were instead diverted to camps in East Africa and Mauritius. In 1940 the *Patria,* a ship chartered by the British authorities to transship illegal Jewish immigrants from Palestine to Mauritius, was blown up in Haifa harbor by Jewish terrorists, causing 268 deaths amongst helpless Jewish passengers. In 1942 the *Struma,* a ship full of Jewish refugees from Europe, was held up off Istanbul while the governments of Turkey and Britain negotiated over its disposal. The Turks ordered the ship to return to a Black Sea port, but an explosion occurred and the ship sank with all 760 Jewish passengers, a Masada-like gesture of despair and defiance.

Because of the British policy of not allowing Jewish refugees to land in Palestine, and despite the fact that both the Haganah and the IZL were fighting and cooperating with the British, Abraham Stern broke away from the IZL with a small group of dissidents to form the Fighters for the Freedom of Israel (FFI) or Lochmei Herut Israel, known as "Lehi" or more commonly as the Stern Gang. It began to carry out a series of sabotage operations. Abraham Stern was shot and killed in 1942 in a clash with the police.

In 1944 the IZL, now in open disagreement with Jewish Agency policy, resumed operations against the British authorities in Palestine. In February there were explosions in the Immigration Offices at Jerusalem, Haifa, and Tel Aviv, and the following month in the Criminal Investigation Department (CID) in Jaffa and Haifa. The CID was charged with tracking down and arresting the IZL terrorists. In April the government broadcasting station at Ramallah was seized by terrorists, and in August an attempt was made to assassinate Sir Harold McMichael, the British High Commissioner of Palestine.

On 6 November 1944 two members of the Stern Gang, Eliahu Hakim and Eliahu Bet-Zuri, killed Lord Moyne in Cairo. Moyne was the British resident minister in the Middle East, and the reason given for his execution was that he was alleged to be anti-Zionist, although official records released under the British thirty-year rule have shown this was not so. The assassination was condemned by Jews and Zionists as well as by gentiles on the Allied side. It was also openly condemned by David Ben Gurion, head of the Jewish Agency. The two killers were caught, tried, and executed for their crime the following year. At their trial in Cairo, the two assassins pleaded that "the Jews tried everything, but nobody heard them. Some of us came to the conclusion that it was necessary to sacrifice ourselves in a savage act, so as to appeal to the world to save our people." Hakim had witnessed the blowing up of the *Patria* in Haifa harbor.

The bodies of the two assassins lay in Egyptian graves until 25 June 1975, when they were exchanged for twenty Egyptian prisoners held by the Israelis. They then lay in state in the Hall of Heroes in Jerusalem, a museum containing relics and souvenirs of the IZL and the Stern Gang, and were given a state funeral. Both men were posthumously granted the rank of major in the Israeli army.

The murder of Lord Moyne was a great setback to the Zionist cause, and at the time Chaim Weizmann, later to become the First President of Israel, said that "it is one of the worst disasters to befall us [the Jews] in recent years." Winston Churchill, the British prime minister, said, "If there is to be any hope of a peaceful and successful future for Zionism, these wicked activities must cease, and those responsible for them must be destroyed root and branch." It had the immediate effect of causing Churchill, a personal friend of Lord Moyne, and until this time extremely favorable towards the Jews and a supporter of a national home for them in Palestine, to lose interest in their cause.

In December 1943 a plan had been submitted to the British war cabinet for an independent Jewish state to be founded in the

Middle East. The British plan was for a ready-made Jewish state to come into being on VE (Victory in Europe) Day in 1945. Moyne's death caused this to be shelved. The two Stern Gang murderers thus delayed the birth of Israel for three years and were responsible for the loss of full British backing. The Jewish Agency, still cooperating with the British, provided information that assisted in detecting and forestalling a plot by the IZL to bombard, with delayed-action mortar bombs, the King David Hotel in Jerusalem, then the headquarters of the British forces in Palestine.

In 1942 a conference of Zionist leaders in America met at the Hotel Biltmore in New York and produced their so-called Biltmore Program. It definitely expressed the view that there should be a Jewish state in Palestine. When World War II ended, the full realization dawned on the world that Hitler had been responsible for the massacre of some six million Jews. If the world was stunned, the Zionists were more so, and they became more determined that Jews should have their own state in which they could live in security—and that state must be in Palestine. Since the British government tried to enforce its policy of limited Jewish immigration, there were painful scenes when British soldiers carried out the repulsive task of either preventing Jewish immigrant ships from docking in Haifa, forcibly removing immigrants from the ships, or deporting them from Palestine to camps in Cyprus and elsewhere if they had succeeded in landing illegally. President Roosevelt had considered drafting a plan to absorb all displaced Jews into America and other Western countries, but this met with extreme Zionist opposition and the idea was dropped because it was "undermining the Zionist movement" and would have "eliminated Zionism's sole humanitarian—rather than ideological—justification."*

On 4 October 1945 the Haganah radio transmitter Kol Israel (Voice of Israel) opened up, pouring out propaganda against British policy. So began a two-and-a-half-year insurrection that developed into a three-cornered contest. The mobilized Haganah was not only openly fighting against the British security forces, but also against the Palestinian Arab groups as it jockeyed for position hoping to seize control of Palestine.†

Concurrently, the IZL and the Stern Gang mounted a campaign of terror against the British security forces, and a period of

*See Abdullah Schleifer, *The Fall of Jerusalem.*
†See Edgar O'Ballance, *The Arab-Israeli War: 1948-49.*

Zionist terrorism began. From October 1945 until November 1947, 127 British soldiers were killed by Zionist terrorists, and another 331 wounded. There were now some 650,000 Jews in Palestine as against some two million Arabs.

Zionist terrorists carried out numerous exploits, placing bombs and explosives in cafes, buses, and hotels, and shooting and kidnapping. Of the major incidents that can be mentioned, two occurred in July 1946. One was an explosion at the King David Hotel, in Jerusalem, in which ninety-one people (including fifteen Jews) were killed and forty-five were injured. Gideon Paglin, chief of operations of the IZL, later said of the King David Hotel incident that the attack was carried out during a rare period of "operational cooperation" between the Haganah and the IZL.* In the other exploit, five British officers were seized from the Navy, Army, and Air Force Institute (NAAFI) Club in Tel Aviv.

In January 1947 a British judge was seized from his court as a hostage against the execution of a terrorist convicted of murdering five people. The judge was released after an ultimatum by the high commissioner. On the 31st the Zionist terrorists threatened to "turn Palestine into a bloodbath," after which all British women, children, and nonessential civilians were evacuated. British soldiers, ostracized by the Jews, tended to remain in their cantonments and camps, so freedom of movement in the countryside was given over to the Jews and Arabs. In March an explosion at the Goldsmith Officers Club in Jerusalem killed thirteen and injured sixteen, and in June two British soldiers were kidnapped and hanged at Nathanya, their bodies being booby-trapped. Just before British troops were finally evacuated in April 1948, there was an explosion at the Semiramis Hotel in Jerusalem that killed twenty people, and another in a house at Tiberias that killed fourteen.

Zionist terrorists instituted a campaign of sending parcel bombs and letter bombs through the mail. Yaacov Eliav, the bomb expert with the IZL, claimed that he simply smoothed out a stick of gelignite between two sheets of stiff cartridge paper and wired it to a percussion cap that was connected to a tiny battery placed inside the folds of the paper.† This was posted in a large official-looking envelope, which when opened released a spring that closed

*In an interview in *Yediot Abaronot*, 15 September 1977.
†According to the *Sunday Times*, September 1972.

the electric circuit and triggered the explosion. Generally, the amount of explosive was excessive for the purpose.

The first Zionist postal bomb in Britain exploded prematurely on 3 September 1947 in a London postal sorting office, injuring two people and causing damage to the building. It was addressed to a senior officer serving in the British Military Intelligence Branch at the War Office and was labelled "Scientific Instruments." At first its origin caused some confusion, since the parcel bomb had been posted in Eire and there was speculation as to whether it had been sent by Irish Republican Army terrorists.

However, there was no doubt about the origin of eight letter bombs posted at Turin, Italy on 5 September 1947, addressed to prominent British politicians and senior army officers in Britain. One, addressed to Arthur Greenwood, then a minister without portfolio, was handled by someone else who felt the wires inside the letter. His suspicions were aroused and the letter bomb was made safe. A police alert went out warning personalities who might be, or had been, involved in the Palestine issue to examine all their mail carefully before opening it. All eight of the letter bombs were detected in time and defused. Other addresses had included Clement Atlee, the prime minister, Sir Stafford Cripps and John Strachey, both ministers, and General Sir Edward Spears, who had been the British resident minister to Syria and Lebanon.

The British postal service operated a rudimentary X-ray apparatus to check suspected mail, and several more parcel bombs and letter bombs were detected in the following weeks. However, this form of terror almost ceased after 29 November 1947, when the Partition Plan was passed by a UN resolution. It was probably thought by the Zionist terrorists that there was no longer any point in continuing this terror-by-post campaign, as Britain had handed the Palestine problem over to the United Nations.

But there was a sting in the tail of the Zionist terrorists. Motivated by revenge, they sent a number of parcel bombs in May 1948, just before the State of Israel emerged. One of these killed Rex Farran in England. It was intended for his brother, Major Roy Farran, who had been involved in antiterrorist operations in Palestine and had been acquitted by a court-martial of murdering a Jewish youth. The Stern Gang had openly threatened to kill him. Another security alert went out to prominent people who had incurred Zionist displeasure to examine their mail carefully before opening it. One such person was Ernest Bevin, the British foreign secretary. Two weeks later a parcel bomb was delivered in England to the home of General Sir Evelyn Barker, a former general officer commanding in Palestine. He had gained the enmity of the Zionists by his instruction to his soldiers not to buy anything Jewish, and to "hit the Jews where it hurts—in their pockets." His wife partly opened the parcel bomb, saw the connecting wires, and called the police. It contained a three-inch stick of gelignite, wired to a detonator, and had a small dry-cell battery. That was the last known Zionist parcel bomb or letter bomb received in England during that period.

As British troops successively evacuated areas of Palestine, concentrating upon keeping open only certain major communications, the Haganah rushed in to occupy the vacated territory whenever it could. Early in April 1947 the Haganah, now virtually the Zionist regular army, launched Operation Nachshom to open the road from the coast to New Jerusalem, where the Jewish population was besieged.* New Jerusalem was that part of the city that had grown up with the Jewish immigration, built and occupied by Jews. Three platoons of the IZL and about two hundred armed fighters of the Stern Gang took part in this operation. They both agreed to take the Arab village of Deir Yassin, to the west of Jerusalem. On 9 January the initial attack on this village ran into trouble, and the IZL and Stern Gang sought Haganah help. Haganah troops then attacked. They successfully captured Deir Yassin, heralded as the first village to be seized in Arab territory. The Haganah withdrew, leaving the IZL and the Stern Gang in possession. The Zionist terrorists then killed the inhabitants of Deir Yassin—254 old men, women, and children, whose bodies were thrown down wells. Most of the younger men were away from home at this time. This terrorist exploit, still the largest in the Middle East in regard to the number of victims, was carried out deliberately. The object was to frighten the Arab population away from villages and areas the Zionists wanted to occupy as British troops withdrew. Deir Yassin is now in Israel, having been renamed Beit Shaul; it is occupied by Israelis.

The IZL and the Stern Gang then held a secret press conference announcing their action at Deir Yassin and stating that it was the beginning of the Jewish conquest of Palestine and Trans-Jordan.

---

*Named after the first of the Children of Israel to obey the command of Moses and jump into the Red Sea during the biblical Exodus.

The political program of both organizations was that Trans-Jordan, which lay to the east of the River Jordan, was to be included in the Jewish state. Writing later, Menachem Begin (who had become prime minister of Israel in June 1977), leader of the IZL, said: "The massacre was not only justified, but there would not have been a State of Israel without the victory at Deir Yassin." David Ben Gurion, as head of the Jewish Agency, sent a message of sympathy to King Abdullah of Trans-Jordan. He was at pains to point out that the IZL and the Stern Gang were independent entities, and although they had agreed to take part in the operation, they were not under Haganah command.

In retaliation, on 13 April the Arabs ambushed a Jewish convoy of vehicles passing through the Jerusalem suburb of Sheikh Jarrah, killing seventy-seven people before British soldiers were able to intervene.

On 14 May 1948 Israel came into being as an independent Jewish state, and the remaining British troops withdrew, leaving the Israelis to face the Arabs in a battle for survival. Military contingents from Egypt, Trans-Jordan, Syria, Iraq, and Lebanon moved in to help the local Palestinian Arabs. On 6 June members of the IZL seized six officials of the Jerusalem Electric and Public Service Corporation, who were under UN protection, from their offices and handed them over to the Israeli government, alleging they were spying for the Arabs. The six were put on trial, one was convicted and sent to prison, and the others were acquitted and released. The First Truce came into effect on 11 June 1948, which gave the hard-pressed Israelis a breathing space. They had succeeded in holding back the combined Arab contingents. Israel as a state had survived.

Meanwhile, in an effort to find a solution, the UN intervened in the conflict, and on 20 May 1948 Count Folke Bernadotte, a Swedish member of the International Red Cross organization, was appointed UN mediator. His proposals were that the Negev, the southern part of Palestine that had been largely occupied by the Israelis after a cease-fire, be given to the Arabs; that Jerusalem and the ports be put under UN supervision; and that Jewish immigration cease. This made him unpopular with the Israelis. On 17 September 1948 Count Bernadotte was assassinated in a Jerusalem street by three men who were never officially identified, but were generally assumed to be members of the Stern Gang. For twenty-four hours no action was taken by the Israeli government, and then Prime Minister Ben Gurion ordered the arrest of members of the Stern Gang. About four hundred of them, including the leader, Friedmann-Yellin, were detained.

On 9 October the warders at Jaffa Prison, where a majority of the Stern Gang were held, were overpowered and the members of the Stern Gang were all released from their cells. Some of them escaped immediately, but others, including Friedmann-Yellin (today known as Nathan Yellin-Mor, a member of the Israeli Knesset), remained in the prison building to hold a celebration party. The press and friends were invited. There was no sympathy for the dead Bernadotte in Israel. There the matter seemed to end, as the assassins have still not been identified and brought to trial.

An interesting sidelight was thrown on the Bernadotte incident by Michael Bar-Zohar, who wrote a biography of David Ben Gurion.* He was given access to Ben Gurion's private diaries, and in one of them he came across the names of four men mentioned as being suspected of being involved in Bernadotte's murder. Apparently, Ben Gurion had tried hard to find out who the culprits were, and had asked Isser Harel, the head of Israeli intelligence, to help. Harel gave him the four names, but said he could provide no proof as to their guilt. In later years one of the named men had become a close friend of Ben Gurion, and Bar-Zohar drew Ben Gurion's attention to this name while working on the diaries. Ben Gurion told Bar-Zohar that he was the "one who pulled the trigger." Ben Gurion took his secret to the grave, but as Bar-Zohar (and others too, perhaps) know it, it remains extant. One day it may be revealed. Later, the Israeli government paid about fifty-five thousand dollars in compensation to the UN, Countess Bernadotte having waived her right to it. The murder of Count Bernadotte closed the first episode of Zionist terrorism. In 1948 IZL merged with the Revisionist Party to become the Freedom Party— the Herut.

*Michael Bar-Zohar, *The Armed Prophet.*

3 The Israeli Mossad

There are men who — it is a biblical phrase, and I am not quite
sure of it in English — are marked to die.
Isser Harel, head of Mossad from 1952 to 1963

ONCE THE STATE of Israel was established, its government, under the leadership of David Ben Gurion, faced problems of security, including the twilight ones of espionage and counterespionage. An organization had to be formed to carry out these functions. The Israelis were fortunate in that Zionists had gained considerable experience in the field of intelligence gathering over a period of years, dating back to the Arab Revolt of 1936-9, or even before that when it was necessary for Jewish immigrants in their isolated settlements to obtain as much information as they could about hostile Arab gangs that roamed the countryside, as well as about Mandate and Arab policy. The Haganah formed its own intelligence branch, which gathered what might be termed military field information, but there was also a political intelligence branch in the Jewish Agency under the direct control of Ben Gurion, whose agents infiltrated every department and at every level of the British Mandate administration. These Zionist intelligence services were helped by contacts made with sympathetic Jews serving in other national security services, and were successful in obtaining a flow of vital information from a wide variety of sources.

During World War II Zionist intelligence services that maintained contacts on the Axis side were at work trying to trace missing Jews in Germany and elsewhere. The Allies did not scorn to use them at times. They had even succeeded in prizing a few Jewish refugees from Occupied Europe — no mean feat in itself. Immediately after the war was over, the Zionist intelligence services worked both to hunt down Nazi war criminals and to smuggle Jewish refugees into Palestine. An element known as the Ha-Mossad La-Aliya, more familiarly called the Bricha, developed for this purpose.

"Bricha" was simply a code name which does not seem to be easily translatable into English.

During the Israeli War of Independence of 1948–9 the Israeli espionage services obtained both battlefield and political information, and were also active in the diligent worldwide search for arms. Jewish communities in Arab countries were a rich source of information. Even when the bulk of these Jewish communities were "ingathered" into Israel, sufficient agents and contacts remained behind. Within a very short time the Israeli espionage service had achieved a high reputation for efficiency and accuracy, and soon several other national security services were only too willing to trade information with it.

The head of the Jewish Agency espionage service, responsible to Ben Gurion personally, was Shaul Avagur, of whom Golda Meir wrote: "I have never known Shaul write an unnecessary note, or say an unnecessary word. Whatever he did, or ordered to be done, was carried out with the maximum secrecy, and everyone was suspect in his eyes of possible indiscretion."* Shaul Avagur left the espionage service in 1948 to enter politics, and he eventually became a minister. His place was taken by Isser Beeri, who left in disgrace in 1952 when it was alleged that he had faked evidence against a political leader. He was accused of creating the Israeli equivalent of the Dreyfus Case, but neither details nor circumstances have been made public.

Beeri's place was taken by Isser Harel, then in charge of the counterespionage branch. Born in Russia in 1912 and brought to Palestine in 1923, he had been a longtime member of the Haganah military intelligence branch, after which he worked with the Shai, the Jewish political espionage service during the last years of the Mandate. In 1952 the Israeli espionage service took much the same shape as it has today, being firmly under the personal control of the premier. As chairman of the Committee of Security, Harel was the executive and technical head of all the Israeli intelligence elements. Collectively, it is known as the Mossad Merkazi Lebitahon Umodiin, usually translated as the "Institution for Security and Intelligence." It is universally known as the Mossad, or "Institution," the head of which, unnamed and unknown to Israelis generally, was known as the Menuneh, or "Supervisor."

*Golda Meir, *My Life*.

Much has been written about the Israeli espionage and intelligence service, some of it fact, much of it shrewd guesswork, and some of it fiction. The dramatic impression of thoroughness, efficiency, and effectiveness was tacitly encouraged by the Israeli government in its desire to present to the Arabs generally, to Arab terrorists in particular, and to the world at large a picture of an infallible machine, the like of which had never been seen before.

In reality the Israelis developed an espionage, and a counterespionage organization that operates on the same basic lines as those of any other state which feels it needs a service of this character. In addition the Israelis have always had, from pre-Haganah days, a "dirty tricks" department, for want of a better expression, which undertook assignments that were illegal, transgressed national boundaries, or were beyond the unspoken, but accepted, bounds of the unwritten rules of the twilight world of James Bond.

Broadly, the Mossad consisted of four main sections and several offshoots. Its main tasks were espionage and counterespionage. Each of the main sections was known by the initials of its Hebrew title, the principal one being the Shin Beit, whose task was to ferret out subversion and deal with general security threats within Israel. Another was the Agaf Modiin, loosely translated as "Military Intelligence Branch" and more usually known by its initials as Aman. Aman is basically the foreign military intelligence-gathering section. It began as a branch of the General Staff and worked in a conventional manner, gaining information through the Israeli military attachés overseas who came under its control. Another section, responsible to the foreign minister, dealt with general international research and worked more openly through Israeli diplomatic missions abroad.

The fourth main section came under the direction of the minister of police and dealt with criminal intelligence, acting as liaison with special branches of other national police forces. This section had antiterrorist squads in Mandate days to protect the outlying isolated kibbutzim. Yet another smaller element was the Reshud, or Special Branch, which was involved in counterespionage operations. While each of these sections was an entity for its own particular specialized task, Isser Harel kept a firm grip over the coordination of all espionage and counterespionage activity. With direct access to Prime Minister Ben Gurion, and having gained his confidence, his was the voice that had the final say.

The Mossad had developed a network of agents in adjoining Arab countries and seemed to be progressing well when, in 1954, it suffered a setback that severely jolted the Israeli government. This became known as the Lavon Affair (Pinhas Lavon was nominated minister of defense in January 1954 by Prime Minister Moshe Sharrett), and escalated into a disputed *cause célèbre* that dragged on for years, bitterly dividing the coalition governments and ministers. Even today, it remains an issue of decided interest in Israel, particularly perhaps because many questions remain unanswered in the name of "national security."

On 6 October 1954 eleven Jews were arrested in Cairo and accused of being members of a "Zionist espionage and sabotage organization" that had been operating in Egypt since 1951. Their trial before a military court began on 11 December 1954. Amongst other charges, it was alleged that they had committed arson and caused explosions at the U.S. Information Center in Cairo and at cinemas and public buildings in both Cairo and Alexandria.

The leader was named as Max Bennet, a West German citizen, and the others were alleged to have operated in two groups. Doctor Mousa Marzouk, of Tunisian origin but holding a French passport, was alleged to be the leader of the group based in Cairo, and Samuel Azar, a teacher, was alleged to be the leader of the group based in Alexandria. Marcello Nino was said to be the liaison officer between the two groups. She admitted she had taken money from one of the accused, an Israeli Mossad officer who had introduced her to the others, but denied she knew it was for obtaining classified information. Two of the accused, Victor Levy and Philip Natanson, were alleged to have bought cases in which to transport explosives, and another, Robert Dassa, was said to have been ordered to set fire to theaters in Cairo. Four of them—Levy, Dassa, Natanson, and Azar—admitted setting fire to the U.S. Information Center in Cairo and a post office in Alexandria.

The trial ended on 5 January 1955 and the verdicts and sentences were announced on the 21st, the day Max Bennet committed suicide in his cell. Marzouk and Azar were condemned to death and were executed on the 31st despite appeals for clemency from several governments and influential bodies. Two people were acquitted, and the others were sentenced to varying periods of imprisonment. On the 31st the Egyptian minister of national guidance issued a statement on "Zionist espionage in Egypt" together with reproductions of "confessions."

The Israelis had launched this terrorist operation to try to disrupt diplomatic relations between America and Egypt, which were becoming cordial. The hope was that a series of attacks against American property in Egypt, seemingly by Egyptians hostile to U.S. policies, would sour them again. They also hoped the resultant appearance of internal unrest would encourage the British to keep their troops in the Suez Canal Zone as insurance against insurrection and instability in Egypt, which might, in turn, set alight a political conflagration in other Middle Eastern states. British troops left Egypt on 13 June 1956.

The importance of the operation to the Israelis can be judged by the fact that when Marcello Nino was married in Israel in October 1972 (she had been released just after the 1967 War), both Prime Minister Golda Meir and Defense Minister Dayan attended the wedding ceremony. Meir praised her as an "Israeli heroine," while Dayan said that "the war [of 1967] was a success enough that it had led to your freedom." However, the Mossad had not lived up to its reputation. Its operatives had been caught and its prestige slipped several notches. It had been a bungled affair, with an unfortunate ending. There the matter should have rested, but there were unexpected political repercussions.

The Israeli government was deeply concerned that the sabotage operation had misfired and that three Jews had died as the result. It wanted to pin responsibility upon someone. The finger was pointed at Lavon, the minister of defense, whose responsibility it was, but he said he had not been consulted, had not given his consent, and knew nothing at all about it. When this was disbelieved, Lavon demanded an inquiry, and a military one was opened in secret. Colonel Benyamin Gibli, the head of Aman, testified that Lavon, in a conversation at which no one else was present, had ordered him to carry out the operation. He also submitted a letter containing the phrase "according to Lavon's orders." Lavon denied that any such conversation had ever taken place. Both General Dayan and Shimon Peres, who were in almost open conflict with Lavon over policy matters, gave evidence. Peres expressed the view that Lavon was unfit for his position as minister of defense. (It should be noted that Isser Harel, appointed to head the Mossad by Ben Gurion in 1952, was in those days very much a Ben Gurion man.)

In view of the conflicting evidence the military court of inquiry was not able to reach a decision. Lavon immediately demanded the removal of Shimon Peres from his post as director general, and also the dismissal from the army of Colonel Gibli. When Prime Minister Sharrett refused these demands in February 1955, Lavon promptly resigned. His place as minister was taken by Ben Gurion, who later in the year, after an election, also resumed leadership as well. Lavon became secretary general of the Histradhut, the General Confederation of Labor, an important and influential post. No reason for this reshuffling of posts was given to the Israeli people, who were kept in ignorance of the power struggles within the cabinet. One result of the military court of inquiry was that the Aman, which had been part of the General Staff, was created as a separate department with even stronger links with Isser Harel, head of Mossad. The Lavon Affair simmered on for over five years, during which time Ben Gurion remained as prime minister and defense minister, while Lavon retained his position at the Histradhut.

To continue the story of the Lavon Affair, it seemed as though the unsatisfactory matter was over and done with and was being allowed to fade into obscurity until unexpectedly, in August 1960, fresh evidence came to light when someone (never officially named) was being secretly tried for a criminal offense in Jerusalem —itself an interesting procedure. During the course of his trial he stated that two military officers had urged him to give false evidence against Lavon before the military court of inquiry held in 1955. Lavon, still smarting under what he considered to be a rank injustice, demanded that the case be reexamined.

This fresh evidence resulted in the assembly of a special military committee of inquiry under Justice Haim Cohen, which reported on 23 October 1960 that a reserve officer (unnamed), with the approval of a regular army officer (meaning Colonel Gibli, who was also not specifically named), had instigated a third man to give false evidence against Lavon at the 1955 inquiry. The third man was the unnamed criminal, who was eventually sentenced to twelve years imprisonment on 20 November. This military committee did not express an opinion on Lavon's responsibility for the Egyptian operation, which it stated was a matter outside its terms of reference.

By this time the Lavon Affair was dividing the government and even threatening the coalition, as some ministers were in sympathy with Lavon while others supported Ben Gurion's line that Lavon had been responsible for the unfortunate terrorist mission. Lavon alleged that a "whole clique of people in the Ministry of Defense, all appointed by Ben Gurion" had conspired to oust him. This turned Ben Gurion hard against Lavon, and great man though he was, there is no doubt that during the last decade of his life Ben Gurion became dictatorial and difficult to deal with. When a spokesman of the left-wing Mapam (Lavon's party), represented in the ruling coalition, openly compared the Lavon Affair with the Dreyfus Affair, Ben Gurion became enraged and opposed the suggestion of yet another inquiry.

However, on 31 October 1960 the cabinet decided to appoint a Ministerial Commission representing all the parties in the coalition to inquire into the Lavon Affair. Ben Gurion did not attend this cabinet meeting and thus was not able to block its decision. Earlier, he had strongly opposed the Lavon Affair being handled on a political level, insisting that the correct procedure was to establish a judicial commission. On 16 November 1960 Ben Gurion had already admitted in the Knesset (the Israeli parliament) that he was the only member of the cabinet who objected to the Ministerial Commission.

The Ministerial Commission eventually reported that "Lavon did not give the order on which the senior officer relies" and that the "unfortunate episode" was carried out without his knowledge. On 25 December the Israeli cabinet accepted the findings, a decision that split the cabinet. Saying that this amounted to condemning Colonel Gibli without a trial, Ben Gurion walked out and did not vote. Ben Gurion refused to attend any more cabinet meetings, causing some of his senior colleagues to become displeased by his attitude and actions, and at least two of them, Foreign Minister Golda Meir and Minister of Commerce Pinhas Saphir threatened to resign. They said that Ben Gurion was the prime minister of Israel, and this was no way for a responsible prime minister to behave.

On 1 January 1961 Moshe Dayan, then minister of agriculture, produced two documents for the cabinet to examine, which he insisted showed that Lavon had given false evidence. Dayan attempted to prove they showed that the army sometimes carried out operations without political approval, but the cabinet was not impressed. On 10 January it was announced that a senior officer involved in a "disastrous security operation" had been discharged from the army, but there had been insufficient evidence to bring any charges against him. This was Colonel Gibli, who became Israeli military attaché in London.

On 31 January 1961 Ben Gurion called a cabinet meeting—

the first one he had attended since his walkout—at which he announced his resignation. He said he could not agree with the cabinet decision to accept the findings of the Ministerial Commission. The president of Israel immediately called on him to form another government. Ben Gurion was not able to form a coalition, so a general election was held in August, which enabled him to return once again as prime minister. He removed Lavon from his post as secretary general of the Histradhut, thus banishing him into the political wilderness. By this time many were in sympathy with Lavon, feeling he had become a victim of the prime minister's spite.

In June 1963 Ben Gurion finally resigned as prime minister of Israel, to be replaced by his nominee, Levi Eshkol, a longtime political colleague who he thought would continue his policies. He especially wanted Eshkol to follow his lead in relation to the Lavon Affair, but was disappointed. Eshkol accepted the decision —that the government of the day knew nothing of the Israeli terrorist operation in Egypt. However, Ben Gurion, who retained his position on his party's (the Mapai) central committee, continued to make virulent attacks on Lavon. The bickering within the government on this issue intensified.

On 4 November 1964 Dayan, a pro–Ben Gurion and anti-Lavon man, resigned. Three days later a group supporting Lavon broke away from the Mapai party because of Eshkol's hesitation. Eshkol was essentially a man of compromise, and although he had publicly stated that the 1960 decision to strip Lavon of the office of secretary general of the Histradhut had become "meaningless" and that there was no reason why Lavon should not reenter political life, he could not bring himself to nominate Lavon as a candidate for the Knesset in the elections due in 1965.

On 15 November 1964 Ben Gurion resigned from the central committee of the Mapai party after being outvoted on the Lavon issue, but the controversy raged on. On 14 December Prime Minister Eshkol resigned following internal disputes within his government over the Lavon Affair. By this time Eshkol, and many other ministers and political leaders in Israel, had had enough of what had developed into an undignified squabble between Ben Gurion and Lavon. The people of Israel knew of this personal quarrel, were saddened by it, but knew little or nothing of its basic causes, owing to censorship. Many of Ben Gurion's friends urged him to overcome his antipathy towards Lavon and allow the matter to subside and be forgotten; but he refused to do so. On 17 December 1964 Eshkol expressed the feelings of many in a broadcast to the nation in which he said: "In this case the two sides to the dispute are aware that the courts are open to them, but they have not appealed to the courts." On 2 December 1964 Eshkol formed a new government. Ben Gurion died in December 1973, and Lavon in January 1976. The Lavon Affair still continues to fascinate and divide Israelis, and is remembered mainly as a personal quarrel between Ben Gurion and Lavon, and not for its real cause, which was the failure of the Mossad to live up to its reputation. Had the Jewish agents involved in the Israeli terrorist operation in Egypt not been detected, there would not have been a Lavon Affair.

The Mossad, however, continued operations with other terrorist campaigns. When Isser Harel took over the leadership he reformed and activated the "dirty tricks" section. During 1955 and 1956, when President Nasser of Egypt began officially to support the Palestinian guerrillas who raided Israel from both the Gaza Strip and Jordan, Isser Harel brought this section into action and eliminated several Arab personalities. Israeli cover was good, and responsibility was not placed at the door of the Mossad. Two such incidents occurred in 1956. In one, on 11 July, Lieutenant Colonel Mustafa Hafez, the Egyptian director of Palestinian guerrilla operations in the Gaza Strip, was killed by a parcel bomb. In the other, on 14 July, Colonel Saleh Mustafa, officially the Egyptian Military Attaché in Jordan but actually director of Palestinian guerrilla operations in that country, was assassinated in Amman, also by a parcel bomb. The Muslim Brotherhood was vaguely blamed, but the Mossad had been responsible.

Part of the Mossad's activities were directed to tracking down Nazi war criminals and passing the information on to Allied governments. The Israeli government then pressed for their extradition to Germany, to be tried for war crimes. The Mossad's greatest achievement in Israeli eyes was kidnapping Adolf Eichmann in Argentina and smuggling him back to Israel for a showpiece trial. This abduction was masterminded by Isser Harel himself, who later wrote a long, dull, step-by-careful-step account of this operation, omitting many vital details.* Eichmann was kidnapped sometime in May 1960, probably on the 11th of that month. His trial in Israel

---

*Isser Harel, *The House on Garibaldi Street*.

lasted from 11 April to 14 August 1961. He was sentenced to death on 15 December 1961 and hanged at Ramallah prison on 31 May 1962.

Isser Harel also directed his attention to Egypt, where President Nasser, now securely installed as its ruler, was appalled by the rising military strength of Israel.[†] Nasser was particularly alarmed by reports that the Israelis were working on missile and nuclear projects. On 5 July 1961 Israel fired its first rocket, known as Shavit "Meteor" II, an unguided multistage meteorological rocket which rose to a height of about fifty miles. It is not known what happened to Shavit I. Shavit I made Israel the seventh nation to launch a rocket into space. It was a solitary effort, as the Israeli program ran into difficulties, apparently mainly because of an unsatisfactory directional device. It did not suit the United States for Israel to become too advanced in this field, as that would have upset the balance of power in the Middle East. Therefore, vital technical assistance was refused. Israel was not able to go it alone.

In 1959, when the French and Israeli governments were well disposed towards each other, drawn together by mutual national interests—the French were faced with insurrection in Algeria, and Nasser was supplying arms to the insurgents—Prime Minister Ben Gurion persuaded President de Gaulle to provide Israel with a nuclear reactor.[*] This was established in secrecy at Dimona in the Negev. The French did not impose any restrictions, and the Israelis were free to make any use of it they wished. The French-Israeli secret was well kept and was not discovered by U.S. intelligence until 1963. The nuclear installation had been passed off as a textile factory.

Like other Arab countries, Egypt had its own intelligence service, which while not as efficient as the Israeli Mossad was nonetheless reasonably competent. It learned that the Israelis were engaged in producing missiles and had obtained a nuclear reactor. This provoked Nasser to compete in these fields. For this purpose he hired German scientists to work in Egypt, some of whom had dubious war records and were glad to find this haven. With German technical assistance the Egyptians produced two long-range rockets capable of striking into the heartland of Israel. The first was fired

[†]In 1958 Egypt formed a union with Syria, which became known as the United Arab Republic (UAR), and although this union was dissolved in 1961, Egypt retained that designation until 1972, when it reverted to the name Arab Republic of Egypt.
[*]See Edgar O'Ballance, *The Algerian Insurrection*.

in July 1962 (a year after Israel's Shavit II). The first rocket was eventually known as Al Zafir (Victory) and was reported to have a 1,000-pound warhead and a range of up to 235 miles; the second was named Al Kahera (Conqueror) and had a larger warhead and a range of up to 375 miles. An even more powerful prototype was produced, but no details were released. Like Israel's rocket, the Egyptian rockets had directional problems, and this missile program was later phased out under Soviet pressure. Commencing in 1955, the Soviet Union supplied Egypt with arms that included sophisticated missiles, which, however, remained under Soviet control.

German scientists also worked on two nuclear projects in Egypt. One was known as Project Ibis, which was a scheme to scatter nuclear waste (cobalt-60 and strontium-90) along the Israeli frontiers. This idea was probably taken from the MacArthur Plan of 1951, part of which involved laying a belt of radioactive material across the northern part of the neck of the Korean Peninsula to prevent Chinese troops pouring southwards during the Korean War. The other was known as Project Cleopatra, which was to manufacture and assemble a crude nuclear bomb. Little real progress was made on either project, but the knowledge that they existed worried the Israelis.

Isser Harel, who was extremely anti-German as well as anti-Nazi, persuaded Ben Gurion to let him use the Mossad to frighten away the German scientists working in Egypt. In November 1962 two parcel bombs and a letter bomb were sent from Hamburg, West Germany, to Egypt. On the 27th one parcel bomb resembling a technical manual addressed to Professor Wolfgang Pilz, a scientist working on the missile projects, exploded and seriously injured his secretary, who lost an eye. The next day another parcel bomb was delivered to the factory manufacturing the missiles. It exploded, killing six Egyptian technicians. There was little doubt the bombs had been sent by the Mossad. Later, Harel said of these victims, "There are men who—it is a biblical phrase, and I am not quite sure of it in English—are marked to die."*

The Mossad also began to operate in West Germany against the scientists working for the Egyptian government. On 11 September 1962 Doctor Heinz Krug, a former Wehrmacht officer, who was in charge of the purchasing organization that bought equipment and materiel in Europe for the Egyptian missile program, was kid-

*According to Michael Bar-Zohar, *Spies in the Promised Land.*

napped in Munich. His body was never recovered. A short while afterwards two other German scientists, believed to be working for the Egyptian government, also disappeared under circumstances that amounted to murder. However, the Mossad met with failure when its agents tried to kill Doctor Hans Kleinwachter at Lorrach, West Germany, near the Swiss border.

At the request of the West German government, Swiss police monitored a meeting at Basle on 2 March 1963 between Fraulein Goercke, daughter of Professor Goercke, a scientist employed at Cairo University, and two Mossad agents who tried to compel her by means of threats to go to Egypt to persuade her father to abandon his work there. The Mossad agents were named as Doctor Otto Joklik, an Austrian nuclear scientist, and Joseph Ben-Gal, an Israeli, and they were arrested by the Swiss police. No announcement was made of this fact until 19 March.

The next day, the 20th, Foreign Minister Meir delivered a violent denunciation in the Knesset of the German scientists and technicians who were helping to develop "offensive missiles and armaments banned by international law" in Egypt, which, she alleged, were for use against Israel. She called upon the West German government to take immediate steps to end their activities. These remarks, made in the absence of Premier Ben Gurion, caused something of a political crisis in the Knesset, as Ben Gurion was trying to develop better relations with the West Germans. Ben Gurion was displeased by rumors, allegedly instigated by the Mossad, that the West German government tolerated the development of chemical and bacteriological weapons by German scientists in Egypt because such weapons were banned in West Germany. Professor Goercke, Doctor Kleinwachter, and Doctor Pilz had stated that their work was restricted to training Egyptian engineers in rocket techniques. They also added that they and their families were being threatened in "a criminal and most evil way."

On 22 November 1963 a government spokesman in Bonn said that a maximum of eleven German experts were working on missile development in Egypt, and that a larger number of Germans, as well as Austrians, Swiss, and Spaniards, were working at a Spanish-Swiss aircraft factory there. He said that the West German government disapproved of Germans engaging in armament activities in "areas of tension" but had no means of preventing it unless the laws of the Federal Republic were violated. On 27 November a government spokesman stated that according to inquiries made by the West German Embassy in Cairo there was no evidence of Germans being engaged in the production of atomic, biological, or chemical weapons in Egypt.

On 2 April 1963 members of all three West German political parties in the Bundestag demanded the recall of all German scientists and technicians working on missile development and aircraft production in Egypt. They proposed that legislation be introduced to make such activities illegal. It was stated that cooperation between West Germans and Egyptians in rocket research was contrary to the constitution, as were activities tending to disturb peaceful relations between nations. However, Israeli secret service activities on West German soil were nevertheless condemned as being incompatible with West German sovereignty.

Ben Gurion, working for closer West German–Israeli cooperation, was opposed by Isser Harel, who wanted the Mossad to continue its line of action. A full debate was called for concerning Ben Gurion's attitude to German scientists working in Egypt and the reason for Harel's resignation. The opposition parties alleged that Ben Gurion had suppressed documentary evidence on the extent of West German assistance in rearming Egypt and had caused the Mossad campaign against them to be toned down.

At a special session, Ben Gurion berated the opposition parties for expecting such matters to be openly debated in the Knesset. He said that measures had been and still were being taken in this respect, and that "they are under discussion both in the Security Committee of the cabinet and the Foreign Affairs Committee of the Knesset," where they would continue to be discussed. He added, "For obvious reasons, it is not desirable that the debate should take place here, for there are certain things which cannot be spoken of here." Ben Gurion won another vote of confidence.

On 9 May 1963 a West German request for the extradition of the two Mossad agents, Joklik and Ben-Gal, to stand trial for the attempted murder of Doctor Kleinwachter was refused by the Swiss authorities. Their trial opened at Basle on the 10th. Fraulein Goercke stated in evidence that the rockets on which her father was working were for launching satellites and not for military purposes, and that he had intended to return to Europe in 1962 but had been deterred by the fate of Doctor Krug. She said that when she met the two accused men they had made threats against her father's life, and that Ben-Gal had told her that although her father was involved in the construction of rockets for use against Israel they wanted to give him a chance because he was not a Nazi, but that Doctor Pilz would not be spared as he was a "Nazi and a criminal." Her evidence was corroborated by her younger brother and a friend who had been present at the meeting.

Joklik, the Austrian scientist, stated in his evidence that he had accepted a scientific post in Egypt in 1961 on the understanding it was not a military one, but that later he had been asked to work on military projects of a "strictly defensive nature." When he realized in 1962 that the quantities of cobalt and strontium ordered by the Egyptians were far in excess of those needed for purely medical purposes and were to be employed "to exterminate the Jews," he returned to Germany. Approached in Salzburg by two Israeli agents, he agreed to assist them to end this alleged threat. Documents were produced in the court that indicated the amounts of cobalt ordered could contaminate the atmosphere above Israel for five years with "fifty times the maximum genetically tolerable amount." Both Joklik and Ben-Gal, the two Mossad agents, were found guilty and sentenced to two months imprisonment on 12 May. As they had already been in custody for that length of time they were released immediately. This was only a limited tactical victory for the Mossad. The terrorist campaign to intimidate the German scientists working in Egypt had been abruptly stopped by Prime Minister Ben Gurion before it really had a chance to get into its stride.

It could be said the Mossad terror campaign was aborted, as the West Germans working in Egypt remained there, and were indeed joined by many others. On 21 October 1964 a West German government spokesman stated that it was well known that West German experts were working in the Egyptian armaments industry without permission. That month West German press reports indicated that at least 120 of them would be leaving Egypt and returning home by the end of that year, but by February 1965 it was estimated there were still between 300 and 400 German scientists in Egypt. Of this number, up to 40 were working on missile projects, the remainder being employed in aircraft production and in engineering. On 13 May 1965 Chancellor Erhardt assured the constantly protesting Israeli government that he would take measures to discourage West German citizens from working in Egypt on such projects.

Gradually the majority of the foreign scientists working on arms development and production left Egypt as their short-term contracts expired and were not renewed. This was due to Soviet pressure, since the Soviet government was arming both Egypt and Syria and did not want competition from local Arab arms industries. The Soviet Union did not like this sort of independence, even to a small degree, in its client states. On 7 March 1965 the West German chancellor announced that his government had decided to seek diplomatic relations with Israel, and they were formally established on 12 May. When this occurred, Egypt broke off its diplomatic relations with West Germany and withdrew its ambassador from Bonn. With a stroke of the pen, Prime Minister Ben Gurion completed what the Mossad terror campaign had failed to accomplish—a breach between the governments of West Germany and Egypt.

The intelligence agencies of Arab countries as well as the Israeli Mossad carried on a considerable volume of espionage and counterespionage during the mid-1960s. One interesting event came to light on 17 November 1964. Cries for help were heard from inside a cabin trunk at Rome airport. The trunk had just been brought to the airport by two Egyptian diplomats and was in the process of being loaded on an Egyptian aircraft bound for Cairo. Addressed to the "Minister for Foreign Affairs, Cairo," it had passed through customs as diplomatic mail. Hearing the shouts, the two Egyptians rushed forward, seized the trunk, hastily put it back on the small truck on which it had been brought to the airport, and raced away. Alerted, the police chased the truck, caught up with it, and took it, the trunk, and the two Egyptians to a police station.

When the trunk was opened a young man was discovered inside, strapped to an adjustable chair, his head encased in a crash helmet and his feet laced tightly in shoes secured to the end of the trunk, while air holes in the side enabled him to breathe. The victim should have stayed under sedation until the plane was airborne, but it had been delayed. He proved to be Mordecai Luk, a Moroccan Jew and a double agent who had worked for both Israel and Egypt. Extradited to Israel, he was tried and imprisoned, while the two Egyptian diplomats were declared persona non grata. The specially converted trunk showed signs that it had been used on previous occasions. It was recalled that in 1962 Lieutenant Colonel Zaghoul Abdul Rahman defected from the Egyptian army and fled to Rome, where he disappeared without trace.

4 The Fedayeen

I am becoming a Fedayeen fighter.
King Hussein of Jordan, 25 March 1968

AFTER THE FIRST Arab-Israeli War about a million and a quarter Palestinian refugees who had fled in terror or been driven from their homes existed in miserable circumstances in camps in the adjacent countries of Lebanon, Syria, Jordan, and the Egyptian-held Gaza Strip.* It was not until 1952 that the United Nations Works and Relief Agency (UNWRA) was formed to look after the feeding, housing, and education of the refugees. The triumphant Israelis hoped the Palestine refugee problem would dissolve, that the refugees would gradually be absorbed into the populations of their reluctant host countries, and that within a generation or so the matter would be little more than a historical memory, leaving them free to consolidate the land the Arab Palestinians had left without being expected either to readmit or to compensate them. The Armenian nation as such disappeared in a somewhat similar way in the chaos of World War I and its aftermath. Certainly, in 1948 the Palestinian Arabs could hardly be thought of as an established nation.

Leaderless, unwanted, an embarrassment to host countries and an affront to Arab pride, the Palestinian refugees squatted, helpless and uncomprehending. Those with any ability, influence, or external contacts quickly left the camps, and of those remaining only 15 percent were literate. The Palestinian students and others who visited the refugee camps were unable to break through the dense cloud of lethargy. A few of the Mufti's followers did try to organize the young refugees into small paramilitary groups to train and educate them, but their enthusiasm soon waned. The educational

---

*According to UNWRA figures (1952), there were about 160,000 Palestinian refugees in Lebanon, 136,000 in Syria, 700,000 in Jordan (of whom 400,000 were on the West Bank), and 300,000 in the Gaza Strip.

program did not really get under way until UNWRA appeared on the scene.

However, all Palestinians did not passively accept the situation, and in small, uncoordinated groups a few occasionally raided Israel on sabotage missions. Although the Israeli armed forces were generally able to contain the raiders, the Israeli authorities did admit, for example, that in 1952 there were "3,742 illegal crossings" into Israel, and that in the course of the year some sixty Israelis had been killed and another seventy injured by Arab infiltrators. The borders of Israel were then not completely fenced off and large sections lay open to infiltration. There were also many peaceful crossings, as Arab farmers who had land on either side of the new border felt they should be able to move across it freely. Yet other farmers, having recovered from the shock of being ejected, tried to return to their farms and villages only to be prevented from doing so by the Israelis.

The Arabs were firmly against fencing the borders with Israel, as that would amount to a de facto admission of a demarcation they did not wish to accept. Egypt, for example, refused an Israeli request made through UN channels to fence off the Gaza Strip. As their armed forces increased in size and efficiency, the Israeli counter to sabotage raids was to make reprisal raids into Arab territory in the area from where it was thought the saboteurs had come.

In Egypt, Nasser faced considerable domestic problems, and it was not until early in 1955 that he was able to turn his attention to what had become known to the Arabs as the Palestine problem. In the meantime sporadic sabotage raids into Israel from adjacent Arab territory continued. Feeling stronger and more confident, the Israeli reprisal policy became bolder and more aggressive.

In February 1955 an Israeli brigade group, taking the Egyptian frontier guards by surprise, moved towards Gaza, where a three-hour battle with Egyptian forces ensued. In this battle the Israelis blew up several houses alleged to have sheltered raiding saboteurs, killed thirty-eight Egyptians, and wounded thirty-one others. From that moment Nasser secretly gave arms, money, training facilities, and regular army assistance to the Palestinian raiders and encouraged them to make forays into Israel. It was not until August 1955 that Nasser openly admitted they were actually paid and controlled by his regular army.

These Palestinian raiders became known as Fedayeen, "Men of Sacrifice," a name deliberately reminiscent of the twelfth century

Fedayeen of the Old Man of the Mountains. Fedayeen raids increased in frequency and size, and progressed from simply being a nuisance to a major problem for the Israelis. Most Fedayeen raids were launched from the Gaza Strip, but after March 1956, when General Glubb Pasha, the British commander of the Arab Legion of Jordan, was dismissed by the youthful King Hussein and his restraining influence removed, they used Jordanian territory as a springboard too. The Israelis hit back. For example, in April 1956 they attacked a Fedayeen training camp near Khan Yunis in the Gaza Strip, killing over 40 Egyptians and Palestinians and wounding 110 more.* The same month the Israelis shelled the Gaza area, killing another 40 people and wounding as many more.

On 23 June 1956 Nasser became president of Egypt. The following month he publicly paraded the Soviet arms and materiel he had received, to the horror and chagrin of the watching Western World, then immersed in the Cold War with the Soviet Union. One of President Nasser's ambitions had been to construct the Aswan Dam to improve irrigation facilities, control the Nile water, and increase agricultural production: pressing needs in arid Upper Egypt with its sparse, sandy economy. He had been hoping to obtain loans for this project from the World Bank, then controlled wholly by America.

The Tripartite Declaration of 1950 by America, Britain, and France, made in an effort to control arms supplies to the Middle East, had forced Nasser to turn to the Soviet Union. This caused U.S. resentment, which resulted in the cancellation of the proposed loan from the World Bank. In desperation, Nasser nationalized the Suez Canal, an act that provoked Britain and France, both fast-fading colonial powers, into mounting a military operation against Egypt. Outraged by such blatant nineteenth century gunboat diplomacy, the United States aborted the attempt.

The Israelis took advantage of Nasser's military involvement with Britain and France to enter a brief war against him. Their columns entered the Gaza Strip and the Sinai to penetrate almost to the Suez Canal. One of the main Israeli objectives had been to eliminate the Fedayeen bases in the Gaza Strip. On the first day of the occupation, the Israelis seized all the Egyptian military and police files, which included lists of Fedayeen organizers, agents, and fighters. The Israeli authorities were able to take action to

---

*Yasir Arafat's brother, Badir, was killed in this raid.

weed them out. The seizure of these intelligence records probably enabled them to "round up and execute close to 250 Palestinians living in the Strip. In one mass execution alone 80 Fedayeen were shot down in the courtyard of a Gaza school."*

Under American pressure the Israelis reluctantly withdrew from the Gaza Strip and Sinai, but they made great propaganda capital of their swift victory in the Hundred Hours War to produce their version of the "invincible Israeli soldier" and the myth that Arabs always run away, which further depressed the Palestinian refugees. None of the Arab states had raised a single rifle to help Nasser in this war, and when it was over they remained as divided and factional as ever before, but Nasser had gained immense prestige by standing up to two colonial powers. Israel now became the main Arab enemy, and Nasser began to emphasize the Palestine problem. During the 1950s the Palestine nation was being forged in the refugee camps. The older, dispirited generation was beginning to lose influence and fade into the background, to be replaced by a new, more abrasive and vigorous one, less acquiescent to its fate.

Israel, too, was increasing its population by ingathering Jews from the Diaspora, but faced economic difficulties. Israel especially needed water to irrigate arid land. Plans were produced to construct a National Water Carrier, a system of pumps, pipes, ducts, canals, and locks to siphon off water from the River Jordan to irrigate the barren Negev in the south. Water is a precious and contentious commodity in the Middle East, and as soon as this project became known the riparian states of Syria and Jordan were alarmed. Nasser, then in the throes of pushing forward his three circles of influence, came to the fore in their defense.†

In January 1964 an Arab conference presided over by Nasser met in Cairo to decide how to react to the Israeli scheme. The conclusion was a sad one. Although all the sources of the River Jordan were in Arab territory, the Arabs were neither singly nor collectively capable militarily of marching against Israel, or even of posing a threat sufficient to compel Israel to reverse its National Water Carrier decision. Nasser said he was not ready to take military action, so the false-fronted, ineffectual United Arab Front was brought into being as a face-saver.

*Abdullah Schleifer, *The Fall of Jerusalem.*
†President Nasser's aim was to forge three circles, all based on Cairo, which would embrace the Arabs, Islam, and pan-Africa.

President Nasser was of the opinion that when the Arabs were ready to launch a military attack the Fedayeen could be used to form the trip-wire to start the war, but that in the meantime they should be firmly restricted. At the January 1964 meeting the suggestion had also been put forward that a Palestine liberation organization be formed to represent Palestinians and to coordinate efforts to recover Palestine from the Israelis. It was not immediately acted upon because King Hussein would not allow Iraqi and Syrian troops to be stationed in his territory. However, Nasser forced the issue and the Palestine Liberation Organization (PLO) came into being about two months later.

On 28 May 1964 King Hussein of Jordan opened the first PLO congress, attended by 350 delegates, at Jerusalem. Ahmed Shukairy, a Syrian who had been active in the service of Saudi Arabia at the UN, was appointed its first chairman. The PLO then took the Palestine seat on the Central Committee of the Arab League. Shukairy was completely influenced by Nasser, and later wrote that he made no move or statement of any importance without first consulting him.*

Work on the National Water Carrier began in July 1964, and at an Arab summit meeting at Alexandria the following month it was decided that the PLO would form a military arm to be known as the Palestine Liberation Army (PLA). This was to consist of small units, formed on conventional infantry lines, to be stationed in the Gaza Strip. Nasser's initial idea was that in this way he would keep a firm influence over them, but afterwards PLA units were also raised and stationed in Jordan and Syria.

Shukairy was soon at loggerheads with King Hussein, as he wanted his PLA units, then forming, to man the Jordanian frontier with Israel. Hussein would not agree. Instead, in 1965, he dissolved his 30,000-strong part-time National Guard, which had carried out that task, and which consisted of West Bank (that is, Palestinian) personnel not completely reconciled to his authority. He replaced it by units of his regular army. Shukairy had been allowed to open PLO offices in Jordan, but as the friction increased, King Hussein closed them down again and arrested many PLO members, alleging they were working subversively against his regime.

The Palestine problem seemed to be constantly festering with the disunited Arab states content to sit idly back and utter plati-

*Ahmed Shukairy, *Dialogues and Secrets with Kings* (In Arabic, Beirut: 1971).

tudes and empty expressions of support. There was plenty of talk, but little action against Israel except for spasmodic internal sabotage and infiltration raids. Then, a new Fedayeen organization suddenly appeared out of the blue on 14 January 1965, when it caused an explosion on the Israeli National Water Carrier. Other similar sabotage operations followed during the course of the year. The new Fedayeen organization was called al-Fatah and was led by a Palestinian named Yasir Arafat.* Its full title was Tahir al-Hatani al Falastin (Movement for the National Liberation of Palestine). (Many Arabs have difficulty in easily pronouncing the consonant *P*, often softening it to *F* or *B*.) The Arab initials THF mean "death," but when reversed to FTH mean "conquest"—hence Fatah.

The birthplace and early life of Yasir Arafat have been deliberately shrouded in myth. He claims to have been born in 1930 in the Old City of Jerusalem; but other, differing sources insist he was born either in Cairo or in Gaza in 1929. Most agree that he is a scion of the powerful Palestinian Husseini family, a fact he now wishes to forget. The earliest undisputed fact is that Arafat entered the Fuad I University in Cairo in August 1951 to study engineering, and while there was politically active on behalf of the Muslim Brotherhood, another fact he wishes to forget.

In 1953 Arafat founded, organized, and became president of the Palestinian Students Union (PSU), and then after a short training course gained a reserve commission in the Egyptian army. During October and November 1956 he was mobilized as a second lieutenant in the Engineer Corps, and was in Port Said when the Anglo-French attack was mounted. Demobilized, Arafat made an official PSU visit to Prague, and from there, using a false passport, he traveled to Germany, making contact with the Palestinian students at Stuttgart University. Despite the fact they were not students, Arafat had taken with him on this European trip Khalid al-Wazir and Saleh Khalif, both of whom came from the al-Burej refugee camp in the Gaza Strip and had been active with Fedayeen groups.

In April 1957 Arafat took an engineering job in Kuwait, where the following year he was joined by Khalid al-Wazir and Saleh

---

*At birth he was named Abdul Rauf Arafat al-Qudwa al-Husseini. Most of those names he has since discarded. At various times he added Mohammed and Rahman, which were dropped; and then that of Yasir, after Yasir al-Birah, a notable Palestinian guerrilla leader in the Arab Revolt, which he retained.

Khalif. The three spent much of their time engaged in political activities on behalf of the Palestinians, raising funds and producing and distributing pamphlets. Several hundred Palestinian university graduates had gone to work in Kuwait, attracted by its oil boom. That summer Arafat and his two colleagues, together with about a dozen or so others, formed the Palestine National Liberation Movement (PNLM), a political organization working openly in the Arab world. All the founders had either been members of the Muslim Brotherhood or had been influenced by it. The Muslim Brotherhood did not oppose Fedayeen movements to liberate Palestine, but wanted to wait until the Arab armies were ready to march against the Israelis; this preparation period might be as long as five years. The Fedayeen groups were less patient. The name of the PNLM was based on a double acronym: Harakat Tahrir Falastin, meaning "Palestine National Liberation Movement," which reversed read Falastin Tahya Huraa, meaning "Free Palestine Lives." Fatah was a separate and secret organization, not connected directly with the PNLM, although several individuals were members of both organizations. The PNLM was finally eclipsed.

Once Fatah was formed it was decided that Arafat would initially remain in Kuwait as the fund raiser, while Saleh Khalif would go to Beirut to establish secret cells in the typical communist pattern, and that Khalid al-Wazir should make contact with the Front de Liberation Nationale (FLN), then fighting for independence against the French in Algeria. Arab revolutionaries generally were impressed and influenced by the FLN at this stage, and were anxious to emulate it. By the early 1960s there was a surge of political awakening in the Palestinian refugee camps, where the UNWRA educational program had begun to produce favorable results. Under pressure of Arab public opinion, Arab states opened the doors of their universities to Palestinian students, as did a few non-Arab ones, such as West Germany.

The period from 1960 until 1964 was one of Fatah expansion, in which it established secret cells, made contact with Palestinian students in Europe and elsewhere, and obtained money, arms, and training facilities. The Fatah objective was to "liberate Palestine," and its view was that since no reliance could be placed on Arab statesmen to help them, Palestinians themselves must work for their own objective. As the Palestinians were not strong enough to defeat Israel on the battlefield, the plan was that Fatah should instigate acts of sabotage and terrorism inside Israel to provoke

Israeli reprisals, which would escalate into the war they were sure the Arabs would win. Fatah insisted that all who joined must give up previous political affiliations, and that the organization must remain aloof and not become involved in any Arab quarrels.

When Algeria won its independence from France in July 1962, Khalid al-Wazir, who had made favorable contact with the FLN, went to Algiers, where he was allowed to open a Fatah office. He also persuaded the government that all Palestinians in Algeria must report to his office before they were granted a work permit. He was also allowed to open training camps for Palestinians, and Fatah made efforts to persuade Palestinian students to attend courses of instruction in commando and sabotage techniques. This project never functioned well, as either the students did not complete the course, or if they did they did not remain dedicated Fatah members, but moved off elsewhere to take comfortable jobs. Only a very small number showed sufficient ideological motivation to become dedicated Fedayeen; most preferred a less rigorous existence.

The Fatah leadership looked for a confrontation country from which to operate into Israel, and received a favorable response from the Syrian government, then in dispute with Nasser. Syria wanted to be seen to outshine Nasser in championing the Palestinian cause. In January 1965 the Syrian government openly admitted it was sponsoring Fatah and that Syrian regular officers were seconded as instructors. Fatah elements settled into training camps in Syria and began to expand.

To be effective it was necessary for Fatah to have a military arm, and this was called Kuwat al-Asifa, meaning "storm troops." It became more simply known as Asifa, the Storm. The actual Fedayeen fighters who would cross into Israel on sabotage missions would be absorbed into the Asifa. Fatah was to be the political leadership, while Asifa was to be the weapon. Fatah was allowed into the Palestinian refugee camps in Syria to recruit for Asifa, but at once had difficulty in finding suitably motivated volunteers. By this time money was being received through its fund-raising activities, and as recruitment to Asifa was slow, Fatah had to buy the services of mercenary thugs. In 1964 Arafat and Khalid al-Wazir traveled secretly to Peking to ask for aid, only to be bluntly told, "When you carry out your first operation against Israel, we will help you." They were equally unsuccessful with the Soviet Union, which dealt only with Arab governments and would not look at Fedayeen organizations.

As becomes a secret organization for reasons of mystique and security, the leaders remained shadowy figures and adopted aliases, which invariably commenced with the prefix Abu, meaning "Father," a respected title in the Arab world. Almost immediately aliases became most essential. Arafat adopted the alias of Abu Amar, Khalid al-Wazir that of Abu Jihad, and Saleh Khalif that of Abu Iyad. The leaders faced the ever-present danger of arrest by governments that disliked their politics (and many Fatah leaders had dubious political careers) and hostility from those hired to undertake their sabotage operations.

Invariably, the mercenaries demanded more payment, frequently threatening their leaders and making off with arms and ammunition for their own nefarious purposes. When sent on a mission they would often simply go close to the Israeli border at night, bury their explosives, sleep until dawn, and then return to give glowing but fictitious reports of damage done and casualties inflicted.

Sometime in 1965 Fatah formed the Jihad al-Rasd, loosely translated as "war information" but later more grandly as the "Research and Information Center." More usually referred to as the Rasd, it developed into the command and intelligence section of Fatah and was headed by Saleh Khalif. Fatah also developed an efficient propaganda section to publicize its operations, real and fictional, and despite the fact that some communiqués were ridiculed by the Israelis, who on occasions produced photographic evidence to prove them false, they were widely accepted and eagerly believed in the Arab world.

At last a Fedayeen organization was seen to be doing something instead of just talking. Despite the many fictitious claims, Fatah carried out sufficient operations inside Israel to worry the Israeli government considerably. Israel admitted that during 1965 there were thirty-one Fatah raids into its territory, of which twenty-seven were made from Jordan. In the refugee camps the Palestinians were finding new hope. Somewhat reluctantly President Nasser gave Fatah air time on Radio Cairo, and so the Saut al-Falastin (Voice of Palestine) was heard by millions—both a bold propaganda tactic and a morale boost for the refugees. However, at the Casablanca Arab summit of September 1965, Nasser asked the Algerians to curb Fatah activities in their country, and this resulted in Fatah offices and camps in Algeria being either closed down or taken over by PLO representatives.

In February 1966 a coup in Syria brought to power an extremely left-wing Baathist government headed by General Salah Jadid, which decided to give more help and support to Fatah, but only on the condition that Fatah raids continued to be launched from Jordanian territory, and not from Syria. His military weakness and the wild popularity of the Fedayeen movement generally deterred King Hussein from clamping down on Fatah activities in his own country. Actually, he would very much like to have prevented raids being made from Jordan into Israel. That February Arafat was allowed to publish his own Fatah newspaper, *Saut al-Asifa* (Voice of the Storm) in Damascus, and it was immediately given a large distribution, thus further spreading the Fatah legend.

In July 1966 the Asifa in Syria came under complete Syrian military control, there being just one active protest that escalated into an armed clash in which four Fatah members were killed. Arafat temporarily bent with the wind, secure in the knowledge that his organization and network of secret cells was expanding successfully in adjacent countries beyond Syrian reach and that elements of his Asifa were enjoying exceptional freedom from national restraints in both Lebanon and Jordan. The Syrian government thought it was using Arafat, but it was the other way round; Arafat began quietly to concentrate his forces elsewhere. In Syria, his Asifa numbered only about five hundred, based mainly in a training camp near Lake Tiberias under the control of Syrian regular officers. Despite the huge wave of Fedayeen popularity, President Nasser gave little support to Fatah apart from a spot on Radio Cairo. On the other hand, the governments of both Lebanon and Jordan were losing control over Fatah personnel in their countries.

The blaze of Fatah publicity and ostensible success caused a few similar organizations to come into being, but they were only pale shadows. One had already appeared in April 1959 in Damascus, when a group of Palestinians under the joint leadership of Ahmed Jabril, Ali Bushnik, and Fadil Zahrur* formed the Palestine Liberation Front (PLF). Jabril had attended the Syrian military academy and was a reserve captain in the Syrian army, while Bushnik and Zahrur were students at Damascus University. Neither was a member of any political party, although Zahrur had some contact with the Syrian Nationalist Party, whose aim was to restore Greater Syria—that is, form a union of Syria, Jordan, Lebanon,

*Often spelled Shrur.

and Palestine under Syrian domination. The PLF organized itself into small, carefully selected cells and sections and began training in 1961. Its military element developed into three commando units: the Abdul Kader Husseini Commando, named after an Arab leader killed in the Battle of Jerusalem in 1948; the Izzidine al-Kassam Commando, named after one of the leaders of the Mufti's militia who had been killed in battle; and the Abdul Latif Zahrur Commando, named after the first member of the PFL to be killed, a brother of Fadil Zahrur. The PLF anticipated a protracted guerrilla struggle.

Meanwhile, Ahmed Shukairy was having difficulty forging his PLO into a viable political organization, being deliberately hamstrung by Nasser, who had no intention of allowing it to develop into a strong, independent instrument that would struggle free from his control. Shukairy also intensified his feuding with King Hussein, and in the hope that Fatah might become his ally he approached Arafat, but although there was some contact between the two organizations, an alliance did not develop.

For eight months Fatah was a grand tonic for the Arab world and an inspiration to Palestinians everywhere, giving them new hope and encouragement, when suddenly disaster struck the Arabs. On 5 June 1967 the Israeli air force made a surprise attack on the airfields of its neighbors and within a few hours it had made ineffective the Egyptian air force, destroyed that of Jordan, and badly mauled those of Syria and Iraq. Without air cover the Arab land forces were pushed backwards by probing Israeli columns that broke through the Gaza Strip, cut into the Sinai to reach the Suez Canal, penetrated the West Bank of Jordan, seized the Old City of Jerusalem, and took the strategically valuable Golan Heights in the north from the Syrians. It was all over in six days, in which time the Israelis had occupied about 22,000 square miles of Arab territory. They now had to administer over one million Arabs.* Only a few Arabs had escaped to swell the already crammed Palestinian refugee camps.

One of the first to recover from the shock of the 1967 defeat was Fatah, which decided to instigate rebellion and insurgency in the Arab Occupied Territories, as the areas occupied by the Israelis in June 1967 became known. Commencing on the West Bank, it

---

*According to an Israeli census taken just after the 1967 War, there were 1,385,000 Arabs, of whom some 300,000 had lived in Israel proper since 1948, as against 2,365,000 Jews.

was decided to emulate Mao Tse-tung and to infiltrate guerrilla fighters—the "fish" who would be able to swim in the "sea" of the Arab population, which would hide, succor, and support them. Arafat and his Fatah leadership set about reestablishing their underground network of secret cells and renewing or replacing intelligence contacts that had been swept away by the Israeli advance. Fatah launched a recruiting campaign in the refugee camps to increase the size of its Asifa.

When this decision was made known to the Chinese, who had shown an interest in Fatah ever since its terrorist campaign in 1965, they gave some help in the form of arms, ammunition, and explosives and accepted a few Fatah members for sabotage and guerrilla warfare training in China. At least three Chinese instructors were sent to Fatah in late 1967 (the language of instruction being English), but they were not popular with the Arabs. The main reason was that they included large chunks of revolutionary propaganda in their instruction, which did not find favor with the Fedayeen, who were religious and nationalistic rather than godless social revolutionaries. The Chinese wanted to send more instructors, but this was resisted by Arafat, and because of this Chinese aid was never received in any volume. However, the Chinese did replace some of Fatah's losses from 1967 up until 1970. There was a dull Arab silence after the 1967 War until the conference in Khartoum from 31 August to 2 September, at which the Arab heads of state agreed that there should be "No recognition, No negotiation, and No peace with Israel." This decision became known as "The Three No's," to which Nasser added a fourth in November—"No [outside] interference in the Palestine issue." On practically all other matters the Arab heads of state attending the Khartoum conference had divided opinions.

By August 1967 Fatah was ready to begin the guerrilla campaign on the West Bank and Asifa troops were filtered in as the "fish." The first incidents occurred on 25 September, when one explosion injured two people and partly demolished a building, and another damaged a factory; others followed. This attempt at guerrilla warfare was a disastrous failure. The terrain was stony, with little cover, and its small size as compared with the vast expanses of China or the deep jungles of Vietnam severely restricted the guerrillas' scope. Additionally, the Israelis had captured Jordanian security files that enabled them to make many vital arrests.

Once they realized what was happening, the Israelis mounted an energetic campaign to catch all the "fish." On 1 October they stated they had already arrested over 100 guerrillas and demolished a number of houses whose occupants had sheltered saboteurs. Within three months they had broken the Fatah guerrilla offensive, which never really got under way. By the end of November the Israeli authorities claimed they had killed 63 armed guerrillas and captured another 350, and the following month they said they had arrested 54 Fatah agents on the West Bank. The "fish swimming in the sea" strategy, as advocated by Mao Tse-tung, so universally accepted and praised, had failed dismally.

Arafat and much (but not all) of his top leadership had never been keen on a "people's revolutionary war," and perhaps the lack of success on the West Bank was in some measure due to this half-hearted conviction. Instead, he favored commando raids and hit-and-run infiltration tactics, so staging camps were established in Jordan close to the east bank of the River Jordan, now largely a de facto border from which small groups of Fedayeen could slip across at night to penetrate into the Occupied Territories, and even further into Israel proper, on sabotage missions. Indeed, on one occasion the raiders penetrated far enough into Israel to be able to lob mortar bombs into Petah Tikva, a town only twelve miles from Tel Aviv and the Mediterranean coast. These Fatah tactics proved more successful, and in the first two months of 1968 the Israelis admitted there had been ninety-one incidents.

The major part of Arafat's Asifa was still supported and controlled by the Syrian government, which insisted even more vigorously than before that no Fatah operations should be mounted from Syrian territory, to avoid Israeli reprisals. King Hussein did not like his country being used for this purpose either but he held his hand and watched Fatah personnel in Jordan warily. Arafat, also in a position of weakness, tried to avoid a head-on clash with Hussein for the moment, saying that "one enemy at a time is sufficient."

To escape from Syrian domination, Arafat established camps in Jordan to train the recruits who now flocked to join Fatah. A fairly large camp had been set up at the small Jordanian town of Karameh, about two miles from the Israeli border, where by March 1968 he had about two thousand Asifa in training. On the 23rd of that month an Israeli reigment-sized group, containing tanks and supported by artillery fire and ground-attack aircraft, crossed into Jordan and advanced towards Karameh. The leading armored column almost ran head-on into Jordanian tanks, and a firefight ensued. The infantry column then sheared off towards the town, where it ran into ambush. Most of the Asifa decamped into the surrounding hills (including Arafat, who happened to be at Karameh at that time), but a group of about two hundred stood fast and fired back despite being heavily pounded by shells, rockets, and bombs. Jordanian artillery joined in the battle, which lasted for fifteen hours, until the Israelis were forced into a fighting retreat. General Dayan, the Israeli Chief of Staff, wrote, "Our forces, mainly armor, did not remain close to their target after capture, as had been planned, but advanced eastward, climbed the ridges, and came up against Jordanian tank units." He also wrote, "Because of persistent ground mist, our heliborne troops could not be flown and landed in time on the hills round Karameh."[*]

Jordanian armor had held and blocked the Israeli tanks, but at some cost. Although the Israelis claimed to have killed 232 Fedayeen fighters and Jordanian soldiers, to have knocked out 30 tanks and to have captured 132 guerrillas, they admitted losing 29 dead and having over 90 wounded, many from Jordanian artillery fire—a fact generally ignored in Fedayeen communiqués and later myth. The Israelis left eight armored vehicles behind and lost one aircraft; the Jordanians had no aircraft, having lost them all in the 1967 War.

Hailed as a victory by the Arabs, the Battle of Karameh revealed a crack in the smooth facade of the image of the Israeli soldier and was a terrific morale boost to Fatah. Dayan said, "Our men encountered tough terrorist opposition." The size of the Israeli attacking force, and its massive use of aircraft, tanks, and guns against a "soft" target, caused Israel to lose some world sympathy. Victory though it was, Fatah training and staging camps were immediately withdrawn some miles back from the border, so any similar Israeli missions would have to spend at least one night on hostile territory.

King Hussein had not wanted his troops to become involved in this clash with the Israelis, and indeed he was far more worried about the increasing strength and intention of Asifa in his kingdom than the Israelis. Only a fortnight previously he had ordered

---

[*]Moshe Dayan, *The Story of My Life*.

Fatah to evacuate Karameh, only to face the humiliation of having his soldiers warned off at gunpoint. Accordingly, he had moved tanks and artillery into positions near Karameh to contain the Asifa. Suddenly faced by Israeli tanks, the Jordanians had instinctively and automatically gone into action against them. Jordanian gunners had deliberately disobeyed their king's order not to open fire. Caught in a cleft stick, Hussein had to echo popular Arab enthusiasm and praise Fatah, reluctantly declaring, "I am becoming a Fedayeen fighter."

The almost mass hysteria that swept the Arab world after the Battle of Karameh solved Fatah's recruiting problems. Suddenly thousands flocked to join. Accordingly, Arafat was able to select those with ideological motivation and dispense with the last of his unreliable and distrusted thugs. All Fedayeen organizations were not so fortunate. On 20 October 1968 Subhi Mohammed Yassim, leader of one group, the Commando Vanguards, was murdered by one of his own men in an argument over pay.

As it confidently expanded, Fatah was able to institute a rigorous training program that included political indoctrination, and its obvious popularity with the masses enabled it to gain greater freedom of movement and activity in Jordan and Lebanon. The money that came from well-wishers or was otherwise obtained by fundraising methods gave a greater measure of independence. Able at last to prize himself free from Syrian domination and dependence, Arafat moved his headquarters from Damascus to Amman. This caused King Hussein some anxiety. By the end of 1968 Fatah had over twelve thousand men and women, all full-time paid soldiers, the majority in Jordan. Realizing their value as teachers and inspirers, Arafat recruited many women and employed them as much as he could on political and military tasks. This was an innovation in itself in Muslim society, and one which many of his early detractors used against him to disparage Fatah. In the refugee camps, Fatah took over existing youth organizations and movements, and where there were none, organized, trained, and indoctrinated youths.

Two days after the Battle of Karameh, Fatah held a press conference on the spot. Never one to hide his light under a bushel, Arafat, appearing for the press as Abu Amar, was able to modify the secrecy that surrounded the Fatah leadership to the extent of revealing code names, but not actual movements and whereabouts of individuals. During the following months a few selected journalists (including myself) were taken secretly to various hideouts to be given dramatic interviews by Arafat. Personal publicity was restricted to a few selected top leaders, who used their code names whenever they spoke to the press or issued statements and communiqués, which they did with increasing frequency, but for the rank and file anonymity was strictly enforced and extrovert individualism repressed.

The wave of enthusiasm generated by Fatah caused at least half-a-dozen other Fedayeen groups to appear, but as before, the small organizations had to struggle hard to survive. One formed in Syria with some government approval was known as the Vanguard of the Popular Revolution which after the Battle of Karameh, under the direction of Zuhair Mohsin, became known as the Saiqa (Storm). This became completely government controlled and concentrated upon recruiting Palestinian Baathists, its strength rising to almost three hundred by the beginning of 1969. Also in 1968, the PLA formed its own Fedayeen group known as the Popular Liberation Force, but this was never effective.

One of the most dynamic Fedayeen organizations that appeared was the Popular Front for the Liberation of Palestine (PFLP), which was formed on 7 December 1967 as a merger of the Heroes of the Return, the Vengeance of Youth, and the Popular Liberation Front. Led by George Habash, a Christian Arab born at Lod (then Lydda), it had a Marxist-Socialist platform rather than a religious one. After qualifying as a doctor at the American University at Beirut, Habash spent some time practicing in the refugee camps after the 1948 War. He then set up a medical practice in Amman in partnership with Wadia Hadad, also a socialist revolutionary. A Christian Arab born in Safad, Hadad was the son of Elias Nasralla, a famous Arab scholar. Habash and Hadad were reputed to hand out propaganda leaflets with their prescriptions.

From Amman, Habash and Hadad moved in 1952 to Lebanon, where they formed the Arab Nationalist Movement (ANM), known generally as the Haraka, from its full title in Arabic, Haraka al-Kuamiyyim al-Arab. At first the ANM tended to have a nationalist character, and for a while Habash worked with Nasser on the theme of Arab unity. During the early 1960s Habash's ANM spread to Syria, Iraq, Jordan, Lebanon, Aden, and Yemen. In July 1966 Habash was arrested on suspicion of being involved in the attempted coup in Baghdad by Aref Abdul Razzak against President Aref.

Michael Aflak, a colleague of Habash's who was a Christian Arab and a social revolutionary, had to flee from the Middle East about this time. After the 1967 War the ANM developed left-wing views.

The PFLP was initially formed as the military arm of the ANM, which by the late 1960s was falling apart after being proscribed in several Arab countries. Neither the Syrians nor the Iraqis liked or trusted George Habash, and both were extremely reluctant to allow the PFLP to operate on their territory. The Syrian government, then backing Fatah, claimed that Habash's ANM was plotting against President Atashi's coalition government. On 21 March 1968, just two days before the Battle of Karameh, three prominent PFLP members were arrested in Damascus.

By this time the various Fedayeen groups were beginning to move into individual refugee camps, staking them out as their own exclusive stamping grounds and using them as headquarters, a refuge, and a recruiting base. For example, the PFLP took over the Baaka Camp, near Amman, and quickly rooted out all opposition. Like Fatah, the PFLP took over existing youth organizations in the camp. An intellectual and revolutionary thinker, George Habash was extremely selective and concentrated upon enlisting the better educated and ideologically orientated person with some degree of sophistication into his PFLP—unlike Fatah, which at this stage was concentrating upon rapid expansion.

Meanwhile, Arafat was astutely active on the political side of the Fedayeen struggle and was maneuvering to take full control of the PLO, which had almost fallen apart during, and immediately after, the 1967 War. Ahmed Shukairy, its chairman, had ignominiously decamped to Damascus to be replaced by a collective leadership held together by Yahya Hamouda. Arafat was also anxious to bring under his control several other Fedayeen organizations that were springing into existence on the crest of the wave of popularity stimulated by his Fatah.

The period from 1967 to 1969 was one of internal poverty for the Fatah organization. Forcible fund raising at this time occasionally amounted to extortion. The PLO received no money direct from the Arab oil states during that period, but was able to persuade them to deduct a small percentage, usually about 5 percent, from the salaries of all Palestinians working in their countries and forward it to the PLO. As Arafat virtually controlled the PLO, he was able to direct the major part of the money to Fatah, only doling out small amounts to other groups to buy their compliance. He gave nothing, for example, to the PFLP, which had to rely upon its own sources to obtain money and materiel support.

When short of money, arms, or facilities, the Fedayeen groups tried to obtain them from external sources, including both the Soviet Union and China. Although the Soviet government openly supported "approved movements of national liberation" that of the Palestinians was not included. The Soviet government considered the Palestine problem to be a refugee one. On the other hand, hostile generally to Israel, the Soviet government did not include Zionism as one of its approved movements either, classing it as a "bourgeois racialist ideology." The Soviet Union had voted for and recognized the UN 1947 Palestine Partition Plan, regarding the map produced with it as defining the legal boundaries of Israel. It had never accepted that some 4,200 square miles of territory outside those boundaries captured by Israel by force of arms in 1948–49 were a legal gain. Since June 1967 the Soviet government had consistently insisted that the Israelis should withdraw from the Occupied Territories.

Terrorism as such, with certain exceptions, generally had little or no support from the Soviet Union, and was regarded by Lenin and the early Bolsheviks as being counterproductive. It preferred a "controlled conflict" in the territory in which a "war of national liberation" of which it approved was being fought. It preferred the means of liberation to be acts of sabotage or resistance rather than naked acts of terrorism. Moreover, the Soviet Union only backed such wars when they had a good chance of succeeding, and did not offer any opportunity for Western participation, intervention, or exploitation, any of which might lead to escalation.

In the 1960s the Soviet Union was only prepared to support resistance action in Israel and the Occupied Territories, by which it meant demonstrations and civil disobedience. It did not like the Fedayeen penchant for terrorism, and certainly strongly disapproved of terrorist acts committed outside Israel and the Occupied Territories, condemning them as "leftist adventurism." Consequently, the Soviet Union gave little aid to the Fedayeen.

Ahmed Shukairy, when chairman of the PLO, had been continually rebuffed by the Soviet government, leaving him no alternative but to turn to distant China to ask for help. Several Fedayeen leaders visited that country in the early 1960s and were favorably received. Indeed, in 1965 Shukairy himself visited Peking and was allowed to open a PLO office there. China wanted to export to the Middle East, and elsewhere, its own concept of a "people's revolutionary war," but this did not appeal to the more traditionally minded leaders such as Arafat, who only obtained miniscule materiel aid. Fedayeen leaders such as Habash and Jabril were more receptive to Chinese political philosophy, although it is doubtful that they interpreted it the way the Chinese did. Even so, they too received only small amounts of help.

It was not until after the Battle of Karameh that the Soviet Union realized that the Fedayeen (and Fatah in particular) were a real factor in the Middle East, an attitude that may have been encouraged by Nasser, then in a pro-Fatah mood. The Soviet Union was basing its Middle East policy firmly on Egypt at that time.

When he visited the Soviet Union in July 1968, Nasser took Arafat with him, only to find that the Soviet government still considered the Palestine problem to be a refugee problem only. Some progress was made in changing this attitude, and the joint Soviet-Egyptian communiqué contained for the first time such phrases as "the Palestine partisan movement" and "the Palestine resistance movement." It also supported the "legitimate rights of the Palestine Arabs." This was a big step forward for Arafat, although the Soviet government would not commit itself to recognizing the PLO, meaning Arafat, as the sole representative of the Palestinians. It was concerned about the many sharp differences within the PLO and tended to favor the Marxist groups such as the PFLP. Arafat was decidedly not a Marxist. After July 1968 the Soviet Union supplied quantities of arms to the PLO for its Fedayeen groups, but not directly, as they were channeled either through East European countries or through Middle Eastern states such as Syria or Iraq.

Yasir Arafat persuaded thirteen Fedayeen organizations to send representatives to a conference with him in Cairo on 20 January 1968. None arrived from the collective leadership of the PLO, while the PFLP representative, after denouncing Arafat and Fatah as being "too nationalistic and parochially minded," walked out of the conference. It was true that Fatah had considerable support from the nationalists, and also from sympathizers with the banned Muslim Brotherhood; in short, it had a broad center section of religious, conservative, middle-of-the-road Arab support. However,

Arafat was able to gain a measure of unanimity from the other twelve groups at his conference for his suggestion that all their Fedayeen efforts should be pooled to liberate Palestine as an entity, and not simply be directed to avenging the 1967 War, which was then the prevailing mood of many.

On 20 March 1968 Arafat was able to cajole Habash of the PFLP and Yahya Hamouda of the PLO to meet him. He tried to persuade them they should all work together, but the Battle of Karameh occurred three days later, so his efforts were nullified, as each Fedayeen group saw an instant opportunity to expand and become influential in its own right. However, Arafat was persistent, and by Fatah infiltration and political maneuvering he managed to gain control of the PLO when it met in July 1968. In the session that lasted from the 10th to the 17th of that month, the PLO produced a document that became known as the Palestine National Covenant. It was a revised manifesto that boldly asserted that the only way to liberate Palestine was by armed struggle. Born in war and fostered in the refugee camps, the Palestine nation at last had a birth certificate. The slogan "national unity, mobilization, and liberation" was coined for the Palestinian people. In November Arafat attempted to establish a coordinating council to control all Fedayeen activity against Israel, but was unsuccessful because there were so many shades of opinion and so many opinionated individuals involved.

At the PLO conference in July Arafat pushed forward the idea of forming a Palestine National Council or Congress (PNC), on which all Fedayeen groups and others would be represented. This came to fruition on 9 January 1969, when an election was held for 104 seats provisionally allocated to the PNC at a meeting of all interested parties. In this contest Fatah gained 33 seats, the PFLP 12, the Vanguards of the Popular Liberation War 12, the PLO Central Committee 11, the PLA 5, the Student Unions and Women's Federations 3, and Independents 28. Having no teeth, the PNC became a talking shop, a sort of parliament-in-exile in which the number of seats was progressively increased, some being merely for observers.

Individualism in the extremist groups was rife, and the PFLP split on 23 February 1969. After much argument and some scuffles, a left-wing faction led by Nayef Hawatmeh, a Christian Palestinian and a member of ANM with distinct Marxist views, broke away to form the Democratic Popular Front for the Liberation of

Palestine (DPFLP). It became known as the Democratic Popular Front (DPF).* Hawatmeh, a founder-member of the PFLP, was a former teacher who had made fruitful early contacts with the Soviet bloc and had also been actively engaged with subversive movements in Aden, then struggling against the British occupation. The platform of the DPF was that Palestine was to be a binational state for both Arabs and Jews. Hawatmeh, who had already visited both the Soviet Union and Hungary, called for greater resistance in the Occupied Territories, the creation of a Palestinian proletariat, and a war of liberation against "Imperialism and Zionism." The order of his priorities was of interest.

Two other splinter groups fell away from the PFLP during 1969 to form their own separate organizations. One became the Front for the Popular Struggle (FPS), led by Ahmed Jabril, one of the founding members of the PFLP and former leader of the PLF. The FPS was often referred to as the PFLP General Command, or the Jabril Front. Another was the Action Group for the Liberation of Palestine (AGLP), led by Fadil Zahrur, also formerly of the PFL. Both were soon to make their mark internationally. Another Fedayeen group that appeared about this time was the Palestinian National Front (PNF), created by the Jordanian Communist Party, led by Abdul Jawad Salah, with some encouragement from the Soviet Union.

The newly elected PNC met in Cairo on 4 February 1969, and Arafat was elected chairman of the eleven-man Central Committee, which consisted of four Fatah members, two Saiqa, two PLO, and three independents. The PLO was not represented at this meeting, so Arafat informally slipped sideways into the office to which he was later formally elected—that of chairman of the PLO. Feeling it was entitled to more than twelve seats on the PNC, as it claimed it had carried out more spectacular terrorist acts than any other Fedayeen group, the PFLP did not attend this meeting either. The following day, the 5th, President Nasser publicly approved the PNC decisions. As Nasser was the most powerful and influential head of state in the Middle East at the time, this gave a wide impression of his solid backing of the Fedayeen movement. Also, Arafat was pleased with Nasser's attitude, reading into it personal praise and support.

On 2 April 1969 Arafat formed the Palestine Armed Struggle

*Sometimes written as Popular Democratic Front.

Command (PASC), which embraced most, but not all, of the Fedayeen groups. Initially, the DPF was not willing to join, but later in the year it changed its mind and became a member. Habash's PFLP did not join it at all. On 16 May 1969 "Palestine Day" was celebrated throughout the Arab world with parades, rallies, and speeches in Arab capitals, cities, and refugee camps. It was a day that was marked by terrorist grenade incidents in Jerusalem, Gaza, and other parts of Israel and the Occupied Territories.

Differences arising between the PLO and the Iraqi government led to the defection of the commander of the PLA, Brigadier Mahdat Budeiry, and in his place Arafat appointed Brigadier Abdul Yahya in June 1969. From his refuge in Iraq, Budeiry still insisted he was the rightful commander of the PLA. It was evident that Arafat was not yet the universally accepted leader of the PLO (and thus of the Fedayeen movement) and that he had many rivals, detractors, and critics when it was announced on 7 July 1969 by a Fatah spokesman in Amman that an assassination attempt had been made against him by means of a parcel bomb. Perhaps the highlight of the year for Arafat came on December 19, when he attended the Arab summit meeting at Rabat, Morocco as an observer. At last he was being recognized as the leader of the PLO and an influence in Middle Eastern affairs by Arab heads of state. Arafat's political scheming was showing results.

Meanwhile, on the ground in the Jordan Valley a sort of stalemate set in. After the Battle of Karameh the Fedayeen had pulled back their training and staging camps some miles. Such Fedayeen activity as occurred was countered by the Israelis, who set up ambushes on paths leading westwards from the River Jordan, studded the area with sensor devices, and erected electronic fencing at certain points to deter or detect intruding terrorists. These measures were not watertight, and the Fedayeen did manage to penetrate Israeli-held territory. For a period Israeli reprisals were limited to artillery fire. In fact, at times activity slowed down until it consisted of little more than occasional artillery firefights across the River Jordan, as Jordanian guns joined in.

5 Hijacking Begins

This is your new captain speaking.
Leila Khalid, on hijacking a TWA airliner, 29 August 1969

WHILE YASIR ARAFAT was concentrating upon expanding his Asifa and training it to carry out sabotage operations inside Israel and the Occupied Territories, George Habash was working on more ambitious ideas for his PFLP. His aim was to seize a world stage from which to generate a universal degree of awareness of the Palestinian cause, and as he was selectively recruiting ideologically motivated individuals who were both educated and intelligent, he was able to achieve it in a dramatic and deadly fashion.

Hijacking of aircraft was not a PFLP invention.* The first recorded incident occurred in Peru on 21 February 1931, when revolutionaries seized a mail plane and used it to drop propaganda leaflets. The second occurred three days later, also in Peru, for a similar purpose. After these two pathfinding exploits, there were no other recorded hijackings until 1947, when a spate of them occurred, mainly perpetrated by refugees from Eastern Europe fleeing West for political asylum. Of the twenty-three incidents recorded between 1947 and 1958, twenty were in this category.

In 1958 Raul Castro's Column Six seized aircraft to harass President Batista's internal communications, and during the next decade there was a rash of aircraft hijackings to and from Cuba, the United States, and adjacent countries. The year 1968 was a bad one, during which twenty-six aircraft were hijacked either from or to Cuba. Another twenty-eight instances were recorded in the first three months of 1969, so despite the acute political friction between Castro's communist regime and the United States, a five-year bilateral agreement was made between the two countries to return hijacked aircraft and vessels.

Hijack was originally a slang American expression meaning "to steal in transit" and came into common use in prohibition days, referring to the theft of truckloads of illicit liquor.

The first Arab hijacking of an airliner was carried out on 23 July 1968 by a PFLP team of three, led by Ali Shafik Ahmed Taha, whose code name was Captain Rafat. Somewhere over the Mediterranean Sea they took over an El Al Boeing 707 with thirty-five passengers and ten crew on board, flying from Rome to Lod, in Israel. Armed with pistols and grenades, the hijackers said they were Palestinians, told the passengers to sit with their arms above their heads, and declared the aircraft to be forthwith named the "Liberation of Palestine." One of the hijackers, a skilled pilot, took over the controls and navigation and flew the Boeing to make a perfect landing at the Dar el-Beida airport near Algiers.*

In a statement issued in Beirut the same day, the PFLP claimed responsibility and insisted that the Algerian government had no prior knowledge of the incident, but urged it to detain both the aircraft and the Israeli personnel on board. The PFLP's objective was to exchange the Israeli hostages for Arab prisoners held by the Israeli government. However, the hijacking caused the Algerian government some embarrassment, and it immediately released the twenty-three non-Israeli passengers, who were flown to Paris, but did detain the Israelis in a nearby military camp with the vague excuse that the Israelis were enemies of the state. The Algerians had declared war on Israel in June 1967, a state of hostilities that still technically existed. Even so, the Algerian government was not very happy about the situation in which it had unwittingly become involved, and on 27 July it released four women passengers, three children, and three air hostesses, who were flown to Geneva on the first stage of their journey back to Israel.

A six-man Arab delegation of representatives of the PLO, Fatah, and the PFLP arrived in Algiers on the 29th, their object being to persuade the Algerian government to continue to detain the remaining twelve Israelis, and only release them in exchange for 1,200 Arabs held in detention by the Israeli government. This figure had been arrived at by the PFLP because the Israelis had said on more than one occasion that "one Israeli life is worth one hundred Arab lives." Then began a period of negotiation between the Fedayeen and the Israeli government through the good offices of the Italian consulate in Algiers, with some International Red Cross (IRC) involvement.

*According to David Phillips, Skyjack.

The Algerian authorities were additionally embarrassed by the Arab hijacking because they already held an important political prisoner who had been landed on them unwanted. He was Moise Tschombe, former leader of the breakaway province of Katanga (later Shaba) of the Congo (later Zaire), and premier of the Congo itself for fifteen months. He had been living in exile in Spain, where he had developed commercial interests that caused him to travel frequently by air. In April 1967 Tschombe had been tried *in absentia* and condemned to death by a Congolese military court, mainly for his activities in leading the Katanganese attempt at secession.

On 30 June 1967, while on a charter flight from Majorca, the plane in which Tschombe was traveling was diverted by Francis-Joseph Bodeman, a French mercenary, to Algiers, where Tschombe was detained. As Bodeman himself had chartered the aircraft, which according to its logbook had once carried David Ben Gurion as a passenger, the incident was technically a kidnapping rather than a hijacking. The Algerians rejected the demand that Tschombe be extradited to Zaire, but appreciating the publicity value of the incident, they restaged the Tschombe kidnapping for their own television propaganda purposes. The hostage value of Tschombe was politically high, and he was probably used to try to persuade President Mobutu of Zaire to expel his Israeli advisers and technicians. Tschombe was still in Algerian detention when he died on 29 June 1969.

On 1 September 1968 the twelve Israelis were freed by the Algerian authorities, and in return, on the 3rd, the Israeli government released sixteen Arabs they had been holding in detention, classed as "infiltrators detained in the 1967 War," hastily emphasizing that it was merely a "gesture of gratitude to the Italian government" for its part in the negotiations. But the precedent had been set, and for the first time the Israelis had openly exchanged Arab prisoners for Israeli hostages. The Israelis took no reprisals.

With this success behind it the PFLP decided to launch a campaign of terror and destruction against the El Al airline, its aircraft, and its overseas offices to deter people from traveling on it and so from visiting Israel. It wanted to hit Israel economically and to sever or seriously disrupt this lifeline. There was also another reason: a matter of prestige. The seven Boeings then possessed by El Al were the flag carriers for Israel, the symbol of the existence of that country abroad, visible at many international airports. This was something the PFLP wanted to eliminate.

The next major PFLP exploit occurred on 26 December 1968 at Athens airport. It was carried out by two young Palestinians named as Mahmoud Mohammed and Maher Hussein Suleiman. One of them suddenly produced a submachine gun from his hold-all bag and began shooting at an El Al Boeing waiting on the tarmac to take off for Paris with fifty-one crew and passengers on board. The other terrorist threw incendiary grenades, which set one of the plane's engines on fire. One passenger was killed by gunfire and an air hostess was injured when she jumped from the aircraft to the tarmac.

The two terrorists, who had arrived in Athens on an Air France aircraft from Beirut an hour before, had waited in the transit lounge for the vital moment to attack. They were arrested, and the fire in the Boeing was extinguished. In a statement issued in Beirut the same day, the PFLP claimed responsibility, saying the reason for the attack was because El Al aircraft had ferried home Israeli pilots who had been training on Phantom aircraft in America. It warned that more such attacks could be expected. The following day, the 27th, it was announced that America would supply fifty Phantom aircraft to Israel; the PFLP timing had been poor. Eventually brought before a Greek court on 27 March 1970, the two terrorists were sentenced to terms of imprisonment, the court accepting their "patriotism" as a mitigating factor.

Although the Israeli government had exchanged Arab prisoners for Israeli hostages in July 1968 and taken no other action, on the ground it continued to pursue a hard reprisal policy of hitting back at Fedayeen camps in Arab-held territory with both artillery fire and aircraft strikes. The advent of the helicopter had given the Israelis a new mobility and a means of lifting commandos into Arab territory for hit-and-run tactics. Already, on 1 December 1968, Israeli troops had made a helicopter raid into Jordan as a reprisal and had demolished a railway bridge some forty miles from the Israeli border.

After the PFLP attack on the Israeli airliner at Athens airport, it was anticipated the Israelis might make a larger scale air strike on PFLP camps than normal, but instead they launched a raid on Beirut airport, one of the busiest in the Middle East, about fifty miles north of Israel.

At 2015 hours on 28 December 1968, led by Colonel Rafael Eytan,* Israeli commandos in four helicopters flew in low from the direction of the sea beneath the radar surveillance towards the airport, which was about five miles from the city of Beirut. Two of the helicopters put down soldiers in blocking positions, while the other two landed on the floodlit tarmac in full view of airport staff and passengers, who took shelter when the commandos emerged to spray the area with bullets. The two helicopters then rose to a height of about 500 feet to fire tracer ammunition at buildings and to drop incendiary bombs on approach roads. Higher overhead flew Israeli fighter aircraft in a protective role.

Using incendiary grenades, the Israelis began destroying the Arab airliners they found on the ground, one of which, waiting to take off for Jedda, in Saudi Arabia, had sixty-eight passengers on board. They were ordered off the plane and into the transit lounge at gunpoint. Within forty-five minutes it was all over. The Israeli commandos were whisked away in their helicopters, leaving behind thirteen Arab airliners that had been destroyed by fire and explosives; the total damage exceeded $30 million.

From a military point of view the raid had been well planned and perfectly executed, and its effects had been sudden and devastating. There had been no loss of life, no injuries caused, and the one non-Arab airliner at the airport, a British one, had not been damaged. There had been no antiaircraft defenses around the Beirut airport to take action against the attackers, and the only shots fired at the Israelis were by a small patrol of Lebanese soldiers who had blundered into one of the Israeli blocking positions. The Lebanese hastily retired when fire was returned. Luck had been with the Israelis, who had only expected to find six Arab airliners on the tarmac at the airport, and the extra planes they found waiting for them were regarded as a bonus. Perhaps their intelligence, generally so good, had been faulty in their favor.

The Israeli government claimed the raid was a punitive one in reprisal for the PFLP attack in Athens. It also claimed Lebanon was harboring Fedayeen fighters, that the Fedayeen recruited in its Palestinian refugee camps had caches of arms and explosives, that they collected funds from the refugees, who were given receipts for the money donated, and that the Lebanese government knew

*Appointed Israeli Chief of Staff in May 1978.

there were terrorist training camps near Tripoli, Sidon, and Tyre, but did nothing about them.

The Israelis pointed out that Abdullah al-Yafi, the Lebanese Muslim premier, had expressed open support for the Fedayeen, and in February 1968 had declared that Lebanon was at war with Israel. More recently, he had attended the funeral of a terrorist. However, al-Yafi said the Israeli action was an "act of international piracy" and constituted "treacherous aggression." He denied there were any Arab bases on Lebanese soil, but added somewhat defiantly that the Lebanese government regarded Palestinian operations against the Israelis to be "legal and sacred."

The Lebanese army was small—less than 11,000 strong—and it did not enjoy a very high reputation for warlike efficiency. Accordingly, many Arabs said that the Israeli raid was merely a "demonstration of weakness" and asked what action the Israelis would have taken had the two PFLP terrorists traveled to Athens from Rome, Paris, or London. Largely owing to the controversy aroused by the Israeli raid on Beirut, Abdullah al-Yafi resigned on 8 January 1969 and Rashid Karami, a former premier, was entrusted with the task of forming another government.

This action by the Israelis brought them one major disadvantage. On 6 January the French government banned all arms supplies to Israel because French-made helicopters had been used in the raid on Beirut airport. This embargo was a total one, and included spares for the French aircraft in service with the Israeli air force. This proved to be a severe handicap.

Although depicted by the Israelis as a glorious achievement showing the Arabs how their long arm could reach out to punish, their raid on Beirut airport was counterproductive in another way. It brought the weakness of the Lebanese government and army to the notice of the Fedayeen, thus encouraging them to expand in Lebanese territory. Meanwhile, on 30 December 1968 the UN Security Council met to consider a complaint against Israel for this raid, and the following day a resolution was passed condemning Israel for its action. This was a setback to Israeli prestige. They were disappointed that the United States had not vetoed it.

The next PFLP exploit occurred on 18 February 1969 at Zurich airport, Switzerland, when four terrorists attacked an El Al Boeing on a flight from Amsterdam to Lod just as it was taxiing up the runway to take off. The terrorists had driven towards the runway in a white Volkswagen automobile, which they had hired in Zurich. The car was partly hidden near a pile of snow about one hundred yards from the Boeing. The terrorists were named as Yusef Ibrahim Toufik, Mohammed Abu al-Haji, Abdul Mohsin Hassan, and a woman, Amena Dahbour, all Palestinians.

The terrorists opened fire with their submachine guns, killing the Israeli copilot and wounding four of the seventeen passengers. One of the passengers was Gideon Rafael, the director general of the Israeli Foreign Ministry, who was unhurt. While the attack was in progress the Israeli security guard on the plane, Mordecai Rachman, slid down the emergency chute to shoot and kill Hassan. One packet of explosives was thrown by one of the terrorists, but it fell short. An airport fire engine rushed to the scene and firemen overpowered both Toufik and al-Haji, but the woman ran away, only to be caught quickly by an airport employee. The three surviving terrorists, who had grenades in their possession, were taken into custody by the police, as was the Israeli security guard. Over fifty bullet holes were counted in the fuselage of the aircraft.

In a statement given out over Radio Beirut, responsibility for the incident was claimed by the PFLP, which stated that it had been carried out because of the "barbaric treatment of unarmed Arab civilians in the Israeli Occupied Territories" and the military character of the Israeli air transport fleet. The PFLP urged the Swiss government to treat their Arab prisoners as "honorable freedom fighters." On 28 February the Swiss government protested to Syria and Jordan that its neutrality had been violated.

King Hussein, who was having difficulties with the Fedayeen, refused to allow the body of Hassan to be brought back to Amman to be given a hero's funeral. A week later the body of Hassan was still at Zurich, and a fortnight afterwards it was being shuttled, unwanted, between Zurich and Amsterdam. Finally it was accepted by the Iraqi government and flown to Baghdad.

The three Arab terrorists were brought to trial at Winterhur on 28 November 1969. Bulletproof glass partitions separated the public from the actual court. The Israeli security guard was refused a separate trial and appeared together with the Arabs. Being Iraqi-born, he understood Arabic and so had the advantage of knowing what the Arabs were saying to each other. He had been released on bail and had returned from Israel to face his trial. The terrorists stated that Switzerland had been chosen as the "military objective" for this exploit because the First Zionist Congress had been held there in 1897. On 22 December 1969 the three Arab terrorists were each sentenced to twelve years imprisonment and the Israeli security guard was acquitted. There was no death penalty in Switzerland.

The PFLP was spreading its hidden tentacles into Europe. The extent to which they had penetrated was revealed in May 1969, when three people were brought to trial at Copenhagen, Denmark, accused of conspiring to assassinate David Ben Gurion during his visit to South America. They were named as Mohammed Razan, an Iraqi; Muna Saudi, a Jordanian girl (both members of the PFLP); and Rolf Anderson, a Swede. The Danish and Swedish security services had worked together to uncover this plot, and the whole of the evidence was given *in camera*. A senior PFLP agent posing as an Egyptian colonel of the PLA had visited Stockholm and made contact with Anderson, who had been recruited into the PFLP while serving with the UN Emergency Force (UNEF) in Gaza.

Anderson was to make the necessary air travel bookings for the two Arabs and to conceal arms and ammunition for them in false-bottomed suitcases. The "Egyptian colonel" produced a large scale map of Rio de Janeiro airport and gave the Arabs detailed instructions on how to kill Ben Gurion. Afterwards Anderson was to arrange safe-houses for them to hide away in, as it was anticipated the Israel Mossad would mount a campaign to find and kill them. All three were sentenced to terms of imprisonment, the two Arabs being later quietly released and deported.

Having once succeeded in forcing the Israeli government to release Arab prisoners in exchange for Israeli hostages, the PFLP tried the same tactic again on 29 August 1969. Two terrorists hijacked an American Trans World Airline Boeing on a flight from New York to Lod after a stopover at Rome. American aircraft did not carry armed security guards. The leader was a girl, Leila Khalid, and her companion was named as Salim Assawi. They called themselves the Che Guevara Commando Unit. (The titles Palestinian hijackers began to adopt were more in the nature of operational code names, which were often assumed for just one exploit.) After some hesitation they directed the pilot to fly his aircraft to Beirut airport. Leila Khalid told passengers, "This is your new captain speaking," and said that the plane had been hijacked because one of the Israeli passengers on board was "an assassin responsible for the death and misery of many Palestinian men, women, and children" who would "be brought before a revolutionary court" for his crime. She did not identify him.

Leila Khalid had been born in Haifa in 1944, one of a large family that had been forced to flee to Lebanon in 1948 when the Israelis took over that city. She became a member of the ANM in 1959, and so began her revolutionary career, joining the PFLP in early 1968. Instead of avoiding Israel, she ordered the pilot to fly low over Haifa so she could again see the city of her birth, of which she only retained early childhood memories. As the hijacked TWA Boeing flew on through Israeli air space, Israeli fighter aircraft attempted to buzz it to force it to land. Despite this, Leila Khalid calmly made the pilot circle low over Lod airport. Speaking over the plane's radio to the Lod control tower, warning the Israeli aircraft to keep clear, she said, "We are from the Front for the Liberation of Palestine. What can you do about it?"

After further indecision—according to her own admission she did not know which Arab airport to make for—she told the pilot to fly the plane to Damascus.* Just before landing there she told the passengers, "Every one of you, regardless of religion or citizenship, is guaranteed freedom to go wherever he pleases as soon as the plane is safely landed. Thank you for your cooperation, and we wish you a happy journey." On landing, the passengers and crew left the plane by emergency chutes, as did the hijackers, who detonated an explosion in the pilot's cabin before leaving.

However, the Syrian government had not been expecting the hijacked airliner and was both displeased and suspicious. The two hijackers were taken into custody. Later, General Tlas, the Syrian defense minister, told me that he thought at first Leila Khalid was an Egyptian agent who had deliberately landed the plane at Damascus to embarrass the Syrian government. The Syrians were also displeased when *Al Hadaf*, the weekly PFLP newspaper printed in Beirut, having learned the destination of the plane, parachuted a photographer into Damascus airport to take photographs of the landing. Both Leila Khalid and Salim Assawi were able to pose, with triumphant smiles, under the damaged nose of the TWA plane. The Syrian authorities allowed all the passengers, except for six Israelis, to remain free, and the following day they were flown out from Damascus airport.

*Leila Khalid, *My People Shall Live*.

On 29 August the PFLP issued a statement in Beirut claiming responsibility for the hijacking, saying it was a reprisal for the American sale of Phantom aircraft to Israel, but made no mention of the assassin alleged to have been on the plane. U.S. Secretary of State William Rogers called the hijacking "an act of international piracy." On the 31st, the day an International Federation of Airline Pilots Association (IFALPA) representative said the pilots were considering a twenty-four-hour strike to focus public attention on the hazard of hijacking, the Syrian government allowed four of the six Israeli passengers, three women and a girl, to leave on a flight for Rome, and thence to Lod. This was a deep disappointment to the PFLP. The two Israelis remaining in Syrian detention were Shlomo Samueloff, a professor of physiology at the Hebrew University, Jerusalem, and Salah Muallen, an Israeli travel agent.

Negotiations through the IRC began, but were lengthy, and it was not until 10 October 1969 that its representative was able to indicate that the Israeli government would be willing to release Arab prisoners in exchange for the two Israelis held in Damascus. Eventually the two Israelis were released on 5 December in exchange for thirteen Syrians held in detention by the Israelis. They were two Syrian pilots whose Mig-17 had landed in Israel on 12 August 1968 owing to a navigational error; five Syrian soldiers captured in border raids; and six civilians, who were handed over, under IRC supervision, on the cease-fire line near Kuneitra on the Golan Plateau.

Meanwhile, Leila Khalid and Salim Assawi had not fared so well at the suspicious, almost hostile hands of the Syrian authorities, who had no love for either the ANM or the PFLP. For the first few days they were kept in detention, and Leila Khalid said her worst day was 4 September, when she heard that her revolutionary hero, Ho Chi Minh, had died. The following day, the 5th, the two were placed under house arrest and held incommunicado for forty-five days, until they were finally released on 11 October to be flown to Beirut and freedom. During this period Leila Khalid went on hunger strikes on three occasions to try to obtain her release or make contact with the PFLP. She emerged a Fedayeen heroine.

A third exchange of prisoners occurred on 7 December 1969 when Egypt released two wounded Israeli pilots who had been brought down over the Suez Canal Zone, in return for an Egyptian pilot shot down on Israeli-held territory, five Egyptian soldiers captured in raids across the Suez Canal, and fifty-two civilians, the majority of the latter being fishermen who had strayed into Israeli-dominated waters. It seemed as though the principle of the exchange of prisoners, for which the Fedayeen organizations were working so hard, was becoming an established one.

The PFLP continued actively with its declared policy of attacking Israeli buildings and offices abroad, and on 29 August 1969 a time bomb exploded in the London office of the Zim Navigation Company; one member of the staff was injured. On 8 September there were three separate attacks when grenades were thrown at the Israeli embassy building in Bonn, West Germany, but no one was injured; at the El Al office in Brussels, Belgium, where four people were hurt; and at the Israeli embassy at the Hague, Holland, where they landed in an adjoining house with casualties. The same day the PFLP announced in Beirut that these grenade attacks had been carried out by their Young Commandos—Asibals or "Young Tigers" of the Ho Chi Minh Section, their youth terrorist organization. The PFLP declared these incidents were the opening of a phase of all-out attacks on Israeli aircraft, buildings, and ships throughout the world. The Asibals were organized and directed by Ali Shafik Ahmed Taha (Captain Rafat), who had led the first PFLP hijacking in July 1968.

The next PFLP attack of this nature occurred in Athens on 27 November 1969 when a terrorist, Elias Derhar Abedian, threw a grenade through a glass-fronted El Al office crowded with passengers waiting to board the airport bus. Fifteen people were injured, one of whom, a two-year-old boy, died two days later. The terrorist was caught by the police after a chase through the city, while his companion, Mansour Murad, was arrested a few hours afterwards at his hotel. Both had Jordanian passports, and a number of Polish-made grenades were found in their possession. The PFLP admitted responsibility.

Not all PFLP hijacking attempts were successful. For example, on 21 December 1969 three terrorists flew to Athens airport with the intention of hijacking a TWA airliner and diverting it to Tunis as a protest against continued American help to Israel. The team was led by a girl, Muna Abu Khalil; her companions were Sami Aboud and Issam Doumidi. Security at the airport had been tightened up after the PFLP attack on the El Al office the previous month, and the suspicions of an airport clerk were aroused when he noticed that all three were carrying identical suitcases. He contacted the police, who found the three suitcases to contain arms, ammunition, and explosives. The three terrorists were arrested.

While the PFLP had committed the most spectacular Fedayeen outrages during 1968 and 1969, a number of major terrorist incidents against the Israelis were carried out by Fatah, which, unlike the PFLP, believed in operating only inside Israel and the Occupied Territories.* In the month of January 1969, for example, Fatah claimed to have made ninety raids into Israel against road bridges, railway lines, and military camps. Speaking in the Knesset on 19 February, Moshe Dayan, minister of defense, said that Arab terrorist organizations had killed 144 Israelis in four years, and wounded 634. An Israeli spokesman later said (19 January 1970) that at least 586 guerrillas had been killed in 1969, of whom 37 percent were from Fatah. The extent of this war of sabotage and terror can be gauged by figures issued by the Israelis on 31 May 1970: since the end of the June 1967 War, Israeli security forces had killed 1,621 Arab guerrillas and terrorists, and 2,500 were still held in detention.

The PFLP was not the only Fedayeen group to disagree with the Fatah policy of striking only at targets inside Israel and the Occupied Territories. The small Action Group for the Liberation of Palestine (AGLP), a splinter from Fatah now led by Issam Sartwi and Fadil Zahrur, tried to emulate PFLP hijacking exploits. After several minor incidents, the AGLP rejoined Fatah and ceased to have an independent existence.

On 21 February 1970 more Palestinian terrorist incidents occurred in Europe when explosives were detonated in two airliners

---

*Although operating on a grand and extensive scale outside the Middle East, the PFLP committed its full share of sabotage and terrorist operations inside Israel and the Occupied Territories. One of the first occurred on 18 August 1968 when a grenade attack in Jerusalem killed one person and injured fourteen; this was followed by an explosion in the Tel Aviv bus station on 4 September that killed one person and injured fifty-one others; on 9 October a grenade thrown near the Tomb of the Patriarchs in Hebron injured forty-two people; on 22 November an explosion in a Jerusalem market killed twelve people and injured another fifty-five; on 21 February 1969 an explosion in a Jerusalem supermarket killed two and injured nine; on 6 March an explosion at the Hebrew University cafeteria in Jerusalem injured twenty-nine students; a bazooka attack that year killed nine pupils and three teachers and injured nineteen children when a bus in which they were traveling in northern Israel was ambushed; and five explosions in Haifa on 23 October 1969 killed two people and injured twenty-three others. The Israeli reaction to these terrorist incidents was to make reprisal raids on Fedayeen camps by aircraft strikes, but after one made into Jordan on 27 March 1969 Israel was condemned (on 1 April) for its action in the UN Security Council.

in flight within a couple of hours of each other. The responsibility for them was attributed to the Jabril Front. Like the PFLP, from which it splintered, the Jabril Front wanted to dissuade all airline companies from flying to Israel and from carrying Israelis or Israeli freight.

One of these explosions occurred in the luggage compartment of a Caravelle of the Austrian Airlines. A gash was ripped in the side of the aircraft, but with great skill and calm determination the pilot was able to turn the plane around and bring it safely back to land at Frankfurt airport. Investigations showed that the explosive device, hidden in a parcel, had been fitted with a delayed action detonator connected to an altimeter, which caused it to be activated when the aircraft climbed to a height of about ten thousand feet.

On 27 February the West German police stated that four Arabs who were suspected of preparing and planting this explosive device had tested the altimeter mechanism during a drive by automobile to the top of the 2,690-foot-high Feldberg, the highest peak in the Taunnus mountain range northwest of Frankfurt. Two of the suspected Arabs, named as Jasser Kassem and Isa Abdullah Abu Toboul, were arrested, but the other two escaped, one having already flown off to Cairo, while the other was believed to have left Germany by automobile.

The second incident had a far more disastrous ending. Just fifteen minutes after it was airborne from Zurich airport on a flight to Lod, a Swiss Coronado airliner crashed into a forest near Wurenligen. All forty-seven people on board, of whom fifteen were Israelis, were killed. The plane narrowly missed a small Swiss nuclear reactor center and an army ammunition depot as it came down. Evidence showed that an explosion had occurred in the luggage compartment when the plane reached a height of about ten thousand feet, a carbon copy of the Frankfurt explosion. The last tragic message from the pilot received at the Zurich airport control tower just before the fatal crash was, "Suspect explosion in aft compartment of aircraft . . . fire on board . . . nothing more we can do . . . Goodbye."

On the evening of 21 February it was reported that a PFLP spokesman had claimed responsibility for the Swiss air disaster, saying that it had been carried out because senior Israeli officials were on board, but this was formally denied by the PFLP in Beirut the following day. On the 22nd a joint statement was issued in the name of all the Arab Fedayeen groups operating from Amman, denying that any of them were either implicated in the Swiss air crash or had in any way been responsible for it, and disclaiming any knowledge at all. The Jabril Front remained silent. Later information indicated that the Jabril Front had posted the explosive parcel, expecting it to be carried to Israel on an El Al aircraft.

Following these two incidents certain restrictions were placed on the entry into Switzerland of Arab nationals, and European police began to show a far greater interest in Arabs living in their countries. Several airlines stopped carrying Israeli mail or freight, but as this ban lasted only three days, the main aim of the Palestinian terrorists was thwarted. The Zurich crash gave an impetus to enforcing and tightening up airport security, sweeping away much of the remaining reluctance of passengers to allow themselves and their luggage to be searched at airports. Equipment for X-raying luggage and freight was installed at all major airports in Europe. Always security conscious, the El Al Airline had the pilot's cabin and the luggage compartments protected by armor plating, and made a rule that pilots' cabins were to be locked on takeoff on all its aircraft.

Another incident of this type occurred on 15 March 1970, for which an adequate and convincing explanation has yet to be forthcoming, when an explosion occurred on an Egyptian Anotov airliner flying from Cairo to Athens about four minutes after takeoff from Alexandria. The aircraft was able to return safely to Alexandria airport and none of the twelve passengers on board, or crew, was injured. In October 1968 an explosion on a similar Egyptian Anotov airliner flying over the Mediterranean caused the aircraft to crash into the sea with the loss of all forty people on board. No adequate explanaton was given for this incident either.

Argument continued within the PLO over whether to restrict terrorist activities to Israel and the Occupied Territories or not. As the PFLP had carried out spectacular operatons outside the area of the Middle East, sometimes acts it had not committed were ascribed to it. This caused the PFLP to issue a statement on 1 March 1970 saying that so far it had been responsible for ten operations outside the Middle East, insisting that no European had been killed or injured as a result of them. A few of the extremist groups such as the Jabril Front and the DPF tried to imitate the PFLP, and a few terrorist acts were carried out by renegade members of Fatah outside the Middle East because of their strong views on this issue, but responsibility for them, and all knowledge of them, was firmly denied by Fatah. One example had come to light on 24 August 1969, when two Palestinian students tried to plant a time bomb at the International Fair at Izmir, Turkey, in the Israeli pavilion, but it exploded in their hands, killing one and badly injuring the other. The survivor, named as Omar Hassan Hammad, claimed that he and his companions were both members of Fatah and were simply obeying Fatah orders. This was promptly denied by Fatah.

On 22 July 1979, as a Greek Olympic Boeing airliner was approaching Athens airport on a flight from Beirut, its pilot sent a radio message to the airport control tower that his plane had been taken over by six Arab hijackers who wanted to communicate with the Greek minister of justice. The hijackers were a PFLP team led by a man named Abdul Abu Meguid, armed with submachine guns and grenades.* When the aircraft landed the terrorists refused to allow the passengers to disembark, threatening to blow up the plane, the fifty-five people on board, and themselves unless the Greek government released seven PFLP members it was holding. The deputy premier spoke to the hijackers on the radio but was unable to persuade them to abandon their intention.

The IRC Middle East representative, André Rochat, who happened to be in Athens at the time, came to the scene as a mediator. The Greek government was willing to release the Arab prisoners it held in exchange for the hostages on the plane, but balked on a point of principle. It insisted that two Arabs who had been responsible for the terrorist act in November 1969 but who had not yet been brought to trial should first of all be dealt with by a Greek court of law. After a seven-hour period of negotiations, André Rochat was successful. It was agreed that the plane, crew, and passengers should be released, and that the seven PFLP prisoners held by the Greeks be set free at the latest by 22 August. This was an extremely delicate arrangement, and one in which trust was involved to a high degree. It came in for much criticism, especially from the Israelis. At one point Aristotle Onassis, owner of the Olympic Airline, went to the airport to offer himself as a hostage in place of the passengers, but this was refused by the terrorists.

The passengers were released, and at once the aircraft with the crew and terrorists on board took off for Beirut, but permission to

*The others were named as Muna Meguid (the leader's sister), Yusef Fakhri, Khaled Abdul Khalid, Abdul Walid, and Mansour Seifeddin; all young Palestinian students.

land was refused, so after circling fruitlessly over the airport they made for Egypt. The plane was allowed to land at Cairo, where the hijackers were received by the secretary of the Arab Socialist Union, Ahmed Farid, who praised the "national spirit they had demonstrated through their determination to attain their aim—the liberation of their colleagues." The Olympic aircraft, its crew, and André Rochat were allowed to return to Athens.

Two days later the trial of Elias Dergan Abedian and Mansour Murad began in Athens. On 26 July both were found guilty and were sentenced to terms of imprisonment. The Greek government then kept its agreement with the PFLP, and on 13 August, under arrangements made by the IRC, the seven detained PFLP terrorists were released and flown to Cairo to receive a hero's welcome. Two of them had been serving sentences for the attack they had made in December 1968. The PFLP was pleased with itself, as it thought it had more firmly established the principle of exchanging hostages for Arabs held in prisons—with the Greek government at least. It hoped this practice would be followed by other European countries, as the PFLP still had six of its members detained in Europe—three in West Germany and three in Switzerland.

In February 1970 Yasir Arafat visited the Soviet Union at the invitation of the Afro-Asian Solidarity Committee, and although he did not meet any high-level members of the Soviet government, his visit was considered to be a success, as the Soviet press referred to the "Arab people of Palestine" for the first time. This was regarded as the beginning of Soviet recognition of the Palestinian political movement. The greater part of the remainder of the year was spent by Arafat in trying to unite the diverse and independently minded Fedayeen groups under his leadership. Fatah had virtually taken over the PLO. On 18 February Arafat had called on the ten main Fedayeen organizations to form a joint permanent command to face opposition in both Jordan and Lebanon. Arafat always fancied himself as a field general, but his proposal was met by stony silence. His next attempt was made on 4 June, when the PNC met in Cairo. The main item on the agenda was to form the Fedayeen into a single command under his leadership. After six days of deliberation and argument, this motion failed.

Meanwhile, a new personality had appeared on the Middle East terrorist scene. Colonel Muammer Gaddafi had led a bloodless coup against King Idris of Libya in September 1969 and assumed the chairmanship of the Revolutionary Command Council, which ruled a country becoming rich from its booming oil production. Coming to power at a time when the fame and mystique of the Fedayeen fighters were sweeping through the Arab world, Gaddafi and his colleagues rushed to embrace openly the cause of the Palestinians. In his naiveté, he could not understand why Arab states such as Egypt, Syria, Jordan, and Iraq, whose total armed forces exceeded in number those of the Israelis, did not immediately march forward to eliminate Israel. He made himself unpopular with his fellow Arab heads of state by telling them so. As the Libyan army was tiny, and his country remote in distance from Israel, there was little he could do in the military sense, but he felt that it was his Islamic duty to support and encourage the Fedayeen organizations. In dispensing his bounty he tended to select those groups that seemed to be achieving something, even if it was only publicity, by their activities.

Gaddafi, still naive, could not understand why the Fedayeen groups would not unite to fight the Israelis together. In January 1970 he persuaded both Arafat and Habash to meet him in Libya. He offered them large sums of money at a time when both their organizations were feeling financially pinched if they would either unite, or if not, at least operate jointly. Gaddafi was not successful, and neither could he persuade Habash to bring his PFLP into the PASC.

The sharp division between the Fedayeen groups, especially the extremist ones, caused a number of incidents, one of which occurred at 0215 hours on 11 July 1970 when a volley of six rockets struck the apartment building in Beirut occupied by Wadia Hadad, of the PFLP, and his family. They were fired from another apartment building about one hundred yards away. Only three of the rockets entered Hadad's apartment, of which only one exploded, slightly injuring Hadad, and causing small burns to his wife and small son. The son was taken to the hospital by Leila Khalid, who was in the apartment at the time planning future PLFP operations while recovering from facial surgery. PFLP members were quickly on the scene, but found the apartment from which the rockets had been fired empty except for the rocket launcher and a message on a note pad, "Made by Fatah in 1970."

Two suspects were identified as Ahmed Batzat, an Iranian, and Ahmed Rauf, a Syrian. These two men had attempted to kill Halel Yasrami, a PFLP leader, a fortnight previously in Beirut. However,

Wadia Hadad, who had only returned to his home in Beirut from France two days before, was of the opinion that the attack on himself and his family had been made by the Israeli Mossad.

On 7 August 1970 President Nasser agreed to a cease-fire across the Suez Canal, and so brought to an end the Egyptian-Israeli War, which had been in progress since the end of the Arab-Israeli War of June 1967. His decision did not please the Palestinian Fedayeen. All the Fedayeen groups wanted action to continue against Israel, although most had only vague ideas as to what form it should take. However, the PFLP was determined to pursue the principle it thought it had established of the exchange of hostages for prisoners. It was anxious to obtain the release of its members held in Israeli prisons, and also the six held in West Germany and Switzerland. To achieve this aim, the PFLP launched its first great television spectacular on 6 September 1970, a day that became known as Skyjack Sunday, when it hijacked three airliners. In addition, it tried and failed to hijack a fourth one. The whole operation was organized and directed by Wadia Hadad.

The first aircraft was a TWA Boeing 707 flying from New York to Tel Aviv with 145 passengers and crew on board. It was taken over by three Arabs, two men and a woman (never named), just after a stopover at Frankfurt. After the aircraft had passed over Cyprus and was heading for Lebanon, the female hijacker gave the pilot a map and directed him to a little-noticed and largely forgotten desert airstrip in Jordan, about forty miles north of Amman. As daylight was fading, the pilot had difficulty in discerning its outline, but he made a safe landing.

The second airliner was a Swissair DC-8 flying from Zurich to New York with 155 crew and passengers aboard. Just after leaving Zurich it was taken over by three Arabs, again two men and a woman (never named), and directed to the same desert airstrip in Jordan, where it landed safely ten minutes after the first one. PFLP commandos were waiting on the ground to receive the planes, so they now held about three hundred people hostage.

This desert airstrip was based on a length of hard sand and surrounded by soft sand and scrub, well away from any settled habitation. It had been created for RAF use in 1947 when Spitfire squadrons were stationed there for short periods to take part in exercises with British troops and the Arab Legion of Trans-Jordan. There were absolutely no landing facilities or buildings, since the RAF took mobile equipment with them whenever they used it. It had never been officially named, but was generally known as Dawson's Field, after Air Marshal Sir William Dawson, the air officer commanding the Levant from 1946 to 1948. The PFLP immediately named it Revolution Airfield, and its commandos dug themselves into defensive positions around the two planes. When Jordanian army patrols approached, they were warned to keep their distance.

The prime intention of the PFLP was to obtain hostages to exchange for its members held in prisons, and Wadia Hadad had guessed correctly that there would be some Germans and Swiss on the DC-8, and perhaps some Israelis on the American TWA plane. To make sure of seizing a fairly large number of Israelis, he additionally ordered the hijacking of an El Al airliner, but this latter part of his plan miscarried. The PFLP plan had been to hijack an El Al Boeing flying from Tel Aviv to New York with 155 crew and passengers on board. Two PFLP terrorists boarded this aircraft at the stopover at Amsterdam. The other two terrorist members of the team of four failed to get on the plane. Leila Khalid, the leader, who already had one successful hijacking to Damascus to her credit, and Patrick Arguello, known to Leila Khalid only as René, were the two hijackers on board.

About fifteen minutes after leaving Amsterdam the two terrorists rose and brandished grenades, making for the first class section. The man, who had produced an automatic rifle, fired a shot as they rushed forward. Leila Khalid shouted to him, "Don't shoot—we have open grenades." The pilot's cabin was armor-protected and had been locked on takeoff according to instructions. However, contrary to instructions, one of the two armed security guards was in the cabin with the pilot; the other was in the body of the plane.

As the hijackers went forward, a member of the air crew rushed at the male terrorist, who shot him with his rifle, five bullets entering his body and leaving him in a critical condition. Arguello was then shot and brought down by the security guard, but not before he managed to draw the safety pin from a grenade he was holding. The grenade dropped to the floor but failed to explode. Arguello was overpowered and bound hand and foot.

Leila Khalid was equally unsuccessful. As the plane lurched she dropped the grenade she was holding. Although the safety pin had been withdrawn, it too failed to explode. Later there was argument as to whether it had been primed at all. A passenger grabbed Leila Khalid, so she too was overpowered. Later she said, "I was knocked down and remembered no more until I came round a few minutes later to find myself tied up." The aircraft touched down at London airport.

At the airport both hijackers were put into an ambulance, in which Arguello died of his wounds. Leila Khalid, by this time sobbing hysterically, was taken to Ealing Police Station, London. In the aircraft there had been a literal tug-of-war between Israeli security guards, helped by the air crew, who wanted to keep her on board to take her to Israel for questioning, trial, and detention, and the British police, who insisted she should be taken into their custody. The instigator of this tug-of-war was General Aharon Yariv, the head of the Mossad, who was traveling incognito (a fact of which Leila Khalid was not aware). Until she became the prime prize of the tug-of-war, she had been the stronger character of the two, as Arguello had suffered an attack of nerves just before the actual attempt to seize the plane and had probably initially fired his rifle in nervousness. The wounded member of the Israeli air crew eventually recovered.

Aged twenty-seven years, Patrick Arguello was born in California to an American mother and a Nicaraguan father, and had been traveling on an American passport; he also had two false Honduran passports in his possession. Well known in Latin American revolutionary circles, he was identified by the FBI from his fingerprints. There had been no prior indication that he had contacts with the PFLP. At a later press conference Leila Khalid claimed the hijacking was a blow against Israeli and imperial interests, adding the interesting comment that "we define our enemies in the following order—Israel, the Zionist movement, international imperialism, and Arab reaction."*

Next, an impromptu hijacking by the two missing members of Leila Khalid's team took place. They were named as Samir Ibrahim and Ali Assayed, and forty-eight hours previously had been refused first-class tickets for the intended El Al airliner because they had somehow aroused suspicion. Determined not to be left out of the operation, they instead purchased tickets on a Pan American Boeing 747 due to leave from Amsterdam that day for New York. They boarded successfully. Shortly after leaving Amsterdam they seized control of the airliner, which had 170 people on board, and ordered it to fly to Beirut, where it arrived with its fuel almost

*Al Anwar, 5 October 1970.

exhausted. At Beirut PFLP commandos had taken over the control tower and were in charge of the airport, while the airport authorities and the Lebanese security forces had to look on helplessly.

Having doubts as to whether the Pan Am plane would be able to land on Revolution Airfield, which was only 1,500 yards in length, the PFLP headquarters in Beirut ordered it to fly to Cairo instead, to be blown up there. Local PFLP personnel came on board with explosives and put them into position inside the plane, wiring them up to detonators. When the Boeing 747 took off again, an additional PFLP man, an explosives expert, was on board. The plane arrived at Cairo International airport and taxied to a position on the open tarmac about 1,000 yards from the airport buildings. Warned they had only eight minutes to get clear, the people on the aircraft hastily slid down emergency chutes to the tarmac, and although the charges were detonated in less than eight minutes, all were safely clear when the plane was blown up. The three PFLP members were detained by the Egyptian authorities, but the crew and passengers were flown back to Europe the following day. This was one hijack Wadia Hadad definitely had not planned.

Meanwhile, back at Revolution Airfield all had not gone quite according to plan, as only two aircraft, instead of the expected three, stood on the desert airstrip. Moreover, Leila Khalid was now held in custody in Britain. Explosives were wired to detonators and placed in position in and around the two aircraft, in which the hostages had to remain uncomfortably throughout the night. The official PFLP reason for the hijackings was that they were in protest against U.S. Secretary of State Roger's peace initiative, and also a "symbolic blow against an American plot to liquidate the Palestinian cause." In Amman, Ghassam Kanafani, the PFLP spokesman, demanded the release of the PFLP members held in Switzerland, West Germany, and Britain, and also an unspecified number in Israeli detention, in exchange for the hostages. He gave an ultimatum, which was to expire at 0300 hours on the 10th. All the Israeli hostages were to be held until all the Arab prisoners had been released.

The following day, 7 September, the hostages had to remain in cramped discomfort in the planes during the morning. By noon the temperature rose to 100°F in the open desert. They suffered from both extremes of cold and heat, as during the night the temperatures fell sharply. During the course of the day the PFLP made an agreement with the Jordanian troops now surrounding them to withdraw to a distance of two kilometers from the aircraft. In return the PFLP allowed the hostages to dismount from the planes for a while. They also released 127 women and children, none of whom were Israeli, who were taken in buses to hotels in Amman. This helped to ameliorate the cramped conditions inside the aircraft somewhat.

The Swiss and West German governments indicated their willingness to exchange prisoners held for hostages, but the British government refused the PFLP demand for the release of Leila Khalid and the body of Arguello. Instead, the British prime minister set to work to persuade the other Western governments concerned to act together on the principle that countries should not deal individually with the terrorists.

By the following day, 8 September, Britain had succeeded, and a committee of the nations involved was formed in Berne, Switzerland—that is America, Britain, West Germany, and Switzerland; Israel attended as an observer only. The Berne Committee, as it became known, decided to send André Rochat, the IRC Middle East representative, to Revolution Airfield to negotiate with the PFLP on the principle of "the release of all hostages or none." The Israelis dissented, being determined not to release a single Arab terrorist they held. In the late afternoon Rochat appeared at Revolution Airfield and made contact with the PFLP hijackers, and also with the PFLP leadership in Amman. He took note of the immediate requirements of the hostages, whose discomfort was increased by overflowing toilets in the aircraft. That evening, after dusk, the hostages were allowed to dig pits under their aircraft to drain away the sewage into the sand.

Wanting to exploit the publicity angle of their operation to the maximum, the PFLP held a press conference at Revolution Airfield at which television teams, photographers, and reporters were allowed to approach to within twenty feet of the aircraft, verbal communication being by bullhorns. The following day, the PFLP commandos allowed food, medical, and other supplies to be brought to the hostages by the IRC.

The original deadline set by the hijackers was approaching, but there was still no sign of the Western governments being willing to deal individually with the PFLP. Moreover, the PFLP did not hold a single British hostage whom they might offer in exchange for Leila Khalid. For two days the PFLP had tried to bluff the British government into believing it held British hostages, but by this time it was obvious the British had been able to check through passenger lists and were aware of this fact. Perhaps this was a contributory factor that influenced Britain to play a leading part in persuading the Berne Committee to hold out on the "all or none" principle of exchanging prisoners for hostages. On 9 September the Israeli government made a request to Britain for the extradition of Leila Khalid.

To rectify the omission of not holding any British hostages, on 9 September the PFLP hijacked a British VC-10 airliner on a flight from Bombay to London with 116 people on board and flew it to Revolution Airfield. The PFLP now had three airliners and still nearly 300 hostages there. Almost immediately, the hijackers released 23 Arabs who had been traveling on the VC-10. In protest, BOAC suspended all its flights to and from Beirut, but they were resumed again on the 13th. The PFLP spokesman stated that the BOAC VC-10 had been hijacked because of "British stubbornness in not releasing Leila Khalid."

On 10 September the PFLP extended the deadline for another three days, that is until the 13th, and released another twenty-three hostages, mainly Asians. Negotiations seemed to have reached a stalemate. The terrorists at Revolution Airfield had only limited communication with their leadership in Amman, by grudging courtesy of the Jordanian soldiers encircling the aircraft, and knew little of what was going on behind the scenes. They listened to various national news broadcasts and were not comforted.

Arafat had arrived in Amman by this time and was trying to dominate the scene, working both to unite the Fedayeen groups under his leadership and to arrange for the release of the hostages, or their exchange. Meetings had taken place on the 10th at which Fatah urged the release of the hostages, being surprisingly backed by the Iraqi government-sponsored ALF. Usually Iraq was a strong supporter of extreme action by the PFLP. The ALF representative urged that hostages should be released for humanitarian reasons. But there was a deeper motive: the hostages could be an excuse for foreign intervention. The PFLP held out firmly against releasing any of the hostages without compensating release of Arab prisoners.

Hearing on their radios that ships of the U.S. Sixth Fleet were steaming towards the Eastern Mediterranean and that U.S. transport aircraft were being made ready to evacuate the hostages, the PFLP commandos on Revolution Airfield became restless and anxious. There were also rumors that the Israelis might make a surprise helicopter raid on the lines of the one they had mounted at Beirut airport in December 1968, a likely event since the Israeli border was less than fifty miles away. Therefore, more explosives were put into position around the aircraft and wired to detonators. Supplies brought up by the IRC for the hostages were turned away, as were a number of buses that had been sent by the PLO to bring the hostages into Amman. The PFLP commandos feared their leadership was weakening.

On the morning of 11 September, at a lengthy meeting in Amman of the Central Committee of the PLO, chaired by Arafat, it was decided that the hostages would be brought into Amman "for humanitarian reasons." The real reason was that the hostages could be guarded more easily in a city. At Revolution Airfield they and their captors were exposed and vulnerable to any Israeli or other rescue operation. This decision was a victory for Arafat over Ghassam Kanafani in Amman and Wadia Hadad in Beirut. That evening the PFLP commandos took eighteen hostages, including Israelis, from the TWA airliner and secretly smuggled them through the ring of Jordanian soldiers into the town of Zerka, some twenty miles away.

PLO orders to bring the hostages into Amman were given to the PFLP commandos on the 12th, who at first would neither believe nor comply with them. Instead they made the hostages get back into the aircraft. Eventually they were persuaded to obey the PLO order, and after six days and six nights in considerable discomfort about 250 hostages were taken in buses into Amman and released, the majority being placed in hotels. However, fifty-five of them, including six rabbis, were split into small groups and held in houses in the suburbs of Amman and in the Wahdat refugee camp.

As soon as the hostages were clear of Revolution Airfield the three aircraft were blown up one after the other; the Swiss DC-8 first, then the TWA plane, and lastly the VC-10. The watching press had been alerted that this would happen, and so the event was recorded and seen on television screens all over the world. The PFLP had made its dramatic appearance on the world stage, and for six days millions of viewers watched as the drama of this cliff-hanging terrorist epic unfolded. They saw on their television screens the three airliners erupt in flames and black smoke, bringing this terrorist operation to a dramatic end.

Ghassam Kanafani held a press conference to explain why the hostages had been brought into Amman. He said the aircraft had been destroyed, "causing a minimum of $30 million worth of damage," because of the "militant and irresponsible actions" of the governments involved. Talks between the IRC and the PFLP ceased, and the PFLP was suspended from the Central Committee of the PLO. On 13 September the Israelis arrested some 450 prominent Arabs in the West Bank and the Gaza Strip as a counter-weight against hostages still in PFLP hands, although they hastened to deny such a motive. Released hostages were quickly flown to Cyprus by RAF aircraft, and thence homewards. About 252 left Amman airport on the 13th, and others were flown out the next day.

On the 15th, Ghassam Kanafani held yet another press conference in Amman at which he said he wanted individual exchanges with Western governments. He declared that as far as the Israelis were concerned the object was to establish that "they accept the principle of exchange of prisoners or hostages." Kanafani said that 375 hostages had been released safely so far, but that the PFLP still held 55, of whom 30 were either Israelis, Jews with dual Israeli-American citizenship, or other nationalities. One, a Norwegian, was released that day. In return for their freedom, Kanafani demanded the release of Bruno Breguet, a Swiss student; two Algerians, Major Khatib Jaloul and Ali Belaziz; ten Lebanese soldiers captured on 2 January 1970; and an unspecified number of Arabs held in Israeli prisons. No time limit was mentioned.

Suddenly, a civil war broke out between the Jordanian government and the Fedayeen, which lasted from 16 to 23 September 1979.* During this period a curtain of silence was drawn across the whereabouts and fate of the fifty-four hostages. By the 18th, the Israelis had released the last of the 450 Arabs they had arrested. On the 25th sixteen hostages were found by the Jordanian army in a house-to-house search of the Wahdat refugee camp, the PFLP base in Amman, and were released unharmed. The following day another thirty-two were released by the PFLP, and on the 29th the remaining six were handed over by the PFLP to the IRC.

The way was now clear for the terrorists held in Europe to be released. On 30 September, after a twenty-three-day period in detention, Leila Khalid left England in an RAF aircraft, which stopped at Munich to pick up the three PFLP members who had been held by the West German government, and at Zurich to col-

*See Edgar O'Ballance, *Arab Guerrilla Power.*

lect the three detained by the Swiss government. The RAF aircraft carrying the seven triumphant terrorists landed at Cairo International airport. The following day the seven terrorists attended the funeral of President Nasser, who had died on the 28th, while they were still in captivity. Leila Khalid had been detained throughout at a London police station, as it was feared that to transfer her to a remand prison might provoke reprisals against the hostages. On 26 November 1970 she married an Iraqi Fedayeen fighter known simply as Hassan. It seemed to be a classical revolutionary partnership, rather than a marriage in the Western sense, as it was formally approved by the PFLP leadership. After only a week together Leila and her husband were sent on missions that caused them to be away from each other for long periods. Since then Leila Khalid and Hassan have seldom been seen together, even at PFLP camps.

This gigantic hijacking epic, the largest in terrorist history, both as regards the number of aircraft and hostages seized, ended with the destruction of the planes. The PFLP had made its point with Western governments on the principle of exchanging prisoners and hostages, but drew a firm blank with the Israelis.

6   The Black September Organization

Money does not matter, and neither do our lives.
BSO terrorist leader at the Munich Olympic Games,
5 September 1972

AT A MEETING of the PNC at Cairo on 5 March
1971, Kamal Nasser, a Fatah leader, said, "Hijacking has not accomplished anything for us," and
his views were echoed by many Fedayeen moderates. Hijacking
spectacularly carried out by the wayward PFLP had brought worldwide publicity to the Palestinian cause, but it had also disturbingly
focused attention on Fedayeen potential and ambitions, which
caused anxiety, not to the Israelis who at this time were contemp-
tuous of them, but to Arab governments. Kamal Nasser's statement underlined the two primary and most pressing problems of
the Fedayeen—unity and survival as a liberation movement.

Two civil wars, one fought in Lebanon in October 1969 and
the other in Jordan in 1970 and 1971, brought home to the badly
shaken Fedayeen, despite all the fine words uttered by Arab governments, the fact that they were regarded as mortal and expend-
able. They stood alone. From a high peak of mass hysterical popularity that had bred overconfidence, the acrimoniously divided
Fedayeen organizations had sunk into a slough of uncertainty
amounting almost to despair.

By 1969 the Fedayeen movement had achieved the crest of a
high wave of popular enthusiasm in the Arab world, unsurpassed
since the days of the initial Muslim expansions and the spread of
Islam. Dazzled by the tumultuous roars of approval from the Arab
masses, the Palestinian Fedayeen organizations failed to realize
that the masses were not democratically represented and that governments in the Middle East were jealous, afraid of rivalry, and
dreaded usurpation. Their smiles were false and their fulsome
praises were meaningless. The seeming strength of the Fedayeen,
its popular appeal, and the sight of the sharp edge of its weapon of
terror made governments cautious and hesitant. This wariness was

not allayed by the behavior of individual Fedayeen fighters, boast-fully swaggering through towns and villages, openly carrying arms, clad in their leopard-camouflaged combat uniforms, and jostling security forces personnel in the streets. Strong and more conservative Arab countries such as Egypt gave only lip service and a bare minimum of facilities, and would not have done that except that each country did not want to be upstaged by the others on this Fedayeen bandwagon. President Nasser, for example, had been quick to withdraw radio facilities when they criticized him. The reason for such grudging, marginal support was the practical one of national security. Israeli punitive raids against Palestinian refugee camps not only caused a heavy toll of casualties, but brought closer the danger of escalation into war, for which the Arabs were not yet ready.

In Syria, when it had some control over Fatah, the government forbade operations into Israel from Syrian soil. Because of the mood of the people in Syria, Fatah was grudgingly allowed a few facilities, such as the use of training camps and a venue for the leaders to meet in Damascus, but all other Fedayeen groups, especially the PFLP, were frozen out.

Although not strictly a confrontation state in the territorial sense, Iraq was certainly a rejection state (rejecting the complete concept of Israel), but would not allow Fatah or any other Fedayeen organization to operate freely on, or from, its soil. As it, too, had to be openly seen to be supporting the Palestinian cause, the Iraqi government had formed its Arab Liberation Front (ALF), which was under military control. Although most of the Fedayeen organizations were generally unwelcome in Iraq, there were at times both sympathy and support for the PFLP, mainly because it too was rejectionist, and more important was also anti-Syrian.

This meant that of all four confrontation states (Egypt, Jordan, Syria, and Lebanon) the Fedayeen were only able to operate freely in, and from, two—Lebanon and Jordan, comparatively small nations with governments reluctant to take overt action that might bring Arab reprobation down on them.

After settling themselves inside the Palestinian refugee camps in Lebanon, the Fedayeen organizations, especially Fatah, tried to expand into the cities and the countryside adjacent to the Israeli border. Fatah managed to infiltrate and occupy a stretch of barren, rocky terrain about one hundred square miles in area known as the Arkoub, which lay against the Mount Hermon Range (Jebel

Sheikh) next to the Israeli-held Golan Plateau and the Israeli north-ern border. From the sparsely populated, desolate Arkoub, which became known as Fatahland, Fatah commandos began to raid into Israel. Fatah policy was to expand its territorial base, but it came up against resistance from the many tiny villages of different reli-gious denominations; Muslim, Christian, and Druse were all inter-mixed. Fatah commando arrogance caused friction and resentment that escalated into a nine-day civil war.*

Encouraged by the Syrian government Fatah tried to make a military push in strength to force open and hold a vital supply route from the Syrian border to Fatahland that became known as the Arafat Trail. It also tried to expand westward to encompass a belt of territory adjacent to the northern Israeli border. Coinciden-tal with this military operation, Fatah organized a supporting dissi-dent campaign in the cities, towns, and refugee camps.

The war began on 23 October 1969 when Arafat ordered his Fatah commandos to "fight against Lebanese intervention to the last bullet." He had not anticipated much serious opposition, but to his surprise, and to that of many a pundit, the disparaged Leba-nese army not only stood up to the Fatah attacks and held them, but also fought the Fatah commandos to a standstill. However, it was not strong enough to completely defeat and eject them all from Lebanese territory, which the government would have liked to do. The war ended on 31 October when Arafat, who had proved himself to be a notoriously unsuccessful field commander, could not persuade his warriors to advance any further to open up the Arafat Trail. Fatah remained in control of Fatahland, but the Ara-fat Trail remained blocked by Lebanese soldiers, who had also held on to their posts along the northern Israeli border, seriously hindering Fatah movement.

Not wishing to see Fatah become too strong and independent, at the same time President Nasser did not want it to be eliminated completely. It was a useful pawn and convenient counterweight to governments and factions, so he intervened and brought about a cease-fire. On 2 November 1969 he persuaded both Fatah and the Lebanese government to enter into what became known as the (Lebanese) Cairo Agreement. Details of this agreement were never made public, but the main ones were assumed to include the con-dition that Fatah commandos return to their refugee camps and

---

*See Edgar O'Ballance, *Arab Guerrilla Power.*

refrain from carrying arms in population centers. In return they were to be allowed to remain in the Arkoub, and to operate from it into Israel. Thus in Lebanon the Fedayeen were halted in their expansionist ambitions, and, chastened, they had to agree to accept restrictions.

In Jordan, as in Lebanon, the Fedayeen had gained control of the Palestinian refugee camps, which they refused to allow Jordanian security forces to enter. They also controlled large sectors of terrain alongside the River Jordan and in northern Jordan. The Fedayeen had many sympathizers amongst the Palestinian refugees living in the towns on the West Bank. Backed by his loyal Bedu army formations and his Bedu population generally, King Hussein opposed and contained the Fedayeen expansion as much as he could. During 1969 and 1970 Fedayeen groups increased considerably in strength, and many instances of friction occurred between the Fedayeen and Jordanian security forces, some developing into clashes of magnitude.

The blatant disregard shown for the authority of the Jordanian government by the PFLP when it hijacked airliners to Revolution Airfield in September 1970 was the actual spark that ignited a fiercely fought civil war. Already, the Fedayeen had gained actual possession of an area in northern Jordan around the town of Irbid, where roadblocks were set up on the 13th to prevent Jordanian security forces from entering the area. On the 15th, Abu Hassan, a political officer of the Asifa and the local Fatah commander, declared Irbid and the surrounding area to be the "First Soviet on Arab territory."* The following day, the 16th, the civil war broke out when the Jordanian army began a series of attacks that drove the Fedayeen from the streets of the capital.† Arafat was quickly on the scene and persuaded the Central Committee of the PLO to name him as the "General Commanding all the Forces of the Revolution." Jordanian soldiers cleared Irbid and other towns despite strong resistance.

Once again President Nasser, not wishing to see the Fedayeen ejected from Jordan, stepped in and persuaded the two sides to accept a cease-fire. On 27 September 1970 King Hussein of Jordan and Yasir Arafat, chairman of the PLO, signed the (Jordanian) Cairo Agreement. Its main conditions were that the Fedayeen

---

*Not to be confused with the other Abu Hassan (Ali Hassan Salameh, of the Fatah leadership).
†See O'Ballance, *Arab Guerrilla Power*.

would evacuate the capital and other towns. This was Nasser's last political act—a peacemaking one—as he died of a heart attack the following day, the 28th. It had indeed been a Black September for the Fedayeen.

Although badly mauled and badly shaken the Fedayeen were neither beaten nor repentant, but their defeat in the field caused Arab governments to harden their attitudes. An example of this occurred on 5 October when a number of armed Fatah commandos attempting to return to Lebanon chartered an Iraqi Viscount air-liner in Baghdad. On arrival at Beirut they were refused permission to disembark. Two Lebanese officers went aboard the aircraft to tell the Fatah commandos they would not be allowed to enter Lebanon, but were immediately seized as hostages. The plane was surrounded by Lebanese security forces, and the airport was closed for three hours. The ambassadors of both Egypt and Iraq came to the airport to appeal to the Fedayeen to release their hostages and return to Baghdad, to which were added the appeals of represen-tatives of the PASC. After eighteen hours delay the Fatah com-mandos agreed. Their hostages were released and they flew back to Baghdad, where they were disarmed and briefly detained. This was a sharp jolt to Fedayeen pride, and a salutary reminder of how they were regarded by Arab governments of even small countries such as Lebanon.

During February 1971 an internal struggle for power took place within the PLO, the culmination of bitterness and recrimi-nation arising from the Black September defeat, between Arafat and the commander of his 7,000-strong PLA, Brigadier Abdul Yahya. There was also a sharp difference within the PLA between Yahya and his Chief of Staff, Colonel Osman Haddad, each of whom sought to dismiss the other. In December 1970 Yahya had resigned from the Central Committee of the PLO because Arafat had criticized the conduct of the PLA during the September fight-ing in Jordan.

In February 1971 Yahya called on the Central Committee to reform the resistance movement radically and set up a commission to determine "who was responsible for past errors." He demanded the dismissal of Arafat as General Commanding all the Forces of the Revolution and insisted that all Fedayeen fighters be brought under his PLA command. Yahya said that "errors committed by the resistance, which have cost the lives of thousands of persons, are seen by certain leaders as a necessary pruning for the movement. In fact, they led us to veritable national disaster." The politically astute (though militarily inept) Arafat won the struggle. Later having gained Egyptian support, on 7 October 1971 he felt secure enough to dismiss both Brigadier Yahya, Colonel Haddad, and twenty-nine other PLA officers who closely supported one or the other. By this time Arafat was on better terms with the Syrian government, but he had to agree to take back Brigadier Madhat Budairy, the former PLA commander, as Chief of Staff and make him acting commander.

On 29 October 1970 Wasfi Tal became Premier of Jordan. He began to apply military pressure systematically on the Fedayeen to ease them from the towns. During the ensuing weeks, Jordanian Bedu soldiers drove the commandos progressively before them, until by the end of January 1971 they had been cleared from Amman and certain other areas. The Fatah field commander in central Jordan, Abu Ali Iyad (his real name was Mohammed Mustafa Shreim), a one-eyed man who sported an eyepatch like Moshe Dayan's, declared that the fighting had cost him "at least two hundred centers in Amman alone." Under such heavy pressure the Fedayeen leaders quarrelled amongst themselves, and as the leaders were highly individualistic, Arafat had great difficulty in persuading them to retain a semblance of unity and continue to operate under his leadership.

When the PNC met in Cairo on 5 March 1971 it accepted in principle George Habash's resolution to bring about a pro-Fedayeen government in Jordan, but decided to postpone Arafat's plan to amalgamate all the Fedayeen groups. A few days later, on the 11th, Kamal Nasser, official spokesman of Fatah, held a press conference in Beirut at which he declared the PNC had agreed to unify all Fedayeen groups to act as one in the political, military, and information fields, as proposed by Arafat, and that any group that deviated from this line would be regarded as dissident. He added that implementation of this decision was to be left to the Central Committee of the PLO. This statement was more hopeful and wishful than true.

Kamal Nasser also said that the Palestinians had no alternative but to "wage a people's armed struggle against Israel" and that the PLO was against the creation of a Palestinian state on the West Bank, but instead wanted a United Front of Palestinians and Jordanians. He said the PLO had decided there should be no more hijacking of aircraft. Those brave words were uttered as the Jordanian armed forces were preparing to eliminate the Fedayeen from their country. As late as June 1971 Arafat was criticized by the Fatah Central Committee for continuing to try to reach an agreement with King Hussein.

In May 1971 Jordanian soldiers turned their attention to the Palestinian refugee camps, which Fedayeen commandos used as bases and in which they sought refuge. One by one they were cleared of Fedayeen fighters. On the 31st of that month Jordanian Bedu troops entered the PFLP-dominated Wahdat camp and destroyed a monument erected over a mass grave of 175 PFLP commandos killed in the fighting of September 1970, known as the Tomb of the Unknown Fedayeen.

During a clash at a DPF-dominated refugee camp at Zerka, about ten miles north of Amman, government troops captured fifteen DPF fighters, but Nayef Hawatmeh's DPF claimed over-optimistically that it had inflicted over one hundred casualties on the attackers. The following day, 8 June 1971, the DPF kidnapped an American, Morris Draper, a political officer at the U.S. Embassy in Amman, and held him hostage, demanding in return for his safety the release of their fifteen commandos. The only response from the Jordanian government was increased military pressure in the Zerka area. After being held for twenty hours, Morris Draper was freed unharmed.

By early July 1971 Abu Ali Iyad, his original force of about eight hundred commandos reduced to less than fifty, was desperately holding out in the Ajloun area in central Jordan. By the 17th even this hard core had begun to crack. On that day the final Fedayeen indignity of all occurred when sixteen of his men deserted to cross the River Jordan to seek sanctuary on the Israeli-held West Bank. Another thirty deserters followed the next day, and by the 19th some seventy-two Fedayeen Self-Sacrifice fighters, dedicated to the destruction of Israel, had slunk across the river to give themselves up to the Israelis rather than fall into the hands of the enraged Jordanian Bedu troops.

So ended the civil war in Jordan. On 19 July Premier Wasfi Tal held a press conference in Amman at which he declared there were no more guerrilla bases remaining in Jordan, that already 2,300 guerrillas had been captured by the security forces, and that only about 200 remained at large. He did not mention how many had died; no one knows exactly, and estimates vary, but it was a great number. For example, the Jordanian Red Crescent organization later estimated that in the period from 16 September to 6 October 1971, 3,444 Fedayeen were killed and 10,840 wounded. The Jordanian government would only admit to a score of its soldiers being killed and twice as many wounded, an estimate generally considered to be far too low. The Fedayeen claimed that Wasfi Tal "killed more Fedayeen in one year than the Israelis had killed in ten" and also pointed out that as no wounded Fedayeen were held by the Jordanians it must follow that the Bedu soldiers had killed all the wounded.

Defeat in Jordan meant a great loss of face for the Fedayeen, but the ten main groups still survived, as did a few other smaller ones.

Shattered, demoralized, and barely surviving as a cohesive liberation movement, the remnants of the Fedayeen organization sought refuge in adjacent countries, mainly Lebanon, and as many as were able filtered back into Fatahland without publicity or fuss. A chastened Arafat was careful not to provoke the Lebanese government openly, as he realized this was the only remaining Arab country from which the Fedayeen could operate. The Lebanese armed forces were still too weak to eject them completely.

At a Fatah Central Committee meeting in Damascus in September 1971, there was debate as to whether Fatah should go underground again to survive, but this measure was not approved, mainly because the leaders, who had vaingloriously exposed themselves to the public gaze in the heyday of their popularity, were now all too well known. Fatah decided to remain overt and concentrate upon survival. Amid the welter of dissension and division within the Fedayeen leadership, Arafat became the prime target for resentment. On 6 October 1971 an attempt was made to assassinate him on a visit to Fatah units in the Golan area. His driver was killed instead. A Fatah spokesman blamed "elements which have infiltrated guerrilla ranks."

The Fedayeen groups were now short of cash, so the newspaper *Fatah* had to suspend publication for financial reasons. At a PNC meeting held in Cairo on 5 July 1971, lack of Arab financial support was commented upon. It was stated that the only contribution received that year by the PLO had been $40,000 from Qatar, and that the nonfulfilled financial commitments to the PLO by Arab states amounted to over $10 million. On 28 June 1972, at a Fatah meeting in Beirut, it was decided to freeze terrorist operations from Fatahland and southern Lebanon generally, but to continue to maintain a terrorist presence there. It was a period of struggle for survival and of comparative inaction.

Meanwhile, on his return from the Far East on 10 November 1970, George Habash was reelected secretary general of the PFLP, and Wadia Hadad remained as his deputy. The PFLP had played a full part in the civil war in Jordan, but owing to its small size, perhaps less than 600 as compared with Fatah's over 35,000, its operations were limited. The PFLP was more resilient and less subdued than the other Fedayeen groups, and while it continued terrorist operations in Israel and the Occupied Territories, it also instigated some unusual ones elsewhere. This PFLP versatility at times both dismayed and confounded Arab states.

One of the PFLP operations unpopular with Arab governments had been to sabotage the 750-mile-long Trans-Arab Pipeline (TAP) that carried the equivalent of half-a-million barrels of oil daily from Saudi Arabia to Sidon, in Lebanon. The TAP oil pipeline, a subsidiary of the American oil firm ARAMCO, ran for a distance of about thirty miles underground through the Israeli-held Golan Plateau, the Israelis tacitly ignoring the flow of oil beneath their feet, perhaps encouraged to do so by the American government, which wished to have friendly relations with Saudi Arabia. In May 1969 the pipeline was fractured by a PFLP explosion just inside the Golan Plateau, and the flow of oil was interrupted.

This was alleged to be an act of spite by the PFLP against Saudi Arabia. Small in size and comparatively poor at the time of Fedayeen affluence, the PFLP was not able to attract sufficient financial donations from supporters and well-wishers, nor to squeeze them from the Arab masses, as the larger Fatah was able to do. Because it had hijacked aircraft, committed terrorist acts outside the Middle East, and would not come to heel in other ways, Arafat, as chairman of the PLO, had ceased to give the PFLP any share of the money donated by Arab states to the PLO. George Habash had sent an emissary to King Feisal of Saudi Arabia to ask for financial support, which was abruptly refused.

The Israelis would not allow the TAP oil pipeline to be repaired, and the stalemate dragged on for a year, until 11 May 1970. At that time King Feisal threatened to suspend the financial aid he was giving to certain Arab states, including Egypt and Jordan, and also to terminate the $1 million he gave annually to the PLO, if the oil did not begin to flow again. Eventually, the Israelis agreed to allow the oil pipeline to be repaired on the understanding that it would not be sabotaged again. Even so, it was not until 28 January 1971 that oil actually flowed through it once more. The PFLP had touched the Arab states on their raw nerve of national interest; America's national interest was also involved.

The next PFLP operation that proved unpopular with Arab states was carried out as the civil war in Jordan drew to its close. It was directed against the Israeli maritime route through the Red Sea and the Gulf of Akaba to Eilat, along which passed, by means of changes of bills of lading and convenience flags, oil from Iran to Israel. On 11 June 1971 the Liberian tanker *Coral Sea,* loaded with oil from Iran and bound for Eilat, was attacked by four members of the PFLP some 1,400 miles south of Akaba, when it had just passed through the Bab el Mendab (Gate of Tears) Straits near Perim Island. Two small speedboats were lowered from a fishing vessel, and from them the PFLP commandos fired bazooka rockets at the ship, causing fires that were soon put out by the crew. In all, nine rockets were fired, of which only two hit the tanker. The PFLP speedboats were immediately chased by Ethiopian naval craft and had to take refuge on the shore of South Yemen.*

Little damage was done to the *Coral Sea,* but the attack alarmed the Israelis, reminding them of the vulnerability of this supply route and causing anxiety in case more attacks of this nature should occur, perhaps with more positive results. The PFLP claimed responsibility, saying the project had been under consideration for two years and had only been delayed because the PFLP was not sure how the South Yemen government would react to Israeli reprisals. Perhaps the real reason was that the PFLP was waiting for the British presence to disappear completely from the Middle East; shortage of cash may have been another retarding factor.

As freedom of navigation in the Red Sea affected the national interests of most Arab states, they were displeased and brought what pressure they could by means of financial action and threats to try to ensure that this type of terrorist operation did not occur again. The South Yemen government was not amused. It detained the four PFLP members (never named), causing the PFLP spokes-

---

*On 30 November 1970 the Republic of South Yemen, formerly the British-controlled Aden Protectorate, was renamed the Democratic Republic of the Yemen.

man in Beirut to announce on 15 January 1972 that his organization was still unable to obtain their release. It was an indication that Arab states, even rather ineffectual South Yemen, would not tolerate such an infringement of their national interests as attacks on shipping in the Red Sea. It also feared that such Fedayeen naval activity might provoke Ethiopian reprisal raids.

However, this solitary incident underlined Israeli reliance on Iranian oil and their dependence upon this precarious route, although the strategic significance did not seem to be fully appreciated by the Arab world. It was not until the War of October 1973 that the Bab el Mendab Straits were successfully blocked by Egyptian naval craft. The PFLP was before its time.

The next major PFLP exploit, parts of which may read like sheer fiction, was aimed at improving its financial position. On 22 February 1972 five members of the PFLP hijacked a Lufthansa airliner with 172 passengers and sixteen crew on board flying (with various stopovers) from Tokyo to Frankfurt, just after it had left Delhi, India. It had been about eighteen months since the PFLP had hijacked an aircraft. One of the terrorists had boarded the plane at Hong Kong, two at Bangkok, and two at Delhi. They diverted the aircraft and landed it at Aden, South Yemen. The hijackers claimed they were a unit of the Zionist Occupation Victims, but Fedayeen groups in Beirut disclaimed all knowledge of any such movement. This was merely an operational code name, a fact not generally realized at the time. The leader of the hijackers was identified as Yusef al-Khatib, but the others were never named.

Initially there were several mistaken guesses as to the reason for this particular terrorist act. The Iraqi government, for example, was of the opinion that it was a reprisal for the amount of reparations sent by West Germany to Israel, which included arms. Amongst the passengers was Joseph Kennedy, the nineteen-year-old son of senator Robert Kennedy (who had been assassinated on 5 June 1968 in California by a Jordanian, Sirhan Bishara Sirhan). Joseph Kennedy had been touring India, and some thought the terrorists wanted him as a hostage to exchange for Sirhan, who was serving a life sentence in America, but this was not so either.

On arrival at Aden the hijackers allowed thirty-six women and children to leave the plane, and after fifteen hours of negotiation between the terrorists and the South Yemen authorities the remainder of the passengers, including Joseph Kennedy, were also allowed to leave the aircraft, to be eventually flown home safely.

The Lufthansa airliner was parked on a remote runway at Aden airport. The sixteen West German crew had to remain on board while the hijackers produced explosives, which they affixed to parts of the plane and wired to detonators. Since they were beyond the range of the normal airport lighting system, the terrorists used a small generator to provide interior lighting.

The true purpose of the hijack was revealed on the morning of 23 February when a letter, written in English and posted in Cologne, West Germany, was received at the Lufthansa head office in Cologne. The letter demanded a sum of money equal to about $5 million as a ransom for the safety of the aircraft and the crew. The letter gave detailed instructions how the money should be handed over. A suitcase containing the money in specified currencies was to be taken by a courier to Beirut airport, where he would be met by a man driving an automobile with a picture of Colonel Gaddafi of Libya on the front windscreen and one of President Nasser on the rear window. The automobile would be driven to a point about twenty-five miles from Beirut, where the suitcase was to be handed over to a man wearing a black jacket and grey trousers and carrying a copy of *Newsweek* in his left hand. If the contents of the suitcase were found to be as demanded, a code word was to be sent by radio to the hijackers in Aden, who would release the aircraft and their hostages.

George Leber, the West German federal minister of transport, was immediately consulted, and it was agreed the ransom should be paid to avoid a "bloody disaster." A Lufthansa agent handed over the money in exactly the manner prescribed, a code word was radioed to Aden, the hostages were released, and Lufthansa repossessed its aircraft. After being held briefly by the Aden authorities the hijackers were freed. Leber said the hijackers belonged to the PFLP, but surprisingly (and falsely) George Habash denied this in Beirut on 14 March 1972. The sardonic twist in this "perfect crime" was that the South Yemen government, desperately short of foreign currency, collected a percentage of the ransom money, thought to be about three hundred thousand dollars. The PFLP had suddenly become affluent, but the South Yemen government, which had helped it to become so, did not hesitate to take a share in this illegal gain, regarding it as a temporary loan. A few months later it repaid the money to Lufthansa, thus tarnishing its political purity in the eyes of revolutionaries.

Meanwhile, the Third PFLP Congress opened in Tripoli, Lebanon, on 5 March 1972. Abu Shihab, who had formed a small group within the PFLP known as the Revolutionary-PFLP (R-PFLP), questioned the legality of the Congress and opposed Habash. He claimed that Ghassam Kanafani, the PFLP spokesman and editor of *Al Hadaf*, the PFLP newspaper, and others supported him. Abu Shihab was unsuccessful in his bid for power, and George Habash was again elected secretary general.

On 20 March Habash, a founder-member of the Arab National Movement, which in theory was the political leadership of the PFLP, was expelled for "subversive and deviationist activities." The PFLP hijacking of the West German plane to Aden had no doubt provoked this decision. The Central Committee of the ANM at the same time announced its support for the PFLP–General Command, instead of Habash's PFLP. Led by Ahmed Jabril, the PFLP–General Command was a splinter from the PFLP and was sometimes also referred to as the Front for the Popular Palestine Struggle, but became more generally known simply as the Jabril Front.

After the Jordanian civil war, which had ended so disastrously for the Fedayeen, a series of terrorist incidents against aircraft of the Jordanian Aliya Airline occurred, undoubtedly committed by embittered commandos, although it never became absolutely clear which group or groups were responsible. Perhaps the acts might have been committed by individuals taking advantage of opportunity targets, as in some instances there seemed to be a distinct lack of the careful preparation that had come to be the hallmark of some Fedayeen organizations such as the PFLP. President Sadat of Egypt organized a conference in Saudi Arabia in an attempt to heal the rift between King Hussein and the PLO, to which both sent representatives. Although the talks themselves failed in their objective, it was believed at the time that these incidents were a protest against the holding of this particular conference.

Apart from minor damage caused by a small explosion to an Aliya aircraft at Cairo airport on 24 July 1971, the first incident occurred on 23 August when an explosion blew a hole in the tail fuselage of an Aliya Boeing 707 just after it had landed at Madrid airport. No one was injured. From evidence collected on examination of the plane, the device was assumed to have been primed to explode while the aircraft was in flight and may have been inexpertly set. The intended victim was to have been Queen Zeina, mother of King Hussein, who had boarded the plane at Amman, but she had disembarked at Istanbul. Fatah and the other Fedayeen groups denied all responsibility.

The next incident occurred on 8 September, when an Aliya Caravelle flying from Beirut to Amman was hijacked by a Fatah commando who diverted the aircraft to Libya. He had been sentenced to death *in absentia* for his part in the civil war by the Jordanian government, was named as Mohammed Jaber, and claimed to be a lieutenant in the Asifa. Despite the hostility existing between Colonel Gaddafi and King Hussein, Gaddafi allowed the Aliya aircraft with its crew and passengers to fly on to Amman, but he briefly detained Mohammed Jaber. Fatah said it had neither planned nor known about this exploit, insisting that Jaber must have carried it out on his own initiative. However, an embittered Fatah spokesman added that Mohammed Jaber had carried out this act "to get rid of the bloodbaths and intimidation to which Palestinian commandos were being subjected in Jordanian prisons and detention camps." After this exploit Aliya aircraft carried armed security guards.

Next, on 16 September, a young Palestinian named as Bilal Abdul Ali, armed with a grenade which he later said he had carried on board the plane in a pair of specially constructed shoes given to him by a Fatah agent in Beirut, tried to hijack an Aliya Caravelle flying from Beirut to Amman. He was overpowered by the security guards and later sentenced to death in Amman. Another failure occurred on 4 October, when two Palestinian terrorists (never named), a man and a woman, tried to hijack an Aliya Caravelle flying from Beirut to Amman. The woman was observed removing a grenade that she had concealed in a wig and was seized by the security guards as she was about to withdraw the safety pin.

The decision not to go underground did not please all the Fatah leadership, and the subject was again brought up at a Central Committee meeting held in September 1971 in Damascus, at which it was also discussed whether or not Fatah should use terrorism and violence to achieve its ends. Arafat and other moderates had all along insisted that diplomatic and political methods should be used, and that while a degree of terrorism was permissible inside Israel and the Occupied Territories whenever necessary, it could be blamed on uncontrollable extremists, thus absolving the leaders from any responsibility.

Some, especially Abu Iyad (Saleh Khalif), the deputy leader of Fatah, were strongly in favor of violence continuing, so as a compromise it was decided that Fatah should form a secret terrorist arm which it could publicly disclaim. Arafat, who only reluctantly agreed to this decision, would remain as head of Fatah to present the Palestinian case openly. In his capacity as chairman of the PLO he could also openly work for a diplomatic solution to the Palestine problem and thus still be able to walk and talk with presidents and kings. In short, Arafat and his Fatah were to form a moderate front as a cover for the secret terrorist arm.

The man chosen to head this new terrorist arm of Fatah was Abu Iyad, who was already in charge of Fatah's Jihad al-Rasd, the "war intelligence section." Half-a-dozen other senior Fatah leaders were selected to control the various branches and elements. One, for example, was Abu Jihad (Khalil al-Wazir), a founder-member of Fatah who had developed foreign terrorist contacts. Another was Abu Motassin (Ahmed Afghani), the official Fatah representative on the PASC, who had control over Fatah finances and supplies. Yet another was Abu Hassan* (Ali Hassan Salameh), whose father, Sheikh Hassan Salameh, had been killed in the fighting in Palestine against the Israelis in 1948 and was already an Arab folk hero. Abu Hassan became the deputy leader of this secret terrorist arm. Others who formed the core of its leadership included Fakhri al-Umari, who became the head of its "killer section," Abu Yusef (Mohammed Yusef Najjar), Abu Daoud (Mohammed Daoud Odeh), Ghazi al-Husseini, and Fuad Shemeli.

This Fatah terrorist arm was called the Black September Organization (BSO), and it was primarily motivated by the desire to overthrow King Hussein's regime in Jordan and revenge the defeat of September 1970 at his hands. The BSO especially set out to avenge the death of Abu Ali Iyad, the Fatah leader who had held out until the last in Jordan and was killed by Bedu soldiers on 23 July 1971. They had reputedly dragged his body through villages behind a tank.

Recruitment for the BSO was entirely (and selectively) from the ranks of Fatah. The men and women who came into the BSO

---

*Abu Hassan, with four other Palestinian commandos, was killed on 22 January 1979 in Beirut. The vehicle in which he was traveling was blown up by a radio-controlled bomb that had been placed in a parked car on his route. Israeli agents were blamed for his death by Fatah.

were formed into small cells on the communist pattern in which each only knew the members of their own cell, and no others. The cell leaders knew only their immediate superiors in a vertical chain of command. Secrecy was emphasized, and BSO commandos were only given information on a strictly need-to-know basis, and then usually not until the very last moment. Operational instructions were also delayed as long as possible, the actual exploit often having begun before the cell leader was authorized to issue the orders he had received. A small number of Fatah personnel had been sent to Egypt in the early 1960s on an army course of instruction that taught terrorist techniques and skills. These men were used to instruct the BSO commandos, who had to train vigorously.

The first terrorist exploit for which the BSO openly took full responsibility was organized by Abu Yusef, who flew to Cairo using an Algerian diplomatic passport. In Cairo he gave instructions to a small four-man BSO cell, all carrying Syrian passports, who had arrived in that city between 16 and 23 November and rented a small flat. They were originally named as Izzat Ahmed Rabah, the leader, who had lost a finger in the fighting in Jordan; Muntzer Khalifa; Jawad Khalil Baghdadi; and Fuad Mahmoud Badran.* Their task was to kill Premier Wasfi Tal, who was due to arrive in Cairo to attend a meeting of the Joint Defense Council of the Arab League; Tal also held the Jordanian portfolio of Defense.

On 28 November 1971 the four BSO commandos waited in a hotel foyer in Cairo for Wasfi Tal to return from his meeting. As he stepped through the hotel doors, Rabah fired five shots from a pistol, wounding Tal, who fell to the ground. Rabah's companions then fired more shots at Tal as he lay on the floor. Abdullah Salah, the Jordanian foreign minister, who was with Tal, was also wounded. Rabah, who was shot in the leg by a Jordanian security guard, was immediately seized, but the other three fled. Khalifa and Baghdadi were caught after a street chase, and Badran was arrested at the flat they had all used. A fifth person, who was never named, was also arrested in connection with this assassination by the Egyptian authorities the following day. Abu Yusef had brought a female member from another BSO cell with him to Cairo. Her task was to remain in the background in the hotel foyer, but to step

---

*At their later trial their names were given as Zaid al-Helew, Mohammed Khairy Khashak, Mohammed Nabil, and Jawad Abu Aziz. Arabs invariably have several names, and do not always use the same ones on all occasions, which tends to confuse a Westerner.

forward and throw a grenade at Wasfi Tal should the others fail in their mission to kill him. When arrested the four BSO commandos had four pistols and one grenade in their possession.

The Egyptian government had initially refused Wasfi Tal permission to enter the country to attend the Arab League meeting because it feared there might be an attempt on his life, so universally unpopular had he become in the Arab world. But he insisted upon attending, and so was allowed to come to Cairo. His body was flown back to Amman on the 29th and was buried with full military honors. President Sadat sent a message of condolence to King Hussein.

Khalifa was reported to have boasted that "I have drunk his blood," which caused Westerners to shudder in disgust in the mistaken belief that the assassin had actually knelt down and lapped up the spilt blood like a cat laps up milk. This was not so, the Arabic expression being a symbolic one used to indicate triumph over an enemy. In his statement, Khalifa said that he and Rabah were walking in Beirut fifteen days before when told that Wasfi Tal had decided to attend the Cairo meeting, adding, "We jumped for joy and embraced, for this was the chance of a lifetime to destroy him after he had killed 10,000 Palestinians." Khalifa admitted that his organization had been waiting for Wasfi Tal for over six months to revenge the death of Abu Ali Iyad, and added that the BSO had plans to kill every Arab leader opposed to the Palestinian cause.

The four assassins appeared briefly before a Cairo Court on 20 February 1972, where they were cheered and applauded. Prominent lawyers from several Arab countries appeared in court to defend the accused, including Ahmed Shukairy, the first chairman of the PLO. The hearing was turned into a political trial of King Hussein. When forensic evidence was produced that none of the bullets that struck Wasfi Tal could have been fired from any of the assassins' pistols, the court immediately released them on bail. All four then lived in Cairo in comfort, first at a hotel and then in private apartments at the expense of Colonel Gaddafi of Libya. After a little while Baghdadi and Badran were allowed to leave Egypt "to carry on the fight"; Khalifa and Rabah remained in Cairo for a while, and then they too disappeared. At their trial the accused claimed that the BSO consisted of about five hundred commandos. Israeli estimates of May 1972 were that the BSO had only about sixty commandos, with up to another hundred in training. The killing of Wasfi Tal was the first resounding BSO success, which gave the Fatah leadership confidence in it. From this moment it was fully approved and supported by Fatah, which openly and flatly denied any knowledge of it or connection with it.

The next BSO exploit was a failure: an attempt to assassinate the Jordanian ambassador in London, Zair Rifai, who was the son of Samir Rifai, a former Jordanian premier. On 15 December 1971 the ambassador left his London home in an automobile for the embassy, and when it slowed down at a road junction a BSO commando standing on the pavement calmly took a submachine gun from under his coat and fired thirty shots into the vehicle. Only one hit the ambassador, slightly injuring his right hand. The terrorist then escaped in an automobile driven by an accomplice. In a telephone call to the Reuters office in Beirut the BSO claimed full responsibility for the incident. The unsuccessful assassin was identified as Frazeh Khelfa, an Algerian, who escaped to France. Britain asked for him to be extradited, but instead the French handed him over to the Algerian authorities, who alleged that Khelfa was wanted by them. The following day, the 16th, the BSO caused an explosion at the home of the Jordanian ambassador in Geneva, but no one was injured.

Other exploits in the first eight months of 1972 that the BSO claimed responsibility for included an explosion on 8 February in the Streuber motor factory near Hamburg, West Germany, and an explosion on the 22nd of that month in an ESSO pipeline, also near Hamburg. Throughout this period Arafat and the overt Fatah leadership denied any connection with the BSO whatever. Arafat found no difficulty in bending with the wind of secret terrorism.

The next major operation carried out by the BSO was also a spectacular first. On 8 May 1972 four of its commandos, two men and two women, hijacked a Belgian Sabina Boeing 707 flying from Brussels to Lod, in Israel, with ninety-seven passengers on board, of whom fifty-five were Jewish. Just after a stopover at Vienna, the pilot was directed to continue on course and land the aircraft at Lod airport. The BSO commandos were flying the plane right into the lion's mouth. It landed safely at 1900 hours. The hijackers refused to let anyone leave the plane and demanded the release of 100 Arabs held in Israeli detention, threatening to blow it up with all on board unless this condition was complied with. The hijackers renamed the aircraft "Victorious Jeddah" and claimed that their leader, Captain Yusef, was a qualified pilot who had taken personal control of the plane. Then began a twenty-two-hour period of negotiation. The Israeli airport authorities asked if they could move the Boeing from the apron on which it stood to another one over a mile from the airport control tower and main buildings. The hijackers agreed, and the plane was towed away to the new position, which was in complete darkness.

The leader of the BSO hijack team was identified by the Israelis as Ali Taha (other authorities identified him as Yusef al-Khatib), who was code-named Captain Yusef for the operation. He had been involved in the first Arab hijack in July 1968, which ended in Algeria. He had then been a member of the PFLP, but seemingly he had since been recruited into Fatah's secret terrorist arm. The other man was named as Abdul Aziz al-Atrasi, a Syrian Druse who was code-named Zacharia. The two women were named as Rima Aissa Tannous, a nurse who had been brought up in Bethlehem; and Therese Halaseh, also a nurse, who had been born in Acre. Both were Christian Arabs who had crossed into Lebanon, where they gravitated into Fatah, eventually being selected for recruitment into the BSO.

After training in Fatah camps in Lebanon, the four had flown separately to Frankfurt, where some of them met each other for the first time. Using forged passports, they then went by air to Brussels, where they received their final instructions and were given weapons and explosives. The women put a grenade each in their vanity cases, detonators in their bras, and were wearing special girdles brought with them from Lebanon, into the lining of which they had each put about six pounds of explosive. Rima Aissa Tannous was the explosive expert in this BSO team. The men carried pistols and batteries for activating the detonators. They all boarded the Sabina aircraft carrying false Israeli passports. Once on the plane the girls extracted the explosives from their girdles in the toilets and then returned to their seats.

After the Vienna stopover the BSO commandos seized control of the aircraft and Captain Yusef pushed the barrel of his pistol into the back of the neck of the pilot and kept it there. The pilot was Reginald Levy, who had served in the RAF during World War II. The other three hijackers, seated in different parts of the aircraft, rose brandishing pistols and grenades. Therese Halaseh spoke to the passengers, telling them the plane had been hijacked, that they were being held as hostages, and warning them the aircraft would be blown up if the Israeli government would not agree to release certain Arabs from detention. The hijackers collected the passengers' passports. Rima Aissa Tannous sat with the detonator box on her lap, dramatically holding in her hands two wires, which she said would cause an explosion if they touched each other.

The hijacked plane remained shrouded in darkness, under which cover two airport employees crawled under it to let down its tires and drain off the hydraulic fluid from the undercarriage and brakes. At 2230 hours the terrorists asked for fuel, not being aware the aircraft had been immobilized. The plane was now surrounded by fire engines and ambulances. During the whole period of this hijack exploit, the normal flow of air traffic continued at Lod airport. At about 0130 hours (on the 9th) the hijackers realized, or were told, what had happened. They insisted the repairs be carried out immediately. At about 0430 hours the terrorists demanded to speak to an International Red Cross representative, and one arrived about an hour later. Captain Yusef said he wanted the aircraft refueled so it could be flown on to Cairo, where he intended to hold the hostages until the demanded Arab prisoners were all released.

Annoyed that negotiations were being protracted, at about 1000 hours Captain Yusef told the two women to wire up the detonators to the explosives, which seemed to take them by surprise. They both burst into tears and embraced each other. That spasm of emotion over, they did as they had been instructed. It would seem that until this moment the threat to blow up the plane had been an idle one. Her task completed, Rima Aissa Tannous went to report to Captain Yusef, who had remained in the pilot's cabin throughout with his pistol still touching the back of the pilot's neck. At this moment the pilot quickly turned and grabbed Captain Yusef's arm and the hand that held the pistol and forced the weapon round so that it was aiming at the terrorist. The pilot pressed the trigger, only to find the safety catch was applied. Abdul Atrassi then appeared in the doorway of the cabin to point his pistol at the pilot, whose gallant attempt had been unsuccessful.

The Israelis were simply playing for time, having no intention of releasing any Arab prisoners. Meanwhile, Moshe Dayan, the defense minister, had arrived on the scene and taken charge. He was planning an assault, but at the same time instituted deception measures. A team of five IRC representatives had arrived at about 0900 hours and were shuttling to and fro between the aircraft and the control tower, where the command headquarters had been established. The senior IRC representative agreed to act as an intermediary between the terrorists and the Israeli authorities.

At about 1200 hours the pilot was allowed by the hijackers to leave the plane and go to the control tower with a sample of the explosive material to try to convince the Israelis they were serious. He was able to give Dayan precise details of the layout of the plane, including the positions of the terrorists and the various exits, which was of great value in planning the assault. For the first time Dayan learned that two of the hijackers were women. The pilot was allowed to make one other trip to the control tower. He was told to give the hijackers the impression that the Arab prisoners would be released, and that the aircraft would be refueled as soon as it was repaired.

A bus full of "Arab prisoners," actually Israeli soldiers with their heads shaved who had been chosen for their darker complexions, was moved up to just within sight of the aircraft. The terrorists thought they were succeeding in their exploit. However, another airliner, out of sight of those in the hijacked plane, was drawn across the path of the Sabina Boeing. Meanwhile Belgian officials had arrived at Lod who were authorized by their government to offer the terrorists up to $600,000 to release the hostages. Dayan would not allow this offer to be made. Earlier, he had offered the hijackers a safe-conduct out of Israel if they would give themselves up, but this offer had been rejected. Of the several alternative solutions examined by the Israelis, one involved the use of nerve gas of the type used in brain surgery, which it was thought could be pumped into the aircraft during darkness. It is an instant action gas. The Israeli cabinet turned this idea down, as medical advisers could not guarantee it would not harm children or those with heart conditions.

At 1515 hours the hijackers allowed an IRC representative, using a vehicle, to take food aboard the aircraft. Then, with the terrorists' agreement, two airport vans, preceded by the IRC representative carrying an IRC flag, started to move towards the aircraft. In the vans were twelve Israeli commandos disguised as airport mechanics, Captain Yusef having agreed that they could come and make the aircraft ready for flight. When the vehicles halted on the tarmac near the aircraft, the "mechanics" alighted. Suddenly the IRC representatives became suspicious and must have communicated their suspicions to the terrorists. Three of the air crew were told to get down and search the "mechanics." While this was happening the IRC representatives stood casually by talking to each other and to the hijackers. Nothing was found in the search, and the "mechanics" were allowed to carry on. In three groups they strolled towards the three emergency exit doors of the plane.

Suddenly, at 1610 hours, they drew their weapons, which had been hidden in their boots, jumped for the doors, and entered the plane. They had rehearsed the operation thoroughly. In thirty-four seconds it was all over. The two male hijackers were killed, and the two women terrorists captured. Therese Halaseh suffered a severe head wound. In the shootout three Israeli commandos were wounded, as were six passengers, one of whom later died; she had been sitting beside one of the female terrorists. Rima Aissa Tannous was overpowered by a passenger as she was in the act of pulling the safety pin from a grenade.

For the Israelis the operation had been a glorious success, demonstrating their hard new policy of not surrendering to terrorist blackmail. To the BSO, which claimed full responsibility, it was a glorious failure, which demonstrated the spirit of the Fedayeen fighters, prepared to give their lives for their cause. Arab newspapers praised the BSO for its exploit, and the consensus of Arab opinion was that it had failed only because the hijackers became so concerned with the welfare of their hostages.

The IRC was rather piqued about the Israeli conduct of the operation, being apparently under the impression that as it had been accepted as the mediator, it should have been in control of events, and consulted and informed of all Israeli intentions and actions beforehand. The senior IRC representative said he had been "completely surprised by the Israeli action" and complained that "there was an abuse of our confidence." The Israelis did not see it quite like that, and Moshe Dayan emphatically denied he had given them any such undertaking at all. The BSO accused the IRC of being in collusion with the Israelis and claimed that the IRC flag had been a deliberate decoy. This was denied. Captain Ola Forsberg, president of IFALPA, who had flown to Lod airport, was also displeased, saying that "the safety of passengers and crew should always be put first, and here it was not." Later, in August

1972, Rima Aissa Tannous and Therese Halaseh were sentenced to life imprisonment.

The BSO leadership was preparing to outshine its rival PFLP, which had launched a television spectacular by hijacking airliners to Revolution Airfield, Jordan, in September 1970. Its chosen site was Munich, West Germany, where the twentieth World Olympic Games had opened on 26 August 1972. The publicity buildup had attracted universal attention and drawn nearly five thousand journalists and television crews to photograph and record the Games. In the city of Munich there were thousands of foreign "guest workers," the largest contingents being those of the Iranians, Greeks, and Yugoslavs, with the Arab one forming a minority.

Just before dawn on 5 September 1972, at about 0430 hours, eight shadowy figures clad in sportsmen's track suits and carrying traveling bags climbed over the metal mesh fence that surrounded Olympic Village, which housed some 12,000 people, mainly competitors, officials, and administrative personnel from over 120 countries. The group was seen entering by passing telephone engineers, a woman cleaner, and a postman, but no one initially paid any particular attention to them, assuming them to be either revelers sneaking back to their quarters after a night out (apparently not an uncommon occurrence) or athletes returning from early morning track training. An Olympics official later told me that "anyone dressed in a track suit could get in with no questions asked."

The eight men, who were BSO commandos, moved from the fence to a three-story concrete building which housed the Israeli, Hong Kong, and Uruguayan Olympic teams, known as 31 Connolly Street, about fifty yards distant. The street had been named after the American hop-skip-and-jump Olympic champion at the 1896 Games. The leader was Mohammed Masalhad, a Palestinian architect who had lived and worked in West Germany for some years. He spoke both German and English fluently. Moreover, he had at one stage been engaged on the construction of the Olympic Village, and had been specially brought over from Libya because of his knowledge of its layout. Two of his companions were actually working in Olympic Village, where, incidentally, the kitchen staff of some 967 people were of eighty-seven different nationalities. The one who worked as a cook and spoke Hebrew was simply identified as Toni, while the other, who worked as a gardener, was named as Abu Halla. Both had arrived from Austria the previous month.

Track suits were stripped off, traveling bags opened, and Kalishnikov AK-47 automatic rifles and grenades taken from them and distributed to the BSO commandos. Their target was the Israeli Olympic team, but they did not seem to know exactly which apartment or rooms it was occupying. Silently they crept from one door to another, to open it quietly if it was not locked, and if locked to knock gently and whisper, "Is this the Israeli team?" in Hebrew. They soon found what they were looking for, but the door of the apartment was locked. However, one Israeli was awake, as he was expecting his companion to return very late and had agreed to let him in. On hearing the knock he thought it was his friend, and so unlocked and partly opened the door. The terrorists pushed hard against it. Instantly the Israeli, who was a weight lifter, realizing the danger, tried to close it again, but was unsuccessful. The scuffling was confused, but the Israeli had a knife, and two of the terrorists received minor wounds. The terrorists shot and killed that Israeli and also another who tried to run past them. Awakened by the shots, the remainder of the Israeli team in another room escaped over their own back balcony, but those in the room the BSO commandos had entered, nine in number, were taken as hostages and their hands tied behind their backs.

The alarm was now fully raised and within fifteen minutes a detachment of police arrived at 31 Connolly Street to cordon off the area. It was now daylight, and as the news spread through Olympic Village television crews and photographers by the hundreds arrived to point their lenses towards the building and to jostle to get as near as the police would allow.

One by one prominent politicians and senior officials arrived on the scene, and a Crisis Staff was established to deal with the situation. One of the first to arrive was Manfred Schreiber, Chief of the Munich Police. He spoke to the terrorist leader, who appeared on the balcony shrouded in a hood, to the delight of the news cameramen. Mohammed Masalhad demanded in exchange for the safety of the Israeli hostages the release of 200 Arabs in Israeli detention; Kozo Okamoto, a Japanese terrorist held by the Israelis; and the two German urban terrorists Andreas Baader and Ulrike Meinhof from prison. He also demanded an aircraft to fly the terrorists and their hostages to an Arab capital other than Amman or Beirut, as well as a helicopter to fly them to Munich airport, where the aircraft was to be waiting. He set a deadline of 0900 hours, saying that if the West German government had not agreed to comply with these conditions, after that moment he would shoot a hostage every two hours until they did agree. Early on the scene was Mahmoud Mestiri, the Tunisian ambassador, who spoke to the terrorist leader and persuaded him to extend his deadline until 1200 hours.

Among the others who arrived were Bruno Merk, the Bavarian state minister of the interior, and the federal minister of the interior, Hans Dietrich Genscher. There was more than a suspicion of coolness between the two men owing to the division of their responsibilities. Later in the day the West German chancellor Willy Brandt also arrived. It was a moment of great embarrassment for the Germans, who had coined the slogan "The Games of Joy and Peace" for this Olympiad.

The Crisis Staff tried to persuade the terrorists to release their hostages by offering a large sum of money, saying they could name the amount. This was later confirmed by one of the terrorists, who said not only had the Germans offered them money, but that an Olympic hostess had offered to "provide us with beautiful German blondes if we would release the hostages."* Mohammed Masalhad's reply was "Money does not matter, and neither do our lives." An offer by West German politicians, and others, to take the place of the hostages was also rejected by the terrorists. The Algerian diplomatic representative, Mohammed Khalid, said his government had authorized him to offer a safe-conduct to the terrorists and to pay them any sum of money they demanded. Willy Brandt got in touch with the Israeli government and urged it to negotiate with the BSO commandos, but it would not do so.

The surrounding police made no attempt to rush the terrorists, who were in an advantageous position to shoot anyone who attempted to cross a stretch of open ground. The BSO commandos mainly stayed inside the shuttered apartment to avoid presenting a target to police marksmen. That day the Egyptian Olympic team left for home, as did Mark Spitz, an American Jew who had won seven gold medals in swimming events.

The reconnaissance and planning for this exploit, which was

*Interview in *An Nahar*, a Lebanese newspaper, 24 November 1972.

named the Berim and Ikrit Operation by the BSO, had been carried out by Fuad Shemali, a founder-member of the BSO who had died of cancer a fortnight earlier in Geneva. His task had been taken on and continued by Fakhi al-Umari, head of the killer section, who had given his last minute instructions to the BSO commandos before slipping out of West Germany into East Berlin to join Abu Hassan, the deputy leader of the BSO. The name of the operation was taken from two Christian Arab villages in northern Israel, which had surrendered without resistance in the 1948 war. The Israeli military authorities persuaded the villagers to leave their homes on "security grounds," promising them they would be able to return within fifteen days. Even though an Israeli high court had later ruled in the villagers' favor, they were still not allowed to return to Berim and Ikrit, where their houses had been demolished and Jewish settlers had taken over their land and were cultivating it.

Also involved in the planning was Abu Daoud, who had deposited eight Kalishnikov automatic rifles and ten grenades in a box at the Munich railway station's Left Luggage Office, where they were collected by the terrorists. It was strongly suspected at the time that the weapons might have been smuggled into West Germany in Libyan diplomatic bags, and later some substance was given to this theory by Major Omar Maheisy, a former member of the Libyan Revolutionary Command Council who had fled to Cairo in 1975 after being involved in an abortive coup against Colonel Gaddafi.* The BSO found it comparatively easy to operate in West Germany because so many of the guest workers were Arab and they could move about the country without exciting undue suspicion.

During the morning glimpses were caught of the hooded Mohammed Masalhad as he briefly appeared on the balcony to talk to one or the other of the officials or to drop notes outlining fresh demands. The West Germans were now required to provide three aircraft to take the terrorists and their hostages to join the prisoners once the latter had been released by the Israelis and flown to an Arab capital. The object was to distribute themselves and their hostages among three planes so there would be less chance of all of them being caught or tricked. As negotiations continued the deadline was successively extended, and the Crisis Staff played for time, ostensibly agreeing to meet the terrorists' demands.

*In a broadcast over Radio Cairo on 18 March 1976.

The telephone inside the besieged apartment was still connected with the exchange and was allowed by the Crisis Staff to remain in use. The terrorists made two calls to Tunis, which were not answered. These were monitored by the West Germans, who asked the Tunisian ambassador, whose offer of his "good offices" as a mediator had been rejected by the BSO commandos, to find out whom the terrorists were trying to contact. After investigation, all the ambassador would say was that it was the number of the residence "of a very highly placed person." The original BSO plan was that the terrorists and their hostages should be flown to Tunis, but something had obviously gone wrong, or someone had backed out. The terrorists made at least two other telephone calls, one of which was traced to a Palestinian refugee organization in Beirut. The other was made during the afternoon to the widow of Fuad Shemali (who had been a BSO member) in Geneva, giving her the facts of the situation and asking her to pass them on to the PLO.

Suddenly, the terrorist leader said they wanted to be flown with their hostages to Cairo, so Chancellor Brandt, who was at the Crisis Staff headquarters, put through a personal telephone call to President Sadat, only to be told the president was not available. Instead, Brandt had to be content to speak to Ahmed Sidky, the Egyptian premier. The chancellor later described this conversation with him as "very disappointing." In short, Cairo would not accept the terrorists. From this moment onwards the Crisis Staff realized that it would have to take action against the BSO commandos. Marksmen were brought up and readied. Later, one of the terrorists said that the federal minister of the interior promised he would give them a safe conduct to Cairo and "that there would be no foul play."*

Meanwhile, from the beginning the Israelis were adamant that they would not release a single Arab prisoner, and urged the West German government to adopt a firm policy of "No negotiation with terrorists." The Israeli government immediately sent General Zvi Zamir, head of the Mossad, who arrived at Munich airport about 1900 hours, bringing with him an Arabic-speaking Mossad officer. They were both included in the Crisis Staff. The Israelis tried to persuade the authorities to abandon the Olympic Games, but there was reluctance despite the gravity of the situation, and

*According to *An Nahar*.

events continued while the siege was in progress. Eventually it was agreed that the Games should be halted for twenty-four hours. This was a disappointment to the Israelis, who had expected a more positive and wholehearted gesture of sympathy and understanding from the West Germans.

Moshe Dayan, the Israeli defense minister, wanted to fly to Munich, but this offer was turned down by the Bonn government. Nevertheless he and another cabinet minister intended to go there all the same, but both were seen at Lod airport by a journalist who reported the fact. The two Israeli ministers were then persuaded to cancel their proposed journey. It was thought that Dayan's presence might provoke the terrorists to kill their hostages.

Early in the evening Kurt Waldheim, the UN secretary general, came into the picture. He contacted Colonel Gaddafi and asked him to mediate at Munich. Gaddafi did not reply, nor did he take any action. However, the UN secretary general telephoned Mohammed Daghely, the Libyan ambassador at Bonn, and told him what he had done, asking the ambassador to pass the information on to the terrorists in the hope they might agree to extend the deadline yet again. Mohammed Daghely, who had a plan of his own, did so, but there was no response. It was now after 2100 hours, and the deadline was due to expire at 2200 hours.

The Libyan ambassador's plan was to try to persuade the terrorists to modify their demands by asking only for the release of 15 Arabs from Israeli detention, instead of 200, which he thought might be more acceptable and face-saving all around. But he had left it too late, as the Crisis Staff had made up its mind to take a hard line. As part of its tactic it told the terrorists that it agreed to their demands, which had been modified to asking for a single aircraft to take them out of Germany, instead of three. They still demanded helicopters to take them to Munich airport. Mohammed Masalhad, who did not know that Cairo had refused to accept them, now additionally demanded an airport bus to take them from the ground floor door of their building to the helicopters, a distance of about a hundred yards. This dismayed the Germans, who were planning to use marksmen to pick off the terrorists, still thought to be only five in number, during this walk.

The Crisis Staff agreed to provide the bus and the hooded Mohammed Masalhad came to the door, grenade in hand, to be shown where the helicopter would land, and the route the bus would take. The airport bus appeared and was thoroughly examined by Toni who appeared to be the deputy leader of the group, and another terrorist who was simply identified as Issa.

At about 2210 hours the terrorists and their hostages emerged from the building and entered the bus. The nine hostages were blindfolded and tied together, and for the first time it was realized there were eight terrorists, not five, which was another setback for the German plan. The bus had darkened windows, and once inside both terrorists and hostages crouched down below window level so that none could become a silhouette target and any bullet fired into the body of the vehicle might just as easily kill a hostage as a terrorist.

Three helicopters were waiting on the selected site, and on leaving the airport bus four terrorists and four hostages got into one of them, and four terrorists and five hostages into the other. Into the third helicopter climbed the Israeli general Zamir, his Arabic-speaking officer, Police Chief Schreiber, and the two ministers of the interior, Genscher and Merk. Under the impression they were being flown to Munich airport, the terrorists had promised not to hijack the helicopters when in flight. Commencing at 2215 hours, the helicopters took off at two-minute intervals. West German police marksmen had hoped for an opportunity to pick off the terrorists when they were leaving the bus and entering the helicopters, but none presented itself as the terrorists made the bus go quite close to the helicopters, and on debussing they mingled with their Israeli captives, all remaining bunched together. Afterwards Schreiber said, "We could never get the terrorists in a group. They were too clever, too professional."

Instead of taking them to Munich airport, the Crisis Staff had arranged for them to be flown to the Furstenfeldbruck military airfield, a NATO airfield that handled all the charter flights for the Olympic Games. The helicopters came to rest on the airfield at about 2230 hours, some fifty yards in front of the control tower, where a police command group had been established. The helicopters were guided in by two policemen disguised as airport ground staff. About 150 yards away was a floodlit Lufthansa Boeing 727; the remainder of the area was in shadow or comparative darkness. Five police marksmen were positioned ready to fire, one being on the roof of the control tower. When a favorable target presented itself, he was to be the first to fire, his shot being the signal for the others to commence firing too.

After a wait of three minutes Mohammed Masalhad and one

other terrorist jumped from the helicopter and walked over to inspect the Boeing, while another terrorist alighted from each of the two helicopters together with their pilots and copilots, who were held at gunpoint. Part of the German plan had been to put policemen on board the Lufthansa aircraft disguised as air crew. This was canceled at the last moment as it was feared that if shooting occurred on the plane there might be heavy casualties. The aircraft was empty of people, the crew being in the control tower, but the aircraft tanks were full. Apparently satisfied with the aircraft, and not suspecting they were not at Munich airport, Mohammed Masalhad and his colleague began to walk back to the helicopters.

When they had reached about halfway, the marksman on the top of the control tower opened fire, and the other marksmen instantly did the same. The terrorist walking with Mohammed Masalhad was killed at once, while Masalhad ran forward and dived into the shadow of one of the helicopters, from where he fired back at the control tower, killing the policeman on its roof. He also damaged radio and radar equipment in the control tower itself. A differing version is that the German policeman was in the act of entering the control tower when he was shot. Another version was that on the walk back from inspecting the aircraft the terrorists had taken with them one of the helicopter pilots, and that on the way back the three of them walked abreast with a few yards distance between each man, the pilot in the center. The pilot was able to signal with a small torch he had, which everyone thought was a lighted cigarette. When fire was opened by the policemen, the pilot dropped to the ground, rolled aside, and then ran behind the control tower.* This account was not confirmed by the West German authorities. The two terrorists standing outside the two helicopters were both killed, but the pilots quickly dropped to the ground and only one was slightly wounded. Firing continued for six minutes, during which time a bullet struck an electric cable, dousing all lights abruptly.

Then followed a period of suspense lasting for over an hour and a half, during which the West German police, speaking through loud-hailers, tried to persuade the terrorists to give themselves up. The Arabic-speaking Mossad officer added his pleas as well, but to no avail. Suddenly, a few minutes after midnight, the remaining four terrorists jumped from their helicopters and turned around

*According to the Sunday Times, 10 September 1972.

and deliberately fired into them at the hostages. One additionally threw in a grenade, which set the machine on fire, causing apprehension in case the fuel tank exploded. A gun battle flared up between the terrorists and the police marksmen, in which one terrorist was killed. Having automatic rifles, the BSO commandos had an advantage over the police, who only had the NATO 7.62 mm self-loading ones.

Firemen rushed forward to try to douse the burning helicopter, which lit up the surrounding area. They were fired on by the terrorists, which momentarily halted them until the police, who had been waiting in the outer darkness in armored vehicles, swept forward to close in on the BSO commandos. Two of the terrorists, both slightly wounded by gunfire, surrendered at once, but the third one played dead until it was discovered he was alive. Yet another terrorist ran away into the darkness. This was believed to be Toni, the Hebrew speaker, who was found some seventeen minutes later hiding under a truck. Toni then escaped again, but was shot minutes later when found under an automobile.

Suddenly it was all over. The death toll was seventeen. Of the nine hostages, eight had died from bullet wounds and the ninth, although wounded by bullets, had actually died of asphyxia from fumes in the burning helicopter. The other dead were five terrorists and one German policeman. Just before midnight came a last-moment tragic message of false hope, when news was given out unwittingly that the hostages were safe, which was taken up without being checked and broadcast on West German television. The equipment in the control tower, damaged by terrorist fire, was later blamed for the false message and for the fact that it was not instantly corrected. At 0300 hours on 6 September a press conference had to be called to correct the false news and announce the black tidings.

A memorial service was held that day in the main stadium, attended by over 80,000 people, and the following day the Israeli contingent was flown back to Israel with its dead. A solitary exception was one of the victims who was a recent immigrant to Israel, whose body was flown back to Ohio, U.S.A. for burial.

The three terrorist survivors were taken into West German custody to await trial. They were named as Ibrahim Masoud Badran, Abdullah Samir, and Abdul Kader al-Dnawy, all young Palestinians who had recently been living in Syria or Jordan. As they remained tight-lipped, little more became known about them, not even if these names were their real ones. Apart from Mohammed Masal-had, none of the other terrorist dead were positively identified, and no country or Fedayeen group came forward to claim their bodies or provide any information about them. Colonel Gaddafi offered to accept the bodies, which were flown to Libya on the 12th to be given a "Hero Martyrs' Funeral." In the wild melee of the shootout it was impossible to determine who killed whom, but later one of the surviving terrorists, Abdullah Samir, stated that "Badran said he threw the grenade that killed the Israelis in the helicopter, and then Dnawy began shooting the hostages."*

The Munich Massacre, as it became generally known, was roundly condemned by Western and other nations, including the Soviet Union, which sent a message of condolence to the Israeli government. On the other hand, Arab governments were silent, the only exception being King Hussein, who spoke out against what he called a sick crime. After a silent pause, Arab governments began to criticize the way the West Germans had handled the incident, and to praise the BSO for its exploit. The BSO survivors openly blamed the federal minister of the interior, Genscher, saying in a later interview that he knew they had grenades and rifles, and that "he also knew we could destroy the helicopters in seconds. Just the same he embarked upon the massacre."* In answer to the comment that the Egyptian government should have accepted the hostages and terrorists, the Egyptian minister of information openly blamed West Germany on 7 September for the Munich Massacre, saying, "It is clear that Egypt had nothing to do with the incident. The commandos and the Israeli hostages were killed in a German ambush, by German bullets, in an American base in Germany." On the 12th, President Idi Amin of Uganda praised the BSO action.

Israeli Prime Minister Golda Meir stated that her government never at any time contemplated releasing a single Arab prisoner, or Kozo Okamoto. The Israelis had previously objected to the general lack of security at the Munich Games and had wanted to send four armed security guards. The West German authorities refused to allow this, saying they did not want to turn Olympic Village into an armed camp. The Israelis nevertheless sent security guards in the guise of training coaches, but they were not armed. The Israeli Mossad had expected a spate of letter bombs to be sent to Israelis at the Games, but had not anticipated such a direct attack. General

*According to *An Nahar*.

Zamir was displeased with the way the West German police had handled the incident and complained of a lack of positive action. The presentation of credentials of the first West German ambassador to be appointed to Israel since 1965 was postponed on 15 September.

On 8 September the Israeli air force made its expected reprisal raids, which lasted about twenty minutes, hitting seven Fedayeen camps in Syria and another three in Lebanon, causing heavy casualties. A Fedayeen spokesman admitted to "60 killed and 200 wounded, not counting civilians." Internally, the Israeli government wielded an axe when on the 16th Premier Meir announced that three senior members of the Israeli security forces, obviously meaning the Mossad, had been compelled to resign "for their shortcomings." It was certainly a loss of face for the Mossad.

All was not yet over, and everyone waited breathlessly for the next episode. The BSO, which had boastfully claimed full responsibility for the Munich Massacre, openly threatened to liberate the three terrorists held in West German detention, saying, "The sky is full of German aircraft." The suspense was soon over. On the morning of 29 October two BSO commandos, named as Kassem Salah and Samir al-Shahed, hijacked a Lufthansa Boeing 727 flying from Damascus to Munich, just after a stopover at Beirut. On board were a West German crew of seven and eleven passengers, of whom nine were Arab. The plane had arrived at Beirut airport about 0300 hours and had remained there for four hours, during which time pistols and grenades had been smuggled on board by local BSO commandos. The BSO headquarters was then in Beirut.

The Lufthansa plane was first flown to Cyprus to refuel, and then to Zagreb, Yugoslavia, to refuel again, before being flown to Munich. On arrival over Munich it circled overhead for half an hour while the hijackers negotiated by radio with the authorities on the ground below. Claiming to belong to the Organization of National Arab Youth for the Liberation of Palestine,* the code name for the operation, the hijackers demanded the release of the three detained BSO members in return for the safety of the Lufthansa aircraft and all on board. The Bavarian state government immediately agreed to their demand.

Originally the hijackers had planned to land at Munich airport, pick up the terrorists, and then fly off again, but when told it

*Not to be confused with a later terrorist organization with a similar name.

would take over ninety minutes to get them to Munich the authorities suggested that they instead be taken to the nearby Reim airfield. In view of the rain and poor flying conditions, the hijackers accepted this alternative. As the Boeing was again low on fuel, the Germans suggested it land at Munich to refuel in the meantime. Suspecting a trick, the hijackers refused to agree, and changed their plan. Instead, they demanded the three detained terrorists be put on an aircraft and flown to Zagreb. With just enough fuel to make the journey, the Lufthansa airliner turned and flew to that city as well.

Handcuffed together, the three terrorists were put into a hired Hawker Siddeley-125 executive plane together with two policemen, two pilots, and the chairman of Lufthansa, Herbert Colmann. The Hawker Siddeley took off and circled Munich airport for a short while, and then suddenly flew off to Zagreb, where it landed a few minutes after the hijacked Lufthansa Boeing. The three terrorists were immediately transferred to the German airliner, which flew off to Tripoli, in Libya. The following day, the German aircraft and its crew and passengers were returned safely to West Germany. In Libya the three released BSO commandos appeared on television to answer questions calmly, showing no trace of fear, pity, or remorse. They all affirmed, without bombast, that if ordered to do so, they would again carry out a similar operation.

Although obviously secretly relieved to be rid of such a potentially explosive problem, there were minor German recriminations. The Bavarian state government alleged the Boeing had left West German air space without permission, but this was contradicted at a press conference, when it was stated that Herbert Colmann, who was in radio contact with the hijacked Boeing and knew that it had very little fuel left, gave his permission. It was not specified from where he, as a private individual, gained his authority. From the BSO point of view the whole operation went smoothly and successfully, and its three commandos had been all too easily rescued from a West German prison. Basking in Arab pride at such fearless dedication, the Fedayeen began to say to each other, "We are all Black September now."

Others were not so pleased with the result. In Israel, Foreign Minister Aba Eban called it a "shocking surrender, a capitulation, and a weakening of the international stand against terrorism." The West German ambassador to Israel, Herr von Puttkamer, replied,

"We are not at war. We have to act according to law, which means to save the lives of citizens. Saving lives is a priority."

It was distinctly noticeable that the West German government attitude had changed from the tough one adopted on 5 September to a milder, almost fatalistically docile one by 29 October. In the former case there had been no German hostages, while in the latter, German lives were at stake. Also, a federal election was due on 19 November, and a mishandling of a hijack situation that might involve loss of lives could prove to be a political football in the election campaign. Shrewdly, the BSO planners had counted on one important factor often overlooked by theorists—that of the national interest, which all too often overrides fine principles.

The Munich Massacre prompted the West German government to consider creating a Federal Anti-Terrorist Force for use in similar emergencies. As the Federal Armed Forces were constitutionally forbidden to aid the civil power, they chose the Federal Frontier Force for this task. This well-armed paramilitary body had developed a reputation for efficiency and had not been involved in any political controversy.

The Palestinian Fedayeen, in the form of the Black September Organization, had turned the West German Games of Joy and Peace into a terrorist Olympiad. The ancient Greek tradition that safe-conduct should be given to competitors by all warring states and that the site of the Games should not be a military target had been violated. The only safe-conduct respected was that given to the three terrorists who had killed their hostages.

7 International Terrorist Contacts

The Front is training Turks in the same way as it trains Ethiopian organizations and revolutionaries from the underground countries.
Leila Khalid, 26 May 1971

SO FAR THE active terrorist elements in the Palestinian Fedayeen had consisted of Arabs, largely Palestinians, who had an emotional interest in dismantling the State of Israel and returning the Palestinian refugees to their former homes. However, their activities attracted a few non-Arab sympathizers who were envious, anxious to learn and gain experience, or wished to be involved in some way for a variety of obscure reasons. Some of them carried out spontaneous and unsolicited acts, others were employed on a mercenary basis, and yet others were unwittingly used by the terrorists.

For example, on 8 January 1970 a French sympathizer, Christian René Belon, hijacked a TWA Boeing 707 on a flight from Paris just before it landed at Rome airport. The hijacker demanded that the plane be refueled, and fired shots into the aircraft galley to hurry the ground crew because he thought the process was taking too long. Belon was armed with an automatic rifle and two pistols. When refueling had been completed, the hijacked plane, with its crew of eight and twelve passengers still on board, took off to land at Beirut airport, where security forces quickly surrounded it. The passengers and crew escaped by using emergency chutes, while Belon fired ten shots into the instrument panel before leaving the plane to give himself up to the Lebanese authorities.

Belon explained that he was in sympathy with the Palestinians but had no affiliation with any Palestinian organization, adding, "I did what I did to spite America, because America helps and encourages the Israelis and her aggression." He also said, "I do not think it was fair that the Israelis should take twenty-one Lebanese prisoners in their raid, for one Israeli prisoner taken by the Palestinians." He was referring to border incidents that had taken place a few days previously. Belon was brought to trial in Beirut in October 1970, and on the 30th of that month was sentenced to nine months' imprisonment, but was immediately released since he had already spent that period of time in detention.

After the Munich Massacre, Arabs studying or working in West Germany became suspect and increasingly came under surveillance. This fact prompted the terrorist organizations to hire mercenaries whenever they could to help them carry out acts of terrorism.

One such example came to light on 25 May 1970 when a young Italian-Swiss student, Christopher Moreau, was arrested as he stepped ashore in Israel from the Greek ship *Enotria*. On being searched he was found to possess five pounds of Soviet-made explosives, one detonator, and a number of labels marked "PFLP." He stated he had been contacted by the PFLP in Beirut, where he had been paid $900 as an advance to take explosives into Israel and to cause explosions in certain buildings. He was to have received another $5,000 when he completed his task. Instead, he was sent to prison for fifteen years. Yet another instance was revealed on 23 June 1970 when a twenty-year-old Swiss student, Bruno Breguet, was arrested as he set foot in Israel, and when searched had explosives in his possession. He too had been recruited by the PFLP as a mercenary and was eventually sent to an Israeli prison.

Five foreigners recruited by the PFLP by its cell in Paris were hired as mercenaries to carry out an operation in Israel code-named Easter Commando. Their task was to smuggle explosives into Israel and then to cause explosions in several hotels during Easter Week, when thousands of foreign pilgrims would be visiting the Holy Land. This group was headed by a woman, Evelyne Barges, a French student.

On 11 April two of them, Evelyne and Nadia Bardali, daughters of an Arab father and a French mother, were arrested as they disembarked from an aircraft at Lod airport. They had explosives in their clothing and luggage. Under interrogation, they revealed details of the other three members of their group. Two of them, an elderly couple named Bourghalter, also French, had arrived in Israel two days previously. They were immediately arrested at the Tel Aviv hotel where they were staying. They too had explosives and detonators in their luggage. Evelyne Barges had given both couples return tickets to Israel and a sum of money that exceeded $1,000. More money was promised when the task was completed.

On 12 April Evelyne Barges herself arrived in Israel, to be promptly arrested. In addition to explosives in her clothing and luggage, she also had a napalmlike solution in her clothing. Detonators were in the hollow heels of the shoes of all the women. All were eventually sentenced to terms of imprisonment. Barges said, "I consider the Palestinians' case against the Israelis the same as that created by the French colonization in Algeria. That's why I want to help them." The Israeli intelligence had some success in detecting non-Arab mercenaries. The explosives were traced to a PFLP illicit factory near Paris in which five terrorist experts manufactured explosive devices of all sorts. The French DST arrested Mohammed Ben Mansour, an Algerian, and René Caudan, a Frenchman, but others escaped. Evelyne Barges was a member of the PFLP Paris cell who a month previously, in March 1971, had blown up three oil tanks at Rotterdam.

Foreign helpers could not always be attracted by money, and indeed the two Bardalis admitted that their young male Arab companions were an additional incentive. Neither was the secret thrill of becoming a member of an Arab Fedayeen organization always enough, so on occasions non-Arabs were used unwittingly to help Arab terrorists. There were two such occurrences in early September 1971, full details of which were not released by Israeli authorities because they did not want to lose their high reputation for aircraft security. On 4 September the Israeli Government Press Office made a brief announcement that saboteurs had tried "to exploit innocent passengers to get explosives onto the aircraft," and that "the attempt had failed."

One of the innocent agents was a Dutch girl who met an Arab in Europe who proposed marriage to her. He arranged to take her to Israel to meet his mother and bought tickets at Rome. He then told her that his business had delayed him and persuaded the girl to travel to Israel to meet his family, where he said he would join her later. He gave her a suitcase to take on the aircraft, saying it was full of presents for his family. The suitcase had a false bottom that contained an explosive device. During the flight to Lod the Dutch girl told an Israeli passenger what she was doing. He became suspicious and alerted the authorities.

The second incident of this nature involved a Peruvian girl who was sent to Israel by her friend, identified only as Roberto, a Brazilian of Arab parentage. She flew from Rome airport and later realized her friend had switched suitcases. The one she took on the plane had a false bottom, which, like the others, contained an explosive device.

The two girls were presented to the press in Tel Aviv on 9 September 1971. The Dutch girl was identified simply as Jetti and the Peruvian as Delia. They were not allowed to answer any questions about what happened on the aircraft. The facts established that the two girls had been duped by members of the Jabril Front to take explosives in suitcases on board El Al aircraft at Rome airport, and that both devices had failed to explode when the plane was in midair. The Israelis would not say how they were detected, or why they had failed to explode. The girls, who were totally innocent, were released. Three suitcases involved were on display to the press. Until this moment El Al staff had only inspected passengers' hand luggage, but after these incidents passengers had to sign statements saying they were acquainted with the contents of every piece of their baggage. This caused long delays.

Another similar incident occurred on 16 August 1972 at Rome airport when two English girls on holiday met two young men who said they were Iranians. They were, in fact, members of the Jabril Front. As a parting present the men gave the girls a record player that contained an explosive device. The device exploded in the luggage compartment about ten minutes after the El Al airliner had taken off for Lod. Little damage was caused because the luggage compartment, as on all El Al planes, was protected by armored plating. The pilot was able to turn his aircraft around and land safely. None of the people on board were injured. The device had been timed to explode when the aircraft reached a height of about 20,000 feet, when the sudden lowering of air pressure within the plane due to a gash in its fuselage would probably have caused it to disintegrate in midair. The aircraft, and all on board, had been saved because it had been twenty-two minutes late in starting.

The two Palestinian students involved were Ahmed Zaidi Ben Baghdadi and Adnam Mohammed Ashem. After seeing the girls off, they had both gone by road to Venice, where they had expected to be met by another member of their cell who was to conduct them safely across the frontier into Yugoslavia. As their contact did not appear, the two men returned to Rome, where they were arrested. They were granted bail, but absconded, causing the Israelis to accuse the Italian authorities of negligence. The Italian police confirmed the existence of suspected Arab terrorist cells in Venice, Trieste, and Perugia.

The PFLP was particularly fortunate in selecting a competent leader to spread its network of secret terrorist cells across Europe.

He was Mohammed Boudia, an Algerian and a Marxist who had been a supporter of Ahmed Ben Bella, the Algerian president. When Ben Bella was deposed by Houri Boumedienne, Boudia had to flee to France. Boudia joined the PFLP in 1969 and was sent to Paris after a period of training in Middle Eastern camps. His task was to form and lead a terrorist cell. He was not only to carry out terrorist exploits in Western Europe, but was to contact other non-Arab terrorist groups, both to assist them and to persuade them to work with PFLP teams on operations. Regarding France as his base and a safe sanctuary where he could live, obtain information, and plan his operations, Boudia, whose cell eventually came to include about ten members (including Evelyne Barges), resisted all Wadia Hadad's urging to attack El Al aircraft on French soil. Boudia also received secret funds from the Soviet KGB, channeled through East Berlin.

One of the first operations carried out by Mohammed Boudia was an act of sabotage. In the early hours of the morning of 4 August 1972 several explosions occurred at the San Dorligo refinery, the Trieste terminal of the Trans-Alpine Oil Pipeline (TAL), which linked Trieste with Austria and Germany. In this exploit eighteen people were injured and five large storage tanks were set on fire and blazed for over two days, causing damage estimated to exceed $3 million.

This raid was personally led by Boudia, who was accompanied by two women, Diane LeFebvre, a Rhodesian, and Dominique Turilli, a Frenchwoman; Chabane Kadem, an Algerian; and an Italian named as Ludovico Cordello. Cordello was caught by the Italian police, but later released for lack of evidence. The other three returned safely to Paris. In a statement put out on the 5th by WAFA, the Palestinian news agency, the PFLP claimed responsibility, although at the time the explosions were thought to have been perpetrated by the BSO, saying the act "was aimed at Zionist and imperialist interests which are enemies of the Palestinian people." This explosion was also thought at the time to have been caused by Croatian nationalists, or even by the Israelis. The oil complex was jointly operated by thirteen oil companies, and shipped large quantities of Libyan oil to Europe.

As the successful are inevitably the envy of the less bold, dedicated, or competent, the Palestinian Fedayeen became a magnet. It had arms, money, and the open support of certain Arab countries that allowed the Fedayeen to live and train in, and even operate from, their territory in security. In the early 1960s there was only scanty, almost accidental contact between terrorist groups of different nationalities, but as this became exploratory, international contacts developed. Eventually representatives from most of the well-known terrorist groups were invited, or invited themselves, to visit Fedayeen training camps in the Middle East. During 1969 a number of foreigners visited these camps in Jordan, Lebanon, and Syria.

One such visit received doubtful publicity when Fatah invited a group of about 145 people, mainly young students from several countries, to live and work with them in their camps in Jordan during July and August 1969. This had unexpected results for the Fatah leadership, as the visitors tended to be impatient, arrogant, and badly behaved. They drank alcohol, would not conform to camp discipline, disliked the spartan conditions and the food, and criticized Fatah ideology and tactics. Moreover, they praised Fatah's rival, the PFLP.

There were many other, more successful visits to both Fatah and the PFLP by smaller parties and even individuals. During 1970 the number of non-Arab terrorists visiting the Middle East increased. Of these foreign revolutionaries, left-wingers, and would-be terrorists who traveled to learn and gain experience, many fell by the wayside or succumbed to bourgeoise comfort, but others returned home to revitalize their own flagging groups and to keep alive, develop, and expand the international contacts they had made.

Libya provided sanctuary and training facilities for some of the extreme Fedayeen activist groups, but was far from the focus of conflict. Egypt would not allow any terrorists to operate in its territory at all, or even to pass through it. After mid-1971 the Fedayeen were effectively barred from Jordan, and increasing restrictions were imposed on them in both Syria and Lebanon. This caused the enterprising PFLP to look farther afield for an openly sympathetic and helpful country.

In November 1967 the British evacuated Aden Protectorate, which then became the independent state of South Yemen. Prior to and immediately after independence there was a struggle for power between the National Liberation Front (NLF) and the Front for the Liberation of Occupied South Yemen (FLOSY). The NLF became predominant, and so formed the first government of

South Yemen, led by President Qahtan al-Shaabi. During the summer of 1968 this interfactional struggle flared up again, and in addition left-wing elements of the NLF rebelled against the government. The government eventually emerged dominant.

On 22 June 1969 President Qahtan al-Shaabi was ousted and replaced by a Presidential Council, which declared open support for the "Palestine Resistance Movement." Marxist in political ideology, this Council approved of, and showed favor to, Marxist-oriented Fedayeen groups. As it lacked natural resources and industrial wealth, the South Yemen government was not able to help materially, but it did offer three immense advantages: sanctuary, and permission to establish headquarters and training camps. These were eagerly accepted by the PFLP and other extreme groups such as the DPF and the Jabril Front. All members obtained freedom of movement within Aden and had no fear of arrest—always two uncertainties in other Arab countries.

In March 1971 Colonel Gaddafi of Libya came out more positively in favor of Palestinian terrorist groups, and favoring the PFLP because of its notoriety, he gave George Habash $1 million. This put the PFLP in a fairly strong position, enabling it to purchase more weapons and ammunition, to expand its external activities, and to give selected training and other assistance to non-Arab terrorist groups. The PFLP soon used up the million dollars, but in February the following year obtained $5 million ransom for a Lufthansa aircraft and crew held at Aden.

By this time, when a degree of cooperation had sprung up between the Fedayeen and non-Arab terrorist groups, a surprising number of political organizations prepared to use violence to achieve their aims were scattered around the world. Most were small, and while some were ambitious and energetic, most were parochial in outlook, ineffective, and puny. A few achieved a terrorist reputation that seeped beyond the borders of their own country. The principal ones with which Fatah, the PFLP, or other extreme Fedayeen groups made or sought to make contact were Trotskyist Fourth International, the Tupermaros of Uruguay, the Montoneros of Argentina, the June Second Movement and the Red Army Faction (the two German groups), the National Iranian Front, the Turkish Peoples Liberation Army, the Omani-based Popular Front for the Liberation of the Arab Gulf (PFLOAG), and the Japanese Red Army. There were others. A brief introduction to each is necessary to show how the Fedayeen groups attracted and inspired them and became the main skein for the threads of international terrorism as it developed.

Until the 1970s terrorists generally grouped themselves together for a common political aim, usually being of the same nationality, race, or political persuasion, each group concentrating on its own ends, gazing intently through narrow blinkers, having little or no knowledge of each other or indeed little in common with each other. Alliances or agreements made between one or more of them were generally short marriages of convenience to obtain some temporary advantage.

Both the Soviet Union and China, as we have seen, had selectively given sparing aid and some encouragement to terrorist groups that looked for guidance or inspiration to either Moscow or Peking. The Trotskyists, whose aim was the vague one of world revolution, were also automatically against whatever happened to be the Moscow line at any given moment in world affairs. After Trotsky's assassination, the Fourth International barely survived in Europe, although it fared a little better in America. However, it was revitalized in the 1960s, when a special effort was made to try to weld together a worldwide alliance of Trotskyist groups. Some progress was made towards forming a central committee to maintain communication with all outlying groups, hopefully to enforce the party line in all corners of the earth.

Eventually the Central Committee of the Fourth Trotskyist International moved its headquarters to Brussels, where it officially disassociated itself from all forms of violence to concentrate upon pumping out propaganda and expanding as an organization. At its 1969 Congress, attended by representatives from over forty different countries, it was decided to adopt a more aggressive stance and to carry out "protracted guerrilla warfare and terrorism" in Latin America. It was the first genuine international organization in the terrorist sense, and it certainly helped Castro export subversion to South America.

The one other organization which had tried hard to band together various terrorist groups was the Afro–Asian–Latin American People's Solidarity Organization, formed in Havana in 1966. It was under heavy Castroite influence. Its intention was to embrace all terrorist groups within these three continents, but in practice it was only effective in South America. It had produced Patrick Arguello, the unsuccessful hijacker of September 1970.

The Movimiento de Liberacion National, more commonly known as the Tupermaros, was founded in Uruguay in 1962, largely by Raul Sendig, a Marxist who gained his original support from among the sugar plantation workers in northern Uruguay. The Tupermaros were named after Tupac Amaru, a Peruvian Indian leader claiming descent from the Inca Macno Capac, who led a revolt against the Spaniards at the end of the eighteenth century and was executed after being captured. The Tupermaros issued their first communiqué in 1965, protesting against American intervention in Vietnam. Their early terrorist activities were mainly confined to armed robberies, which began in 1966, when the organization only had about fifty members. During 1968 the Tupermaros moved into the capital, Montevideo, and as they expanded, recruiting mainly from students and those with middle class backgrounds, they shed their rural character and became urban guerrillas. Contact between the Tupermaros and the PFLP was maintained through the Boudia cell in Paris, but little seemed to develop from it.

The same can be said of the Montoneros of Argentina. Led by Eduardo Firmenich, the Montoneros became perhaps the best known terrorist group internationally. They gained a great deal of support from the trade union movement and workers generally.

In Europe, a fruitful liaison was maintained by the Boudia cell with the two main West German urban terrorist groups, the June Second Movement and the Red Army Faction, more commonly known as the Baader-Meinhof Gang. Fatah also maintained links with these two groups, members of which visited Fedayeen camps. The June Second Movement took its name from the occasion of the visit of the Shah of Iran to Berlin on 2 June 1967, which provoked demonstrations of protest in which Benno Ohnesorg, a student, was shot and killed by the police. Led by Rolf Pohle and Ernst Wilfred Bose, its platform was an anarchistic one. Pohle, a lawyer and the son of a former rector of Munich University, had organized the theft of seventy-five U.S. M-26 grenades in June 1971 from a U.S. army depot in West Germany, while Bose ran a left-wing publishing house known as Roter Stern. Bose was the main contact with the Boudia cell.

At first the June Second Movement set out to win the support of workers in West Germany, and was selective in its terrorist exploits to avoid alienating them. As this policy did not succeed, the organization took a harder line, its robberies and explosions becoming less discerning. In one explosion, at the British Yacht Club in Berlin, a German worker was killed. On 4 June 1972 it executed one of its members, Ulrich Schumucker, a student who was accused of being a traitor to the movement and of passing on information about it to the police while in prison. Many of the leaders and activists of the June Second Movement were arrested by the West German police.

The other notorious West German terrorist organization was the Red Army Faction (Rote Armee Fraktion), founded and led by Horst Mahler, a West Berlin lawyer. After an unsuccessful attempt had been made to kill Rudi Duetschke, a left-wing student leader, in April 1968, the so-called Extra-Parliamentary Opposition, a loose body of left-wing opinion, split up into a number of small groups, one of which became the Red Army Faction (RAF). The RAF professed anarchistic aims and was influenced by the activities of the South American urban guerrillas. Its terrorist activities began on 2 April 1968 when twenty-eight-year-old Andreas Baader and Gudrun Ensslin, the daughter of a clergyman, set fire to a supermarket in Frankfurt as a protest against capitalism. Both were arrested and imprisoned. On 17 May 1970 Ulrike Meinhof, a journalist, led an armed rescue team that snatched Baader from the Berlin library where he had been allowed to continue his studies under escort. Until this date the organization did not seem to have a definite title, but after this exploit it was dubbed the Baader-Meinhof Gang by the press. The title Red Army Faction came some time later. Many members of the leadership element of the RAF escaped to East Berlin, and in the summer of 1970 several of them spent some time in Fedayeen camps in the Middle East.

In the winter of 1970 the Baader-Meinhof leaders returned to West Germany, and for about eighteen months the group embarked upon a campaign of urban terrorism that included armed robberies, explosions, and attacks on government buildings and American installations. During May 1972, when the RAF probably had about sixty members, it caused explosions at the U.S. Army European Command Headquarters in Heidelburg, killing three American servicemen, and at the headquarters of the U.S. Fifth Army Corps in Frankfurt, killing an American officer. Other explosions occurred at police stations in Munich and Augsberg and in a building of the right-wing Springer publishing house in Hamburg. The Baader-Meinhof Gang gained much of its terrorist knowledge from *The Minihandbook of the Brazilian Urban Guerrilla* by

Carlos Marighela, a Brazilian terrorist, which had been on sale in Berlin in 1970.

The luck of the leadership ran out in June 1972. On the 1st of that month Andreas Baader and two other leaders, Jan-Carl Raspe and Holger Meins, were arrested in Frankfurt. On the 7th Gudrun Ensslin was also arrested, and on the 15th so was Ulrike Meinhof. The arrest of Horest Mahler followed. Within about a fortnight almost the complete leadership of the Baader-Meinhof Gang had been captured. Another leader, Peter Homan, gave himself up. After these arrests, explosions and other terrorist acts in West Germany ceased while the remaining members went deeper underground for their own survival. On 18 October 1972 Horst Mahler was brought to trial and Peter Homan turned state's evidence. Homan said at the trial that he had fled to East Berlin in 1970, and from there went to Jordan to join other members of the RAF, where he saw Horst Mahler, Ulrike Meinhof, Andreas Baader, and other West German terrorist leaders in Fatah camps. This confirmed links between the Palestinian Fedayeen and both the June Second Movement and the Baader-Meinhof Gang.

On 9 November 1972 Holger Meins died while on hunger strike in a prison hospital. The following day an armed group broke into the West Berlin apartment of Judge Gunter von Drenkmann and killed him. The judge had taken no part in either the Meins trial or the preparation for it. It was not certain whether this was a deliberate assassination or the June Second Movement members responsible had meant to hold the judge as a hostage and had shot him in the struggle.

The Boudia cell in Paris also kept in touch with other smaller and less well-known terrorist groups, giving them at times some selective help. One of these was the Basque terrorist organization Euzkadi Ta Ashatasuna, or "Basque Nation and Liberty" (ETA), which was seeking autonomy for a separate Basque state. The Boudia cell provided the explosives that were used to make the gigantic land mine that killed Admiral Carrero Blanco, the Spanish premier, in December 1973. Other national terrorist groups with which the PFLP or Fatah was in touch were the Breton Liberation Front and the Corsican Liberation Front, as well as the Irish Republican Army. While in theory the PFLP accepted the international concept of Marxist revolutionary warfare, in practice it remained intensely nationalistic, adhering rigidly to its single-minded aim of dismantling the State of Israel. This was often a point of acute disagreement which surprised and often disappointed Marxist visitors to the Fedayeen camps.

The Palestinian Fedayeen terrorist elements also had a close liaison with the National Iranian Front (NIF), formerly the Iranian Liberation Movement, which was mainly Muslim and nationalist, with Marxist tinges. Money and support were given by Fatah and the PFLP. Iranian terrorists trained in and visited Fedayeen camps. Confirmation of this came on 2 July 1971 when a joint statement was issued by Fatah and the NIR that gave news of the death of an Iranian terrorist. It said, "An Iranian fighter, Ali Zefani Frehani, has died of torture in an Iranian prison. He fought alongside the Fedayeen in Palestine. Frehani trained, together with a group of young Iranians, at Arab Fedayeen bases, and participated in Fedayeen actions against the enemy. He reached the rank of officer in the resistance forces before transferring to the Iranian Front." More confirmation came on 22 October 1971 in the Algerian newspaper *El Shaab*, which reported that "The Iranian revolutionary movement had established a Palestine group composed of forty-five Iranian fighters who fought alongside their Palestinian breathren. Some of these fighters have returned to Iran, after obtaining combat experience and advanced training."

On 19 December 1971 the Lebanese newspaper *El Ahad* reported that "the Palestinian Revolution has opened the way for many Iranian fighters to benefit from practical training in the use of arms. This aid first began in 1968 when a contingent of the Iranian revolutionary movement left Iran for training with the resistance movement. On their return to Iran, they began to train other members. Owing to the direct influence of the Palestinian struggle, revolutionary groups began to study armed struggle and to carry out armed actions inside Iran." This periodical went on to report that the Iranian authorities had recently arrested seventy-five members of a single group, many of whom had participated in action in the "conquered territory." The PFLP newspaper *Al Hadaf* regularly reported actions alleged to have been carried out by the NIF. However, while there was undoubtedly a degree of Fedayeen assistance given to the NIF, it does not appear to have been very great. This tended to be surprising, as the Iranian government was shipping oil to Israel by means of transferred bills of lading and flags of convenience.

Another national terrorist organization to which Fatah and the PFLP gave assistance was the Turkish People's Liberation Army (TPLA). In May 1960 a military coup had ended a democratic regime in Turkey, and after a short period of military rule free elections were held in October 1961. A series of coalition governments followed. The political freedom of 1961 allowed a proliferation of political parties to spring into existence, in particular student unions of both the left and the right. Political violence began in June 1968, when four students were killed in scuffles with the police, and escalated. The reasons for the spasms of political violence were the combination of the sudden release of pent-up political expression and the slow pace of land and economic reforms, aggravated by worldwide student unrest.

The Turkish government banned all student organizations having a political aim. This caused the right to fall apart, while the left went underground within the university campuses, where disorders and demonstrations continued. In 1970 over eighteen students were killed in clashes with security forces, and many more were injured. The splintered left came together under the umbrella of the Dev Genc, or Great Youth (sometimes mistranslated as Revolutionary Youth), which after a while split into two factions—the theorists and the activists. The theorists gained control of the Dev Genc, while the activists, still keeping some contact with the Dev Genc, formed an organization in January 1971 that became known as the Turkish People's Liberation Army.

Led by Nahit Tore and Mahir Cayan, and seldom consisting of more than 300 to 400 members, the TPLA was based on student support, its members being Marxist-Leninist oriented and usually drawn from comfortable middle-class backgrounds. Its platform was that the liberation and complete independence of Turkey could only be achieved by an armed struggle. It particularly wanted to free Turkey from what it considered to be American domination. Mahir Cayan, who became the leader, was a twenty-five-year-old student at Ankara University who had trained with the PFLP in Jordan and claimed to have taken part in a PFLP sabotage raid into Israel.

The TPLA tried to precipitate a military coup, after which it hoped the military might initiate administrative reforms. The first stage was to wage a type of guerrilla warfare on the lines laid down by Mao Tse-tung, and a few base camps were set up in southeastern Turkey, in Kurdish territory. Some help was obtained from the Kurds and from exiled Kurdish groups in Sweden and Switzerland. There were about three million Kurds in Turkey (within a population of twenty-eight million), but they were oppressed and politically unrecognized. However, the TPLA plan to wage guerrilla warfare did not materialize, and so instead it had to resort to urban terrorism, including explosions, kidnapping, and armed robbery. The Turkish authorities clamped down heavily on these urban terrorists, and many were arrested.

The first major act of sabotage had occurred in November 1970, even before the TPLA was officially formed, when the Cultural Palace in Istanbul was set on fire. This was followed in March 1971 by the shooting of a Turkish policeman who was on guard duty outside an American-owned building. That same month the TPLA kidnapped two American servicemen, demanding a ransom of one million dollars for their safe release. The Turkish government stood firm and would not negotiate. After four days, the Americans were set free. On 16 April martial rule was imposed on certain Turkish provinces, and on 1 June all youth movements were banned.

The TPLA sought contacts with the PFLP and Fatah, which had the one vital requirement it did not possess—the almost open use of training camps in certain Arab countries. In an interview with a Turkish journal,* Leila Khalid confirmed that this type of help was given. She said, "The Popular Front is sending instructors to Turkey in order to train youth in urban guerrilla fighting, kidnapping, and plane hijackings, and in other matters, in view of the fact that it is more difficult than in the past for Turks to go and train in Front camps. The Front is training Turks in the same way as it trains Ethiopian organizations and revolutionaries from underground countries. The Front trained most of the detained Turkish underground." The Turkish authorities classified and identified all Palestinian assistance as being from Fatah, blaming Arafat for supporting the dissidents, but in fact the major portion of such help was given by the PFLP.

On 17 May 1971 Ephraim Elrom, the Israeli consul general, was kidnapped in Istanbul, and the TPLA demanded the release of its members in detention in return for his safety. The government refused to negotiate with the TPLA. On the 23rd, during a house-

*Hurryet, 26 May 1971.

to-house search by 30,000 troops and police, Elrom's body was found in a room in Istanbul. He had been taken there by the TPLA and, while strapped to a chair, shot and killed in cold blood by Mahir Cayan. Cayan was arrested in August and brought to trial, together with another twenty-five TPLA terrorists. On 30 November the police also arrested Nahit Tore, who was also wanted in connection with the Elrom murder. That same day Mahir Cayan escaped from detention by tunneling his way to freedom. Altogether, during 1971, 3,759 people stood trail before military tribunals in Turkey, mainly for political or terrorist offenses.*

There was a certain amount of sympathy in Turkey with the aims of the TPLA, especially in the army, which may help to account for a number of escapes. On 13 March 1972 fifty-seven officers and soldiers were arrested for supplying arms to the TPLA and helping TPLA members to escape from military prisons in Istanbul.

On 26 March 1972 the TPLA kidnapped three NATO technicians, two British and one Canadian, from a NATO base at Unya, near the Black Sea. Seven others were tied up and left behind. The three were held as hostages for the freedom of three TPLA members under sentence of death for kidnapping two American servicemen in March the previous year. The TPLA justified its action by saying the technicians were part of a foreign occupation force.

Again, the Turkish government would not bargain, and the following day the kidnappers were cornered in a small village about fifty miles from Unya. In the ensuing gun battle with the security forces nine TPLA men were killed, including Mahir Cayan; one survivor escaped, but was later captured. The three NATO technicians had been murdered about two hours previously when the terrorists saw that the situation was hopeless. This loss practically decimated the TPLA leadership. On 23 April twenty-three TPLA members were arraigned for the murders of the NATO personnel. Once comparatively popular with the Turkish masses, from this moment the TPLA began to lose their support, mainly because it now indulged in indiscriminate terrorism. Members of the public began to pass information on to the police, which resulted in many more arrests.

Emulating the PFLP, on 3 May 1972 four TPLA terrorists seized a Turkish airliner at Istanbul airport with sixty-eight people

*According to the Anatolian News Agency, 12 March 1972.

on board and forced the pilot to fly the plane to Sofia, Bulgaria. The hijackers demanded the release of six terrorists in exchange for the safety of the plane and all on board. Once again the Turkish government would not negotiate. The following day, the 4th, the hijackers released their hostages and were granted political asylum in Bulgaria. The next TPLA hijacking occurred on 22 October 1972, when four TPLA terrorists took over a Turkish aircraft with over seventy people on board and forced the pilot to land at Sofia airport. Again, the terrorists demanded the release of twelve prisoners, but again, the Turkish government was adamant and would not negotiate. On the 25th the hijackers released their hostages and sought sanctuary in Bulgaria.

The TPLA was seen by the Palestinian Fedayeen activists to be a virile, aggressive terrorist organization that appeared to be achieving something and therefore merited assistance and encouragement. The fact that Turkey was close at hand and had a common frontier with the Arab states of Syria and Iraq could be seen as an additional advantage which facilitated communication and liaison. The Turkish government complained bitterly about the help given to the TPLA by the Fedayeen. On 24 May 1972 the Turkish military authorities announced that fourteen Turkish terrorists had been seized in a Fatah boat in Turkey's southern waters near the Syrian coast. They were returning to Turkey after being trained in a Palestinian camp. The Turkish spokesman said, "These anarchists were trained by Fatah agents to undermine the Turkish Republic and its national unity, and to serve Marxist-Leninist aims." A Turkish newspaper commented plaintively that "Turkey now faces open attacks by Fatah, which has been granted the status of a semi-state by certain Arab nations. It is known in which states Fatah is active, but we still retain friendly relations with states recognizing the organization and giving it protection."*

Another terrorist organization with which the Fedayeen, especially the PFLP, kept in close contact was the Popular Front for the Liberation of the Arab Gulf (PFLOAG, formerly the Popular Front for the Liberation of the Occupied Arab Gulf), which had been active in Oman since 1963. It was led by Moussilim bin Nufal, and its strength seemed to hover at about the one thousand mark. Originally it was a nationalist movement, but in 1967 it was taken over by Marxists, and the following year was reconstituted on

*Yeni Istabu, 27 June 1972.

Marxist lines. In December 1971 Mohammed Abdullah, a member of some of the most active and violent terrorist groups with which based in Aden, announced that it had absorbed the National Democratic Front for the Liberation of Oman and the Persian Gulf, which had been inactive for over eighteen months.

In May 1972, at the Badawi refugee camp near Tripoli, Lebanon, Geroge Habash of the PFLP held a meeting of representatives of some of the most active and violent terrorists groups with which the PFLP had made contact. Representatives attended from the June Second Movement, the Baader-Meinhof Gang, the IRA, the TPLA, the NIF, and several South American terrorist groups. The Japanese Red Army was represented, and the BSO sent Abu Iyad and Fuad Shemali. Considerable care was taken to smuggle these delegates into Lebanon, and then out again once the conference was over.

The most important decision reached at this meeting at the Badawi refugee camp was that the terrorist groups represented would not only continue to help each other in every way they could, but that additionally they would whenever possible carry out exploits in countries other than their own for other terrorist organizations when required to do so. The object was to minimize risk of detection of members of a national terrorist group by their own security forces. In short, it meant that foreign terrorists could enter a country, commit an act of terrorism, and then quickly slip out of it again. The PFLP remained the dominant organization in what had become a form of international terrorism. The Central Committee of the PFLP was reshuffled, but remained under the leadership of George Habash. Other prominent members were Wadia Hadad, the operations director; Ghassan Kanafani, the propaganda director and editor of the PFLP newspaper *Al Hadaf;* and Abu Riyad, the PFLP commander in Lebanon.

8 The Japanese Red Army

You must prove your sincerity by your readiness to die.
Maxim of the Japanese Red Army

THE OTHER TERRORIST organization that developed a close liaison with the PFLP was that which eventually became known as the Japanese Red Army (JRA). Born of Japanese student unrest of the 1960s and springing from the left-dominated Japanese Student Federation, the JRA was conceived by people who mixed a craving for modernization with a nostalgia for tradition and a dissatisfaction with what was thought to be deliberate restrictions imposed on the country by the Allies in the peace treaty after World War II.

The Communist Party and other left-wing parties were legal in Japan and operated openly, vigorously, and vocally, but generally within legal limits, until extremists lost patience with what they considered to be smug governmental complacency. In October 1968 a spate of student demonstrations, riots, and violence began at Japanese universities and continued until November 1969. In June 1969, at a meeting of the Central Committee of the Japanese Communist Party, a group of dissidents led by Takoya Shiomi, wanted to form a militant arm to bring about world revolution, but this was not accepted. It was a time of dissent and dispute within the party, exacerbated by the mounting background struggle between the differing doctrines of Soviet and Chinese political ideology, some members supporting one, and some the other.

Takoya Shiomi and his followers broke away from the Japanese Communist Party to establish an extreme anarchist organization whose first title was the Red Army, later referred to as the Red Army Faction. The majority of its members had university backgrounds and came from comfortable middle-class families. The Red Army declared it would start the "world revolution" on 1 September 1970, but its leadership was hopelessly unprepared and uncomprehending, not having the slightest conception of what

147

such an undertaking involved. Takoya Shiomi was arrested for possessing explosives, and while he was in detention his followers were able to do little more than make a puny gesture against authority by throwing crude Molotov cocktails at police boxes in the city of Osaka and at a police station in Tokyo.

However, realizing their complete ineptitude, nine of the leaders of the Red Army hijacked a Japanese Air Lines Boeing 727 on 31 March 1970, which after a few hiccups flew them to North Korea. They became known as the Samurai Nine because they carried and waved about at every opportunity the traditional Samurai warriors' curved, two-handed sword. They stated they wanted to visit this communist state "to learn new tactics on how to conduct a revolution." In their naiveté they had not determined whether they would be helped in their ideal, and had not even bothered to inform the North Korean government they were arriving in a hijacked plane. The North Koreans were not at all pleased to see them, and ushered them into detention after an icy reception.

The Red Army set out to inculcate its members in the stern moral code of the Samurai warriors and to encourage the spirit of self-sacrifice. The Kamikaze (Divine Wind) complex is something peculiar to the Japanese character. Ritual suicide as a national phenomenon was given a boost on 25 November 1970 when Yukio Mishima killed himself. He was one of Japan's best-known authors and had organized the Society of the Shield, which was dedicated to reviving Samurai traditions and the martial spirit associated with them. Mishima, with four of his followers, broke into an army headquarters building in Tokyo. After tying up the Chief of Staff, he tried to persuade officers and soldiers to carry out a coup against the government in protest against the "pacifist constitution" which, he alleged, had been forced upon his country by the Americans. Failing to incite mutiny, Yukio Mishima and one of his followers committed hari-kari (known as *suppuku* to the Japanese).

Hari-kari is a form of ritual suicide reputed to be the most painful death known to man; the person plunges a dagger into his own stomach and disembowels himself. Part of the ritual is that a male relative, usually the eldest son, or a friend stands ready with uplifted sword to instantly cut off the person's head with one massive stroke to end his life and suffering once the disemboweling has been effected. The three other members of the Society of the Shield gave themselves up and were tried in April 1972. They were sentenced to terms of imprisonment. Because of their involvement in the beheading process, one of the charges they faced was that of "murder by request," brought for the first time before Japanese courts.

This incident fanned the flames of fanaticism, and the Red Army merged with another left-wing militant group, the Keihin Ampo Kyoto, to form the United Red Army. Towards the end of 1971 a group of twenty-eight of its members, men and women (women invariably formed between one-third to half of the organization), moved into hideouts in the snow-covered mountains near Katuisawa, about eighty miles from Tokyo, to prepare to launch a countrywide campaign of guerrilla warfare against the authorities. Instead, under the urging of Hiroko Nagata, the daughter of a respectable businessman, they became involved in a frenzy of self-criticism and accusation that got horribly out of hand. Those judged to have faults were tortured and killed in a ghastly manner. Fourteen in all suffered this fate, killed by their comrades for having "bourgeois tendencies" or "antirevolutionary failings." One sixteen-year-old girl was murdered because she wore earrings. These deaths became known as the Snow Murders.

In February 1972, in their search for terrorists wanted mainly for bank robberies, the police flushed out five United Red Army members from the mountains. The terrorists stole guns and ammunition from a sports shop and were eventually cornered by the police in a holiday chalet at Katuisawa, holding the caretaker's wife as a hostage. A dramatic ten-day siege ensued in which over twelve hundred police were involved, and which was recorded by television cameras. After demolishing part of the building, the police eventually moved in to arrest the terrorists, but were fired upon and had to withdraw again. Two policemen were killed. A second police assault at night was successful. The terrorist marksman was named as Kunio Bando. Interrogation of the arrested terrorists revealed the extent and horror of the Snow Murders. Sixteen were brought to trial, of whom six were women. All were sentenced to terms of imprisonment.

Police arrests and pressure and internal dissension caused the United Red Army to fragment into half-a-dozen small groups, each with Red Army in their title. At its peak the United Red Army had consisted of about thirty hard-core terrorists and about another one hundred active supporters. The strongest of the fragments called itself the Japanese Red Army.

Lost in admiration for the mass hijacking in September 1970

by the PFLP, still thirsting for world revolution, and being anxious to learn, the JRA sought contact with the Fedayeen group in the Middle East. A few Japanese communists and terrorists, fleeing from Japan, had already found refuge in Fedayeen camps. The JRA sent one of its founder-members, a woman named Fusako Shigenobu, to Beirut in February 1971 to make contact. She met both Habash and Hadad, who agreed that the PFLP would accept a small number of JRA members for training. The contact made, Fusako Shigenobu returned to Japan, to be imprisoned for carrying explosives.

In October 1971 the PFLP sent Ruyashi Ghanem and Bassam Abu Sherif to Japan to talk to the JRA leadership and possibly to recruit Japanese terrorists for exploits in the Middle East. These two Arabs were hosted by Fusako Shigenobu, who by then had been released from police detention. The two PFLP leaders were shown a film entitled *Declaration of World War,* the theme being that only violence can change world society. One of the actors in the film was Fusako herself, then twenty-six years old.

Fusako Shigenobu's father, variously described as a school-teacher, shopkeeper, and insurance broker (perhaps he may have been all three in succession), was a revolutionary, although a right-wing one, who in the 1930s had joined the Blood Oath League, which believed it should cleanse Japan by selective assassination of corrupt politicians and businessmen. He served a term of imprisonment for his involvement with the League before World War II. Fusako Shigenobu attended the Meiji University and became the leader of its students' union. She became a convinced Marxist and later taught at the Tokyo University, where she was involved first with the Japanese Communist Party and then became a founder-member of the JRA. It has been widely reported that at one stage of her life she was a go-go dancer at a night club in Tokyo's Ginza district, but perhaps this is more fiction than fact, although it is continually held against her.

It was agreed that the PFLP would train JRA members at its Middle East camps, and would select a few, if suitable, to join its exploits. The PFLP also agreed to give sanctuary to JRA terrorists on the run and to help the JRA establish cells in Beirut and elsewhere in Europe. Some persuasion was necessary, as initially the PFLP was reluctant to meet all the eager demands of the Japanese terrorists because the two Fedayeen representatives were astounded at their helpless idealism and this impractical approach to real terrorist problems. They were skeptical of their amateur approach and immature enthusiasm. On the other hand, the Japanese terrorists were not impressed by the moral fiber of the PFLP and thought that they too had an important contribution to make to international terrorism—to instill the spirit of self-sacrifice.

Fusako Shigenobu was selected by the JRA leadership to go to Beirut to establish a Middle East headquarters and to arrange for JRA members to reach Beirut and for their training with the PFLP. She was also to set up cells in Europe, especially in Paris and Berlin. Her organization became known as the Arab Committee of the JRA, and she was practically given a free hand in her task; soon a trickle of JRA terrorists was reaching her in Beirut. She maintained a close liaison with both Habash and Hadad, both of whom gave her considerable help. At the time when it was customary for female terrorists and revolutionaries to slouch about like hippies, unwashed and unkempt, Fusako Shigenobu was extremely fastidious about her personal appearance and dress, and soon became known as the Red Queen.

As JRA members were trained they were sent out to cells. The one established in Paris was led by Takahashi Taketomo and Mariko Yamamoto. Takahashi, a professor from the Rikkyo University, Tokyo, was an expert on eighteenth-century French literature. Mariko was a graduate of the Tokyo Women's Christian College, and her cover was to work as a salesgirl in the Mitsukoshi gift shop in the Avenue de l'Opera, which was visited by hundreds of Japanese tourists daily and thus was a convenient terrorist post office. Anxious that her JRA be allowed to prove themselves, Fusako Shigenobu quickly agreed to Habash's suggestion that they take part in a suicide mission in Israel. Research and planning was carried out by the operational section of the PFLP, controlled by Hadad, and three Japanese terrorists were involved as the action men.

The leader was Takeshi Okudaira, who had joined Fusako in Beirut, and although he was reputedly her husband she had no hesitation in sending him off on a suicide mission.* He was an electronics student at Kyoto University. The second man was Yasuyuki Yasuda, an architecture student at Kyoto University

*This is the Israeli version, the marriage allegedly taking place in Japan in early 1971. The Japanese police insist this is not so and that Fusako Shigenobu was married to Osamu Maruoka, a JRA terrorist, in Japan in February 1971.

who arrived in Beirut in December 1971, while the third man was Kozo Okamoto, an agricultural student at Tokyo University who did not arrive in the Middle East until April 1972.

Once the three terrorists were assembled they were kept in a safe-flat in Beirut, whence each day they were taken by automobile to a PFLP training area near Baalbeck in the Lebanese mountains. There they practiced firing live ammunition, threw grenades, and learned how to set an aircraft on fire with phosphorous bullets, as well as other essential terrorist techniques. The mission was called Operation Arguello, after the South American terrorist who had been killed in the attempted hijack of September 1970. The leader, Fusako's supposed husband, was code-named Jaro.

Training completed, the three Japanese terrorists left Beirut on 25 May 1972, traveling by air first to Paris and then on to Frankfurt. They were given forged passports by a PFLP messenger. From Frankfurt they went by train to Rome, where, in the quiet Pension Scalighera, weapons, ammunition, and grenades were given to them by Fusako Shigenobu in person. She had come to give last minute instructions and to bid them all farewell. The weapons were packed in individual suitcases, ready to be taken to the airport.

On the afternoon of 30 May the three terrorists arrived at Rome airport, where their false passports aroused no suspicions. Their suitcases were checked in and put onto the conveyor belt to be taken to the aircraft without being opened and examined. Having valid tickets to Tokyo via Lod, they passed through a newly installed metal detector screen and came out "clean," indicating they had no weapons concealed on them. The PFLP had tested this detector screen two days previously when a female Lebanese member carrying two pistols concealed in her clothing had been detected by the same device. This was why the JRA weapons were in their suitcases and were not carried by the terrorists themselves.

With nineteen other passengers, the three men boarded an Air France Boeing 707, flight number 132, which left Rome at 1850 hours to touch down at Lod airport just after 2200 hours. During the flight they had attracted no special attention, as Japanese abroad were invariably polite, unassuming, and well behaved.

At Lod airport the three terrorists, with other passengers, alighted from the plane and entered the airport bus, which took them all to the immigration entrance of the airport buildings. Again their false passports were accepted as genuine and duly stamped by the official on duty, indicating they could stay in

Israel as tourists for up to three months if they wished. At least two hundred Japanese were working on Israeli kibbutzim, and there were others in the country as students and tourists or engaged in research work. Israel, too, was becoming used to Japanese visitors.

Their aliases were Torio Ken (Takeshi Okudaira, the leader), Sagisaki Kiro (Yasuyuki Yasuda), and Namba Daisuke (Kozo Okamoto). Namba Daisuke was the name of a Japanese revolutionary character who had attempted to kill Emperor Hirohito in 1923 and had gone to the gallows shouting, "Long live the workers." Japanese school children knew all about him, but not the average Israeli immigration official.

Once through the immigration section they entered the customs hall to wait for their baggage to arrive on the conveyor belt from the plane, and when one impatient lady passenger pushed her way forward, one of the Japanese politely stood aside. As their suitcases appeared the Japanese stepped forward, took them from the conveyor belt, and walked away with them, spreading out from each other as they did so. Then they stopped, put down their suitcases, stooped down, unfastened them, and from each took a Czech 7.26 mm automatic rifle, the VZ-58; several magazines, each filled with thirty rounds of ammunition; and two or three grenades.

Straightening up, they commenced firing into the crowded customs hall, and after a few bursts (some three hundred rounds were fired by them in all), they each threw one or two grenades at the people, who were momentarily stunned. The shuffling and murmuring bustle of waiting passengers watching for and collecting their baggage suddenly gave way to instant pandemonium as death, injury, and pain were brought into a concentrated area in a way that seldom happens even on a battlefield. The rattle of automatic fire and the cracking thuds of exploding grenades gave way to cries and moans. Within seventeen seconds over twenty people were killed and nearly eighty wounded.

Having wrought this massive carnage, the three terrorists then moved towards the open exit doors leading to the tarmac, where two aircraft had been waiting for some minutes for permission to move off. One was an El Al airliner and the other a Scanair plane, both of which had passengers on board. As they did so Jaru, the leader, came within the line of fire of his comrades' rifles and was killed at once. Then Yasuyuki Yasuda, who had a grenade grasped in his hand, tripped over a baggage trolley, which caused him to release the grenade. Before he recovered himself it exploded, blowing his head into a mass of bloody pulp; he must have died instantly. One witness later stated that Yasuyuki Yasuda had been killed by a grenade he threw that bounced back from a wall it had struck to explode near him. He had already thrown one grenade, but it was the second one that killed him.

The third terrorist, Kozo Okamoto, ran out the exit door onto the tarmac after throwing two grenades and was firing his rifle at the standing aircraft when he was seized by an airport official, who held on to him until security guards rushed to his aid. Recovering quickly from their momentary stunned surprise, the airport staff and others swung into emergency action. Okamoto was secured, doctors, nurses, and ambulances began to arrive, and the injured were tended.

Okamoto did not resist, and remained expressionless and impassive, his self-control slipping only when he was taken to identify the bodies of his two dead comrades. He broke down and wept briefly, but having shed his tears he regained his composure quickly. Many of the victims were Puerto Rican Christian pilgrims visiting the Holy Land, but one of the Israelis killed was Professor Ahron Katzur, a famous scientist and brother of Ephraim Katzur, shortly to become president of Israel. There was so much blood and human debris in the customs hall that when cleaners were brought in to clean it up several of them had to be treated for shock.

The intention of the Japanese terrorists, after firing their rifles into the crowded customs hall, was to run towards the two aircraft on the tarmac, set them on fire with phosphorous bullets, and then jump into the flames to commit suicide in a dramatic kamikaze so that their bodies would be burnt beyond recognition. Then the full responsibility could be claimed by the PFLP. In its first international terrorist exploit, the JRA seemed content simply to prove itself and to show that it could live up to its maxim: "You must prove your sincerity by your readiness to die." Just before opening their suitcases to take out their weapons, the three terrorists had each torn the identity page from his passport and put it in a separate pocket. They anticipated that in this way there would be more chance of their identities, even though false, being completely destroyed by fire than if they were between hard passport covers. The following day, 31 May, the PFLP claimed full responsibility for the atrocity and said it was a reprisal for the death of two Black September terrorists who had been killed by Israeli security forces on 5 May when they had forced a hijacked plane into Lod airport.

The survivor, Kozo Okamoto, repeatedly asked to be allowed to commit suicide, a request which was, of course, refused. While in detention he was extremely uncommunicative, and little information was obtained from him. The chief interrogator was no less a person than Major General Rehaven Zeevi, commanding the Central Command, who by way of a trick offered to leave a pistol and one round of ammunition for Kozo Okamoto if he would make a statement. This offer was eventually withdrawn as being unproductive. At his trail Okamoto, whose brother had been one of the Sumurai Nine, pleaded guilty to all the charges against him, refused to undergo a psychiatric examination, and barely tolerated the defense lawyer nominated to defend him, who was Mordecai Kreitzman, once a member of the underground Irgun Zvi Leumi. Okamoto asked for the death penalty. The Israelis had abolished the death penalty in 1954 for all offenses except those of treason and genocide.

Kozo Okamoto made an eighty-five-minute long speech in which he explained why he, a Japanese, had committed this crime, saying, "It was a means of propelling ourselves onto the world stage in preparation for the world revolution that will produce a classless society." He further explained that "the Arab world lacks spiritual fervor, so we felt this attempt would probably stir up the Arab world." Found guilty on all charges, he was sentenced to life imprisonment. The final toll of the Lod Massacre was twenty-six killed and seventy-six injured.

Since the Lod Massacre Fusako Shigenobu has worked hard to build up the image of the husband she sent to his death into that of a glorious revolutionary, a perfect kamikaze who out-kamikazed the Japanese aircraft pilots of World War II, instead of admitting he was accidentally shot and killed by his comrades. Now the undisputed leader of the JRA in the Middle East and Europe, Fusako Shigenobu was joined by other members of the organization who were driven from Japan by police pressure. These she placed in PFLP training camps, and as they became efficient and capable she sent them to widely scattered cells. She continued to maintain a close liaison with George Habash, Wadia Hadad, and other PFLP leaders.

The next time the JRA was involved in a major terrorist exploit was on 20 July 1973, when five terrorists hijacked a Japanese Air Lines plane flying from Paris via Amsterdam and Anchorage, Alaska to Tokyo with 145 passengers and crew on board. The hijackers were four men and one woman. One of the men was a Japanese, Osamu Maruoka;* two others were named as Mohammed Abu Hassan and Abu Laghad (Yahya Hassan), both members of the PFLP, while the fourth, traveling on an Ecuadoran passport, was simply known as Carlos. The leader was a woman, an Iraqi member of the PFLP who was traveling under the name of Mrs. Peralta.† She and one of the Arabs were posing as a newly married couple, both having Peruvian passports. It was an international terrorist team at work.

Soon after taking off from Amsterdam, as the purser was serving champagne to the "newly married couple" in the first-class section, the woman produced a grenade, which immediately exploded, killing her and injuring the purser. On hearing the explosion the other three terrorists, brandishing automatic rifles and grenades, rushed from the tourist part of the plane and took it over. Confusion now reigned amongst the terrorists, as none of them knew what to do next: the woman leader, now dead, was the only one who had been entrusted with the full instructions. The terrorists neither knew their destination nor that they were expected to demand a huge ransom. However, they asked permission to land at Beirut, but this was refused, so the airliner was diverted to Basra, where again permission to land was refused. It then made for Dubai. Whilst over the Mediterranean, the hijackers said they were Sons of the Occupied Territories, the code name for the operation, and that they were awaiting instructions from their headquarters. They explained they were a "Palestinian commando and members of the Japanese Red Army" and were demanding the release of Okamoto from his Israeli prison. The Israelis feared the aircraft might make a kamikaze crash landing in the heart of Tel Aviv. However, the airliner landed safely at Dubai, where the terrorists kept the crew and passengers on board.

On 22 July the president of the Japanese Air Lines and the Japanese deputy minister of transport arrived in Dubai. After contacting the hijackers they held a press conference at which they

*Fusako Shigenobu's husband?
†According to Christopher Dobson and Ronald Payne her name was Katie George Thomas.

stated that so far the terrorists had not yet outlined their demands and that no money had been offered to, or been demanded by, the hijackers. Both Japanese offered themselves in exchange for the hostages, but this was refused. The president of the United Arab Emirates also tried unsuccessfully to negotiate with the terrorists, but all appeals to release the injured purser, a young child in ill health, and four elderly passengers who were suffering from the extreme heat were refused. However, the terrorist demands were soon forthcoming; they received coded messages from West Germany, all in English. They demanded the release of Kozo Okamoto and fifty other JRA members in Japanese prisons, together with a ransom of $4 million for the safe release of the aircraft and all hostages.

On the 23rd the hijackers demanded that the aircraft be refueled, and when this had been completed, after releasing the purser, the child, and the elderly passengers and taking on board a coffin containing the dead female terrorist, the plane took off. The body of the dead terrorist had been taken from the aircraft, but was demanded back again. The airliner was refused permission to land at several Arab airports, but was allowed to put down at Damascus to refuel. It eventually landed at Benghazi, Libya in the early hours of the 24th. Minutes later the plane was blown up, all on board having managed to scramble to safety using the emergency chutes. The body of the female terrorist was recovered from the wreckage later.

The WAFA News Agency in Beirut received a message on the 26th from the Sons of the Occupied Territories, who accepted full responsibility—this, of course, meant the PFLP. The exploit was claimed to be in retaliation for the Japanese government paying compensation to the victims of the Lod Massacre. The message urged the Libyans "to treat our men as revolutionaries and fighters against tyranny." The Libyan minister of information announced they would be put on trial and dealt with according to Islamic law, but the Arabs were released almost immediately, while Osamu Maruoka was kept in detention for about a year before being quietly deported.

The next major terrorist incident involving the JRA and the PFLP began on 31 January 1974 in Singapore when four terrorists, two Japanese and two Arabs, persuaded a boatman to take them to the island of Bukom, where an oil refinery was situated. On arrival the terrorists tied up the boatman and detonated plastic explosives against three of the oil storage tanks, but the resulting fires were quickly brought under control; only one tank was burnt out. The Japanese terrorists were identified as Haruo Wako and Yoshiaki Yamada, while the two Palestinians were never positively identified.

Next, the four terrorists seized the *Laju,* a ferryboat owned by the oil company, and ordered its crew of five to sail for international waters, but naval and police vessels forced it to stop. The terrorists threw out a note contained in a plastic bag so that it floated, which was picked up by the police. It said they were members of the JRA and the PFLP and declared their attack on the oil refinery had been carried out to show solidarity with the "Vietnamese revolutionary people" in order to create a revolutionary situation. They demanded a safe-conduct for themselves, failing which they would kill their hostages.

The Japanese ambassador, Tokichiro Uomoto, was taken out in a boat to talk to the terrorists. On the evening of the 31st the Singapore cabinet decided to meet the terrorists' demands for safe-conduct to an Arab capital as "no life had been taken and minimal damage caused." That night the terrorists allowed two of their hostages to jump overboard and swim to safety. Although the terrorists threatened to take drastic action against their three remaining hostages, nothing happened during 1 and 2 February. The pause was due to the difficulty in finding an Arab government willing to accept the terrorists and an Arab aircraft to fly them to such a sanctuary.

On 3 February the terrorists rejected an offer by the Singapore government to refuel the ferryboat and allow it to sail with the hostages into international waters. The following day, the 4th, the Singapore authorities again refused to provide a Singapore aircraft to fly the terrorists to a sanctuary. They did say they would allow them a safe-conduct to go into any of the twelve diplomatic missions in Singapore while a solution was being worked out. Then they could go to the airport, provided the ambassador concerned agreed and they released their three hostages. On the 5th the terrorists asked for asylum in the North Korean consulate.

Thousands of miles away, in Kuwait, five Arab PFLP terrorists burst into the Japanese embassy on 6 February and held the ambassador, Ryoko Ishikawa, and his staff of twenty-eight hostage. The building was surrounded by Kuwaiti security forces, but the terrorists said they would execute their hostages if any attack was made on them. They sent a message to the Japanese foreign minister, Massayoshi Ohira, saying the groups involved in this exploit were the PFLP, the JRA, and the Sons of the Occupied Territories. The latter was simply a code name for the exploit, last used when a Japanese airliner was hijacked in July 1973. It said they would kill the second secretary within an hour unless the Japanese government agreed to send an aircraft to Singapore to fly the JRA and PFLP terrorists there together with their hostages and weapons. They threatened to kill their hostages one by one until this demand was met. The Kuwaiti government stated it would not give landing permission, as it wished to avoid further complications.

The Japanese government capitulated. On 7 February a Japanese airliner flew from Tokyo to Singapore to pick up the terrorists on the ferryboat, who released their hostages and were given safe-conduct to board the plane. Accompanied by certain Singapore officials, they flew off towards Kuwait. In Kuwait, on the morning of the 7th, the terrorists released three women and a boy from the embassy building. In the evening the Kuwaiti government reversed its decision not to allow the Japanese airliner to land on its territory on condition the terrorists free all their hostages when the plane touched down and that the eleven terrorists immediately leave Kuwait on the aircraft. This being agreed, the Japanese airliner landed at Kuwait. On the morning of the 8th the terrorists freed the remaining hostages and allowed themselves to be taken to the airport. All nine of the terrorists were then flown to Aden, where they were met by senior government officials and taken to an undisclosed destination. As usual the PLO denied all knowledge of, or connection with, the exploit.

Meanwhile, in Japan, the remnants of the JRA were surviving underground, and although Fusako Shigenobu retained contact, she remained virtually independent and aloof from internal dissents. The JRA soon split again, this time into two factions known as the Kakamara (Revolutionary Marxists) and the Chukuka group (core faction). There was considerable friction and many clashes between the two. This strengthened Fusako Shigenobu's independence, and being in contact with both, she played one against the other to her own advantage. An efficient organizer, she strengthened her cells, and the one based in Paris became particularly active. In January 1974 she moved to Paris so as to be less dependent upon the PFLP. She had ideological differences with the PFLP, in as much as she wanted to work for world revolution, whereas the PFLP had limited national aims. At this time she had approximately thirty trained and dedicated members in Europe.

As she was short of funds, her plan was to kidnap Japanese businessmen in Europe (but not in France itself) and hold them for ransom. For this purpose she asked that money, false identification papers, and other aids be sent to her in Paris. In July 1974 Yosiaki Yamada, who had been involved in the recent Singapore exploit, was stopped by customs officials at Orly airport, Paris. His suitcase, which had a false bottom, was found to contain $10,000 in forged U.S. bills, false passports, and coded instructions relating to the kidnapping plans. The news of his arrest was not immediately released by the French police, who when they had decoded the instructions realized that Mariko Yamamoto, who worked at the Mitsukoshi gift shop, was the main contact and post office. Her flat was watched, and during the following week Takahashi Taketomo and other JRA members were arrested. This was the first inkling the French police had of the existence of the JRA cell in Paris, its extensive activities, and its potential. Yamada was held in detention in the hope he would reveal more information about the JRA under interrogation, but the others, fourteen in all, were simply deported from France. The documents in Yamada's suitcase contained codes, names and addresses of contacts in France and safe-houses, and instructions.

In the interests of international terrorist cooperation, the PFLP Boudia Commando in Paris was ordered to assist the JRA to obtain the release of Yamada. A combined plan was drawn up, and on 13 September 1974 an attack was made on the French embassy at The Hague, Holland. Although the three terrorists involved were Japanese, most of the planning and backup arrangements were made by the Boudia Commando, as the JRA Paris cell had been shattered by arrests and deportations. The JRA terrorists were named as Haruo Wako, who had been involved in the Singapore exploit, Junzo Okudaira, brother of the Lod killer, and Jun Nishikana, a student. They seized the French ambassador, Count Jacque Senard, and ten other people who were in the embassy and held them hostage. In the initial exchange of fire between the terrorists and armed police who had followed the JRA men into the building, one policeman and one policewoman were wounded. The police then withdrew from the actual building to form a cordon around it.

The terrorists dropped a note from a window outlining their demands, saying that if they were not agreed to by 0300 hours (on the 14th) they would execute their hostages at intervals. They demanded that Yoshiaki Yamada be released and brought to them at The Hague, and that a Boeing 707 with full fuel tanks, together with a pilot and copilot, be readied at Schipol airport, Amsterdam, at their disposal. A period of protracted negotiations began in which the French and Dutch governments were both involved. The French minister of the interior, Michel Poniatowski, agreed to the demand, and Yamada was flown to The Hague in a French military aircraft. As he was unwilling to join his comrades in the besieged embassy, he remained in the aircraft. The French were also reluctant to allow him to set foot on Dutch soil as the Dutch authorities wanted, as he would have technically passed into Dutch custody.

The terrorists agreed to extend their deadline but made further demands. These were that they should retain their arms (pistols, grenades, and explosives) when they left Holland, that the French ambassador must accompany them out of Holland as a hostage, that Yoshiaki Yamada be paid $1 million by the French government as compensation for his arrest and detention, and that Yamada be flown back to Paris to collect certain documents that had been taken from him by the French police.

At this point differences arose between the French and Dutch authorities over the handling of the incident, the French wishing to take a much harder line than the Dutch. On the 15th the French released a statement insisting that all the hostages be released on Dutch territory under guarantee of the Dutch government in exchange for Yamada. The French agreed to produce a Boeing 707, and to fly out the terrorists, but said that the crew must not be French. A volunteer crew consisting of a Dutch pilot and copilot and a British flight engineer was found, and the following day the JRA terrorists released two female hostages from the embassy building.

To emphasize that the terrorists meant business and to deter any long-drawn-out negotiations that might tend to wear down the resolve of the JRA, on the 15th the leader of the Boudia Commando threw a grenade at Le Drugstore, a tobacconist's shop in the center of Paris, which exploded and killed two people, injuring thirty-four others. The Boudia Commando did not openly claim responsibility because it did not want to deflect any limelight from the JRA, but French press laid the blame on the Palestinians.

On the 17th an agreement was reached between the JRA terrorists and the two governments by which the terrorists retained their arms and their hostages until they were on board the aircraft containing Yoshiaki Yamada. It was agreed to accept $300,000 instead of $1 million. The money was produced by the French government and handed over. In the afternoon the terrorists and six of their hostages were taken to the airport. After some negotiation the hostages were released when the terrorists entered the aircraft to join Yamada.

The French plane flew off to Beirut, but when it was refused permission to land there it changed direction and landed instead at Aden, where the authorities would not allow anyone to leave it except the British flight engineer, who was permitted to supervise refueling. No contact was permitted with the waiting Wadia Hadad either. The plane took off again, but Arab country after Arab country refused to accept it, and it was only when the aircraft began to develop faults that permission was reluctantly given for it to land at Damascus.

Once on the ground at Damascus airport, no one was allowed to leave the aircraft and several hours of tense negotiations ensued. The Syrian authorities were not happy at the terrorists taking ransom money, as this savored of the criminal and not the political. In return for a safe-conduct the Syrians insisted that the ransom money be handed back. It was given to the aircraft crew, who handed it to the French ambassador. After brief detention the JRA terrorists were allowed to leave for Beirut. This exploit was regarded as a triumph by the Boudia Commando, but it depressed Fusako Shigenobu and her JRA members, as they had lost the much-needed ransom money required to finance JRA-style world revolution. Her coffers were almost empty.

9 Terror by Post

... interesting novelties ... a device which sprays the person ...
with curare snake poison.
West German intelligence report

DURING 1972 AND 1973 deadly spates of letter bombs were dispatched by both Israelis and Arabs to one another. Started by the Israelis, the Arab terrorists responded quickly and soon warmed to their work. The advantages of this terror by post are that there is little personal danger to the sender and distance is no object. If the letter bomb reaches the addressee and explodes, it will kill or badly injure him; and if it is detected in transit, it causes fear and apprehension, which bring with them the burden and inconvenience of extra tedious security precautions. The terrorist simply needs to know the address of his intended victim, which is most probably listed in a telephone directory, possess the necessary ingredients, and have the technical knowledge to assemble them into a lethal device. If he has neither the technical knowledge nor the ingredients, his organization may be able to obtain ready-made letter bombs through international terrorist contacts.

In July 1972 the Israeli Mossad sent at least ten letter bombs to Palestinian leaders, most of whom had overt, legitimate jobs apart from their nefarious terrorist activities. As mail addressed to the top Fedayeen leadership would most likely be examined and screened by subordinates and never reach an intended victim, they were not included. The ten letter bombs were in yellow envelopes, about four by eight inches in size, and each bore a commemorative stamp that concealed a tiny detonator. When these envelopes were opened, a slender wire was broken, which released a spring that in turn set off the explosion.

On 8 July a senior official at the Rifbank in Beirut was injured when trying to remove the commemorative stamp from the letter bomb. The following day a second similar letter bomb, also received in Beirut, exploded and injured Anis Sayegh, director of the

163

PLO Research Center. These two explosions caused alarm, and in Beirut and other Arab cities letters were carefully and delicately examined by addressees before being opened. Security precautions and detection equipment were brought into operation at Lebanese postal sorting offices.

The Israelis had used the parcel bomb and the letter bomb on previous occasions, but the Arabs had not indulged in this form of terrorism until about 1966. The first Arab revolutionary group to do so was FLOSY, struggling against British occupation in the Aden Protectorate. FLOSY, which had been given support from East European sources, had been taught how to assemble book bombs and instructed in the techniques of mailing them. However, FLOSY did not make much use of this terrorist medium and was content to rely mainly upon the hand grenade in its terrorist campaign against British servicemen and their families.

As contact between Fatah and FLOSY materialized, this specialized knowledge was passed on to the Fedayeen terrorists, who only used it on one occasion against the Israelis. This was on 2 January 1967, when a total of fourteen parcel bombs were posted by them from Vienna, Zagreb, and Belgrade to Israelis whose addresses had been randomly selected from telephone directories. These packages, which were fairly crude parcel bombs, arrived in Israel between the 26th and 29th of that month. All were detected in time and defused, with the exception of one that exploded while being examined by an Israeli policeman.

It was not until September 1972 that Arab terrorists hit back hard at this terror-by-post warfare, and one of the first fatalities was Ami Shachori, an agricultural counselor at the Israeli embassy in London. He was killed on the 19th of that month at his desk while opening a letter bomb. Two other letters, identical in every detail, had been held back for further examination by a suspicious official at the embassy, but somehow the third one got through to the victim's desk.

Immediately after this explosion the Israelis alerted their diplomatic missions worldwide to be on the lookout for letter bombs. The result was that in Paris that day two letter bombs addressed to members of the Israeli embassy staff were detected and rendered harmless by the police. The same evening another four letter bombs addressed to Israelis on the diplomatic staff were discovered at a postal sorting office and defused by the police. The following day, the 20th, another seventeen sent to members of Israeli diplomatic missions in Brussels, Geneva, Vienna, Montreal, and New York were discovered in time. By the 23rd, forty-two letter bombs in all had been detected in cities as far apart as London, Montreal, New York, Buenos Aires, and Kinshasa, and also in Israel. Of the seventeen sent to Israel, one had been addressed to Shimon Peres, then minister of communications. On 25 September it was announced from Australia that five letter bombs addressed to Israelis in Canberra and Sydney had been discovered.

All these letter bombs looked like ordinary airmail letters, were postmarked Amsterdam, and contained a sophisticated explosive device. The British police contacted the Dutch police to try to trace the originators, but the Dutch authorities said they believed the instigators had already left Holland. No Fedayeen organization claimed responsibility so far, but the finger of suspicion pointed to the BSO. Previously, on the 20th, a Fedayeen broadcast from Syria, calling itself the Voice of the Central Committee of the Palestinian Revolution, claimed that the Fedayeen fighters "have in their armory more sophisticated devices than bombs, devices that are subtle and cannot be detected by those who protect Israel."

Suspicion that the BSO was the originator of this round of terror-by-post warfare was confirmed to some extent when on 23 September 1972 four letter bombs posted from Amsterdam and addressed to Jordanian officials in Amman were detected in the Amman sorting office and made safe. The Jordanian government and those who served it remained high on the hate list of the BSO.

While the parcel bombs used by Arab terrorists in 1967 had been crude devices, the letter bombs they used in 1972 showed a marked advance in techniques and sophistication that amazed the Israelis. The view of the Israeli Mossad was that apart from the two superpowers the only other nations capable of producing such advanced letter bomb mechanisms were Czechoslovakia and East Germany. Moreover, the Israeli authorities openly accused the governments of these two countries of manufacturing them for and supplying them to the Arab terrorists.

The letter bombs used by the Arab terrorists were all of the same pattern and in every instance contained what is commonly known as a "number 8 industrial detonator" to trigger the device. It had been squeezed in a vice to make it fit the slim-line type of airmail envelope without making a noticeable bulge. This squeezing process made the bomb less stable and accounted for premature explosions that injured two people in Beirut and another in India. When the flap of the envelope was opened it released a spring to which had been soldered a percussion striker, which caused a flash that touched off the detonator. In the chain reaction the detonator triggered the plastic explosive, perhaps less than one ounce in weight.

A high level security meeting held at Bonn, West Germany on 6 October was warned by West German intelligence personnel that apart from the explosive inside letter bombs, some of them might contain "interesting novelties, including a device which sprays the person who opens it with curare snake poison." The meeting was also told that Fatah was about to unleash a wave of letter bombs of a "new, and hard to detect, type" to prominent citizens and public figures, mainly of American, French, and West German nationality.

In all, the Arab terrorists released at least four separate spates of terror by post to Zionists. The first was from Amsterdam, and the others were successively from Malaysia, India, and Singapore. The flush of letter bombs in October 1972 was dispatched by Arab terrorists from Penang, Malaya. One of the first was addressed to the director (a Jewish woman) of the Rome branch of a Jewish organization. It was received on the 4th and was detected because it had not been franked. Additionally, this letter bomb contained some curare, a deadly South American snake poison used by the Indians to tip their arrows in battle, which was mixed in with the explosive. It also contained a brief message from the BSO, leaving no doubt as to its origin.

In mid-October 1972 letter bombs from Penang containing similar messages from the BSO were received in London, Rome, Dusseldorf, New York, and Rhodesia, but they either failed to explode or were detected in time. The one sent to Dusseldorf was found to contain curare and had been addressed to an elderly Jew in an old people's home who had died several months earlier. On the 11th two letter bombs from Penang were received in New York by two senior members of the Hadassah, an American Zionist women's organization, and were opened by them, but failed to explode, as did a similar letter bomb received by a Jew in Rhodesia. On 15 October a letter bomb injured a postal worker in New York. The flap of the envelope had worked open, and it exploded when he tried to seal it down again. A letter bomb was received and detected at the Israeli embassy at Bonn that contained cyanide, which when exposed to the air emitted a lethal gas. On 23 October 1972 the Israeli police gave out a general warning to everyone in Israel to beware of suspicious letters or parcels.

On 2 November it was announced from Kuala Lumpur, the capital of Malaysia, that an Arab-Malay group was responsible for the letter bombs that had been mailed to Jewish organizations and individuals from Penang. It was stated that thirty-five outgoing suspicious letters had been intercepted and examined at postal sorting offices, of which fifteen had been found to contain explosives. On the same day Abu Yakub, the Fatah representative in Kuala Lumpur, discovered forty letter bombs, contained in two paper packages, in his flat. He informed the Saudi Arabian embassy, and Saudi officials told the police, who collected them. No explanation was given, but this tended to confirm the Israeli Mossad theory that the letter bombs were obtained in bulk, stored in diplomatic missions, and delivered by diplomatic means to the terrorists. It is interesting to speculate whether there was some disagreement between the various terrorist groups in this instance and whether someone had backed out. This incident seemed to put an end to the terror-by-post phase from Malaysia.

On 24 October 1972 Ribhi Halloum, a Palestinian traveling on an Algerian passport from Damascus to the Algerian embassy in Buenos Aires, had his luggage searched when he disembarked from an aircraft at a stopover at Schipol airport, Holland. He was found to possess letter bombs identical to those recently posted from Amsterdam in his suitcase. The Dutch authorities allowed him to leave the country immediately, but did not release the news until the following day, when they announced that one of his suitcases contained eight kilograms of plastic explosive, five grenades, and twenty-one letter bombs, while the other suitcase contained five pistols and some ammunition. The angry Israeli government made a formal protest, pointing out that a diplomatic passport only carried immunity in the country to which the holder is accredited. The Dutch police replied they had allowed Halloum to continue his journey because they could not establish that he was aware his suitcases contained these items.

On 26 October 1972 the Israeli police arrested Dennis Feinstein, an American Jewish tourist, on suspicion of mailing three letter bombs from Kiryat Shimona that had been detected at an Israeli postal sorting office. They were addressed to President

Nixon, U.S. Secretary of State Rogers, and U.S. Secretary of Defense Laird. This puzzled many for some time, and one explanation was that notorious crimes of an unusual nature, such as terror by post, inevitably attracted imitators.

On 1 February 1973 the Israeli authorities stated they had just unearthed a spy ring whose members were based in the area of the occupied Golan Plateau, and that some of them had been posting letter bombs to ordinary Israeli citizens, hoping to demoralize the population. They added that most of them had been discovered in time, except for one addressed to a woman teacher who was injured when the letter handed to her by a postman exploded. The Israelis also alleged that this spy ring had been responsible for sending the letter bombs to President Nixon and his two cabinet members.

Meanwhile, the Mossad retaliated in kind, and during the third week in October 1972, just a fortnight or so after the Munich Massacre, it sent letter bombs to Arab Fedayeen personalities, most of which were posted in Belgrade. On the 25th and 26th six Arabs were injured by them, some seriously. In Egypt a security official had his hand blown off when examining suspicious letters addressed to the Cairo PLO office. In Lebanon a postal sorter was injured by one, as was a woman secretary, but the cause of both these explosions was attributed to rough handling and over-sensitive mechanisms. In Libya Mustafa Awadh Abu Zeid, the PLO representative, was injured outside the central post office in Tripoli when he opened a letter bomb addressed to him. In Algiers Abu Khalil, the Fatah representative, was hurt when opening one, as was Rafiq Nitcha, an arms dealer and a member of the Fatah Rasd in Beirut. On 26 October Arafat presided over an impromptu conference of Arab Fedayeen leaders in Damascus at which ways and means of countering Israeli terror by post were discussed.

The next spate of letter bombs was dispatched from India to Jewish addresses taken at random from the Zionist Year Book. The first was received on 10 November 1972 by a Jewish diamond broker in London, who was injured when he opened it. The same day twelve more, posted either in Bombay or New Delhi, were received in Belfast, and five others to Zionist organizations were received in Geneva. In all fifty-one letter bombs were identified as originating from India in this spate. Of the ten addressed to London, two were sent to the Egyptian embassy, one of which was an incendiary device. Practically all were detected and defused.

Others were detected in Canada, Jamaica, Switzerland, Denmark, and France.

On 11 November 1972 twenty-five letter bombs were discovered in a Bombay postal sorting office, one of which exploded, injuring a postal sorter. On the 18th a suspect letter bomb addressed to David Ben Gurion at Sde Boker, his desert retreat in the Negev, was detected in an Israeli postal sorting office. It was handed over to the police, who did not confirm whether it was in fact an explosive device.

Many of the letter bombs from India bore stamps in excess of the required amount of postage, which made them obvious and singled them out for examination. Each of them contained a brief message from the BSO. They were activated by a spring release mechanism, a small device about an inch in length that could not be detected by touch when the envelope was sealed. The various national police authorities warned people not to open suspicious letters nor to put them in water, as water would cause the gum on the flap to become moist and so allow the flap of the envelope to slowly open, and, of course, to explode.

During November 1972 a few letter bombs were posted from Beirut to Arabs in Europe, the origin and purpose of which have never been made absolutely clear. They could have been sent to execute those considered by Arabs to be traitors, or by rival Fedayeen groups to each other; or again Mossad agents in Beirut could have posted them. Two were received on 29 November, one by Omar Sufan, a Palestinian student in Stockholm, who was injured when he opened it, and the other by Mohammed Mustafa, an Arab medical student in Bavaria, who was also injured. Mohammed Mustafa had been politically active in Arab student circles in West Germany and had been ordered to leave the country for this reason. He had been granted a respite to complete his final examinations. On the 30th a Palestinian in Copenhagen was severely injured by a letter bomb that had been posted in Beirut.

Next, a few letter bombs were dispatched from Singapore to Jewish individuals and organizations, but this spate came to an abrupt stop on 10 December 1972 when a postal worker was arrested in the act of putting letter bombs through the sorting office.

After this there was a lull in the terror-by-post warfare, broken only by occasional exceptions such as the episode on 30 January 1973, when it was announced in Tel Aviv that postal security staff had intercepted "two more letter bombs, posted from Turkey,

bringing the number detected during the last two days up to ten."
This slackening off of the terror-by-post phase may have been
partly due to improved security measures and alertness on the part
of the police and postal authorities worldwide, the high rate of
detection of letter bombs before they reached their addressees,
and to the seizure of so many letter bomb mechanisms. Perhaps
the Arabs had just run out of stock, and their Eastern European
suppliers were reluctant for some reason or other to provide more.
On the Israeli side, the reason was that the Mossad was directing
its attention and efforts into another anti-Arab terrorist channel.

10 Twilight Terror

We are considering measures yet untried against Arab terrorist organizations.

Prime Minister Golda Meir, speaking to the Knesset on
12 September 1972

F OR SOME TIME Prime Minister Golda Meir had been urged by some of her ministers and advisers to strike back at the Arab terrorists. Moshe Dayan, echoing the mood of the Israeli people, once told her that "unconventional war should be combatted by unconventional means." She had invariably refused, and said they never could be certain that one day a mistake would not be made. But there must have been exceptions to this rule, because she either directly or indirectly gave her consent to what virtually became a campaign of twilight warfare between Israeli agents and Arab terrorists. Although the Israeli Mossad was responsible for the terror-by-post campaign against Arab terrorists, its existence was never admitted by the Israeli government, despite the overwhelming weight of evidence of its presence and activities, until after the Munich Massacre of September 1972. Until the Munich Massacre it seemed as if there had been almost an unspoken agreement between Israel and the Arab states not to use violence against individual leaders. The Arab Fedayeen had broken this unspoken conventional code of international conduct. While no government knew quite how to deal with them, none played their game of assassination with its bland disregard for national boundaries.

The Israeli Mossad was appalled at the way the Munich Massacre had been handled by the West German police. On his return to report to Prime Minister Meir, General Zamir recommended that the Israelis activate their assassination squads and send them out to track down and kill the terrorist leaders, and in particular those who had been involved in the planning of that massacre. Prime Minister Meir agreed. She said, speaking in the Knesset on 12 September 1972, that "we are considering measures yet untried against Arab terrorist organizations." She appointed General

Aharon Yariv as her Special Advisor for the Coordination of Counter-Terrorist Activities, and he worked closely with General Zvi Zamir. The Mossad had been directed since 1968 by General Zamir, while General Yariv had been the head of Aman since 1964.

In September 1972 a special antiterrorist group known as the Wrath of God was formed and placed under Yariv's direct control. This group would be able to call upon any specialists it required for any particular operation, and could assemble and disperse them as necessary. The specialists would come from the Mossad, the armed forces, or any other source that might be able to produce a person with the skills or techniques temporarily required. Yariv was responsible to three people: Prime Minister Meir, Ygal Alon, the deputy prime minister, and Israel Galili, a minister without portfolio who was a former head of the underground Haganah. Yariv had to report daily to Alon. This new group caused a struggle as to who should control such a vital and potentially dangerous instrument. Prime Minister Meir solved the personal power controversy by assuming direct authority herself, which rather upset Moshe Dayan, who as minister of defense thought the responsibility should be his.

The Mossad provided the information required about Arab terrorist targets, but Wrath of God detachments, known less dramatically as Squad 101, were responsible for providing the personnel to make last minute preparations, such as reconnaissance, surveillance of intended victims, hiring automobiles, making hotel reservations, and other essential local arrangements. Like the Libyans and the Algerians, the Israeli diplomatic embassies and missions abroad provided a safe refuge and cover for personnel when required and a safe cache for arms and explosives, which were carried in diplomatic bags across national frontiers. More important still, Squad 101 provided the assassination section, known as Aleph (first letter in the Hebrew alphabet), and the getaway section, known as Beth (the second Hebrew letter), whose task was to enable the Aleph section to escape and create a diversion if necessary.

The first known Arab terrorist victim of the Israeli Squad 101 was Abdul Zwaiter, who was regarded by the Mossad as the head of the BSO in Italy.* Zwaiter's cover was that he worked as a clerk at the Libyan Embassy in Rome and raised funds for the Palestinian cause. A Marxist and a nephew of Akram Zwaiter, the Jor-

---

*Sometimes spelled Zuaiter.

danian ambassador in Beirut, and a distant relative of Arafat, he had come to the attention of the Italian police and had been questioned on several occasions in connection with terrorist incidents.

Zwaiter arrived home late in the evening of 16 October 1972 with a girl friend and was shot dead as he entered the doorway of the block of flats in which he lived. One assailant fired three shots that wounded him, and the other fired nine more into his body. Witnesses stated they saw two men and a woman drive off in an automobile, which was later found to have been stolen. A Fatah spokesman openly accused the Israelis, saying that it was "part of a Zionist campaign of terror carried out by the enemy throughout the world."

The second victim of Israeli Squad 101 was Mahmoud Hamshari, who was thought to be the head of BSO operations in France. The Israelis alleged he had been involved in the assassination attempt against Ben Gurion brought to light in Copenhagen in 1969. Hamshari was the official PLO representative in Paris, where he lived with his wife and children. Israeli agents entered his apartment when it was empty and affixed an explosive device to his telephone that could be detonated by an electronic signal. A member of an Aleph team telephoned Hamshari, and when Hamshari identified himself the device was activated, fatally wounding him. Hamshari died on 9 January 1973.

The next victim was Hussein Abad al-Chir, whom the Israelis believed to be the main contact between the BSO and the Soviet KGB. An explosive device was planted in his bedroom at the Olympic Hotel, Nicosia, Cyprus. On 24 January 1973, as Chir went to bed and switched off his light, it was activated by an electronic signal transmitted by an Aleph member. The next important victim was Doctor Basil al-Kubaisi, a professor of law who had taught at the American University in Beirut. He was a member of the PFLP, but not of the BSO. Kubaisi was in charge of procurement, storage, and distribution of arms and explosives for the PFLP in France and had only been living in Paris for a few weeks. On the night of 6 April 1973, when walking back to his hotel near the Madeleine Church in Paris, Kubaisi was overtaken by two members of an Aleph team and shot at point-blank range.

The PFLP spokesman in Beirut admitted that Basil al-Kubaisi was one of its leaders on "an important mission in Paris." The PFLP statement was critical of the French police and complained of "the persistence of the French authorities in overlooking the activity of the Israeli intelligence and its gangs on French territory." The spokesman added, "It is the third crime, following the assassination of Ben Barka (the Moroccan opposition leader) and Mahmoud al-Hamshari, to be carried out by imperialist intelligence and Zionists in the French capital within sight and hearing of the French authorities." There was a general feeling about this period that, with their large resident Algerian population, the French authorities were not looking for trouble, and did not want to become involved in what to them seemed to be a form of underground gangster warfare.

On 9 April 1973 an Israeli Aleph team in Cyprus killed Abu Sami (Ali Ahmed Abdul Khair), the BSO replacement for Hussein Abad al-Chir. The method was the same. An explosive device was placed under the victim's bed in the Hotel Olympia and detonated by an electronic impulse when Abu Sami switched off his light to go to sleep. Cyprus was then a center of espionage activity, with the Soviet KGB fully involved.

Knowing a high level meeting of Fedayeen leaders was to be held in Beirut on 9 April 1973, Yariv planned what amounted to a commando raid on that city, intending to kill as many of them as he could. It was a combined operation involving not only the Mossad, but the Israeli air force and navy, and perhaps also the army. A week or so earlier, at least half a dozen of Yariv's men with false passports booked into Beirut hotels to carry out certain preparations. Preceded by frogmen, about thirty Mossad agents and commandos slipped quietly ashore on the beach to the south of the city at about 0130 hours on the 9th. Dressed in casual civilian clothing, they divided into three teams and drove off in six hired automobiles.* In all they had seven objectives. At the same time a small team of Mossad agents and commandos made a diversionary landing at Sidon, on the coast about twenty-five miles south of Beirut, where they blew up some buildings alleged to have been used by Fedayeen terrorists.

One Israeli team drove into the center of Beirut to the area of the Rue Verdun and divided into two assault groups, each entering separate building blocks. They killed three PLO sentries. On one block, after shooting the lock from the door, the Israelis burst into the apartment occupied by Kamal Adwan. Adwan was able to seize his Kalashnikov automatic rifle and fire at the attackers, wounding

---

*On 22 December 1974 a Beirut court sentenced a Frenchman named as Francois Rangee to death, alleging he had hired the automobiles for the Israelis.

two of them before he was killed by this Aleph team. An elderly Italian woman living in the next apartment, hearing the noise opened her door to see what was happening and was shot dead.

The other Aleph team burst into the apartment occupied by Abu Yusef, where he lived with his wife and children. Caught in bed, he was shot and killed as was his wife, who tried to shield him with her body, while their two children watched. In yet another building, another Aleph team broke into the apartment occupied by Kamal Nasser, a bachelor, who was killed as he sat writing at his desk. The Israeli raiders then ransacked the rooms, taking papers and files away with them. At least one complete filing cabinet was taken off. Because it was locked, the Israelis did not want to risk damaging the contents by shooting it open.

Belatedly, Lebanese security forces arrived on the scene just as the Israelis were leaving. Shots were exchanged. Overhead an Israeli helicopter dropped crows' feet (small steel spikes) onto the roadways to puncture the tires of vehicles that followed. One witness later said there was a woman in the Israeli team who shouted orders. Two Lebanese police vehicles drove up as the Israelis were leaving, causing at least two of the Israelis to be wounded, as were two Lebanese police. In the Rue Verdun area it was all over in twenty minutes.

This was both a triumph and a disappointment to Israeli Squad 101. It had been a triumph because it had eliminated three of the top Arab Fedayeen leaders, each deeply involved in planning terrorism. Abu Yusef was third in the Fatah hierarchy, in charge of its political department. A BSO leader, he was also a member of the PLO Executive Committee and chairman of the Higher Committee for Palestinian Affairs in Lebanon, responsible for liaison between the some three hundred thousand Palestinians in the country and Lebanese authorities. Kamal Adwan, Fatah's chief spokesman, was in charge of all Fatah and BSO operations inside Israel and the Occupied Territories, while Kamal Nasser, a member of the PLO Executive, was a thinker and a poet rather than an activist, and was head of the PLO Information Department.

The Israeli disappointment was that both Yasir Arafat, chairman of the PLO and leader of Fatah, and Abu Iyad (Saleh Khalif), leader of the BSO and deputy leader of Fatah, had escaped their clutches. A meeting of the Executive Committee of Fatah on the 8th had ended about 2000 hours, when it was arranged that Arafat should stay with Kamal Nasser, and Abu Iyad with Abu Yusef.

However, in the evening an urgent call was received from Damascus that the presence of both top leaders was required there. Both set out by automobile for that city straight away and so escaped death.

One of the other groups of Israeli raiders in Beirut moved towards a Palestinian refugee camp in the Sabra area, near the airport adjacent to the coast, to attack a six-story building known to be the headquarters of the DPF. Two DPF sentries in an automobile were shot and killed, but the sound of the gunfire alerted the Arabs, who fired back at the Israelis from the upper windows. A gun battle ensued during which the Israelis managed to place explosive charges near the building. They also fired rockets at it. After a while the Israelis withdrew with the loss of two dead and two severely wounded. At least four DPF men were killed, and several injured. Yet another Israeli group attacked the house of the Arab Mukhtar (village headman) at the coastal village of Ouzai, south of Beirut, blowing it up, killing the Mukhtar and three other people. Elsewhere a few buildings were demolished by explosives because it was believed they were used by Arab terrorists. One of them was alleged to be a small arsenal.

At least one Israeli helicopter landed to take off a badly wounded Israeli officer, the filing cabinet, and the stacks of files and documents that had been seized. During this raid Israeli strike aircraft flew overhead. Within ninety minutes it was all over. The Israeli raiders had either been taken on board helicopters or, having left their automobiles where they found them, returned the way they came to the waiting Israeli naval craft lying a few miles offshore. They took their dead and wounded with them. General Elazar, the Israeli Chief of Staff, said that no prisoners had been taken by them.

The shock and national chagrin caused by these audacious Israeli raids into the heart of Beirut brought recriminations, and there were complaints about the alleged inactivity of the Lebanese security forces. Premier Saab Salim, who for over two years had headed a government (which was reasonably stable for Lebanon) whose platform was "law and order," offered his resignation. It was accepted on the 13th, but he stayed on as caretaker premier. The Lebanese officially admitted their casualties as two killed and ten wounded. Reports of greater casualties on both sides which were given out about this period were not later substantiated. The Israeli raid was condemned by the UN Security Council. In Lebanon it was announced that three Israeli agents had been arrested, having been detected with radio transmitters, together with about twenty other suspects.

On 12 April the funeral of the three assassinated leaders was held in Beirut. A three-mile long procession walked through the streets of the city to the Palestinian Martyrs' Cemetery on its outskirts. In addition to the three coffins containing the bodies of the Fedayeen leaders, another four appeared in the funeral procession as well. Kamal Nasser was a Christian Arab, a fact which helped to prevent an outbreak of violence between the Muslims and the Christians in Lebanon on this occasion. Symbolic funerals were held in Cairo, Baghdad, Damascus, and Kuwait. In Cairo the symbolic funeral procession was led by two of the BSO assassins of Wasfi Tal, the Jordanian premier.

For some time the three dead terrorist leaders had considered moving from Beirut, which from a security point of view was far too close to Israel and swarmed with Israeli agents. Anticipating individual assassination attempts being made on them, but liking the cosmopolitan atmosphere, the good accommodations, good schools for their children, and other city amenities, they had procrastinated. They had not, however, anticipated an attempt at mass assassination, as so far the Mossad had moved against individuals only. After this raid Fatah, BSO, PFLP, and other Fedayeen groups in Beirut began to move their headquarters to Damascus and Baghdad, cities with far less scope for Israeli agents and far less vulnerability to Israeli commando raids.

The Israelis were triumphant, and speaking in the Knesset, Prime Minister Golda Meir said, "We killed the murderers who were planning to murder again." As a military operation this raid was a boost to morale, but there was far more to it than that. It had, in fact, been a gigantic espionage scoop, such as had seldom been seen in recent intelligence history. Kamal Adwan, deeply involved with the Fatah Rasd, had been in possession of details of operations, future plans, lists of Fatah and BSO agents inside Israel and the Occupied Territories, and more important still, the codes for communicating with them. These included details of a rash of sabotage incidents planned for 7 May 1973, the twenty-fifth anniversary of the founding of the State of Israel.*

It had been the practice of Fatah, and of course the BSO, to

---

*The Hebrew calendar differs slightly from the Western one, and so the date varies each year. The actual original date was 14 May 1948.

broadcast over Saut al-Asifa a daily program of coded messages. This was the system of communication they employed in the underground in Israel and the Occupied Territories, one that had been in use since the 1967 War. On 11 April Saut al-Asifa canceled its daily program of coded messages and announced, "Until a new system is worked out, do not heed any orders by the old code because the enemy might use it to expose cells." On the 12th the Israelis arrested about thirty-five Fedayeen agents, having obtained their names from captured lists. They were small fry, but it was hoped that their interrogation might produce more vital information. Also, while they were out of circulation their espionage network was either ineffective or inoperative. Other arrests followed.

On 12 April an Aleph team struck in Greece. In the early hours of that day Moussa Abu Zeid, a BSO terrorist, was killed in an Athens hotel by an incendiary bomb that exploded in his room. It also slightly injured a German tourist. The Greek police thought this was an accidental explosion, but Mossad agents let it be known that Yariv's men had been at work again.

Documents captured in Beirut had shown the Israelis how important Boudia's cell in Paris was, and that although technically a member of the PFLP, Mohammed Boudia was in contact with the BSO and other terrorist groups. He was virtually heading a miniature terrorist international. It was confirmed that Boudia, an Algerian, had been involved in the planning of several anti-Israeli terrorist acts, and that he was in close touch with the Soviet KGB. On 28 June 1973, after visiting a friend in the Latin Quarter, he was blown up and killed as he entered his automobile.

To enhance their prestige, Yariv and his Squad 101 wanted to eliminate successively all the BSO members involved in the Munich Massacre. The one they sought most was Abu Hassan (Ali Hassan Salameh), the deputy leader of the BSO, who it was thought bore the ultimate responsibility for the exploit. Strangely enough, the Israeli Squad 101 did not seem to demonstrate the same zeal in tracking down Abu Iyad (Saleh Khalif), the actual leader of the BSO. Perhaps it did, but as the Mossad was not successful, this particular hunt was not publicized.

Mossad information pointed to the fact that Abu Hassan would be operating in Scandinavia, so members of the Aleph and Beth teams were sent there to kill him. For some time the Mossad had been expecting the BSO to carry out some spectacular exploit in that part of Europe, being alerted to this probability by the almost chance arrest at London airport on 24 December 1972 of Mohammed Abdul Karin Fuheid, a BSO messenger traveling on an Algerian passport. He had carelessly assumed that as it was Christmas Eve he could walk through the customs nothing-to-declare exit with impunity. He was unlucky and was stopped and searched. When his suitcase was opened it was found to contain pistols and explosives.

Brought to trial in Britain and sentenced to a term of imprisonment, he confessed he was a lieutenant in Fatah and that he had come to London only because it had been necessary to change aircraft there on his journey from Damascus to Stockholm. Stockholm was then an international terrorist center, with members of the PFLP, JRA, and other groups operating in, and from, that city. This fact, together with information gained from documents taken in the Beirut Raid, convinced the Mossad that Abu Hassan was about to travel to Scandinavia to organize a terrorist exploit.

In July 1973 Mossad agents thought they had sighted Abu Hassan in Norway, and tracked him to the small fishing town of Lillehammar, where they waylaid and killed the wrong man on the 21st. The victim was Ahmed Bouchiki, a Moroccan waiter. The overconfident team had mistaken his identity, and worse still, because of carelessness and tension, they left several clues that resulted in six of them being arrested by the Norwegian police and brought to trial. The trial was something of a showpiece and revealed the responsibility of the Israeli government for sending out assassination squads into foreign countries. The names of the accused were given as Dan Aerbel, Sylvia Rafael, Marianne Gladnikoff, Abraham Gehmer, Zwi Steinberg, and Michael Dorf.* Michael Dorf was acquitted, but the others were found guilty and sentenced to terms of imprisonment. From the high peak of the success of the Beirut Raid of April 1973, Yariv's Squad 101 had sunk to this miserable failure, which did untold harm to the Israeli cause

---

*Dan Aerbel, reputed to be a longtime Mossad agent, in anticipation and expectation that the Norwegian government would release them all if they could persuade it they were Israeli government agents, told what details he knew of the Plumbat Affair. This concerned some two hundred tons of uranium missing while in transit from Hamburg to Genoa by sea in 1969. The suspicion was that it had been transferred to Israel. At the trial the Norwegian prosecutor forbade the Norwegian police to make any mention of this incident. Details of the Plumbat Affair were not leaked to the world until April 1977.

throughout the world. On 14 August 1973 the Norwegian government expelled an Israeli diplomat for having sheltered two of the Mossad team involved in the murder of Bouchiki at Lillehammar.

From its inception, the BSO was bitterly hostile to the Jordanian government and those who served it, and hit out against them as often as it could. This conflict quickly spread to Europe, and on 6 February 1972 two BSO members knocked at the door of an apartment in the Bruhl district of Cologne and were admitted by one of three Turks sharing the flat with five Jordanians. The terrorists shot all five Jordanians. Two died instantly, and the other three on their way to hospital in an ambulance helicopter. The two terrorists threw away their weapons, a British Sterling submachine gun and a pistol, and fled to seek refuge in the Libyan embassy at Bonn, from which they escaped to Libya. The BSO alleged the Jordanians were spying for the Israelis, although other sources indicated they might have been working for Jordanian intelligence.

Meanwhile, Arab terrorists kept up their spasmodic campaign against Israeli targets, and when they realized that the Mossad was out to kill their leaders and other selected personnel, they in turn hit back in a like manner. One of the first of these incidents occurred on 10 September 1972 in Brussels, only four days after the Munich Massacre, when a member of the Israeli diplomatic staff, Ophir Zadok, was lured to a street cafe by a telephone call from an Arab who said he had information he wanted to impart about a planned Fedayeen attack on Israeli property in Belgium.

Ophir Zadok went to the cafe and sat waiting at a pavement table. A gunman shot and wounded him, and then escaped. The Belgian police later said the terrorist was Hassan Joudat, a Moroccan who had just been released from prison for stealing passports and threatening to kill the Moroccan ambassador in Brussels. Mohammed Boudia's Paris cell was behind Joudat's operations.

One of the greatest losses to the Mossad occurred when Baruch Cohen was killed in Madrid by a BSO terrorist on 28 January 1973.* Cohen was a senior Mossad officer who it is thought was on the track of the BSO network operating in Spain. He was in

*He was also known as Uri Molou and Moshe Hanan Tahai.

Madrid because it was anticipated the BSO might strike at the new Madrid Trade Center, which had largely been financed by Jewish money. The shooting occurred in broad daylight in the Grand Via outside a cafe owned by a Syrian. Cohen was fatally wounded after being shot in the stomach and left arm, but was able to shoot back, and one Spanish bystander was injured. The assassin, who had used a pistol with a silencer, was able to escape even though the incident was seen by many people. A list of all his Mossad agents in Europe was found on Cohen's body and was somehow obtained by the BSO, although it was never revealed quite how; but the killing did take place outside a Syrian-owned cafe. Cohen was a master spy, and a tribute was paid to him by an Israeli spokesman, which was unusual. The death of Baruch Cohen brought home to the Mossad that it was hunted as well as being the hunter.

The next Mossad casualty of note, perhaps in revenge for the death of Hussein Abad al-Chir (killed on 24 January 1973) occurred on 12 March 1973 when a Mossad agent, Simia Gilzer, posing as a businessman, was shot dead on the steps of the Palace Hotel, Nicosia, Cyprus. A former IZL member, he was a senior Mossad officer on a routine tour of inspection.

The BSO made their mistakes too, such as one that occurred on 27 April 1973 when a BSO member named as Zaharia Abu Saleh shot and fatally wounded Vittorio Olivares, who worked at the El Al office in Rome. Abu Saleh shot his victim twice outside a department store in the city center. The BSO terrorist then ran away, but was caught and disarmed by two policemen. Olivares, who had been mistaken for the deputy chief of the El Al office, died on his way to hospital.

Meanwhile Arab terrorists kept up their campaign against Israeli targets in Europe and America. On 9 January 1973 a large bomb exploded at the entrance to the Jewish Agency building in Paris, and several automobiles were damaged, but no one was hurt. The Jewish Agency still handled all Israeli immigration. When Prime Minister Meir visited New York on 16 March 1973 the BSO planted three bombs, two of which failed to explode because of technical failures. The third was found fifteen minutes before it was due to explode and was defused. One was in a hired automobile outside the Israeli Discount Bank in Manhattan and was found by chance by a representative of the leasing company. When checking the vehicle, he saw the bomb in the trunk and informed the police. The second was discovered in an automobile outside the

First Israel Bank and Trust Company. Both vehicles had notes in them from the BSO. The third was found near the El Al Terminal at Kennedy airport and defused. The FBI, which handled these incidents, said that had the three bombs exploded, they would have caused death or injury to hundreds of people. The FBI was looking for an Iraqi, Khalid Dahham al-Jawari, in connection with this crime.

In February 1973 the Mossad, and indeed the world in general, gained a good deal of information about the BSO with the arrest of Abu Daoud, a senior leader of the BSO who had been involved in the preparations for the Munich Massacre. He, with sixteen other BSO terrorists, went into Jordan intending to plan an operation to attack government offices, seize the premier and other members of the government, and hold them hostage for the release of Fedayeen still in Jordanian detention.

On the 13th he was caught while making a reconnaissance, as were successively the other sixteen members of the BSO. On the 18th the Israeli Mossad released the news, since the Jordanian authorities had said nothing. On the 19th Abu Daoud appeared on Jordanian television to make a full confession of his intended exploits and to give the first real information about the BSO, confirming what was then only suspected—that it was a part of Fatah, and controlled by Fatah. Abu Daoud said in his television interview that the BSO "is not a separate organization. It is a group of people from al-Fatah itself."*

Yasir Arafat denied that the BSO was part of his Fatah, but added, "I see nothing strange in Fatah elements joining Black September." A Fatah spokesman said that Abu Daoud was merely passing through Jordan, that the voice on television was not his, and that the words must have been dubbed onto film taken during Abu Daoud's interrogation. Abu Daoud admitted he had taken part in the preparations for the Munich Massacre while traveling in Europe under the name of Saad ad-Din Wadi. He confirmed that Libyan embassies held the explosives and arms for the terrorists, especially the embassy at Bonn, and also confirmed that the BSO European headquarters were housed in the Algerian consulate at Geneva. He said the Libyans freely gave false passports to BSO

*On 29 January 1973 an unidentified Arab had appeared on West German television to state there was no difference between Fatah and the BSO, but little credence was given to his statement.

members, sometimes even diplomatic ones, which enabled them to move freely about Europe.

On 21 February Abu Daoud and the other sixteen BSO members were sentenced to death, and this was confirmed by King Hussein on 4 March 1973. The following day the Emir of Kuwait sent a special envoy to Hussein to try to persuade him to rescind his decision. Then followed some behind-the-scenes bargaining in which King Hussein said he would spare the lives of Abu Daoud and the other condemned terrorists on condition the BSO and Fatah would refrain from entering into, or initiating, any more conspiracies against him, and cease hostile propaganda. The several Fedayeen groups grudgingly made a vague statement to the effect they would not interfere in Jordanian internal affairs, and would work solely for the Arab cause. On 14 March King Hussein announced he had commuted the death sentences "on humanitarian grounds," and "in response to pleas from foreign and Arab friends." Eventually, Abu Daoud and his fellow conspirators, together with some 970 Fedayeen fighters in Jordanian detention, were released on 19 September 1973 as part of the buildup of Arab solidarity preparatory to the October War.

The next Israeli victim to fall to Arab terrorists was Colonel Yusef Alon, the air attaché at the Israeli embassy in Washington. On 1 July 1973 he was shot outside his home at 0100 hours. The assassin escaped. The PLO radio, Saut al-Falastin, claimed that Alon was killed in revenge for the assassination of Mohammed Boudia three days previously. At Alon's funeral in Israel Defense Minister Dayan said, "We shall continue to hit the terrorists whenever they can be reached, as we have done in the past."

Resigning in July 1973 from his post as Special Advisor for the Coordination of Counter-Terrorist Activities to stand as a political candidate in the forthcoming general elections (scheduled to be held on 30 October but postponed until December owing to the Yom Kippur War in October), Aharon Yariv handed over his duties to Brigadier Israel Lior, who had been military secretary to successive prime ministers since 1966.

During the mere eleven months he had held the job, Yariv had built his Squad 101, the Wrath of God teams, into living Israeli legends; their successes were remembered and praised, while their failures were never mentioned. Although supposed to be a secret service, the existence of the Mossad was no longer secret—it was a source of extreme pride to the average Israeli, who loved to hint at its exploits and embellish what was known of them.

The Mossad was keen to eliminate George Habash, leader of the PFLP, and had already made one attempt to do so in February 1973, when an Israeli seaborne raiding force struck at two Palestinian refugee camps near Tripoli, in Lebanon. The camps were that of Badawi, a PFLP-dominated one, and Nahr al-Bared, a Fatah one. The Israelis knew that Habash was scheduled to hold an important PFLP conference at the Badawi camp, and the main aim of the operation was to kill or capture him. However, Habash, who had a heart condition, was taken ill. The conference was postponed for six hours, so he evaded death or capture.

The next serious Israeli attempt was made on 12 August 1973, when the Mossad learned that Habash and three other PFLP leaders were due to fly from Beirut to Damascus in a Lebanese Air Lines aircraft. While this aircraft was in flight it was diverted by four Israeli fighter planes and forced to land in Israel. To the intense disappointment of the Israelis, George Habash was not on board. In this instance Prime Minister Golda Meir, after consulting her cabinet, had given her permission for this act to be carried out. Amongst the eighty-three passengers on this plane, the majority of whom were Arabs, was the Iraqi minister of planning. The airliner, with its crew and all its passengers, was allowed to fly off to its intended destination. Even Israeli opinion was not completely in agreement with this exploit of forcing a Lebanese airliner from Arab air space to come down in Israel; not so much on legal or moral grounds, but because it might provoke Arab nations, some well beyond the physical reach of the Israeli air force, to try to forcibly divert Israeli airliners in retaliation.

The general reason given for his not catching that plane was that George Habash had taken ill at the last moment and was unfit to travel. The real reason, not liked by the Israelis, was that he had been tipped off about this hijack by a member of the Lebanese government. The Israelis liked to boast that their Mossad agents had infiltrated all the Fedayeen organizations and thus knew in advance what was about to happen. This converse example showed that sometimes the Fedayeen groups did the same. The Fedayeen groups also had Lebanese sympathizers in high places. The incident was good for Habash's popularity with the Arab masses. Although a Christian, he was credited with having the Baraka, the "Protection of Allah," or, as we might say, was blessed with sheer good luck.

On 30 August 1973 the International Civil Aviation Organization (ICAO) severely censured the Israeli government at its convention held in Rome for intercepting and diverting an aircraft of another nation on a routine flight by eighty-seven votes to one (that of Israel). There were only four abstentions. Israel was also condemned for this act by the UN Security Council, and indeed forfeited much international good will, while at home the Mossad reputation took a knock.

The Italian government took advantage of this incident to get rid of four Arab terrorists they were holding, two of whom had been arrested in April for an attempted attack on an El Al building in Rome. The two others had been detained in June for possessing explosives. This angered the Israelis, and their spokesman bitterly declared, "This is an inexplicable way of treating the matter. For the second time people who have been caught *in flagrante delecto* have been released, against any legal procedure known to anyone." Moshe Dayan said, "Of the 110 terrorists caught so far in the world, 70 have been released after a short time. We do not know how much ransom money had been paid, or what overt or under-the-counter agreements states have entered into with them."

For almost a year the Israeli government had authorized and operated what almost amounted to open twilight warfare in Europe and elsewhere against Fedayeen terrorists, especially those in the BSO. Realizing it was losing too many friends and too much vital international support, the resignation of General Yariv was a convenient moment to bring the illegal underground war to an end. Squad 101 was disbanded, but the capability of quickly bringing together experts in various fields in case of emergency or in case of a reversal of this decision was retained. The Mossad, of course, continued its normal intelligence-gathering activities. If indeed there was further killing of Fedayeen terrorists, and there might still have been, it was carried out with more discretion, and any traces of Israeli implication were obliterated. So with the resignation of General Yariv the Israeli Wrath of God teams passed into Israeli mythology. In cold, practical terms, their usefulness had been little more than morale-boosting to the Israeli nation, downcast by the Munich Massacre and other Arab terrorist exploits. Excluding the Beirut Raid, on balance the Israeli Squad 101 had lost more agents than it had killed.

11 A Year of Hijacking and Horror

We do not want our territory to be used as a battlefield in the Arab-Israeli conflict.

President Makarios of Cyprus, 10 April 1973

THE YEAR 1973 was one of hijacking and the taking of hostages, and ended in horror. The Arab terrorists continued with their policy of seizing aircraft and buildings and treating the people caught in them as hostages. Few incidents ended without bloodshed and hardship to innocent victims. Indeed, this sequence of terrorist acts began a few days before the start of 1973 on 28 December 1972. On that date, about noon, four BSO terrorists entered and occupied the Israeli embassy in Bangkok, Thailand and remained in possession for about eighteen hours. The ambassador, Rehavem Amir, was away attending the official investiture of Prince Vajiralongkorn as Crown Prince. Two of the terrorists, dressed in full morning dress, as were most diplomats that day, strolled through the embassy gates. The Thai policeman on duty assumed they were Israelis returning from the investiture. Almost at the same moment two other BSO members leaped over the embassy compound wall, but were seen by the Thai policeman, who raised the alarm.

It was too late. The four terrorists forced their way into the building, seized the six occupants, and held them hostage. They were Shimon Avimor, Israeli ambassador to Cambodia, who was visiting Bangkok; the first secretary and his wife; Dan Beeri, an attaché, and his wife; and Pinhas Levi, an administrative officer. They were bound hand and foot and spent the next few hours in a second-story corridor. The BSO terrorists had not done their homework properly, as they had hoped to seize the Israeli ambassador himself.

The embassy was soon surrounded by troops and police. The terrorists threw down a letter outlining their demands from a window. They threatened to blow up the building, together with the hostages and themselves, if thirty-six named persons, of whom

187

thirty-two were Arabs alleged to be held in Israeli prisons, were not immediately released and flown to Cairo. They included Kozo Okamoto and three women: Rima Issa Tannous, Therese Halaseh, and Fatima Barnawi, the latter serving a life sentence for placing a bomb in a Jerusalem cinema in 1967. They also demanded that the bodies of Abdul Aziz Atrassi and Ali Shafik Ahmed Taha, killed at Lod airport in May 1972, be released to the men's families.

At first the terrorists refused to accept mediation by Thai officials but eventually changed their minds and agreed to talk to the Thai deputy foreign minister, Air Marshal Chunchai Chunhawan. The Israeli government would not agree to release a single prisoner, but asked the Thais to allow the terrorists to go unpunished, provided they freed their hostages. The air marshal, who was in Munich at the time of the Munich Massacre, went unarmed into the embassy to talk to the terrorists. Food was taken in, and he sat down with them to eat it, thus gaining their confidence. A Thai airliner was standing by ready to fly the BSO members to any Arab capital. Eventually, the air marshal persuaded the terrorists that Israel would never comply with their demands. He talked them into letting the hostages go and surrendering their arms in return for a safe-conduct to the airport and an aircraft to fly them to either Cairo or Beirut.

On the morning of the 29th the Egyptian ambassador, Mustafa el-Essawy, was asked if Cairo would accept the terrorists. He entered the building to talk to the BSO men—this was thought to be the first time an Egyptian ambassador had officially entered an Israeli embassy. The arrangements were officially agreed upon and accepted, but the terrorists held on to their hostages until they reached the airport. There they were released. Once aboard the Thai aircraft, the BSO men surrendered their arms, and were flown to Cairo together with the Egyptian ambassador and eight Thais. The BSO terrorists were detained for four days in Egypt and then were flown to Damascus. According to *Al-Goumhuriya,* they were to face a Palestinian Resistance court to answer charges of failing in their mission to blow up the embassy building if the Israelis did not release the prisoners demanded. This abortive exploit meant loss of face for the BSO, as these particular BSO members, who were never officially named, obviously lacked the spirit of self-sacrifice expected of them. What happened to them is not known. The Israeli government stated on the 5th that in appreciation for the conduct of the Thai government in this situation it would hand over the bodies of the two terrorists killed at Lod airport to relatives in East Jerusalem and Hebron respectively.

On 21 February 1973 a Libyan Boeing 727 on a regular flight from Tripoli to Cairo with a French air crew strayed too far eastwards when coming into Cairo airport, due to a navigational error, and was shot down by the Israelis about twelve miles to the east of the Suez Canal. The Israelis claimed that for fifteen minutes the Libyan plane had been under warning by them to land, but had not done so. It was thought that the French pilot, when he realized where he was and how close he was to Egyptian-held territory, tried to make a run for it. However, the Israelis did admit the weather was bad and that they also believed the aircraft might be off course, but stated that as Fedayeen terrorists had threatened to carry out suicidal air missions over Israel they could not be sure it was not going to crash-land on some Israeli target.

Colonel Gaddafi threatened to make an aerial raid on an Israeli city, but was persuaded to think better of the project. On 6 March 1973 the Israeli government announced compensation payments to the families of victims of this disaster. One hundred and six people had been killed. The bodies of the victims were handed to the Arabs through IRC arrangements at Kantara.

Previously, in the early hours of the same day, the 21st, Israeli aircraft had raided Fatah camps in Lebanon, where the final death toll was 108. At the same time the Israelis also mounted a seaborne naval commando raid on the Nahr al-Bared refugee camp, which was about five miles from Tripoli, Lebanon, where BSO terrorists were training. In this raid the Israelis captured a Turkish Kurd named as Faik Buluk, who under interrogation gave information that future BSO targets included Jordanian ones, and also other Arab embassies abroad. Until this moment the Israelis had assumed that all BSO targets would be Israeli ones. On 8 August 1973 the captured Turk was sentenced to imprisonment.

The next major BSO exploit ended in tragedy. At Khartoum, capital of the Sudan, at about 1900 hours on 1 March 1973, eight BSO terrorists burst into the Saudi Arabian embassy, where a diplomatic party was in progress, and held a number of people hostage. The terrorists were variously described as being a university teacher, a doctor, a student, a government clerk, and Libyan embassy employees.

The Soviet, French, and British ambassadors, when they saw what was happening, managed to escape over the compound wall in the initial confusion, but five other diplomats present were captured. They were Sheikh Abdullah al-Malhouk, the Saudi Arabian ambassador, the doyen of the Khartoum diplomatic corps; George Moore, the retiring American ambassador, in whose honor the party was given; his successor, Cleo Noel; Guy Eid, the Belgian chargé d'affaires; and Adly al-Nasser, the Jordanian chargé d'affaires, together with a number of wives and children.

In return for the safety of the hostages, the BSO terrorists demanded the release of Abu Daoud and his sixteen colleagues, then in a Jordanian prison, together with other terrorists arrested since Abu Daoud, and also fifty Palestinian Fedayeen who had been in Jordanian detention since 1970; the release of Sirhan Bishara Sirhan, the Jordanian who had killed Robert Kennedy, held in an American prison; the release of all the Baader-Meinhof members held in West German jails; and the release of all female guerrillas held in Israeli prisons.

The BSO terrorists gave a twenty-four-hour time limit for their demands to be complied with, threatening to blow up the embassy building if any rescue attempt was made. The hostages were kept on the second floor of the embassy. The Saudi Arabian and Jordanian diplomats were not tied up, and were later told they would not be killed, but Cleo Noel, the American who had been wounded in the initial attack on the building, was tied to a chair, while the other two, George Moore and Guy Eid, had their wrists and ankles bound and were placed face downwards on the floor. After contact with the governments concerned, President Numeiry of the Sudan telephoned King Feisal of Saudi Arabia and informed him that the governments of America, West Germany, Jordan, and Israel had all said they would not give in to blackmail.

The following day, 2 March, the terrorists dropped their demands on the governments of America, West Germany, and Israel, but insisted on the release of Abu Daoud and other prisoners held in Jordan. The hostages later said that the terrorists were calm and reasonably relaxed until the evening of the 2nd, when suddenly their attitude changed after the receipt of a radio message. They became hard and tense. The message, monitored by the Sudanese security service, was, "Why are you waiting? The blood of the people of Nahr al-Bared cries out for vengeance." Just before 1900 hours, the two Americans and the Belgian were untied, given paper and pens, and told to write their last letter to their families. They were then taken to a cellar and four long bursts of automatic fire were heard. Later evidence showed that George Moore had been beaten and kicked in the face before being killed.

Immediately after the killings, just twenty-four hours after the incident began, the Saudi Arabian ambassador was allowed to use his embassy telephone to speak to General al-Bagaara Ahmed, a Sudanese first vice-president and minister of the interior, to tell him that the diplomats Moore, Noel, and Eid had been executed. On the third day the terrorists, who were in touch with the Sudanese government by telephone, tried to bargain, but President Numeiry insisted upon unconditional surrender. That day a man and his wife, friends of Sheikh Malhouk, the Saudi Arabian ambassador, boldly walked into the embassy to demand the release of Mrs. Malhouk and her four children. The children were freed, and although the terrorists offered to allow Mrs. Malhouk to leave as well, she chose to remain with her husband.

The BSO leadership in Beirut sent a message to the besieged terrorists to surrender, which they received about 0300 hours on 4 March. At 0600 hours, after a sixty-hour siege, the BSO terrorists gave themselves up and released their remaining hostages unharmed. Numeiry said the terrorists must stand trial, something that no Arab government had been bold enough to do so far. The bodies of the two Americans were flown to the United States on 6 March, while that of Eid, a naturalized Belgian who had been born in Egypt, was flown to Cairo for burial. That same day, the 4th, King Hussein confirmed the death sentence on Abu Daoud and his colleagues in Amman.

President Numeiry openly accused Fatah of instigating the exploit, at a time when it was thought the BSO was a separate organization. He claimed that Kawaz Yassin, the Fatah representative in Khartoum, who had diplomatic status and had left the Sudan in a Libyan aircraft for Tripoli just a few hours before the terrorist attack on the embassy began, had planned the operation. He said that Yassin's assistant had driven the terrorists to the embassy in his landrover and had actually led the assault himself.

Immediately, Arafat issued a statement denying that either the PLO or Fatah were implicated in the plot at all, and accused President Numeiry of "launching an American-inspired campaign against the Palestinian guerrillas." He stated he had asked Abu Yusef (who was later killed by the Israelis in their Beirut Raid of April 1973) to conduct a Fatah inquiry into the Khartoum embassy killings; but this statement was made for public consumption only. No

Fatah inquiry was held. In Libya, Syria, and Iraq the Khartoum incident was not mentioned at all in the press or on the radio. In Egypt the only criticism was the mild one that it was the "latest in a series of mistakes made by the Palestinian organization."

On 7 March 1973 the Sudanese security authorities made public an eight-page BSO battle plan entitled Operation Tariq, complete with a map showing the layout of the embassy, which they had seized together with many other incriminating documents when they raided the PLO office in Khartoum. The plan had been written by Kawa Yassin (also known as Abu Marwin) and gave details of the precise objectives that each of the terrorists was to achieve. For example, one man was to command the initial assault squad, another was to read a statement to the diplomats, another to control the telephone communications to and from the embassy, another was to select the diplomats to be killed, another was to be the executioner, and so on.

Omar Haj Musa, the Sudanese information minister, said that six Sudanese named in the incriminating documents had been arrested and would stand trial. He added, "We will give him [Arafat] the facts. It was his men and an al-Fatah car. And the plans were found in the Fatah leader's drawer after he fled the country before the attack. We are prepared to give them [the PLO] all the documents. We want them to give us the men who fled." The weapons had been provided by Libya.

On the 9th the Sudanese security authorities stated that the main target of the BSO operation had been Emperor Haile Selassie of Ethiopia, who was visiting the Sudan at the time. Pretending to be Saudi Arabian officials, the terrorists had telephoned Haile Selassie's secretary several times both before and during the diplomatic party on 1 March to try to persuade him to attend or even to put in a brief appearance. Haile Selassie had been the mediator a year previously in the negotiations that brought about a ceasefire in the seventeen-year long civil war in southern Sudan, when the Arab north was ranged against the Black south.* He had been invited to the Sudan as the guest of honor on the First Sudanese National Unity Day. The Saudi Arabian invitation to the diplomatic party was declined by the emperor, even though the dinner in his honor was not due to start until one hour after the party was due to end.

*See Edgar O'Ballance, *The Secret War in the Sudan*.

President Numeiry alleged that Fatah activities in the Sudan were directed against his regime and were particularly aimed at disrupting his good relations with the Ethiopian government, saying, "We have documents to prove that Fatah men in Khartoum worked more to foment troubles in Ethiopia than for the cause of Palestine." This was true, and the real BSO aim had been both to create a rift in the new Sudanese-American relations and to isolate the Sudan from Black Africa by seizing and killing Emperor Haile Selassie.

Previously a strong supporter of the Palestinians, President Numeiry now banned all Palestinian organizations and activities within the Sudan. Because the issue was so potentially explosive, President Numeiry was under considerable pressure from Arab states not to bring the terrorists to public trial. Numeiry was stubborn. After a postponement in June, the eight BSO terrorists appeared before a court in Khartoum on 25 September 1974, but after a brief hearing the trial was adjourned.

Because of its geographical position Cyprus attracted both Mossad agents and Arab terrorists. On 9 April 1973 there were two exploits on the island. In one, three Arab terrorists in a hired automobile drove up to a block of flats in Nicosia in which the Israeli ambassador lived. They placed explosives on the ground floor, ran back to their vehicle, and had started to drive away when Cypriot policemen opened fire at them. In an exchange of shots one policeman was killed. The explosion damaged the ground floor apartments, but those on the second floor, where the ambassador, who had left only minutes before, lived, were undamaged. His wife and children, who were in the flat, were unharmed. The three terrorists were subsequently captured by the police.

In the second exploit, Arab terrorists attempted to hijack an Israeli Arkia Viscount aircraft. They drove in two landrovers through the entrance barrier at Nicosia airport. One vehicle circled the aircraft while the terrorists fired at the plane, which was waiting to take off for Lod, although neither the crew nor passengers had yet boarded. An Israeli security guard standing on the tarmac near the door of the plane fired his pistol at the attackers. He then entered the aircraft and emerged again with an automatic weapon, which he fired at them, killing one and wounding the other two.

The landrover then crashed into a mobile generator parked near the tail of the plane. Cypriot police were now on the scene and seized the two wounded men as they jumped from their vehicle, although one of them knocked out a policeman by hitting him on the head with a grenade.

The second landrover had been forced by police action to swerve, and it crashed into the airport entrance gatepost. The three men in it were arrested. In all, one terrorist was killed and seven were captured that day. One of the landrovers contained over fifty pounds of explosives. The police found a hand-written note identifying the terrorists as being members of the National Arab Youth. This was the first mention of this title, which was thought to be merely an operational code name. Part of the contents of the note were meant to be read to the passengers of the Arkia aircraft once it had been taken over. Another part was addressed to the Cypriot people, apologizing for carrying out the exploit on Cypriot territory. The terrorists had badly mistimed their airport operation.

On 10 April President Makarios said, "Cyprus has its own problems; we do not want our territory to be used as a battlefield in the Arab-Israeli conflict." The seven Arab terrorists were eventually sentenced to terms of imprisonment. On 3 December 1973 President Makarios signed a pardon for them, and they were released to the PLO by being flown to Cairo on the 6th.

On 14 April 1973 four masked men overpowered the guards at the Zahrani terminal of the TAP Oil Pipeline at Sidon, Lebanon, and took them together with other employees to the beach, where the raiders were joined by fourteen other men. Explosives were then affixed to eighteen oil storage tanks and detonated. Only two tanks were destroyed by fire. The other explosive devices either failed to detonate or were defused by Lebanese army experts. Nails were scattered by the raiders on the main road running through the oil installation complex to delay pursuing vehicles.

After a short but confused silence, the Lebanese Revolutionary Guard claimed responsibility for this outrage, saying that the intention was to cut off "oil shipments which feed imperialism and are transformed into American weapons, which are given to the Israeli enemy." Nothing was known of such a Palestinian dissident organization. The general opinion at the time was that it was a PFLP code word for the operation. The oil came from Saudi Arabia, and the PFLP still bore a strong grudge against the Saudi Arabian government.

Greece also remained the scene of Arab terrorist exploits. On 19 July 1973 an Arab terrorist who was never positively identified, armed with an automatic rifle and grenades, attempted to enter the El Al office in Athens, but a Greek police guard, seeing the rifle, prevented his entry by closing an inner door quickly. The gunman was seized by bystanders, but escaped and ran to the near-by Amelia Hotel, where he held about twenty people hostage, including three Greek policemen. Three of the hostages managed to slip away. The terrorist demanded to speak to the Greek deputy premier, who refused to meet him.

Both the Libyan ambassador and the Egyptian chargé d'affaires were brought into negotiations with the gunman, which lasted over four hours. At one point there was a sudden alarm when the pistol of a Greek policeman was discharged as he was entering the hotel to speak to the terrorist. His weapon caught against the doorway, wounding him. This caused the terrorist to produce a grenade, pull out the safety-pin with his teeth, and give another twenty-five-minute deadline for a safe-conduct for himself. Eventually the Arab diplomatic representatives persuaded him to release the hostages in return for the demanded safe-conduct. The Arab terrorist was taken to the airport and put on an aircraft, which flew to Kuwait. He still refused to reveal his identity and departed by road for Iraq. The embittered Israelis pointed out that Greek economy was completely dependent upon supplies of Arab oil.

The next major BSO terrorist exploit also occurred in Greece, on 5 August 1973, in the crowded transit lounge at Athens airport. Two BSO members, Talaat Hussein and Jihad Mohammed, waiting in the queue to have their luggage searched, suddenly took grenades from their suitcases and threw them across the floor. Next they produced automatic weapons and fired them indiscriminately into the crowd. They killed three people and injured fifty-six, one of whom later died. Three of the dead were Americans, and the other was an Austrian.

The two terrorists then herded about fifty hostages into a corner of the transit lounge and attempted to bargain with the police. After about two hours they surrendered. They told the police that they had been instructed to attack passengers embarking on an Israeli-bound TWA flight, but had made a mistake and instead attacked those waiting to embark on a flight to Geneva and New York. They were sentenced to death by a Greek court on 24 January 1974. They admitted to being members of Black September, but both the PLO and Fatah denied all knowledge of them.

At about 1000 hours on 5 September 1973, the first anniversary of the Munich Massacre, five BSO terrorists broke into the Saudi Arabian embassy in Paris, seized control of the building, and held fifteen people hostage, including four women. Stating they were from Al-Eqab (punishment), which was merely a code word for the operation, they demanded the immediate release of Abu Daoud and his colleagues as well as a safe-conduct for themselves to leave France in an aircraft that would fly them to an Arab capital. They threatened to blow up the building, themselves, and their hostages if their demands were not met. Several deadlines were set, which successively expired without the threat being carried out.

The ambassadors of Egypt, Algeria, Iraq, Libya, and Kuwait attempted to negotiate with the terrorists without success. In the late evening one of the hostages escaped by jumping through a first floor window, but injured himself. During the night the French authorities agreed to provide a plane for the terrorists and the male hostages if the women were released. Early the next day, the 6th, Maama al-Naam, the Iraqi ambassador, went into the embassy as a voluntary hostage to try to ensure the safety of those inside. At 1030 hours a Syrian Caravelle aircraft sent by President Assad to fly the terrorists out of France arrived at Le Bourget airport. As the terrorists had agreed to release the women at the airfield, the hostages, bound and shackled, were led out from the embassy building and put in a bus with its blinds drawn. This was a moment of tense drama reminiscent of that of the previous year at Munich, when hostages had been led in a similar manner to their deaths.

However, at the airport the BSO terrorists freed all their hostages except for five Saudi Arabians, whom they took with them on board the Syrian aircraft, which flew off to Cairo, where it had been given permission to refuel. At the Cairo international airport the terrorists refused to make contact with the control tower, but instead sought permission to land in Libya, only to be coldly told that both the Tripoli and Benghazi airports were closed. The Caravelle was then flown to Syria, where it circled over Damascus until suddenly the terrorists changed their minds. Instead of landing, the aircraft flew off to Kuwait, where it arrived soon after midnight. It is believed that Abu Nidal, leader of the breakaway Fatah Revolutionary Council, masterminded this operation. If this were so, the five terrorists may have had good reason to shy away from Damascus in view of the hostility between the governments of Iraq and Syria. Perhaps President Assad had this in mind when he sent an aircraft to bring them to Damascus.

At Kuwait the BSO terrorists demanded that the Syrian Cara-velle be replaced by a Kuwaiti Boeing. When this was done both terrorists and hostages moved into the Boeing aircraft and took off, making first of all for Riyadh, the Saudi Arabian capital. During this flight over desert terrain, the terrorists threatened to throw their hostages out from the plane one by one unless Abu Daoud was released. As there was no response from either Riyadh or Amman, the BSO terrorists then ordered the pilot to fly back to Kuwait again, where the aircraft landed at about 0300 hours on the 7th, to be instantly surrounded by troops and police. After more negotiation, more deadlines, and more threats, the terrorists released their Saudi Arabian hostages at noon. Later that afternoon they surrendered themselves to the Kuwaiti authorities. As had become customary, the PLO and Fatah condemned the exploit and claimed they had never heard of Al-Eqab.

On 5 September 1973, the same day as the seizure of the Saudi Arabian Embassy in Paris, the Italian police announced they had arrested five Arabs the previous evening just before they were planning to shoot down an El Al airliner coming into Rome airport with ground-to-air missiles. The police had raided a flat at Osia, near the airport, and arrested a Lebanese who had in his possession two SAM-7s, complete with launcher and missiles. Later, another four Arabs were arrested in a Rome hotel in connection with the same offense. The leader was named as Atef Bisaysu. The Mossad traced the SAM-7s by their serial numbers and found they were part of a consignment from the Soviet Union to Syria.

Despite Palestinian Fedayeen threats of reprisals, the five BSO terrorists were brought to trial for illegally being in possession of weapons of war and were sentenced to imprisonment by a Rome court on 27 February 1974. Two of the terrorists had already been released provisionally and deported to Libya. The remaining three were expelled from Italy on 1 March 1974 after a sum of money equal to about $13,000 each had been paid to the court on their behalf by an unknown source.

The leaders of Egypt, Syria, and Jordan met in Cairo on 10 September 1973. The October War was approaching and President Sadat of Egypt wanted to bring King Hussein of Jordan back into the Arab fold, from which he had been banished for ejecting the Fedayeen fighters from his country in 1970 and 1971, to establish some form of "Third Front" against Israel. This was a momentous meeting, as just over two years previously Syrian and Jordanian tanks had been fighting each other in northern Jordan. However,

President Sadat achieved his aim, diplomatic relations were restored between Jordan and both Egypt and Syria, and some vague form of military cooperation was agreed upon. The three Arab countries were to form a united front against Israel, and the several issues dividing them were to be put aside.

For example, the Syrian government withdrew the facilities it had allowed Fatah for the use of a radio transmitter at Deraa, near the Jordanian border, which was churning out anti-Hussein propaganda, and arrested the station's director and five of the staff, all Fatah members. King Hussein also had to make concessions, the major one being the release of political prisoners, principally Abu Daoud, the BSO leader for whose freedom several terrorist exploits had been specially mounted. Another prisoner freed at this time was Colonel Hindawi, who had plotted with the BSO to overthrow King Hussein.

In preparation for the October War, which was to begin on the 6th of that month, Presidents Sadat and Assad kept as tight a rein on terrorist activities as they could, as they did not want the terrorists to carry out any extraordinary exploits that might provoke the Israelis into launching a premature attack on the Arab states. However, one terrorist exploit did occur, which later both presidents claimed was really part of the overall deception plan against the Israelis.

On 28 September 1973 two members of the Syrian Saiqa, named as Abu Ali (Mustafa Soudeidan) and Abu Salim (Mahmoud Khaldi), boarded the daily train that ran from Moscow through Kiev and Bratislava (on the Czech-Austrian frontier) to Vienna, Austria. It was generally known as the Chopin Express. On this occasion the train was carrying about seventy passengers, thirty-seven of whom were Jews emigrating from the Soviet Union. Since the Soviet government had eased its emigration restrictions in 1971, about 70,000 Russian Jews had traveled on this train to the West. When the customs and passport checks at the frontier had been completed and the train had crossed into Austria, the terrorists seized two Austrian customs officers, but one escaped by jumping from the slow-moving train. As the train got under way the terrorists went into the sleeping coaches, awoke and seized four Jews, and held them hostage. The terrorists, who had Lebanese passports and carried automatic weapons and grenades, claimed they were Eagles of the Palestinian Revolution, a code name for the operation, which they later said was carried out because "the immigration of Soviet Jews forms a great danger to our cause."

The two terrorists had actually traveled on the same train on 8 September as a rehearsal. A surprising fact was that the terrorists had managed to smuggle their arms through Czechoslovakia, a country in which at that period searches and close surveillance of Arabs was customary.

The train stopped at Marchegg, a station about four miles from Vienna, where the terrorists demanded a vehicle to take them to the airport. They were given an Austrian Railways truck, which they made the captive customs officer drive. It was only at this point, as the vehicle drove off, that the police were alerted to what was happening. At the Schwochat airport the truck was surrounded by police and security personnel, and a period of negotiation began in which the ambassadors of Egypt, Iraq, Lebanon, and Libya participated. The terrorists demanded that the Schonau Castle transit camp near Vienna be closed down and that all facilities given to Jews emigrating from the Soviet Union by the Austrian government be withdrawn. They handed a statement to the police, which was given to the Austrian government. In the early hours of the 29th, Otto Kreisky, the Austrian chancellor, himself a Jew, agreed to comply with these demands. Israeli Prime Minister Golda Meir, who was in Europe at the time attending an International Socialist Conference, visited Chancellor Kreisky in an attempt to persuade him to remain firm and not give in to terrorist blackmail, but she failed.

The government also promised safe-conduct for the terrorists and an aircraft to fly them from Austria. The plane provided was a private Cessna, flown by its volunteer owner, which had to make three refueling stops at Dubrovnik, Yugoslavia; Palermo, Sicily; and Cagliari, Sardinia because no Arab state seemed willing to accept the terrorists. In turn the governments of Algeria, Tunisia, and Libya refused permission for the plane to land on their territory. However, Malta said it would accept the aircraft, but this did not please the terrorists, who threatened to blow up the plane along with the pilot, the hostages, and themselves unless an Arab government would give them sanctuary. Eventually, Libya changed its mind "for humanitarian reasons" and the Cessna landed in that country. Later that day, the 29th, the two terrorists were presented at a press conference, at which one of them said, "Moshe Dayan has stated publicly that he would attack the Palestinian Fedayeen wherever they may be. Therefore, we are determined to attack Zionists everywhere in the world."

Chancellor Kreisky asked the secretary general of the UN to

take over Schonau Castle, but he refused, saying he had no authority to do so, as the Soviet Jews were technically not refugees. This action of the Austrian chancellor shocked the whole Israeli nation and became the main talking point there, even overshadowing the forthcoming general election. Certainly, the Israeli government seemed more preoccupied with this incident and the Fedayeen terrorists in general than the possibility of a conventional Arab military attack.

The October War suddenly hit at 1400 hours on the 6th of that month when the Egyptians and Syrians simultaneously attacked Israel on two fronts, initially catching the Israelis by surprise and tumbling them backwards.* For several days it was touch and go, but they recovered and regained most of the territory they had lost. The October War was a shock to the Israelis, as the myth of the invincibility of the Israeli fighting soldier in the Middle East had taken a knock. It was a terrific morale booster for the Arabs. The war was in fact a draw in which both sides lost and gained territory and claimed to have won. There was a cease-fire with the Syrians on the 22nd and with the Egyptians on the 24th, but on both fronts a war of attrition continued in which ground forces virtually remained static in their basic positions, but fought each other with guns, tanks, and combat aircraft. This war of attrition lasted for 34 days on the Syrian front and for 129 days on the Egyptian front.

On 25 November 1973 a Dutch KLM jumbo jet with about 288 people on board, mostly Japanese returning from from visits to Europe, was hijacked by three Arabs just after leaving Beirut. At Beirut twelve passengers had boarded the aircraft, three of whom were the hijackers. The terrorists, who said they were from the National Arab Youth, demanded that the Dutch government close the transit camps on its soil for Russian Jews, stop Soviet Jewish emigration through Holland, stop Dutch volunteers fighting for the Israelis, and stop Dutch arms deliveries by air to Israel.

The Dutch government emphatically denied it had any transit camps for Soviet Jews on its territory, that Soviet Jews passed through Holland, that it ever supplied arms to the Israelis during the October War, and that its KLM aircraft had carried arms to Israel.

After being diverted to Damascus for refueling the aircraft was then flown to Libya, where the terrorists had a meeting with the

*See Edgar O'Ballance, *No Victor, No Vanquished.*

Dutch chargé d'affaires on the 26th. After that the plane was flown to Malta, where after a talk with the Maltese authorities the hijackers agreed to release all 247 passengers and three air hostesses in exchange for being refueled. That day the Dutch government stated that Dutch volunteers fighting with the Israeli armed forces would lose their citizenship. On the 28th the jet flew off again from Malta towards the Middle East, but was successively refused permission to land at Cairo, Baghdad, Kuwait, Bahrein, and Aden. Because it was running short of fuel, it was eventually allowed to land at Dubai, where the terrorists surrendered to the authorities. The nine-man crew, a relief pilot, and a KLM representative were released unharmed. The three hijackers were alleged to have come from the Gulf Sheikhdoms of Bahrein and Ras el-Khaimah.

This was the second mention of the National Arab Youth, which claimed responsibility for the exploit. The first was on 9 April 1973 in Greece, when it was thought to be merely a code name for the operation. More information had since been revealed. It had been formed by Colonel Gaddafi of Libya earlier in the year as a terrorist group because he was unable to influence existing Fedayeen terrorist organizations sufficiently, despite the large sums of money he gave them. He wanted one of his own that would do his own bidding without question. The National Arab Youth (NAY) had been formed and was led by Abu Mahmoud (Ahmed Abdul al-Ghafour), a longtime member of Fatah who had been in charge of the Libyan Fatah office. As an activist, Abu Mahmoud disagreed with Arafat's policy of restricting terrorism to Israel and the Occupied Territories, and because of a personality clash had not been selected for the BSO, which might have been an outlet for his vicious energies. Perhaps it was because of this slight that he left Fatah and agreed to work for Colonel Gaddafi. He recruited proven and capable terrorists by poaching them from the existing Fedayeen terrorist groups such as Fatah, BSO, PFLP, and DPF. The money he was able to offer tempted many of the discontented and greedy. NAY, which was completely supported and controlled by Colonel Gaddafi, later claimed responsibility for the two attacks in Cyprus on 9 April 1973 against the home of the Israeli ambassador and the Israeli airliner and for the attack in Greece on 5 August 1973, when two terrorists opened fire in a crowded transit lounge at Athens airport.

As if to mark the end of a terrorist year, on 17 December 1973 (the day the five Arab terrorists who had been arrested in Rome for possessing the SAM-7s were brought to trial), one of the worst terrorist exploits committed so far occurred. It was anticipated that the Fedayeen terrorists might stage a terrorist spectacular to disrupt the forthcoming Geneva Peace Conference, due to meet on the 21st, which had been called by the United States and the Soviet Union and was to be attended by representatives of the belligerent states in the October War.

As five Arabs were having their hand baggage examined at Rome airport they took out automatic weapons and grenades and opened fire indiscriminately. They then rushed out onto the tarmac towards an Air France aircraft about to leave for Beirut, which had on board Mohammed Osman, the Moroccan premier. Seeing what was happening, the air crew managed to slam the plane's door shut in time. The terrorists then turned and made for a Pan American airliner waiting for the signal to take off with some ninety people on board, including Moroccan ministers, all with their safety belts fastened. It was afterwards revealed that they thought Henry Kissinger, the U.S. secretary of state, was on that plane. This was not a very clever deduction, as Kissinger invariably carried out his famous shuttle diplomacy with a "circus" of about five or six aircraft, he himself usually traveling in the U.S. president's personal plane, Air Force One. The terrorists threw incendiary bombs at the Pan Am plane. Within seconds it became a blazing inferno. In this blaze thirty-four people died and another forty were seriously injured; the dead included two Moroccan ministers. Emilio Tayeani, the Italian minister of the interior, resigned after this incident.

Next, taking several Italian airport staff hostage, the five terrorists entered and seized a Lufthansa plane that was standing nearby, killing an airport worker in the process. The hijacked Lufthansa aircraft took off carrying the five terrorists, six Italian hostages (five airport policemen and an airport worker), and a crew of seven, of whom three were air hostesses. The pilot was directed to fly to Beirut, but when that airport was barred to them he was told to fly to Athens. The terrorists demanded the release of two Arabs, Talaat Hussein and Jihad Mohammed, who had killed four people and injured fifty-five in August 1973. The Greek government was beginning to take a harder line against terrorists and refused to release these two prisoners, so the hijackers selected at random an Italian policeman, shot him, and flung his body out onto the tarmac. During the flight the hijackers had threatened to kill their hostages one by one if their demands were not met, although at that point it was not clear precisely what they were.

The hijacked Lufthansa airliner took off again, this time heading for Beirut, but again was refused permission to land there. It was also refused permission to land at Baghdad, but eventually, after refueling at Damascus, it flew to Kuwait. The Kuwaiti authorities did not want the aircraft, so the runway was unlit and blocked by placing vehicles on it. Determined to land, the hijackers forced the pilot to descend and land, which he managed to do, narrowly avoiding vehicles, although the plane itself was damaged. No one on board was seriously hurt. Then for an hour there was silence, without any contact with the control tower, as the hijackers and their hostages waited inside the plane. Eventually, the Kuwaiti authorities made contact, demanding that the hijackers and their plane leave Kuwait immediately. The hijackers replied, saying they insisted on staying in Kuwait, that the pilot was too tired to fly any more, and that it was not certain the aircraft could take off in its present condition. After some three hours of negotiation the terrorists surrendered, freeing their twelve hostages unharmed.

The Italian government asked for the extradition of the five terrorists, which was refused as the crime was allegedly a political one, but the Kuwaiti government stated they would be handed over to the PLO. The PLO and Fatah, as usual, expressed regret to the Italian government but disclaimed any knowledge of the exploit or the hijackers. The West German pilot, who had been at the controls all the time the aircraft was in flight with the barrel of a gun pressed into the back of his neck, the crew, and the hostages were all flown back to Rome. Later, on 2 March 1974, the five terrorists were handed over to the PLO, and two days afterwards the Palestinian news agency (WAFA) reported that they would be questioned by a special Fatah commission. No evidence was forthcoming that they ever were. The Soviet Union was displeased because this Arab terrorist incident had coincided with the preparations for the Geneva Peace Conference.

12   Carlos the Jackal

Violence is the one language the Western democracies can understand.

Carlos the Jackal, 22 December 1975

T HE OCTOBER WAR of 1973 not only broke the deadlock of the Palestine problem and the Arab frustration which had in large measure produced Fedayeen terrorism, but also brought about a change of tactics and emphasis on political fronts. Possessing a shrewd political acumen, Yasir Arafat decided that the moment was opportune for him to become "respectable and responsible," and while he secretly continued to support the BSO and its violence, he openly condemned all Arab terrorist activity and gave the impression he sought to control his own hotheads and extremists.

The October War marked the watershed in Fedayeen fortunes, as it seemed to have dulled the mass enthusiasm for the ideal of the Fedayeen spirit of self-sacrifice. Lip service was still fulsomely paid to this idea, but in fact the inherent jealousies, rivalries, and suspicions among the Arab states soon rose up again, phoenixlike, and caused a hardening of attitudes towards the Arab Fedayeen groups, especially those over which they had minimal influence or none at all. Arab states selectively restricted the movements of the Fedayeen terrorists, making their lives and freedom precarious and uncertain, and the Fedayeen terrorist never quite knew which way the political wind of any particular Arab state might swirl to sweep him into silent detention.

The holding of Arab terrorists incommunicado was a bitter complaint from extreme activist groups such as the PFLP. When terrorists were selectively or grudgingly given sanctuary in some Arab country, they were all too often detained for indefinite periods, themselves virtually held as hostages against further terrorist excesses or pressure. Operating on an international scale, Arab terrorists were increasingly hampered by the refusal of Arab countries to accept hijacked aircraft and hostages. Arab governments wanted little to do with terrorism that was so far removed from their control.

One of the main organizers of the international aspect of Arab terrorism was Wadia Hadad, the deputy leader of the PFLP, who developed into something of a secret mastermind, forever plotting and planning behind the scenes and pulling strings to activate his terrorist puppets. Later, towards the end of 1974, Hadad differed with George Habash and took up residence in Aden, where his Marxist political philosophy was generally in accord with that of the government of South Yemen. Hadad, however, never completely broke with Habash. The government of South Yemen gave Hadad support, facilities, and certain freedom of action, although there was a limit beyond which it would not allow him and his terrorists to trespass. Wadia Hadad and the South Yemen government both tolerated and used each other warily. Hadad made periodic secret trips to Middle East capitals and PFLP camps to attend conferences and briefings. His main cells based in Lebanon were well established. His main European cell in Paris had been developing satisfactorily under Mohammed Boudia until June 1973, when Boudia was killed by an Israeli assassination team.

Hadad's problem of replacing Boudia was solved for him by the Soviet KGB, which produced a candidate who not only picked up the threads where Boudia had dropped them, but fostered and developed the international aspect of terrorism, operating successfully with such groups as the JRA, the Baader-Meinhof Gang, the TPLA, and other prominent revolutionary groups.

The man recommended to Wadia Hadad was Ilich Ramirez Sanchez, a Venezuelan whose father, paradoxically, was both a rich lawyer and a convinced Marxist. Sanchez was soon to achieve notoriety as "Carlos," and he also acquired the nickname "the Jackal."* Born in 1949, Carlos had been sent with his mother, who was separated from her husband, and his brothers and sisters to live in London. In 1969 his father sent him to Moscow to absorb Marxist-Leninist tenets, and he was enrolled in the Patrice Lumumba University, where he first came into contact with Palestinian students. These contacts led to a visit to PFLP camps in the Middle East in 1970, where he was nominally recruited into George Habash's PFLP by Michael Waheh Moukarbel—Wadia Hadad's European courier, scout, and liaison officer.

*Taken from Frederick Forsyth, *Day of the Jackal,* in which a terrorist known as the Jackal attempts to assassinate President de Gaulle.

Returning from the PFLP camps to the Patrice Lumumba University, Carlos led a gay student life and was "sent down" for "bourgeois activities and anti-Communist tendencies." Whether this was a deliberate KBG buildup as a cover for Carlos to enable him to operate later as a revolutionary agent in Europe without exciting suspicion is not known with certainty. Clearly, Carlos liked the good life and enjoyed parties, girls, and drink, and as his father was wealthy he was able to indulge himself in these delights. This playboy exterior was useful to him as a serious revolutionary terrorist. However, he heartily disliked the spartan discomforts of the PFLP training camps, and his opinion of the people in whose name he had enlisted was extremely low. The expression "dirty Arabs," according to many witnesses, was frequently uttered by him. Carlos was a terrorist by vocation, not by dedication.

After discussions with Hadad, Carlos was sent to Paris to take over the cell, now officially named the Boudia Commando, on a temporary basis until he proved himself to be a competent terrorist. So far he had not been involved in any major terrorist exploits.* Hadad also emphasized that the Boudia Commando was expected to operate against targets in France, when selected, as well as elsewhere, something Hadad had not been able to persuade Boudia to do. Boudia thought that if his terrorists did not attack French people, aircraft, or property and confined their activities to Zionists only, the French Direction de la Surveillance du Territoire (the DST, responsible for dealing with foreign terrorists and espionage activities on French soil) would leave them alone as much as possible and not become involved in what was considered to be a private Arab-Israeli squabble.

In Paris Carlos spent several months picking up the pieces of the Boudia Commando, as many of its members and contacts had gone underground after the death of Boudia. Being on probation, so to speak, Carlos took the first opportunity to prove himself. He traveled to England to carry out his first solo exploits. As a starter he decided to assassinate a prominent British Jewish member of parliament. On 18 November 1973 he shot and wounded Alan Quartermaine, an insurance broker, when his Rolls Royce automobile stopped at a traffic light. Carlos had shot the wrong man, as Quartermaine was not Jewish and had nothing to do whatsoever with the Palestine problem; he had been mistaken for the real target, who was somewhat similar in appearance and drove a similar

*The Carlos of the hijack of July 1973, page 156, may or may not have been him.

car. Not discouraged, Carlos planned another solo exploit to prove he had the necessary killer instinct and nerve.

Next, on 30 November, he forced his way into the London home of Joseph Seiff, a prominent British Zionist who had entertained Menachem Begin,* then a member of the Israeli Knesset. Carlos fired at Seiff with his pistol, wounding him in the mouth, before quickly fleeing. The following day a PFLP spokesman at Beirut claimed responsibility for the exploit, saying that Seiff had been shot by "one of our freedom fighters." Carlos had proved himself, but remaining in London for a while longer, he committed one more solo act. On 25 January 1974 he threw a bomb through the doorway of the Israel Bank of Hapoalin that caused considerable damage and injured one person.

The next exploit that can be directly attributed to the Boudia Commando happened on the night of 2 August 1974 in Paris when explosions occurred at the offices of *L'Aurore, Minute,* and the United Jewish Social Fund, which all caused damage, but no injuries. A fourth device, which had been placed at the Paris office of Telediffusion de France (TDF), the French broadcasting corporation, had failed to explode. A communiqué issued in Paris by the Boudia Commando claimed responsibility, alleging that the two newspapers and the TDF had become "instruments of the Israeli secret service by constantly condemning Palestinian actions while condoning the activities of Israeli agents." These were the first real Arab terrorist attacks on French property, and they attracted the attention of the DST. As if to emphasize the international character of the Boudia Commando, on the 27th of the same month an explosion occurred outside the Israeli Tourist Office in Frankfurt, West Germany that damaged the building and several parked vehicles, but no one was injured.

Meanwhile, under the leadership of Abu Mahmoud (Ahmed al-Ghafour), the National Arab Youth, sponsored and instigated by Colonel Gaddafi, remained active, so Carlos made contact with it. On 8 September 1974 a TWA Boeing crashed into the Ionian Sea with the loss of all eighty-eight people on board. NAY announced that one of its members on a suicide mission had detonated the explosive device that caused the crash. Later (on 10 January 1975) the U.S. National Transportation and Safety Board confirmed that an explosion on the plane caused the disaster.

---

*Appointed prime minister of Israel in June 1977.

In keeping with his new image of "respectability and responsibility" and aided by a degree of chagrin and spite, Yasir Arafat set up a PLO tribunal to try Abu Mahmoud, Abu Nidal (of the Iraqi-supported Fatah Revolutionary Council), and half-a-dozen other defectors and renegades. Most were tried *in absentia*, and some, including Abu Mahmoud and Abu Nidal, both of whom had openly criticized Arafat's policy, were condemned to death. On 29 September 1974 Abu Mahmoud was shot and killed in a street in Beirut by a BSO assassination team. Arafat was trying to enforce his control over the extremists by either eliminating them or bringing them to heel. Abu Nidal remained beyond Arafat's reach in Iraq, whose government was strongly opposed to Arafat's new policy.

Although Abu Mahmoud was eliminated, his Libyan-backed NAY remained active. It became concerned about two of its members who had been involved in the hijacking and eventual destruction of a British airliner at Amsterdam airport in March 1974. On 6 June they had been sentenced to imprisonment, and were now languishing in Dutch prisons. Armed with two pistols and three knives, one of the NAY members, together with an Algerian and two Dutch prisoners seized twenty-two people on 26 October 1974, including women and children as well as two unarmed warders, in the chapel of Scheveningen Prison, Holland. The chapel was immediately surrounded by police, and negotiations with the terrorists began.

In response to terrorist demands, the other NAY Palestinian was taken from his prison on the 28th and brought to Scheveningen, but he refused to join his colleague in the siege situation on the grounds that the PLO had condemned individual guerrilla actions outside Palestine. The terrorists then released the captive children, but retained sixteen adults as hostages. On the 29th they demanded an aircraft to fly themselves and the other Palestinian out of the country. The following day they released a hostage who had a heart condition.

The siege ended suddenly in the early hours of the 31st when a specially trained group of Dutch marines, formed for this type of security situation, stormed the chapel, firing their guns into the air and making as much noise as possible. Within a few minutes the three terrorists were captured without anyone being injured. Later, on 6 November 1974, a Benedictine monk was arrested by the Dutch police for allegedly smuggling two pistols into the prison, which had been passed to him at a clandestine meeting with a prostitute in the monastery garden.

The next NAY exploit was more successful. On 21 November 1974 four NAP members dressed as airport mechanics seized control of a British VC-10 aircraft on a flight from London to Bombay shortly after it had touched down at Dubai. Running from the transit lounge and firing their automatic weapons as they charged forward, the terrorists wounded an Indian air hostess in the process. Once inside the aircraft they ordered the pilot to fly the plane to Tunis. It took off carrying twenty-five passengers, nine air crew, and ten Dubai airport staff who had been servicing the plane. After a refueling stop at Tripoli, Libya, the VC-10 landed at Tunis, where the terrorists released two women, three children, and all the Indians with British passports.

The hijackers, who were in touch by radio with their headquarters, said they were of the Abu Mahmoud Commando, the operational code name in honor of their former leader. They demanded the release of fifteen named prisoners, saying they would kill a hostage every two hours if their demands were not met. They also demanded that the British government make a public apology for the Balfour Declaration and accept responsibility for the "destitution of the Palestinian people." The prisoners whose release was demanded were the eight BSO terrorists who had been involved in the attack on the Saudi Arabian embassy in Khartoum in March 1973. The "Khartoum Eight" had been sentenced to life imprisonment by a Sudanese court, but this had been commuted to lesser terms by President Numeiry, who handed them over to the PLO. The other five men whose release was demanded were those who had hijacked the West German aircraft to Kuwait after killing thirty-four people at Rome airport. The "Rome Five" had also been handed over to the PLO. All thirteen men were in Cairo under a loose form of house arrest, which gave them considerable freedom. The NAY headquarters in Beirut additionally demanded that the two NAY members in Dutch prisons should also be released.

On 23 November, on the expiration of one deadline, the hijackers shot and killed a West German passenger and threw his body down to the tarmac. In Holland the Dutch premier, Joop den Uyl, said that if it were demanded and innocent lives were at stake the two Palestinian prisoners his government was holding would be released. The following day the Rome Five NAY terrorists arrived in Tunis from Cairo, as did the two from Holland, which caused the hijackers to release their thirty-six hostages, retaining just the three crew members, the two pilots, and a navigator.

During the morning of the 25th the hijackers threatened to blow up the airliner, the crew, and themselves unless a guarantee was given that they would not be handed over to the PLO or brought to trial in Tunisia. Later in the day they surrendered to the Tunisian authorities. The Egyptian government refused to release the Khartoum Eight, as it did not wish to compromise its relations with the Sudan. Throughout, the British government had ignored the terrorists' demand that it renege on the Balfour Declaration. At a press conference Habib Chatti, the Tunisian foreign minister, said that the four hijackers and the seven released Palestinians had given themselves up without any guarantee as to their subsequent treatment, and were then in Tunisian custody. Later, on 7 December 1974, all eleven of them, after signing a declaration collectively placing themselves at the disposal of the PLO, were handed over to PLO representatives and flown to Cairo.

This hijacking had coincided with the voting on the Palestine issue in the UN General Assembly, on which Yasir Arafat had made his "Gun or Olive Branch" speech, and the PLO was not amused.* Its Beirut spokesman said that "these operations reflect great harm to our people and our struggle. The operation in Tunis was especially damaging, particularly after the international recognition we have obtained at the UN." He added, "When we have the necessary evidence we will try those responsible in public so that everyone will see that the PLO has passed judgment and meted out punishment." Both the Iraqi and Libyan governments would have liked the Khartoum Eight released to embarrass Arafat, the PLO, Egypt, and the Sudan, all being considered antirejectionist.

On 27 November the PLO spokesman in Beirut announced that "twenty-six guerrilla rebels have been arrested in a number of Arab countries in response to the PLO pledge that those responsible for the Dubai-Tunis hijacking would be brought to public trial." There was a growing concern about whether terrorists who surrendered to Arab governments were to be punished or immediately allowed to go free. On 24 November the Egyptian government called for the convening of a high-level conference to draw up "demarcation lines between acts of legitimate resistance and criminal acts that only serve the enemy's objective." The PLO accused the Iraqi government of sponsoring the Rome Five through the Fatah Revolu-

---

*"I have come bearing an olive branch and a freedom fighter's gun. Do not let the olive branch drop from my hand."

tionary Council, led by Abu Nidal (who was under a PLO death sentence), which was only partly true, as he had only collaborated with the Libyan-backed NAY.

Later, in an interview with the French periodical *Le Monde* on 21 February 1975, Colonel Gaddafi confirmed that terrorists had been handed over to the PLO and said that Abu Iyad (leader of the BSO) had personally conducted the inquiry and assumed responsibility for their fate. In answer to a question as to whether Libya was training Palestinian guerrillas, Gaddafi replied, "I refuse to supply information by way of a newspaper interview," adding, however, "I can tell you we disapprove of hijackings, as well as violence against civilians. Nevertheless, those who perform such acts are in our eyes excusable; they enjoy extenuating circumstances."

Meanwhile, back in Paris, the Boudia Commando made two attacks at Orly airport in January 1975. The first occurred on the 13th, when the terrorists chose the wrong aircraft. A white automobile was hired by Johannes Weinrich, a German terrorist. He drove two of Carlos' men, who had two RPG-7s (rocket propelled grenades) and pistols, onto the open public terrace at the airport. The two men alighted from the vehicle and loaded and aimed their RPGs at a Yugoslav DC-9 airliner. They hit the aircraft with two grenades, injuring three people. The recoil from the second RPG caused the weapon to break the windscreen of the vehicle and the terrorist holding it to drop his pistol. The two men got quickly into the automobile and escaped. The vehicle was found abandoned later with two grenades in it. A telephone call made to the Paris office of Reuters News Agency stated that the act had been committed by the Boudia Commando. It ended with, "Next time we will hit our target." At the time of the incident an El Al airliner bound for New York with 147 people on board was taxiing to take off. Carlos' attention to detail, although good, was not yet perfect. After this exploit security measures were tightened up at Orly airport.

Despite the extra precautions, the second attack by the Boudia Commando on Orly airport occurred about 1600 hours from exactly the same open public terrace on 19 January 1975. Three hooded gunmen suddenly appeared. One was spotted by a policeman who opened fire at him with his automatic weapon, wounding the terrorist in the arm. One of the other hooded figures leaned over the terrace and dropped grenades into the crowded passenger lounge below. A shootout flared up between the terrorists and police, lasting some fifteen minutes. After wounding about thirty people in all, the terrorists seized ten hostages, including a four-year-old girl, whom they held in the airport lavatory for about eighteen hours. An El Al aircraft bound for Tel Aviv had been waiting nearby ready to take off. Once again Carlos' attention to detail was at fault.

Michel Poniatowski, the French minister of the interior, arrived on the scene and took charge. Negotiations began when the terrorists pushed notes outlining their demands under the doors of the lavatory. There was confusion as to precisely what they wanted until the Egyptian ambassador arrived and spoke to the terrorists in Arabic. He obtained the release of the young child and her mother. They demanded an aircraft to take themselves and their hostages out of the country. During the night the French police bugged the terrorists electronically, using new sophisticated listening devices, to hear what they were saying to each other. This was the first occasion this tactic had been used by security forces in such incidents. Eventually the demand was agreed to, and on the 20th the three terrorists and eight hostages were put on a French plane manned by a volunteer crew, which took off for the Middle East. Most Arab capitals contacted refused them permission to land, but the aircraft was finally accepted at Baghdad, where the hostages were freed and the plane and its crew allowed to return to France. This exploit was counted as another success for the Boudia Commando, and for Carlos in particular.

In Baghdad the three terrorists were detained in custody, although on 25 January 1975 the Iraqi government had indicated they would be handed over to the PLO for trial. The Central Committee of the PLO had indeed met on that same day in Damascus to decide what disciplinary action to take and how to enforce it. The Iraqi ambassador in Paris, speaking on 4 February, confirmed that the three terrorists, whom the Air France pilot had identified only as a Palestinian, a Lebanese, and an Algerian, remained in Iraqi detention. It was reported that Abu Nidal, who had a loose working arrangement with the PFLP cells in Beirut and Paris, was trying to persuade the Iraqi government to hand the terrorists over to his organization instead of to the PLO.

Meanwhile, in Paris, Carlos had been progressing very well in leading the Boudia Commando when disaster struck. On 11 June 1975 Michael Waheb Moukarbel, the PFLP courier, was arrested in Beirut while posing as a Lebanese businessman. During interrogation he divulged information that was passed on to the French police authorities, either directly by the Lebanese police or by the Israeli Mossad. Moukarbel was released and traveled to Paris, arriving there on the 15th, but this time he was under close police surveillance. For ten days he was watched and followed, so that his contacts (who of course included Carlos) could be identified. Until this moment French police were unaware of Carlos and his importance.

Moukarbel was persuaded by the police to take them to Carlos. On the 27th Carlos was giving a party when three French policemen and Moukarbel arrived at his flat. There was a shoot-out in which two policemen were killed and one was wounded. Then Carlos deliberately killed Moukarbel, shooting him in cold blood, alleging that although a sophisticated Lebanese he was a traitor and a "dirty Arab." The Soviet KGB helped Carlos to escape through East Berlin to Beirut, where he lay low for a short period before returning to Paris again.

The French police hunt for Carlos was now in full cry. Three Cubans who lived in the flat below that of Carlos were arrested and deported, although the Cuban government officially denied they were involved in any espionage activity. Some of Carlos' contacts were also arrested and imprisoned or deported. For example, weapons and documents belonging to Carlos were found in the flat of a revolutionary named as Angela Ortaola Baranca in London on 1 July 1975, and she was later sent to prison for a year. Again, also in London, on 25 October 1975, an accomplice of Carlos named as Maria Nadya Romero de Tobon, a Colombian revolutionary, was sentenced to imprisonment for possessing forged identity cards. She was alleged to be his "banker," holding money and documents for him.

By this time Wadia Hadad was not only pleased with Carlos but also proud, going to the unusual length of issuing a statement from his Beirut office on 9 July 1975 confirming that Carlos Martinez was a "long-standing member of the PFLP" whose "revolutionary organization had done its best to support the Palestinian struggle."

By the end of 1975 the Arab states were ranged into two opposing blocs, the Rejection Front, still consisting mainly of Syria, Iraq, and Libya, and the more conservative ones led by Egypt, Saudi Arabia, and Kuwait. The Rejection Front wanted a hard line to be taken against Israel, and especially wanted to use the "oil weapon." It was appalled by what it saw as the surrender of some Arab oil states to Western (and thus indirectly Israeli) interests. Colonel Gaddafi, and perhaps other Arab leaders of the Rejection Front, also giving their subversive support, called in Carlos to lead an exploit to teach moderate Arab countries a lesson and to try to persuade them to use the oil weapon to the Palestinians' advantage. The mastermind behind the plan was Wadia Hadad, who was supplying German terrorists with money and arms, the latter by means of Arab diplomatic bags. He forced the Baader-Meinhof Gang and the June Second Movement to work together. According to one of the terrorists who took part in this exploit, "The idea for the OPEC raid came from an Arab president whose country also provided all essential information to carry out the raid. It was represented at the OPEC meeting."* The terrorists refused to name the Arab president.

At about 1100 hours on 21 December 1975 Carlos launched his television spectacular when with five other terrorists, one woman and four men, he burst into the headquarters of the Organization of Petroleum Exporting Countries (OPEC) in Vienna, Austria. After training together as a team in the Middle East, the terrorists had been driven into Austria in an automobile, after which the automobile and its driver disappeared. Weapons and explosives were picked up in Vienna, and according to one of the team, "I picked up a very large diplomatic bag stuffed with weapons, which an ambassador had hauled through Rome customs, at the ambassador's private residence in Vienna. . . . [Then] we simply took the tramway, getting off at OPEC's front door."†

The six terrorists shot their way into the OPEC building, in which a regular quarterly ministerial meeting was in session, and which was guarded only by one policeman and an elderly Austrian doorman. The latter was fatally shot. In the initial shooting two other people were also killed, one of whom was Yusef Ismari, a Libyan economist working at OPEC headquarters, who was killed by Carlos himself. The other was an Iraqi security guard. The Austrian and the Iraqi were both killed by the female terrorist, identified as Gabriele Krocher-Tiedemann. Two people were wounded in this initial affray: Suhail Nasser of the Kuwaiti delegation and a terrorist identified as Hans-Joachim Klein, who had been on the West German Police wanted list since 1974.

---

*An interview with Hans-Joachim Klein in *Der Spiegal*, 6 August 1978.
†Klein interview.

In the main conference room were eleven oil ministers, with their staffs, representing Algeria, Ecuador, Gabon, Indonesia, Iran, Iraq, Kuwait, Libya, Nigeria, Saudi Arabia, and Venezuela; as well as Ali Jaidah, who was an alternate for the Qatar minister. Said Maneh Said el-Oteiba of the United Arab Emirates had left the session of the previous day and so escaped this shattering experience. All the people in the building, numbering over seventy, were rounded up and held as hostages by Carlos and his team, who threatened to kill them if their demands were not met. Within a few minutes the building, in which OPEC occupied only the second floor, was cordoned off by the police.

By means of the telephone in the building, Carlos asked for the Libyan ambassador to act as the negotiator, but as he was not in Vienna he agreed to accept Riyafh al-Azzawi, the Iraqi chargé d'affairs. Al-Azzawi went to the OPEC building and made contact with Carlos. First of all he asked him who he was, and what he represented. Carlos replied, "We are revolutionaries, not criminals. We are the Arm of the Arab Revolution." Al-Azzawi replied in astonishment, "But you are not an Arab?" to which Carlos replied, "We are all fighting for world revolution." He added, "I am from Venezuela, and my name is Carlos. They all know me. I am the famous Carlos."

Carlos gave al-Azzawi a communiqué containing eight basic points, which he demanded should be read over Austrian radio at two-hour intervals, and in all OPEC countries. It also stated that the terrorists were from the Arm of the Arab Revolution and that their action was directed against a "high-level plot aimed at obtaining recognition for the legality of a Zionist presence on our territory" and was "designed to confront the conspiracy, to strike at its support, and to apply revolutionary sanctions to all personalities and parties involved." In brief the eight points were:

1. Reaffirmation of the Three No's enunciated at the Khartoum Conference of 1967 (No Treaty with, No Recognition of, and No Negotiation with Israel);
2. A denunciation of all compromise with Israel;
3. A condemnation of attempts to persuade the Palestinians to go to the negotiating table at Geneva;
4. A condemnation of the Disengagement Agreements and the reopening of the Suez Canal;
5. The formation of a Northeast Front comprising Syria, Iraq, and the PLO;

6. Arab states to work for unification;
7. A declaration of full sovereignty over oil; and
8. A declaration of support in Lebanon against the Zionists.

The full text of the communiqué was read out over the Austrian radio in French for the first time at 1820 hours and took twenty minutes to complete. The same day a similar statement, issued by the Arm of the Arab Revolution, was found in a public lavatory in Geneva. Other demands from the terrorists included a DC-9 aircraft with full fuel tanks to be ready by 0700 hours the following morning to take the terrorists and their hostages out of the country, and a bus with curtained windows to be ready to take them to the airport. The wounded terrorist was also to be taken to the airport, whether dead or alive.

The Austrian cabinet met in emergency session under Chancellor Otto Kreisky, who got in touch with certain Arab governments to see whether they would accept the terrorists. Algeria was agreeable to doing so on the condition that all hostages were immediately released when the aircraft arrived there. The Austrian cabinet decision was that "all consideration must be given to saving lives," and the government agreed to provide the demanded aircraft on two conditions. One was that a written declaration be produced indicating that all hostages were leaving Austria of their own free will, and the second was that all Austrian hostages, believed to number ten, who worked at the OPEC headquarters were not to be taken from Austrian soil. These terms were passed on to Carlos, who spoke to the hostages. In a short space of time fifteen letters were written by the oil ministers and others asking the chancellor to meet the demands of the terrorists, all saying the writers were willing to be flown out with them. The chancellor agreed, and the necessary preparations were made. About 0200 hours the Venezuelan ambassador went to the OPEC building and was allowed to speak to the Venezuelan oil minister, and also to Carlos. He confirmed the casualties.

Early on the 22nd the six terrorists together with thirty-three hostages were taken by bus to the airport, where they were joined by the wounded Klein, who was brought there by ambulance. It had been a terrorist condition that the departure be televised live. After Carlos had carefully inspected the aircraft and announced that it was acceptable, the terrorists and the hostages went on board. The Austrian minister of the interior, Otto Rosch, was personally supervising the departure. As the last man to board the aircraft, Carlos briefly spoke to him, and then shook the Austrian minister by the hand as he left. This handshake, shown on television, caused immediate hostile reaction to the minister, who defended himself by saying that it had been an involuntary action in a country where handshaking is a frequent and automatic greeting and habit. A Kurdish doctor, Wiriya Ravenduzi, had volunteered to go on the plane to look after the wounded terrorist, who was so dangerously ill that the medical authorities strongly advised against moving him at all. The aircraft took off for Algeria, and on the journey the pilot, Manfred Pollock, asked Carlos why he carried out an operation which involved killing and injuring innocent people. Carlos replied, "Because violence is the one language the Western democracies can understand."

The aircraft touched down at the Dar al-Beida airport, Algiers, at about 1700 hours, where Carlos released the so-called neutrals, that is the oil ministers of Ecuador, Gabon, Indonesia, Nigeria, and Venezuela, but refused to let the other hostages leave the plane. The only exception was the Algerian oil minister, who accompanied the wounded terrorist to hospital. He returned and voluntarily rejoined the hostages. President Boumedienne of Algeria was under the impression that all the hostages would be released, and when this did not happen, sudden alarm began to be felt for the safety of some of the oil ministers, especially Sheikh Ahmed Yaki Yamami of Saudi Arabia and Jamshid Amouzegar of Iran.

At 1900 hours the aircraft, still with hostages aboard, took off, and two hours later landed at Tripoli, Libya. Here the command of the operation was taken over by one of the other terrorists, known simply as Khalid. Another terrorist was known only as Yusef, while the other, who wore dark glasses all the time and was believed to be a South American, was not addressed by a name at all in the hearing of the hostages.

Khalid and the oil ministers of Algeria and Libya went to the control tower, while all the others, including Carlos, remained in the aircraft. At first Khalid asked that the Austrian DC-9 be changed for a Boeing 707, which had a much greater range, but was told by the Libyans that they did not have one. It seems that the plan at this juncture was to take the oil ministers of the moderate Arab states, and of Iran, on a tour of the rejection state capitals to show them off and to demonstrate the latent power of the Rejection Front. According to Hans-Joachim Klein (from an interview in *Liberation*, 4 October 1978) Carlos told him that the aim of the exploit was twofold: to extract a pro-Palestinian statement from each of the oil ministers, and to execute the Iranian and Saudi oil ministers.

Khalid seemed extremely hostile to Yamami and Amouzegar, and as negotiations continued they concentrated upon bargaining for a ransom for the lives of the oil ministers of Saudi Arabia and Iran. This was done partly through President Boumedienne, who had a hot line to the Shah of Iran that had been installed some months previously when Boumedienne was a mediator in the Iranian-Kurdish-Iraqi dispute. The governments of Saudi Arabia and Iran eventually agreed to pay a ransom to the terrorists amounting to $25 million each. Later, on 22 March 1976, Chancellor Kreisky confirmed the ransom (although not the exact amount) while speaking at the Vienna Press Club on the OPEC exploit when he said, "The two countries have paid a "war tribute" for the return of their oil ministers."

The terrorists then released the Algerian and Libyan oil ministers and the other hostages, but still retained nine, including both the Iranian and Saudi Arabian oil ministers. The aircraft took off again at 0400 hours on 23 December and returned to Algiers. By this time the radioed acceptance from the Saudi Arabian government had been received, so the terrorists released all their remaining hostages, including Yamami and Amouzegar, and gave themselves up to the Algerian authorities. Khalid had dropped into the background again and Carlos resumed his position as leader of the team. The following day the five terrorists traveled to Libya, where they were personally welcomed by Colonel Gaddafi. A fortnight later Hans-Joachim Klein was sufficiently recovered to join his colleagues in Libya, where he reputedly received a sum equivalent to $200,000 for himself.

Neither Carlos nor Khalid had been open and frank with Colonel Gaddafi, and President Boumedienne had been at a loss when the terrorists refused to honor the pledge he thought they had given to release all their hostages in Algeria. Gaddafi clearly wanted the blood of the Iranian oil minister, whose country was shipping oil to Israel, and that of the Saudi Arabian oil minister too, whose country was openly aiding the economy of the West, especially America, and so indirectly of Israel. Gaddafi perhaps had some pressure from Arab heads of state put upon him, causing him to hesitate, and then agree that their lives could be ransomed. During the tense inter-Arab government negotiations, Abdul Beliad

Abdesselam, the Algerian oil minister, in consultation with President Boumedienne, had promised the terrorists their freedom on the condition they spared the lives of Yamami and Amouzegar. Colonel Gaddafi must have obtained secret satisfaction in helping to squeeze a huge sum of money as "war tribute" out of the governments of Iran and Saudi Arabia, which regarded him with ill-concealed hostility. For Carlos this was his biggest and most successful exploit so far, and the world press was now billing him as "the Jackal" and lauding him as the premier international terrorist. Some governments condemned the weak attitude of Chancellor Kreisky, but he defended his decision on the grounds that otherwise the terrorists would have killed several important people. The Algerian government defended its actions on much the same grounds.

13 Fedayeen Sacrifice and Failure

I cannot promise that the terrorists will let us live in peace. But I can, and do, promise that every government of Israel will chop off the hands of those who want to cut short the lives of our children.

Prime Minister Golda Meir, 16 April 1974, after the Maalot Massacre

FROM OCTOBER 1974 through to the end of 1975 several terrorist exploits caught the breathless attention of the world. Those that were successful, in that terrorists escaped capture or were exchanged for hostages, encouraged terrorists to pursue their course. Those that ended in disaster for the terrorists were all too often regarded by them as the epitome of the Arab ideal of self-sacrifice, and an inspiration to all.

A typical example occurred on 11 December 1974 when a PFLP member entered Israel on a false passport, smuggling in explosives and detonators in the lining of his suitcase. He made explosive devices in his hotel bedroom out of soft drink cans, which he packed full of locally bought key rings and pieces of metal toy automobiles. Entering a Tel Aviv cinema, he threw five of his homemade grenades into the audience from a balcony, killing himself and three other people, and wounding fifty-five. This exploit was claimed to be a reprisal for a rocket attack on the PLO offices the previous day in Beirut, and to mark the seventh anniversary of the founding of the PFLP. In Beirut rockets had been fired by remote control from the roofs of three parked vehicles, aimed at the offices of the PLO and the PFLP. A fourth vehicle was discovered, and the rockets on its roof were made safe in time. The Arabs blamed the Israeli Mossad for this attack, alleging its agents had escaped by motorboats from south of Beirut.

Friction between Arab governments and Fedayeen groups was abrasive, and the constant bitter complaint of the extremist organizations was that all too often their members were detained by Arab governments instead of being helped and allowed to return quickly to their headquarters. There was continuing pressure put on Yasir Arafat and his thirteen-man PLO Executive Committee by Arab governments to control the Fedayeen terrorists and punish

221

them when they attacked Arab property, carried out attacks on Arab territory, and either killed Arabs or put their lives in danger.

Although Arab terrorist exploits were piously condemned by the PLO, and Arafat personally gave repeated assurances that terrorists would be brought before the PLO Revolutionary Court, there was no positive evidence they ever were until after the October War of 1973. The first known trial with the press admitted was held in August 1974 in Beirut. Nine people were freed, accused mainly of defecting from Fatah, as well as other crimes; several were condemned to death *in absentia* for "sabotaging the revolution." Two of the latter were Abu Mahmoud (Ahmed al-Ghafour), who had defected to Colonel Gaddafi to form NAY and was alleged to have plotted to kill Khalid Hassan and other Fatah leaders (he was executed by a BSO team in a Beirut street the following month); while the other was Abu Nidal, of the Iraqi-backed Fatah Revolutionary Council. Arafat was rewarded for staging this show trial by being invited to the Arab summit conference held at Rabat in October 1974, where it was agreed he would speak for all Palestinians. Arafat had scored over King Hussein, of Jordan, who thought he held that role, but he also incurred the enmity of the rejection governments and Fedayeen groups.

On 26 September 1974 the PFLP announced it was withdrawing from the PLO Executive Committee because of the PLO's "historical deviation," but that it would remain a member of the PLO through its membership in the Palestine National Council. On 14 October 1974 the leaders of the PFLP, the Jabril Front, the Iraqi ALF, and a new terrorist group known as the Popular Struggle Front, led by the Goseh brothers, met to see if they could establish an umbrella organization that would rival, and then oust, the PLO. They wanted a popular congress of all Fedayeen parties and groups to elect a new Palestinian leadership. In other words, their aim was to push out the "moderate" Arafat and block all Arab contact with Israel. These groups were later joined by NAY and the DPF. On 8 August 1975 the Jabril Front also suspended its membership on the PLO Executive Committee. Members of these Fedayeen groups, who had met in Baghdad, became even more apprehensive over how they would be treated if they were handed over to the PLO for trial, which in practice meant Arafat's Fatah.

On 29 January 1975 the Fatah spokesman in Beirut, Zaid Abdul Fatah, announced at a press conference that for the first time five would-be hijackers had been brought before a PLO revolutionary court and sentenced to a total of fifty-seven years imprisonment with hard labor. He also stated that the PLO had a "correction camp" about four miles east of Damascus and that they were seeking the three "Orly terrorists" (of the Boudia Commando in Paris), who had taken refuge in Baghdad, to bring them to trial. Journalists were shown a cell in which there were eight mattresses on the floor. The spokesman said there were over seventy persons in this correction camp, imprisoned for offenses that ranged from drinking on duty to "sabotaging the resistance." There had always been a form of kangaroo justice within most of the Fedayeen organizations, but it was invariably administered in secrecy.

Non-Arab governments, previously timid in their dealings with Fedayeen terrorists, often being only too glad to deport them, were becoming bolder. For example, in 1973 the Greek government had not only put two terrorists on trial, but had condemned them to death—although they were released quietly later.

Iran had always taken a hard line against terrorists. When two Kurds and a Kurdish sympathizer hijacked an Iraqi aircraft flying between Mosul and Baghdad on 1 March 1975 and wanted to land it at Teheran, permission was refused. Although the airport was closed down and its runways were obstructed, owing to shortage of fuel the pilot crash-landed. The terrorists, who had demanded the release of eighty-five Kurdish prisoners held by the Iraqi government and a ransom of $5 million, became involved in a gunfight with the Iranian police when they landed. One of the terrorists was killed and the other wounded. Six days after this incident the leaders of Iran and Iraq concluded an agreement at an oil summit conference at Algiers by which Iran would withdraw all its support from the Kurds, who were in revolt against the Iraqi government. On 7 April 1975 the two surviving terrorists were executed by a firing squad.

Many instances of what can be termed terrorist failures came to light during the three-year period from 1973 to 1975 in what was ostensibly the era of the successful terrorist. A few examples will put Fedayeen activities in their proper perspective.

On 10 January 1973 four BSO terrorists with false Afghan passports were taken from the Italian cruise liner *Messalia* when it called at Cyprus. It was alleged they were on a suicide mission to be carried out at Haifa, the ship's next port of call. They were deported quietly to an Arab country. No government liked to have unwanted terrorists any longer than could be helped.

On 21 January 1973 three BSO members were arrested in Vienna, Austria with a plan of Schonau Castle, the transit camp for Jews emigrating from Russia, in their possession. They were interrogated, and the next day three of their colleagues were arrested by the Italian police at a border post and handed back to the Austrian authorities. The six men were nominally brought to trial and then quickly deported. After this incident precautions were tightened up at Schonau Castle and police protection increased until it became too tough a nut for terrorists to crack directly. The Israeli Mossad was of the opinion that the three men arrested on the Italian side of the border were on their way to Paris to be briefed by the Boudia Commando and given weapons and explosives for their mission, which was to attack Schonau Castle in some way. All the BSO members had false passports. On 31 January two other BSO terrorists, also with false passports, were detected traveling through Austria and were arrested and deported.

In February 1973 Bisham Lutfi Yusef, the assistant military attaché at the Jordanian embassy in Beirut, was arrested on the seafront by the Lebanese police. He was carrying plastic explosive, a detonator, and a timing device. He was suspected of being the leader of a detachment of Jordanian Saiqa, special troops then ostensibly in Beirut to guard the Jordanian embassy, and of planning to strike back at the BSO, whose headquarters were then in that city. Because of his diplomatic immunity, Yusef was simply expelled from Lebanon.

In March 1973, two months before the Israeli Mossad killed Mohammed Boudia, his cell in Paris suffered a severe blow when several of its members were arrested. On the 14th two Arabs named as Talab al-Jabari and Adib Sadat Salem Hussein, were arrested by the Italian police near Como on information provided by the Israeli Mossad. In their suitcases were details, photographs, and plans of the railway station, the airport, and the El Al office in Milan. They were interrogated. The following day, the 15th, two other Arabs, named as Omar Tabab and Raed Talb, were arrested by the French police near Lyon. Their automobile contained sixteen pounds of plastic explosive, detonators, and timing switches. They also talked.

A few days later, on 19 March, as a result of information collected, the French police arrested two people near Briancon, and in the vehicle in which they were traveling was a quantity of explosives, detonators, and timing switches. One was named as Jamil Abdul Hakim, identified as a senior member of the BSO, and had three false passports. His companion was Doctor Diane Le Febvre, who had accompanied Mohammed Boudia on his exploit to blow up oil storage tanks in Trieste in August 1972. The Mossad was of the opinion that the group was on its way to blow up the Jordanian embassy in Paris. Both Hakim and Le Febvre were deported on the 22nd, he to Syria and she to England.

Diane Le Febvre, also known as Diana Campbell, was born in Rhodesia in 1942, but had no Jewish or Arab background. She qualified as a doctor, and originally had Jewish friends in South Africa, but for some unknown reason she became violently anti-Jewish and pro-Arab. Coming to England in June 1968, she worked at several hospitals, but took holiday trips to Lebanon. Le Febvre had been in Paris since January 1973, working closely with Mohammed Boudia. She was on the suspected terrorist list of the French DST and had been taken in for questioning at the time of the murder of Khodr Kannou, the double agent, in 1972.

On 17 June an automobile described by the Italian police as a "mobile arsenal" exploded in the Piazza Barberini in Rome, injuring two BSO members who were in it. It had contained a dozen cigarette packets, each filled with nitroglycerin, and a four-and-a-half pound packet of explosive material. The BSO members were named as Abdul Hamid Shibi and Abdul Hadi Nakaa. One source claimed that Yariv's Aleph men had caused the explosion by remote control,* but the Rome police put the cause down to unstable detonators. These arrests tended to appease the exasperation of the Israeli government, always complaining of the unwillingness of the Italian authorities to crack down on terrorists on its soil.

On 5 September 1973 the Dutch police thwarted an Arab terrorist exploit when they arrested four Arabs as they were about to board the train that ran from Moscow to Amsterdam when it stopped at Amersfoort station, Holland. A number of Jews emigrating from Russia were traveling on it. The terrorists, only two of whom were named (Amin Salameh and Joseph Assad Azar) by

*David Tinnin, *Hit Team.*

the Dutch authorities, admitted they had been trained in sabotage techniques in the Soviet Union and were members of Abu Nidal's Fatah Revolutionary Council. They intended to seize the train as it left Amersfoort station, hold the Jews on it hostage, and demand that Holland cease helping Israel. The Dutch government conducted all diplomatic contact with the Soviet Union on behalf of Israel and thus was a focus of Arab terrorist attention.

The international terrorist network in Europe suffered another blow in December 1973 when the French DST announced that it had arrested thirteen terrorists, of whom ten were Turks, two Palestinians, and one Algerian. They were charged with possessing arms and explosives, manufacturing explosives, and forging passports and official documents. On the 19th the French police arrested an Arab at Mondane, on the French-Italian frontier, as he was attempting to leave France in an automobile. When the vehicle, which the Arab had driven into France a few days previously, was searched, it was found to have tailor-made secret compartments for smuggling arms and explosives—but all were empty.

The Arab, who was not named, was interrogated, and on the basis of the information obtained the DST entered a villa near Paris on the 20th, where they arrested the ten Turks. In the villa they found quantities of plastic explosive, grenades, detonators, letter bombs, and book bomb mechanisms. A few hours later, in Paris, the DST seized the Palestinian and the Algerian. The Turks admitted to being members of the TPLA. One of them was the widow of Maher Cayan, the late leader of the TPLA, who had been killed in March 1972. In accordance with Arafat's new policy of "responsibility," on 26 December 1973 Ezzeddine Kalak, the PLO representative in Paris, denied that any of the people arrested had any connection with the PLO, remarking that "it is merely a Turkish affair."

Most important of all, perhaps, the DST found plans in the villa for future terrorist attacks, information that caused at least three major security alerts. One was at Rome airport on 25 and 26 December, the second at Brussels airport on the 28th, and the third at London airport on 5 January 1974.

In January 1974 the Italians were particularly embarrassed owing to the information that emerged from the trial of the six Israeli Mossad agents at Lillehammar, in Norway, the "Lillehammar Six." They were obliged to issue warrants for the arrest of fourteen people, mainly Jews or Israelis, as suspects or accomplices in the murder of Abdul Zwaiter in Rome in October 1972. The Italian police relied heavily upon the Israeli Mossad to keep them informed of details and movements of Arab terrorists in their country.

One of the most important Israeli detection successes occurred when Archbishop Hilarion Capucci, the Greek Catholic archbishop of Jerusalem, Judea, and Samaria, was arrested at the frontier on 25 July 1974 just after crossing into Israel from Lebanon. Quantities of weapons, ammunition, and explosives were concealed in his automobile. He was remanded in custody. Protests from religious leaders flooded the Israeli government from many quarters, some alleging that the archbishop had been framed because of his outspoken anti-Israeli views and pro-Arab attitude. The Greek Catholics, who numbered about thirty thousand in Galilee (their main strength was in Lebanon) with another four thousand in Cappuci's diocese, had broken away from the Greek Orthodox Church and sought and gained communion with the pope in Rome. They followed the Byzantine rites, but their liturgy was in Arabic.

Israeli suspicions of the archbishop had been aroused earlier in the year when he complained to the police that the sum of $75,000 had been stolen from his residence. Police inquiries elicited the fact that the sum missing was more like $750,000. This raised the suspicion that the archbishop was buying arms for the terrorists operating in Israel and the Occupied Territories. He had a diplomatic passport issued by the Vatican and thus was not searched whenever he crossed into Lebanon and returned.

Archbishop Capucci was brought to trial in East Jerusalem on 20 September 1974 before a female judge, Mrs. Miriam Ben-Porat, who rejected his claim of diplomatic immunity and his contention that the court did not have jurisdiction over him. The prosecution produced a confession that the archbishop insisted had been extracted from him by fear, as his Israeli interrogators had told him he must confess or be killed. The defense contention that the confession was inadmissible was also rejected. The prosecution alleged that the archbishop, on his visits to Lebanon, had made contact with two leading Fatah terrorists, Abu Jihad and Abu Firas, and agreed to buy arms for Fatah and smuggle them into Israeli-held territory. Abu Firas was then directing BSO operations in the West Bank area.

An interesting aspect of this case was that three Arab brothers, Mohammed, Zuhair, and Zaki Malabi, were brought as witnesses for the prosecution. They had been arrested in May 1974, accused of murdering a Jerusalem taxi driver and then putting explosives with a detonator and timing switch into the vehicle and parking it on a busy street during rush hour. Fortunately, it was discovered and defused in time. The brothers were also accused of positioning three Katyusha rockets aimed at the King David Hotel in Jerusalem on 15 May 1974, when U.S. Secretary of State Kissinger was staying there. The Malabi brothers had turned state's evidence, but changed their minds in court and had to be treated as hostile witnesses. Zuhair Malabi, for example, denied he ever told the police that he obtained the Katyusha rockets from the archbishop, saying that he had found them under a bridge. The defense refused to call any witnesses, not accepting the court's jurisdiction over Capucci, who, on 9 December 1974, was sentenced to twelve years imprisonment. Eventually, on 6 November 1977, after serving three years of his sentence, Archbishop Capucci was released by the Israelis on the intervention of the pope, who had addressed a letter to the "President of the Jewish State." This was taken by the Israeli government to be a de facto recognition by the Vatican of the State of Israel—its first. Archbishop Capucci was deported to Rome, and then traveled to South America.

The Israelis had another detection success in September 1974 when two female Dutch tourists coming into Israel from Jordan over the Allenby Bridge were arrested. In their possession was found a Fatah code written in invisible ink between the lines of a Dutch poem in a notebook. The two women were brought to trial on 10 October 1974 and sentenced to imprisonment. The code had been written by George Stefan, a Christian Arab and Fatah agent who was also later arrested by the Israelis.

On 2 August 1974 the Lebanese intercepted a terrorist who was believed to be a member of NAY when he walked into the Beirut office of Pan American Airlines and deposited a bag that contained an explosive device and a timing switch. This was almost instantly detected by mechanical means, and security guards arrested the unnamed Arab as he was about to escape. No other details were given.

Other Arab governments also succeeded against terrorists. For example, Abu Iyad, head of the BSO, had planned to assassinate King Hussein in October 1974 at Rabat, Morocco, where a summit meeting of Arab heads of state was being held. The plot was discovered, and the Moroccan police arrested nineteen BSO members, but Abu Iyad had slipped out of the country the previous day. The BSO terrorists detained by the Moroccans were released again on 11 November, when the meeting was over and all Arab heads of state had dispersed. On 19 November Abu Iyad, speaking to an audience in Beirut, admitted the plot against King Hussein, saying that "two groups went to Rabat to kill Hussein, but failed and were arrested and tortured."

The Israeli general election due to be held on 30 October 1973 and postponed because of the outbreak of the October War was eventually held on 31 December. Israel had been badly shaken by the October War and was in a bitter and recriminatory mood, but despite that a Labor coalition was returned to office under Golda Meir, then seventy-five years of age. However, she indicated she wanted to leave political life, and resigned as prime minister on 4 June 1974. Meanwhile, the Central Committee of the Labor Party had chosen Yitzhak Rabin to succeed her after he gained a narrow victory over Shimon Peres in a ballot. Rabin formed his government with Peres as his defense minister and Aharon Yariv as his minister of information. The previous July, on leaving his post as Special Adviser for the Coordination of Counter-Terrorist Activities, Yariv had stated that during his term of office (about eleven months) he knew of "sixty-seven planned attacks by Arab terrorists, of which forty-eight had been thwarted, and that of the forty-eight known Arab terrorist plots against Israeli targets thirty-one had failed." His distinction between "plots" and "attacks" was not too clear, but assuming his figures were correct, only a comparatively small proportion of them had come to light officially. This was some confirmation of the failure rate of Fedayeen terrorism. Commenting upon these figures, while contesting their accuracy, Arab newspapers in Lebanon said that Israel was at least admitting the Arabs had made nineteen successful attacks and eleven successful plots. Yariv estimated that the Fedayeen groups in total had between thirteen and fourteen thousand active terrorists.

A new Israeli prime minister inevitably made certain changes in key personalities and policies. Prime Minister Rabin would not permit the activities of the Mossad assassination teams to recommence. On 29 September 1974 he appointed Major General Rehavan Zeevi, formerly of the Central Command, who had so energetically interrogated Kozo Okamoto after the Lod Massacre, to head the Mossad. The key figures in the Mossad were always shadowy ones, their identity being carefully shrouded; whenever any of them left

Israel they used false identities and passports. General Zamir, who had headed the Mossad since 1968, was not known as such to the Israeli people, and his name had never been mentioned publicly in the Israeli media in connection with it. Few would have known that Prime Minister Rabin was changing the head of the Mossad, or who the new man was, except that information leaked to the press that a farewell party had been arranged for Zamir on 1 September 1974. This was duly reported. As it had somehow been preempted, the government, for the first time, released Zamir's name and appointment and announced the fact that he was retiring. His successor was Yitzhak Hofi. Among other key changes, General Zeira, who had been head of Aman, the military intelligence branch, and had been quietly dropped after the October War for faulty intelligence assessments, was replaced by General Shlomo Gazit.

The Israeli response to terrorist blackmail demands that Arab prisoners held in Israel be released in exchange for the safety of hostages had been strongly resisted, especially by Prime Minister Meir and Defense Minister Dayan. Since the war of 1967 the Occupied Territories had always presented a security problem to the Israelis, there being frequent incidents of bomb throwing, sabotage, and other terrorist activities. After the October War terrorist incidents increased considerably, particularly those committed by small groups of Arabs who crossed into Israel and the Occupied Territories on suicide missions. Shlomo Hillel, the Israeli minister of justice, stated that in the year from April 1974 to March 1975 guerrilla incidents caused eighty-two deaths, while for the preceding twelve months the number of deaths from those causes was only nine.

One of the first major Fedayeen suicide missions occurred on 11 April 1974, the first anniversary of the Israeli commando attack in Beirut in which three Fedayeen leaders were killed, at the northernmost Israeli settlement of Kiryat Shimona, and involved three terrorists of the Jabril Front. Kiryat Shimona (the town of eight) was named after one of the early Zionist heroes, Captain Yusef Trumpeldor, who was killed along with seven comrades by the Arabs in 1924 while defending the nearby settlement of Tel Hai. The intention of the three terrorists, named as Mounir Maghrebi, Ahmed Mahmoud, and Yasin Mouzani, had been to break into the school and hold a number of children hostage, but they had miscalculated, not realizing that it was Passover and the school was closed. They then broke into an apartment building and went from flat to flat shooting at everyone they saw with Kalashnikov automatic rifles, and when cornered by security forces they fired on both troops and people below. Israeli soldiers stormed the building and killed the three terrorists, but the cost was eighteen Israeli dead.

Claiming responsibility, a Jabril Front spokesman in Beirut calling himself Abu Abbas, a few hours afterwards said that the incident at Kiryat Shimona was "the beginning of a new campaign of revolutionary violence and revolutionary suicide inside Israel." Israeli vengeance was swift, and a few hours after the terrorist attack Israeli troops raided across the border into Lebanon to assault six villages suspected of harboring Fedayeen terrorists. They blew up twenty-four houses and a waterworks and brought back with them thirteen people, whom they accused of collaborating with the terrorists. On 24 April 1974 the Israelis were condemned by the UN Security Council for a "violation of Lebanese territorial integrity and sovereignty."

Another similar incursion by three DPF terrorists into Israel from Lebanon occurred just over a month later on 15 May 1974, the day after the anniversary of the founding of Israel, at the northern village of Maalot, which had about four thousand inhabitants. The leader of the group was named as Ali Ahmed Hassan, who spoke Hebrew, having been born at Haifa, and his two companions were named as Ahmed Saleh Nayef and Zaid Abdul Rahmin, born in Jerusalem and Safad respectively.

In the early hours of the morning the terrorists shot at a truck in which Arab women were traveling, killing two and injuring eight. Although wounded himself, the driver kept the vehicle moving and so escaped. Next, about 0400 hours, the terrorists went to the nearby hilltop school, where 103 Israeli children, mostly girls between the ages of fourteen and seventeen, were sleeping. The majority of these children were on a three-day tour of Galilee and were from Safad, about thirty miles away. They were escorted by three teachers, a female lieutenant, and two soldiers. In the initial confusion of the incident, two teachers, twelve children, and the two soldiers escaped from the building. The soldiers were unarmed, as no weapons were allowed inside universities or schools. The remaining children were held as hostages, and explosives were placed inside the main entrance and in the classrooms and wired to detonators.

By 0800 hours Defense Minister Dayan and Chief of Staff Gur had arrived on the scene, and an hour later the first negotiations by means of bullhorns began. Shortly afterwards the female lieutenant, Narkis Mordechai, was released to take a note outlining the demands of the terrorists to the Israeli authorities. They demanded the release of twenty-six prisoners held in Israeli custody. Six were named, two of whom were to select ten others each, for a total of one prisoner for each year of the existence of Israel. They said they would release half the children when the freed prisoners arrived in Damascus. The remainder of the children and other hostages were to accompany the terrorists in an aircraft to be provided by the Israelis, which would fly to an Arab capital upon receipt of a code word from Damascus. The code word was to indicate that the Israelis had agreed to their demand and that the released prisoners had arrived at Damascus. The terrorists also demanded that the French and Rumanian ambassadors monitor the exchange of personnel. Indeed, letters to this effect had already been delivered to the two ambassadors.

The prisoners whose release was demanded included two Jews, Rami Levin and Mali Leiberham, of the Red Front, an Israeli underground organization that supported the Palestinians. The terrorists set a deadline at 1800 hours, saying that if the code word had not been received by them by that time they would blow up the school and everyone inside it. The code word was to be given by a DPF representative in either Damascus or Beirut to one of the ambassadors.

Then followed a period of negotiation over which there is some argument as to what actually happened. Later a DPF representative named as Abu Aud, a member of its Central Committee, stated that two sets of demands had been sent to the Israeli authorities, one by the terrorists in the school and the other from Damascus; but the Israeli government denied receiving any such letter. Abu Rubbah, the deputy leader of the DPF, stated that six letters outlining their demands had been given by the terrorists in the school to the negotiators. They were for the Israeli military local headquarters, one each for the French and Rumanian ambassadors, one for the municipality of Maalot, one to the IRC, and one for the families of the hostages. The Israelis say the letters were never delivered, although afterwards it was alleged that General Dayan had received one, but had not read it. The basic confusion was that the terrorists believed that receipt of the code word meant the prisoners had beeen released and were being flown to Damascus, while the Israelis thought, or hoped, it meant the start of negotiations.

Dayan flew from Maalot to be present at the Israeli cabinet meeting, which met in routine session at noon, and at which a decision to release twenty prisoners was made, but it was not a unanimous one. Later, both Prime Minister Meir and Dayan declared they had voted against it. Once this decision was reached, the Israeli problem remained how to get the children to Damascus. No Israeli aircraft could make the trip, as the temptation for the Syrians to either shoot it down or impound it would be too great. Other nations were reluctant to become involved. Eventually a UN aircraft was located at Jerusalem, but it could not be made ready to fly until 1800 hours.

The French ambassador arrived at Maalot, but as he did not have the required code word, the terrorists became suspicious and refused to extend the deadline. At 1700 hours the Rumanian ambassador was told that Cyprus would accept the terrorists and the hostage children, but this message does not seem to have been acted upon. The Israelis had suggested Bucharest, Rumania, as a neutral destination for the release of the prisoners. This caused the terrorists to think the Israelis were simply playing for time; and again they refused to extend their deadline.

At 1725 hours Israeli troops moved in for the assault, and it was all over within a few minutes, all three terrorists being killed. However, as the Israeli soldiers commenced the attack, two of the terrorists (one had been killed by sniper fire as the attack commenced) turned their guns on and threw grenades at the child hostages. The toll was twenty-two children killed and seventy injured. The code word that never came was "Al-Aksa," the name of the mosque in Jerusalem, the third most holy in Islam.

On 16 May Nayef Hawatmeh, leader of the DPF, held a press conference in Beirut at which he claimed responsibility for the Maalot Massacre, saying that its object had been to sabotage the Kissinger peace mission, and that he had chosen the twenty-sixth anniversary of the establishment of Israel for the operation to show that Israel's so-called "secure borders cannot withstand Palestinian determination." Prime Minister Meir's answer was, "I cannot promise that the terrorists will let us live in peace. But I can, and do, promise that every government of Israel will chop off the hands of those who want to cut short the lives of our children."

On the 16th and 17th the Israeli air force made a number of reprisal raids on Fedayeen camps in Lebanon, in one of which thirty-six Israeli aircraft were used. Some Lebanese antiaircraft fire was encountered, but the Israeli pilots said it was ineffective. The Lebanese authorities stated that 27 people had been killed and 138 wounded, and that 20 were missing as the result of the air raids. On the 19th the Israelis shelled the Rashidyah refugee camp, a DPF stronghold just south of Tyre, the Lebanese spokesman claiming that 5 people were killed and 12 wounded. On 20 May a symbolic funeral was held in Damascus for the three Fedayeen fighters killed at Maalot. Three empty coffins were carried at the head of a long procession. (U.S. Secretary of State Kissinger was in the city at this time.) The platform on which Abu Rubbah, deputy leader of the DPF, was giving the funeral oration collapsed, some shots were fired in the air as was customary at Arab funerals, the crowd panicked, and many people were injured.

The Israeli government formed a committee under General Horev to inquire into the conduct at the Maalot Massacre, and its report, twice delayed, was finally issued on 10 July 1974. It was critical of Defense Minister Dayan and Chief of Staff Gur, saying they had ignored the demands of the terrorists, which led "to tragic confusion and a waste of precious time." It accused Dayan of not reading the letter from the terrorists and wanting to negotiate on the spot. With a new government to implement its recommendations, the report brought about a change in the decision-making process in such emergencies. Instead of the whole cabinet of twenty-three ministers having to meet and decide what to do, as was the case under Prime Minister Meir, Prime Minister Rabin set up a small committee consisting of himself, the defense minister, and three other ministers, which would be empowered to act in a situation like the one at Maalot. Another comment in the report criticized Israeli radio reporting, which had given a minute-by-minute account of the siege. Since the terrorists in the school had transistor sets, much vital information was relayed to them in this manner. An important aspect of this incident was that the Israelis seemed willing to release twenty prisoners they were holding, a departure from their normal hard line. The massacre had occurred because the terrorists insisted upon sticking to their deadline, while the Israelis were playing for time.

Not the least discouraged by the outcome of the Maalot Massacre, an eight-man group from the DPF infiltrated from Syria into

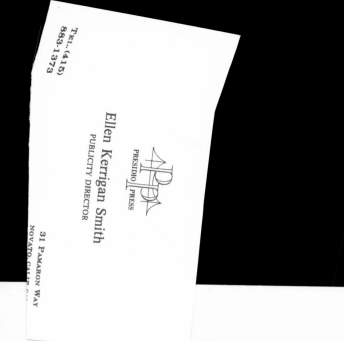

the Israeli-held Golan Plateau on 23 May 1974, where it was intercepted by Israeli troops. In the clash, six of the terrorists were killed, and the other two captured. They admitted they were in two cells and that their mission had been to capture the kibbutzim of Ein Gev and Ha-on, take hostages, and bargain for the release of prisoners held by the Israelis. This Fedayeen operation was to be on a similar pattern to the Maalot one, except that this time they wanted the French, Rumanian, and Japanese ambassadors to be not only involved in the negotiations, but to supervise the release of prisoners. Again, the terrorists were to await a code word before they would release their hostages.

The next DPF exploit of this nature occurred on 13 June 1974 when four terrorists crossed the Lebanese border near Mount Hermon and attacked the kibbutz of Shamir, killing three women they encountered. The terrorists then made for the children's dormitory, but were headed off and killed by armed members of the kibbutz Civil Guard. In the frontier settlements all the children slept in special dormitories, usually underground, for protection against rockets or bombs. On this occasion the Israelis did not make immediate reprisal raids on camps suspected of harboring Fedayeen fighters, as President Nixon was in Israel on a Middle East fact-finding tour. After President Nixon left, between the 17th and the 20th, the Israeli air force made its usual heavy strikes against Palestinian camps in southern Lebanon, killing twenty-four people and injuring ninety-four.

A few days later, on the night of 23 June 1974, there was another Fedayeen incursion from Lebanon, this time from the sea. Three members of the DPF landed on the beach at Nahariya, just south of the Lebanese border, in a small boat. They broke into a block of flats and killed a woman and her two children, but they themselves were killed in exchanges of fire with the Civil Guard and soldiers. On 9 June Israeli naval forces attacked the harbors of Tyre, Sidon, and Sarafand, all frequently used by Fedayeen groups, and "sank about thirty small boats" to prevent any repetition of the Nahariya raid.

A tragic incident occurred on 19 November 1974 when three DPF terrorists, dressed as Arab workmen, with their arms and explosives in sacks, came from the Occupied West Bank to the small town of Beit Shean, about three miles from the Jordanian border in lower Galilee, in the early morning. Calling themselves the Abu Bakh Commando, they first of all attacked a block of flats at about 0500 hours, and the alarm was given by two children who escaped. In the wild rush to get out of the building, four Israelis were killed and twenty-six injured by the terrorists, who had apparently been hiding on the West Bank for up to a month. The terrorists were all killed when troops rushed the building they were in.

The inhabitants of Beit Shean, which had also been attacked in 1971 when Katyusha rockets hit the school and killed three children, were now further enraged. When the shooting stopped, a number of them brushed aside the security forces, entered the building, and threw the bodies of the dead terrorists down to the waiting crowd below, which burnt them. There were insufficient police available to prevent this. The body of an Israeli who had been killed in the incident was also burnt in the belief that it was that of an Arab. Leaflets carried by the terrorists indicated they were to take hostages, demand the release of twenty prisoners, including Archbishop Capucci, who was then standing trial, and involve the ambassadors of France and Austria in the negotiations. The funeral oration for the victims was given by Aharon Yariv, now minister of information, who called for more volunteers for the Civil Guard.

The PLO as usual denied all knowledge of the Beit Shean incident, but it is of interest to note that Ahmed Abdul Rahman, a PLO spokesman, said, "Our political battle has been highlighted by the appearance of our chairman at the United Nations. Events in the West Bank, where the Arabs are raising their voices against the enemy, show the success of the struggle of our masses, but this does not mean that military action should not continue at the same time. After all, the Viet Cong continued their struggle in the field while they were talking peace in Paris."

Another incident occurred on 1 December 1974 when two DPF terrorists, crossing into Israel from Lebanon, attempted to take hostages in the Muslim Circassian village of Rihaniya, near the frontier. In an exchange of fire one was killed, while the other was wounded and captured. They carried leaflets demanding the release of Archbishop Capucci and five other prisoners held by the Israelis.

Perhaps the most dramatic terrorist incident of 1975 of a Fedayeen self-sacrifice nature occurred on 5 March, when eight BSO members in two small rubber dinghies landed on the beach at Tel Aviv seafront. After killing an off-duty soldier, they fired into a crowd leaving a cinema before bursting into the small Savoy Hotel just off the seafront to seize hostages. They barricaded themselves on the top floor. There was a two-hour gun battle before negotiations began. The terrorists called themselves the Abu Yusef Commando (after the Fatah leader killed in the Israeli raid on Beirut in April 1973) and demanded the release of ten named prisoners, who again included Archbishop Capucci. They also demanded a UN aircraft to fly them to Damascus, and a foreign ambassador to go with them as a guarantee of safe-conduct. Later this was modified to merely a safe-conduct for themselves.

Israeli troops attacked the hotel just before dawn on the 6th. As they did so the terrorists detonated explosives that demolished the top floor. The Israelis searched the rubble for bodies and survivors, and at first it was thought that all the terrorists had been killed. However, about six hours later, one who had survived and had remained hidden opened fire with his automatic rifle, but he was captured alive. He was identified as Musa Jumaa (the others were not named). He claimed the terrorist group had sailed from Egypt, but later changed his story and admitted it had come by boat from Sidon, Lebanon, after training in Syria. He admitted the purpose of the mission was to embarrass the Egyptian government, then about to sign the second disengagement agreement. In all, the death toll was eighteen. That day, the 6th, the Israeli navy located a 150-ton ship about forty-five miles offshore, without a name or a flag, which was escorted into Haifa harbor with its crew of six Arabs. It had carried the BSO terrorists to Tel Aviv. The Arabs on board confirmed the survivor's second story. In Beirut, Abu Iyad, leader of the BSO, said, "There can be no peace in the Middle East without the Palestinians."

At the northern village of Kfar Yuval, on 15 June 1975, four members of the Iraqi-sponsored ALF attacked a farmhouse, took the family hostage, and demanded the release of certain named prisoners, including Archbishop Capucci. Israeli soldiers attacked the building and killed all four terrorists, who were not named, but simply identified by the Israeli authorities as "a Turk, a Moroccan, an Iraqi, and a Palestinian." The toll of casualties also included three Israeli civilians killed and five injured.

Another similar exploit by the ALF occurred on 18 July, when three terrorists were intercepted near the northern Israeli town of Metulla during the night after a chase by Israeli troops in which aircraft dropped flares to light up the ground. All three Fedayeen fighters were killed. On their bodies were found leaflets in Hebrew and Arabic and instructions for them to take hostages and demand the release of prisoners in exchange for their safety. The year 1975 was not a very profitable one for either the DPF or the ALF, although both groups made political capital of the self-sacrifice aspect of their ideal.

However, the Jabril Front also came darkly into the picture on 4 July 1975, when a terrorist placed an explosive device in a refrigerator outside a store in Jerusalem. It exploded, killing thirteen people and injuring seventy-eight. A similar incident had occurred in November 1968, when a bomb was thrown into a Jerusalem supermarket, killing twelve people.

14 The Entebbe Legend

What I consider worthwhile and important for the public to know—you will know.

General Gur, Israeli Chief of Staff, 8 July 1976

DURING THE 1960s the Israelis had worked hard to gain good relations with the emerging Black states of Central Africa, the object being to establish a friendly cordon that would contain the northern, Muslim part of Africa. A degree of success was obtained with such countries as Uganda and Kenya, and also Christian Ethiopia. The Israelis provided expertise in the form of teams to help organize armed forces and police and to improve health and agriculture. Within their limited means they also gave material aid. Israel also maintained friendly relations with the government of South Africa, and its El Al airline ran a regular service to Johannesburg, usually with a stopover at Nairobi, Kenya. These flights inevitably attracted the attention of Palestinian terrorists.

On 18 January 1976, as the result of information passed to them by the Israeli Mossad, the Kenyan security forces arrested three Arab members of the PFLP on the perimeter of Nairobi airport, armed with two Soviet SAM-7 ground-to-air missiles. They were awaiting the arrival of an El Al airliner flying from Johannesburg to Tel Aviv with 110 people on board, with the intention of shooting it down. Kalashnikov automatic rifles, pistols, and grenades were found in their automobile. They had false Lebanese passports stamped with a visa to enter Kenya issued by the British embassy passport section in Beirut. (Britain acted for Kenya in this diplomatic respect.) The three men were arrested, but no announcement of the incident or the arrest was made by the Kenyan authorities. Two of the terrorists were alleged to have been involved in the attacks on Orly airport, France, in January 1975.

The PFLP, or rather Wadia Hadad's breakaway section of that organization, rose to the bait. When nothing was heard of their three terrorists, they sent Brigitta Schultz and Thomas Reuter,

239

two West Germans, to Nairobi on the 21st to find out what had gone wrong and why the Israeli aircraft had not been shot down. On arrival in Nairobi, both were arrested by the Kenyan police. Again, no announcement was made by the government, and nothing was leaked that could be picked up by either the PFLP or the world press. The woman, Schultz, had been ordered to find the three terrorists and instruct them to continue in their efforts to shoot down an Israeli airliner.* Kenyan liaison with the Israelis was good, but covert. President Kenyatta secretly allowed Mossad agents to interview the five terrorists on 3 February. He also agreed to hand them over to the Israelis, glad to be rid of them in case they attracted terrorist reprisals in Kenya if he continued to hold them or Western anger if he released them. Two days later they were spirited away to Israel and silent detention, and nothing more was heard of them for many months.

To follow this particular incident through, after making numerous unsuccessful inquiries in Kenya and other African and Arab states, Brigitta Schultz's mother received the first news of the whereabouts of her daughter on 23 August 1976. She received an anonymous letter stating that Brigitta and her companion, Thomas Reuter, had both been arrested in Nairobi and taken to Israel. The letter also alleged that while in Kenya they had been tortured under interrogation in the presence of Israeli agents. In due course, on 1 December 1976, the West German ambassador in Israel was officially instructed by his government to ask the Israeli government to investigate this allegation. In January 1977 the West German ambassador received a reply stating that the Israeli government had no knowledge of the two West Germans referred to and was certainly not holding them in detention.

Gradually, more information was gained by Reuter's parents, who announced they would hold a press conference on 15 March 1977, stating that Thomas Reuter and Brigitta Schultz were detained by the Israelis. This prompted the Israeli government to step in first and announce on the 14th that it was indeed holding the two West Germans, who would shortly be brought to trial. On 17 March the West German government officially protested having previously been given false information about its two citizens.

On 1 April 1977 the Israeli authorities permitted Frau Schultz to have a brief interview with her daughter, who had been held

---

*It was alleged by some sources that Brigitta Schultz had a message to this effect written on her stomach in invisible ink. My Kenyan contacts do not confirm this, but say she did have several incriminating documents in her possession.

incommunicado for about fifteen months. The next day, 2 April, the West German authorities announced they had arrested Monika Haas in Frankfurt, who was known to have close contacts with PFLP cells in Europe. It was alleged she had also been involved in the SAM-7 incident in Nairobi in January 1976. On 15 June 1977 the trial of the "Nairobi Five" (two West Germans and three as yet unnamed Arabs) opened in Israel, *in camera*. Since then the Israeli authorities have made no further official statements about this case.

The Israeli Mossad almost openly alleged that the two SAM-7 launchers and missiles had been given to the terrorists by President Idi Amin of Uganda, who had obtained them from Colonel Gaddafi of Libya, who in turn had received them from the Soviet Union. Landlocked Uganda had gained its independence from Britain in 1962, and for almost a decade was led by Milton Obote, during which time he was friendly with the Israelis, accepting help from them. After General Numeiry came to power in adjacent, Muslim Sudan in 1969, Milton Obote cooled towards the Israelis, as he was concerned about a possible spreading of the civil war in the southern provinces of the Sudan. He wished to appear to be friendly to Numeiry so the situation would not be exploited by the Black African rebels and others. However, the Israelis felt they still had a firm friend in Idi Amin, the Ugandan Chief of Staff, who had risen through the ranks of the local British colonial force to the top military job in his country. General Amin visited Israel in 1968 and was fêted, presented with an Israeli parachute badge, and given a few Soviet armored vehicles captured by the Israelis in the 1967 War to take back with him.

Beginning in 1963 Israeli teams established a small Ugandan air force, trained the army, the Special Security Force, and the police, and also built additions and made alterations to the airport at Entebbe that enabled it to assume international status. In January 1971 Milton Obote left Uganda to attend the Commonwealth Prime Ministers' Conference in Singapore. Before he departed he left instructions that his Chief of Staff should be arrested in his absence. However, General Amin beat him to it, staged a coup, and seized power for himself. It was alleged later by at least one source that Israeli advisers helped Amin in his coup.* When he came to power, Amin was given an Israeli-built Westwind executive jet aircraft as his own personal plane, together with an Israeli pilot.

*BBC TV program "World in Action."

President Amin, as he soon became, visited Israel twice in 1971 in an effort to persuade the Israeli government to help him in his plan to invade Tanzania across Lake Victoria. He asked for more fighter planes and for naval craft to take his soldiers across the lake, but the Israelis refused. This refusal caused Amin to turn against the Israelis, and he became increasingly hostile to them. On 27 March 1972 he ordered all Israelis to leave Uganda immediately, and on the 30th he broke off diplomatic relations. Amongst other allegations, he accused them of planning to poison the River Nile where it ran through Ugandan territory so as to kill Arabs in the Sudan and Egypt. President Amin proved to be a megalomaniac who suffered from delusions of grandeur, but was ill-educated and barely literate. His unpredictability and absurd statements and actions caused him to lose international respect as a national leader and to come into conflict with his immediate neighbors, especially adjoining Kenya. The East African port of Mombassa, in Kenya, was the economic gateway into Uganda, and the majority of Ugandan imports and fuel came through it to be carried by road and rail into Uganda.

Having ejected the Israelis, President Amin turned to Colonel Gaddafi of Libya, who gave him some aid and support, and because of his anti-Israeli posture Uganda received a few Soviet aircraft, vehicles, and weapons. Espousing the Palestinian cause, Amin gave certain facilities to the Fedayeen, mainly the use of training camps. He brought at least three hundred Palestinians into his government service to replace Asians, and he also recruited a Palestinian bodyguard. Amin had already ejected the Asians, who had been the entrepreneurs, businessmen, bankers, shopkeepers, and government officials, having a much higher standard of education and sophistication than the Ugandan Africans. In July 1975, when the thirteenth assembly of the heads of state and government of the Organization of African Unity (OAU) met in Kampala, Idi Amin was elected chairman for the ensuing year, but not without some opposition. On the 28th of that month he invited a PLO delegation to attend the meeting.

Uganda had been the scene of the first East African hijacking situation on 20 March 1974, when an Ethiopian couple hijacked an East African Airways F-27 Fokker Friendship aircraft with thirty-five people on board, the majority being Western tourists on an internal flight in Kenya, about forty-five minutes after the plane had taken off from Nairobi. The Ethiopian wife had concealed a pistol in her coiffure, which she handed to her husband, who forced the British pilot to fly to Entebbe in Uganda. The hijackers held the pilot and passengers hostage, protesting against the "3,000 years of slavery in Ethiopia" and the dictatorial rule of Haile Selassie. The two hijackers first of all wanted to fly to Libya, and from there be flown to the Soviet Union. When the plane landed at Entebbe it was encircled by soldiers, and President Amin appeared on the scene to take charge personally. He eventually persuaded the hijackers to surrender, and the pistol was thrown down from the aircraft to him. The hijackers were temporarily taken into custody.

Wadia Hadad, leader of the PFLP breakaway group (which was never given an officially accepted designation), who was estimated at the time to have up to five hundred terrorists under his direct control, was planning a large-scale hijacking. For years he had been in charge of the Operations and Foreign Liaison Branch of the PFLP, but in fact had broken away from the main body of the PFLP in mid-1975. The split had occurred when Colonel Gaddafi of Libya offered huge sums of money for more drastic terrorist action. This appealed to Wadia Hadad, whose operations had always tended to be restricted by lack of funds, but not to George Habash, who did not want his political purity to be besmirched in this way, nor did he want to be at the beck and call of a foreign head of state. The break between the two men was not a violent one, but rather a parting of the ways. Contact was maintained between them, and it is a matter of speculation as to how much, if any, help was given by the PFLP to Hadad's breakaway group. Backed by Gaddafi's almost limitless financial resources, together with large sums obtained by ransoms gained from various hijacking exploits (such as the OPEC incident), by June 1976 Wadia Hadad was heading a mini-terrorist international, perhaps the most efficient the modern world had seen so far.

The hijacking was to be set in East Africa, well out of the vaunted long reach of the Israeli air force, in an attempt to obtain the release of terrorists held in Israeli and other national prisons. For this purpose Hadad and his small operational staff moved to

Mogadishu, capital of Muslim Somalia which had become a member of the Arab League in 1973 and accepted so much Soviet aid that it had almost degenerated into a Soviet satellite state.

On 27 June 1976 an Air France A-300B airbus, flight 139, flying from Tel Aviv to Paris with a stopover at Athens, took off from Athens airport about noon carrying 247 passengers and a crew of 12. A few minutes later four armed terrorists, who announced they were the Che Guevara Cell of the Haifa Unit of the PFLP, took over. The passengers were told in English they were being taken hostage in the name of the "Arab and World Revolution" and that the aircraft had just been renamed "Arafat." The French air hostesses translated the message for the French passengers. The same day one of Wadia Hadad's spokesmen telephoned the Reuter News Agency office in Kuwait, claiming that the PFLP was responsible for the hijacking. Hadad still pretended he was part of the PFLP. However, the next day a PFLP spokesman in Beirut denied that it was a PFLP exploit at all.

Later, on 11 July, in an interview published in Beirut, George Habash was quoted as saying that his organization had ceased hijacking operations long ago and had nothing to do with this one. He said it had been carried out by a group of young men who had broken away from him some time earlier.

The hijackers were Wilfried Bose and Brigitta Kulmann, both West Germans; an Iranian calling himself Abu Bardai; and a Palestinian named as Hosni Albou Waiki. The leader, Bose, was a West German lawyer who had been in close contact with the PFLP Boudia Commando in Paris. He had been arrested by the French DST, but released again, only to be arrested in West Germany, to be released yet again. Since mid-1975 he had been involved with Wadia Hadad in planning this exploit. Brigitta Kulmann was a twenty-nine-year-old student teacher from Hanover. Bose, calling himself Bazin el-Nubazi, announced he was the new captain of the aircraft, but the woman was the one who shouted orders to the crew and passengers.

The four hijackers had traveled on a Singapore Air Lines plane from Kuwait that arrived at Athens in the early hours of the morning of the 27th, where they waited for several hours in the transit lounge. There was a lightning strike at Athens airport at the time, which had a detrimental effect on security measures. The terrorists were able to disembark with their weapons—four pistols and some grenades—and take them onto the Air France airbus without being searched or detected.

Although there had been attacks on Orly airport, Paris in January 1975, this was the first French aircraft to be hijacked by terrorists. The pilot was ordered to fly to Benghazi. During this short journey the hijackers collected all passports and other identification documents from passengers, some of whom were also searched. Arriving over Benghazi, the aircraft circled the airport about ten times before being allowed to land by the Libyan authorities. Colonel Gaddafi did not want to seem involved in this exploit in any way. At Benghazi the plane was refueled, and one pregnant woman passenger was allowed to leave it.

After nine hours at Benghazi, the hijacked French airbus, now with 242 passengers, four terrorists, and a crew of twelve on board, flew towards Entebbe, Uganda, where it touched down after a five hour flight at about 0200 hours (local time) on 28 June. The crew and passengers were detained in the aircraft for another six hours. Waiting to receive the hijacked airbus on the tarmac were three more terrorists led by Antonio Dages Bouvier, who immediately assumed command of the whole hijack situation. The other two were named as Jail el-Arka and Tisir Kuba, the latter calling himself Abu Ali. Bouvier was a South American who had joined the Boudia Commando in Paris back in 1971. He generally operated in London, finding safe-houses, selecting Zionist targets, and smuggling arms and ammunition between France and England. Arka had been the PFLP representative in South America until he defected to Wadia Hadad, while Abu Ali had been a senior officer in the PFLP Political Branch.

It seemed to the hostages that the three waiting terrorists had actually taken over control of the airport, but it is not known for certain what degree of collaboration with the airport staff and Ugandan soldiers had been reached at this stage. While it was most likely that President Amin knew the hijacked aircraft was arriving, other Ugandans may not have been privy to this information. Later, on 9 July, Chaim Herzog, the Israeli representative at the UN, claimed that Bose knew that his destination was Entebbe all the time and that on landing he was overheard to say to Brigitta Kulmann, "All is in order, the army is here." It was also disclosed at the same time that Pierre Renard, the French ambassador to Uganda, had been contacted, presumably by terrorists, and had requested that Ugandan authorities allow the hijacked French airbus to land at Entebbe.

At about 0730 hours (all times now mentioned in relation to this incident are local Ugandan time) the hostages were taken from the aircraft, which had been drawn away from the main runway towards the old airport buildings and the control tower, and put into an old transit hall where the terrorists mounted guard over them. The hostages were supplied with food and drink by the manager of the airport cafeteria, who stated he had been expecting them. The building in which the hostages were detained and the aircraft were cordoned off by about thirty Ugandan soldiers, who remained at a distance of about thirty yards.

About an hour later President Amin paid his first visit to the hostages, welcomed them to Uganda, and said that he hoped to obtain their early release. But he added that this would only happen provided the terrorists' demands were met. As the hostages did not yet know what these demands were, they were puzzled and anxious, but initially heartened by Amin's bluff, amiable manner. He appeared again in the evening about 1720 hours, but did not give the hostages any more news or comfort.

Three more terrorists, Fayiz Rahmin Jaber, Abed el-Latif, and Jail Naji al-Arjam, appeared that day from Mogadishu. Like Bouvier and his two companions, they had traveled overland by automobile from Somalia to Uganda, where they joined up with other terrorists at Entebbe. Jaber was the founder of the Heroes of the Return, a guerrilla organization formed in 1966, one of the three that merged to form the PFLP in December 1967. Born in Hebron, Jaber had been in early disagreement with George Habash and had left the PFLP, living for some years in Cairo. He eventually made up his differences with Habash and was reinstated in the PFLP hierarchy sometime in 1975, only to defect again to join up with Wadia Hadad.

On the 29th negotiations were in progress between Bouvier, leader of the terrorists at Entebbe, and Khaled al-Sheikh, the PLO representative in Uganda, in which President Amin was also involved. The communication equipment in the French airbus was used by the terrorists to send code words to several capitals. Also, at about 1130 hours that day, when he again visited the hostages, President Amin announced that he had arranged that forty-seven of them should be immediately released—women, children, and those in need of medical treatment. With the exception of an elderly Frenchman who was taken off to a hospital in Kampala, the other forty-six arrived safely in Paris the following day.

On the 29th the demands of the terrorists were given in full and transmitted to Mordecai Gazit, the Israeli ambassador in Paris. They were also read to the hostages at Entebbe about 1530 hours. At Entebbe, just after 1900 hours, the Jewish hostages were separated from the non-Jews, which caused considerable alarm and brought back painful memories of similar separations in Hitler's Germany. Pierre Renard, the French ambassador to Uganda, became involved in the negotiations. The terrorists demanded the immediate release of "fifty-three freedom fighters" held in various national prisons who were to be flown out to join them in Entebbe. The deadline for this was given as noon on 1 July, and if the named "freedom fighters" had not arrived at Entebbe by that time the hostages would "suffer strict and severe punishment." The following day, the 30th, the hijackers again repeated that the prisoners must be in Entebbe by that deadline or else the hostages would be killed. Of the fifty-three named, forty were alleged to be held in Israel, six in West Germany, five in Kenya, and one each in France and Switzerland. Those named as being held in Israeli prisons included Kozo Okamoto, the JRA killer; the gunrunning Archbishop Capucci; and the Black Muslim woman Fatima Barnawi, convicted of causing an explosion in the Zion Cinema, Jerusalem, in 1967.

The terrorists named as being in a Kenya prison were the Nairobi Five, who had been secretly taken to Israel, a fact apparently not known by Wadia Hadad. The Kenyan authorities blankly denied the existence of any such prisoners, which caused some ridicule to fall on the hijackers and was played upon by the Israelis. On 1 July President Amin again visited the hostages and 101 of them were released. They were mostly French, but all non-Jewish, and arrived safely in Paris on 2 July. This left 98 hostages in the hands of the terrorists, causing considerable alarm in Israel. The French air crew insisted upon remaining with the hostages.

Western and other countries condemned the hijacking outright, as did certain Arab states including Egypt, Jordan, and Syria, but not Libya or Iraq. On 1 July an Arab League spokesman said that the hijacking "was an attempt to tarnish the image of the Palestinian resistance," and the same day Ezzedine Kalak, the PLO representative in Paris, stated that it conflicted "with the general Arab position, which is to strengthen cooperation and friendly relations with France."

By 1 July suspicion that President Amin was either collaborating or actually in league with the hijackers was fully aroused. He was seen talking in an affable manner to the terrorists guarding the hostages. It was known he was involved in the negotiations between the terrorist leader, the PLO representative in Uganda, the Somali ambassador to Uganda, and others, and that he had deliberately allowed the second group of three terrorists to join the hijackers. Also, his Ugandan soldiers surrounding the French aircraft and the building housing the hostages gave the impression that they were more of a backup support for the terrorists than an antiterrorist force waiting to pounce at the opportune moment to free the hostages. The Israelis alleged that Amin had actually embraced the terrorists and had allowed his soldiers to give them some arms and ammunition.

Amin's answer was that he was merely negotiating with the terrorists, that his hands were tied, and that any rescue attempt by his men would provoke a bloodbath, as the hijackers would kill their hostages. He flatly denied that he was cooperating with the terrorists and insisted, "I wish all the hostages to be released." However, he was firm on the major issue that the problem could "be settled if Israel showed understanding," or in other words released the demanded prisoners.

During this tense period of negotiation, President Amin had several long-distance telephone conversations with a retired Israeli colonel who lived in Tel Aviv, Baruch Bar-Lev, who had at one time been the head of the Israeli military mission to Uganda.* Bar-Lev had gained Amin's confidence. Talks were encouraged, being of course carefully monitored by the Mossad to obtain as much information from Amin as possible. In effect, little was obtained from them.

Evidence confirmed that President Amin was in control of the situation at Entebbe, coming and going as he pleased, and the suspicion was that he took a keen delight in annoying Israel and the Western nations by his intransigence. Later, Henry Kyemba, a former Ugandan minister who defected and sought refuge in England,

*Not to be confused with Chaim Bar-Lev, a former Israeli Chief of Staff.

said, "The Entebbe Raid, for example, was never mentioned in the cabinet, because Amin handled the whole affair personally and it would not have been possible to discuss it without criticizing him in some way. No one wanted to take that risk."*

In Israel a small committee of five ministers was set up as a decision-making body to deal with the Entebbe hijack situation, which at first echoed the usual Israeli hard-line policy of no negotiation with terrorists. The committee consisted of Prime Minister Rabin, Defense Minister Shimon Peres, Minister of Justice Chaim Zadok, Minister of Transport Gad Yaakobi, and Israel Galili, a minister without portfolio. There was considerable anxiety in Israel for the safety of the Jewish hostages, and when it was known that the Jews had been separated from the non-Jews, the protests and demonstrations of relatives and friends in Israel became loud and clamorous, verging almost upon the hysterical. They demanded that the Arab prisoners called for by the terrorists be immediately released and that Jewish lives be saved at all costs.

This pressure, together with the fact that Entebbe was some 2,500 miles from Israel, separated by hostile Muslim states, caused a change of policy. It was decided that the government would negotiate with the hijackers for the lives of the Jewish hostages, which was a reversal of the previous policy for dealing with Arab terrorists. In a television broadcast on 1 July, Gad Yaakobi announced that the Israeli government would commence negotiations for the freedom of the hostages in exchange for a certain number of prisoners held in Israel. He explained that "Israel had been forced to chose between respect for human lives and the refusal to give in to blackmail." The negotiations were to be through the good offices of the French government. This Israeli decision was communicated to the hijackers just before noon on the 1st by Hashi Abdullah Farah, the Somali Ambassador to Uganda, who went with President Amin to see the hostages. Noon on 1 July was the first deadline the terrorists had set. When they received information that the Israelis would negotiate, the hijackers extended their deadline until 1100 hours on 4 July.

On 2 July President Amin flew off to Mauritius to attend the fourteenth assembly of heads of state of the OAU, of which he was the outgoing chairman. He was gone from 2 to 6 July. While

*Sunday Times, 12 June 1977.

he was away from Uganda things seemed to remain static at Entebbe, where conditions for the hostages were now extremely uncomfortable. With Amin away, authority to issue any instructions or make local decisions seemed to be absent.

Meanwhile, Defense Minister Peres and his Chief of Staff, General Gur, were investigating the possibility of military action to rescue the hostages from Entebbe, and a careful examination of the technicalities of flying aircraft such a long distance and a major intelligence-gathering operation were mounted. Anyone who could possibly know anything about Entebbe airport and the situation was carefully questioned, including released hostages, Israelis who had served in Uganda, and Abbie Nathan.

Abbie Nathan, an Iranian Jew and a rich restaurateur in Israel, was regarded as a harmless, eccentric character and spent much of his time preaching peace between the Israelis and the Arabs. In 1966 he had tried to fly his private aircraft, on which was emblazoned "Shalom-Salaam" (meaning "peace" in both Hebrew and Arabic), from Israel to Cairo to talk peace with President Nasser. He had to crash-land at Port Said, where the Egyptians repaired his aircraft, refueled it, and sent him back to Israel. During the 1973 war he had outfitted a small ship, which he called *Shalom*, as a floating radio transmitting station, and sailed it into the dangerous wartime East Mediterranean waters, broadcasting pop music and messages of peace to both Arabs and Israelis. Abbie Nathan had actually flown into Entebbe on the 2nd. The Israeli Mossad urgently persuaded him to return to Israel, where he was pumped of information about the situation at Entebbe, the positions the terrorists occupied, their numbers, the precise layout of the airport, and where the Ugandan soldiers were positioned.

The Ugandan army, consisting basically of infantry, was about 21,000 strong. About half of it was stationed in and around Entebbe and Kampala, some twenty-one miles distant from each other, with up to 100 soldiers at the airport. The army was well equipped with small arms, mortars, and howitzers, and had about 267 Soviet armored troop carriers and 27 old tanks. In addition, its small air force of some 48 combat aircraft included about 30 MiG-17s and MiG-21s, about half of which were at Entebbe.

A lifesize model of Entebbe airport was constructed in the Negev desert, and about two hundred Israeli soldiers made a practice raid on it on the 2nd.

There was also an attempted coup in the Sudan against President Numeiry on 2 July, which was suppressed by local troops, although there was considerable loss of life and damage to property in Khartoum. On the 3rd Numeiry made a broadcast blaming Libya for organizing the attempt, which he alleged was carried out by "hired African and other mercenaries." He thanked President Sadat of Egypt and King Khalid of Saudi Arabia for their attitude and support.

On 3 July President Amin cut short his stay in Mauritius and returned to Uganda.

On the morning of the 3rd, General Gur told Prime Minister Rabin that a military rescue operation to Entebbe was feasible, and that he was ready to launch one instantly if this was required. In the early afternoon, Prime Minister Rabin put the project to the whole cabinet. The risks were discussed, the main one being that if it failed, not only would the setback to morale be terrific, but the hostages, now all Jewish (except for the French air crew), might be killed and the rescue force also be lost.

On the positive side were the following: since President Sadat of Egypt disapproved of the hijacking in principle, his air force would be unlikely to interfere with any Israeli aircraft flying over the Red Sea; the Sudan was in the aftermath of an attempted coup, and all radar stations (except one) in the southern Sudan were closed down, with the Sudanese air force temporarily grounded; Ethiopia was torn apart by civil war on two main fronts and was too involved in this struggle to worry about Israeli aircraft flying to Entebbe, and in any case the government at the time was vaguely sympathetic towards Israel; and the Israeli government had a secret agreement with Kenya that allowed its aircraft to use Kenyan airfields in certain circumstances.

Also, it was thought that President Amin would have to remain in Mauritius until the 6th, as the outgoing chairman would have to close formally the session of the heads of state and government assembly of the OAU. The Israeli cabinet voted unanimously for the project to go ahead. It was to be known as Operation Thunderbolt.

At about 1600 hours on 3 July 1976 five Israeli aircraft—three C-130 Hercules carrying between them about 200 combat troops, of whom 33 were doctors in anticipation of heavy casualties; and two Boeing 707s, one fitted out as an ambulance plane and the other as a flying communications-command post—flew southwards from Israel. They flew over the Red Sea and then turned westward across radar-blacked-out southern Sudan into Kenya.*

At about 2300 hours the ambulance Boeing landed at Nairobi airport "without permission," as the Israelis insist, but the three Hercules flew into Uganda to Entebbe, arriving there just after midnight and landing in swift succession. At Entebbe there was some thin rain and ground fog. The initial surprise was complete, the landing lights were on, the area was floodlit, and the building in which the hostages were detained and the control tower were illuminated. Despite being caught by surprise, once the first Israeli plane had landed the control tower doused all the landing and other lights in the vicinity. The huge doors of the first Hercules opened and out rolled a black Mercedes automobile, similar to the once used by President Amin. It contained Israelis with blackened faces wearing uniforms that were replicas of those worn by Amin and his bodyguard. The vehicle drove swiftly to the command post headquarters of the airport security force near the control tower. Thinking it was President Amin himself, the Ugandan soldiers saluted, only to be killed by the disguised Israelis, who took over the command post.

Also, two jeep-like vehicles and at least two halftrack armored vehicles quickly emerged from each aircraft, together with soldiers firing their weapons. The Israeli troops were well briefed and well practiced, and in small groups they sped to the objectives assigned to them. One group occupied the control tower and another moved to destroy the MiG aircraft standing some 200 yards away with rockets. Other groups made for the perimeter to halt the arrival of reinforcements, others dealt with Ugandan soldiers inside the perimeter fence, and yet others rushed towards the transit hall where the hostages were held under the guard of four terrorists. President Amin was asleep a few miles away.

---

*The Israelis were in possession of certain electronic equipment that was able to neutral-ize radar defenses by what has been described as a "freeze ray." Considerable research work was being carried out by the governments of the Soviet Union and major Western countries on this project, but it was not generally known precisely what progress had been made or whether or not a working version had yet been developed with a practical military capability. Neither was it known whether the Israelis possessed a working model of the freeze ray, but later evidence tends to confirm that they did indeed have one, and that it neutralized radars at military bases between Israel and Entebbe. The inventor of the freeze ray, Sydney Hulwich, a Canadian from Toronto, was presented with the Israeli Medal of Honor in August 1977, and the rabbi who made the presen-tation would only say that the medal had been earned because Hulwich produced a "secret device which saved thousands of Israeli lives in operations of war," which was something of an exaggeration.

The communications-command Boeing aircraft, in which were General Peled, the air force commander, and General Yekutiel Adan, the Israeli Head of Operations and Deputy Chief of Staff who were in strategic control of the operation, circled overhead. The radio equipment carried in the Boeing enabled the small command group not only to be in direct communication with the commander on the ground, but also to listen in to all orders given and conversations held by the ground troops over their own radios. Additionally, it was able to relay all radio traffic back to the GHQ operations room in Israel, where Prime Minister Rabin, other ministers, the Chief of Staff, and other senior military officers were actually able to listen to the flow of battle conversation. The commander of the ground troops was Brigadier Dan Shomron, who was director of the Israeli Commando and Paratroop Branch, and with him was Lieutenant Colonel Jonathon Netahyahu.

It was the Israeli intention to break into the transit hall through several entrances simultaneously. As Israeli soldiers rushed across the tarmac, two Ugandan soldiers appeared and motioned the attackers to stop. They were instantly shot dead. Alarmed by the noise of the aircraft landing and the firing, one of the four terrorists guarding the hostages appeared at the front entrance to the transit hall with his Kalishnikov automatic rifle. He was the first terrorist to be killed.

Bursting into the transit hall, the Israelis shouted in Hebrew to the hostages to lie flat on the floor, and immediately the Israeli soldiers and the terrorists fired at each other over the crouching hostages. The firing lasted for about ten minutes. The other three terrorists guarding the hostages (including the two West Germans, Wilfried Bose and Brigitta Kulmann) were also killed. So also were three of the hostages who had not obeyed the command to lie flat on the floor, not understood it, or panicked and stood up or tried to run away, only to be caught in the cross fire. The terrorists had no time to throw their grenades at the hostages or shoot them, as they were so busy trying to defend themselves. Searching the remainder of the building, the Israeli troops found and killed two more terrorists hiding in a lavatory, and yet another a few minutes later.

The Israelis near the control tower successfully ambushed some Ugandan soldiers who rushed from the building they were in to see what the shooting was about. They thought the terrorists had begun to shoot the hostages. A little later, the Israeli soldiers in position near the airport's main gate ambushed half-a-dozen trucks bringing reinforcements, killing or wounding over a score of Ugandans.

Meanwhile, the Israelis were hurrying the hostages across the tarmac into the Hercules. A Ugandian soldier who had climbed to the roof of the control tower fired on and fatally wounded Colonel Netahyahu, who was supervising the evacuation from the transit hall. The first Israeli plane packed with hostages took off exactly fifty-two minutes after it had landed. At the same time, while Israeli troops were firing rockets at Amin's MiGs, others were attacking the building in which his soldiers were billeted and yet others were grabbing Soviet equipment and machinery, which were packed into the Hercules aircraft.

Abandoning the attempt to refuel at Entebbe, as the process was too lengthy, and taking with them their dead and wounded, the Israelis boarded the two remaining Hercules. Taking off, the aircraft flew to Nairobi, where the badly wounded were transferred either to the ambulance Boeing aircraft or to a hospital in Nairobi. At Nairobi the Israeli raiders met up with their commanders, Generals Peled and Adan, who had been monitoring the operation in the other communications-command Boeing. General Gur later said of the Kenyans, "We forced ourselves upon them, they did not know anything beforehand." This was an extremely suspect statement. General Gur also claimed that the Entebbe Raid was over in fifty-two minutes—but that was only the rescue of the hostages. The whole operation took ninety minutes.

The final toll was seven terrorists killed. The Israelis inferred that three had escaped, including Bouvier, the leader, who they said was away from the airport at the precise time of the raid. Israeli casualties were one officer killed (Colonel Netahyahu, who died of his wounds) and the three civilians who died in the transit hall; while five civilians were wounded, as were four soldiers, one of whom later died in a Nairobi hospital. President Amin stated that twenty Ugandan soldiers had been killed, thirteen seriously wounded, and nineteen slightly wounded. The Israelis destroyed eleven MiG aircraft on the ground. (On 10 July 1976 Colonel Gaddafi of Libya sent a number of Soviet fighter aircraft to Uganda to replace Amin's losses.) One unfortunate Israeli hostage was left behind in Uganda, the seventy-five-year-old Mrs. Dora Bloch, who had choked on some food and had to be rushed to a hospital on 3 July. She was last seen sleeping soundly at the Kampala hospital by Peter Chandley, a second secretary at the British High Commission, when he went to visit her on the 4th. Shortly afterwards she was dragged away by Ugandan security police and never seen again.

The Israeli aircraft began landing at Embakasi airport, Nairobi at about 0100 hours, and after refueling all five took off again between 0200 hours and 0400 hours to arrive safely back in Israel in the morning of 4 July 1976—the day of the American bicentennial celebrations. The Israelis denied that any of their aircraft had refueled at Nairobi on the outward journey to Entebbe. That is the outline story based on the Israeli version. Most of the details were given out at a press conference in Tel Aviv held by General Gur, the Chief of Staff, on 8 July 1976. At this conference General Gur said, "What I consider worthwhile and important for the public to learn—you will know," and he refused to take questions.

On 4 July President Amin returned to the OAU assembly in Mauritius, where he reported what had happened at Entebbe.

The successful audacity of the daring long-distance raid to rescue hostages from the clutches of the terrorists brought mass admiration in the Western world. Amin was the unpopular Goliath, while the Israelis had once again excelled in their role of David. On the 4th both President Ford of the United States and Chancellor Schmidt of West Germany sent messages of congratulation to Prime Minister Rabin. Anxious not to be the odd man out, Kurt Waldheim, the UN Secretary General, vigorously denied on the 5th that he had described the raid as "flagrant aggression," as had been reported in Cairo the previous day.

For a day or so the Arab press withheld comment (only the Egyptian media remarked mildly that the raid was "a terrorist theatrical demonstration"), but it soon became vocal on the issue of "infringement of national sovereignty." In the UN, where the raid was debated on 9 July, majority opinion swung against Israel, which was also denounced for its action by the Soviet Union. On 15 July, voting on the Entebbe Raid in the UN Security Council was inconclusive, as the African states could not muster enough votes to condemn it and America could not obtain enough to condemn hijacking in general.

From the point of view of combating international terrorism, the Entebbe Raid had been a huge success, the hostages (except for the three who were killed and the one left behind) had been rescued, no terrorist prisoners had been released from Israeli or other jails, and seven terrorists, of whom at least four were Wadia Hadad's "top class internationals," had been killed. Hadad and the

Fedayeen world in general were understandably chagrined. International terrorism had taken a severe knock, but what seemed to needle Wadia Hadad as much as anything else was the flat denial by the Kenyan government that it held the Nairobi Five, which caused some ridicule and skepticism to fall on the terrorists. This provoked the PFLP to issue a statement from Beirut on 6 July 1976 admitting it had planned an attack on the El Al airliner in January 1975 (before Wadia Hadad broke away) and that "one of our commando units" had been detained in Kenya. On this occasion the Rasd (war information) Section of the PFLP had failed badly.

The radio communication equipment on the French airbus had been used by the terrorists to transmit and receive code words and messages to and from many parts of the world, and these transmissions would have been faithfully recorded on the aircraft's black box. This black box was an intelligence prize for any antiterrorist security force and must have been eagerly sought. However, as President Amin was anti-Israeli, and as terrorists and Palestinians were in Uganda, the supposition must be that it was retrieved and retained, or destroyed, by either the Ugandans or the terrorists.

Despite the pleas of French authorities anxious to get their airliner back and get their hands on the black box, the French airbus was retained by Amin for some weeks. Amin held on to the plane, valued at $4 million, in an unsuccessful attempt to squeeze some compensation from the Israelis. It was eventually returned to Paris on 22 July, but minus the passengers' luggage, which was presumably looted. The passports and identity documents of the passengers and crew were retained by the Israelis, who had seized them at Entebbe. Later, on 6 September 1976, President Amin's private aircraft, the Israeli-built Westwind, was returned to Israel. It was piloted by two Americans, who boasted they had stolen it from Amin. However, President Amin said he had returned it because Uganda would not take any property without compensation, while the Israelis merely said they had repossessed it because it had not been paid for.

Acute friction arose between Kenya and Uganda, never the best of friends, as the aftermath of the Entebbe Raid. Anti-Kenyan propaganda was pumped out and many Kenyans were expelled from Uganda, while in turn Ugandans were expelled from Kenya. On 8 July the Kenyan government placed a heavy economic embargo on Uganda by demanding that all freight and passenger services from Mombassa through to Kampala be paid for in Kenyan currency. This placed a big strain on Uganda, whose economic position was very weak, and which was short of foreign currency. By the 10th the refusal of Kenyan truck and train drivers to drive into Uganda itself caused a fuel shortage, as fuel vehicles were halted on the Kenyan side of the frontier. On the 20th it was reported that some 2,000 Ugandan soldiers had mutinied near Kampala, as they had not received any pay for months. However, towards the end of July 1976 President Amin sent conciliatory messages to President Kenyatta that temporarily took some of the heat from the situation.

There is no doubt that the Entebbe Raid was boldly planned and efficiently carried out, and deserved to become an epic that any nation would be proud to have in its military annals. Because it is unlikely that the circumstances would ever again be as favorable to the Israelis, it was a once-only operation and could not be repeated without courting almost certain disaster. It is unfortunate the Israelis have not come out with a full factual account for historians to study. They may not want to divulge certain facts for security reasons and may wish to keep the terrorists guessing on certain aspects, but there is much they could, and should, for the accurate record, say about it to prevent distortion.

It would, for example, be of interest to know what happened to the three unaccounted-for terrorists at Entebbe, including Bouvier, the leader of the exploit, who were not killed by the Israelis. The vague indications are that they escaped. They have not been sighted since, which is unusual in itself. The suspicions are that the Israelis captured them and took them back to Israel to keep them incommunicado, as they had done to the Nairobi Five.

President Amin set up his own commission of inquiry into the Entebbe Raid, which reported on 16 November 1976 that there was no collusion between the Ugandans and the terrorists. It also pointed out that the Ugandans could have shot down the Israeli Hercules aircraft as they took off, but had not done so. Another teaser is what degree of cooperation there was between President Kenyatta of Kenya and the Israeli government. It must have been considerable, as the Israelis would hardly have embarked upon such a long-distance raid to a target 2,500 miles away unless they could have been absolutely sure their aircraft would have been given refueling facilities to enable them to return.

As might be expected, several books were rushed out on the Entebbe Raid, while the film industry also showed a keen interest in this exploit. The Israeli government let it be known that it would give exclusive assistance and the use of Israeli soldiers, air-craft, weapons, vehicles, and locations to one major film company. This magnet drew several of the larger film organizations into competing for the sponsorship. It was announced in Jerusalem on 12 August 1976 that Warner Brothers, beating out its rivals, had been chosen to make a film on the Entebbe Raid with exclusive official assistance. It was to have a $10 million budget, the most ever to be spent on making a film in Israel, but the company also had to undertake to produce other films in Israel over a three-year period. It is of interest to note that a few months later Warner Brothers backed out of this agreement because the Israeli government would not release sufficient factual information for it to work with. The Israeli government prefers its legends to remain intact and is not prepared to help anyone question their authenticity.

As films of the Entebbe Raid appeared and were distributed to many countries, Arab protests mounted against their showing. For example, in December 1976 Arab states persuaded Japan, which relied upon Arab oil for its booming economy, not to show the film *Victory at Entebbe.* In other countries there were also Arab-instigated protests that in some cases caused film showings to be canceled, while in others there were incidents including bomb hoaxes and explosions in cinemas. On 3 December 1976, when the American actor Godfrey Cambridge, who was playing the role of President Amin in a film about the Entebbe Raid, collapsed on the film set and died of a heart attack, Amin's comment was that "it was a punishment of God." Another death that occurred while filming the same subject was that of Peter Finch, a well-known film star, which tended to cast a blight on these projects.

The Entebbe Raid not only raised morale inside Israel, which had tended to droop since the October War, but temporarily helped to enhance Israeli reputation abroad. It had suffered setbacks in the UN at the hands of Afro-Asian countries that had ganged up against Israel and condemned Zionism as "racialism." The Israeli principle of no negotiation with Arab terrorists and not yielding to the blackmail of releasing hostages for prisoners remained intact this time. But it had been a close shave, as indeed the Entebbe Raid itself had been—but no one can argue with success.

15   The Volume of Terrorism

It is intolerable for the sons of the Roman middle class to kill the sons of southern peasants.

Francesco Cossiga, Italian minister of the interior,
August 1977

THE ENTEBBE RAID of July 1976 was a milestone in public awareness of the huge volume of terrorism—regional, national, and international. While acts of regional terrorism were well reported locally, news of them seldom reached very far beyond regional or national boundaries, and before the Entebbe Raid only major or unusual terrorist exploits were universally reported. European newspaper readers, for example, had little idea of the volume of terrorism in South America, or indeed in Asia, while American readers saw their own internal terrorist problems writ large, but had only a hazy knowledge of foreign terrorist exploits.

As yet there is no universal, comprehensive catalogue of terrorist groups, their causes, aims, and exploits. When one is compiled it must surely be a work of considerable magnitude. Partial sets of statistics that make impressive reading are spasmodically issued to prove some official point or other. A few of them will be quoted here, together with a few selected exploits, to give an idea of the overall volume of terrorism.

One European country torn apart by political terrorism was Italy, whose problems included unemployment, inflation, falling productivity, and economic difficulties. Of the 1.7 million unemployed, almost half possessed high school certificates or university degrees. The universities, themselves hotbeds of violence, were hopelessly overcrowded, as in the 1960s entry qualifications had been abolished, allowing almost anyone to register as a student. In July 1977 the Italian authorities identified 115 political extremist groups, of which 21 were regarded as being of right-wing persuasion, the other 94 being left-wing. The right-wing groups had barely disguised fascist aims, wanting to establish a strong centrally controlled government in Italy and dedicated to eliminating left-wing opposition. The Catholic Church, an emotive, if not all-powerful, influence in Italian politics, was suspected of sympathizing with and even helping the right-wing groups. In Milan, on 14 July 1977, a priest was beaten unconscious when he refused to give two callers records of a right-wing group with which he was involved. Generally, the right-wing organizations avoided attacking the security forces or the structure of the state, but clashed violently with their left-wing opponents on many occasions.

Of the left-wing groups, two stand out as being most extreme and active. They are the Brigate Rosse, usually translated as Red Brigades (not Brigade), and the Nucleus of the Armed Proletariat (NAP). The general line of thinking of both is that Italian state administration is so corrupt that only a slight push is required to topple it over; they insist they are merely aiding a revolutionary process rather than instigating a revolution. Led by Renato Curcio, the Red Brigades began operating in 1970, committing acts of political and industrial sabotage, kidnapping factory managers, booby-trapping automobiles, and issuing revolutionary propaganda. Operating mainly in northern Italy, the Red Brigades preached the "armed struggle" for communism, but was soon rejected by the official Italian Communist Party. It then advocated violent revolt, trying to incite the working class to rise against a threatened right-wing seizure of government. This ploy failed too, so the Red Brigades changed its target to the political system, which it alleged was run by multinationals.

The other extreme active terrorist group was the left-wing NAP, which first surfaced on 11 March 1975 when a member was killed by his own bomb. Basing itself in Naples, but also operating in Rome, the NAP had a similar history of political violence. The NAP and the Red Brigades were each divided into two sections: the political leadership and the military one, the latter consisting of terrorist cells. The military sections of both groups were decimated by arrests and deaths, but by surviving underground the political leadership was able to recruit replacements. While the NAP and the Red Brigades were separate organizations, they cooperated closely with each other on several occasions, and both were in touch with, and received help from, other European terrorist groups.

On 1 July 1977 Antonio Lo Muscio, leader of the NAP, was killed in a shoot-out with the police near Rome University. Two female members of the NAP who were with him at the time produced pistols from their handbags and joined in the fight. They were both wounded and captured. The three had been about to kill the Rector of Rome University, after which they had planned to seize a judge to hold hostage to try to obtain the release of NAP members in detention. On 3 July the NAP leadership threatened to carry out massacres in the main squares of Rome unless the two women were instantly released, emphasizing that "no one, repeat, no one, should feel safe from reprisals." This provoked Francesco Cossiga, the minister of the interior, to say, "It is intolerable for the sons of the Roman middle class to kill the sons of southern peasants." He was alluding to the fact that a large proportion of the security forces were recruited from poorer families in southern Italy and Sicily, while the majority of Red Brigades members were students from middle class families in Rome and northern Italy. Both NAP women were eventually sentenced to terms of imprisonment.

Renato Curcio, the Red Brigades leader, had been arrested on 8 September 1974, but had been rescued in an armed attack led by his wife, Margarita Cagol, on the prison in which he was held in February 1975. On 5 June that year Curcio, his wife, and other members of the Red Brigades were besieged by the police in a farmhouse in which they were holding an industrialist as hostage for ransom. Margarita Cagol was killed in the shoot-out, but Curcio escaped, only to be recaptured in January 1976. He was put on trial with fourteen other Red Brigades members, and thirty-six others were tried *in absentia* at the same time. The trial was postponed on three occasions, the first in 1976 when the Red Brigades killed the Prosecutor General in Genoa, the second in May 1977 when it killed a lawyer, and early in 1978 when it killed a police officer.

Both the Red Brigades and the NAP waged a campaign of intimidation to try to bring justice in Italy, and the Curcio trial in particular, to a halt. Members began shooting victims deliberately in the legs, a practice that became known as *azzoppamenti*, or "laming." This happened to several prominent justice officers, lawyers, policemen, editors, journalists, and industrialists. At one stage these incidents were occurring at the rate of two or more a week. Additionally, the terrorists carried out selective assassinations, one victim being the chairman of the Turin Lawyers Association. The regulation was that eight "people's jurors" were required for a trial, but most of those summoned to serve on the jury sent excuses for nonattendance. As the law only allowed for three drawings, the Curcio trial had to be postponed. The venue was moved to Milan, where the trial eventually opened amid heavy security precautions, some four thousand police guarding the court and its surroundings against a possible terrorist attack or rescue attempt. The fifteen defendants were manacled together and sat inside an iron cage within the courtroom. On 23 June 1978 Renato Curcio and his fourteen colleagues were all sentenced to long terms of imprisonment.

Interesting figures were released on 17 July 1977 by Premier Andreotti, who admitted the Red Brigades was by far the most effective terrorist group in Italy. He said that 128 of its members were in prison, and that another 14 were sought by the police. Speaking of the NAP, he said that 133 of its members were in prison while another 14 were also on the police wanted list. He stated that 343 members of right-wing groups were in prison, and 65 were on the wanted list. Over 1,200 political crimes of violence were recorded in Italy in 1976, and this figure rose to 2,128 in 1977.

Prisons in Italy were hopelessly overcrowded, largely owing to the slow process of criminal justice. Prison escapes were frequent; there were 513 successful ones in 1976. By the end of 1978 some fifteen prisons had been upgraded and classed as top security ones. A prison fortress to hold the hard-case terrorists and criminals was established on the small island of Favignano, off Sicily. Those on trial could be brought quickly by hydrofoil or helicopter to the appropriate courtroom and then returned to Favignano when court proceedings for the day were over, whenever that was thought to be necessary.

A disturbing aspect of terrorism in Italy was the use of firearms in street demonstrations against security forces and opposing terrorist groups. During demonstrations at Rome University on 21 April 1977, a policeman was murdered by political activists, the first instance of its kind in Italy. Some weeks later, on 16 May, during a left-wing student demonstration in Milan, a small number broke away from the main body and, armed with pistols and grenades, turned their attention to the police. Again, a policeman was killed.

The procurement of illicit arms was hardly any problem at all in Italy. On 15 May 1977 the police announced they had unearthed an import-export firm in Rome that bought weapons, ammunition, and explosives to sell to the Mafia or Italian terrorist groups, or for re-export to Middle Eastern terrorist organizations. If a terrorist had money, he could buy weapons and explosives in Italy.

Apart from the welter of terrorist incidents in Italy, kidnapping for ransom almost became a growth industry. In 1976 there were forty-eight reported cases, with the ransom demanded running into millions of dollars, and in 1977 this figure had risen to seventy-five cases. In an effort to prevent terrorists obtaining funds in this way, the authorities tried to freeze individual bank accounts to stop relatives quietly paying money to kidnappers for the safe release of the victim. This prevention measure was often circumvented, and had the unfortunate result that families of kidnap victims would not inform the police, but instead would secretly pay the ransom. Suspicions were that these unreported instances exceeded reported ones. Another offshoot of kidnapping for ransom was that target personalities began to insure themselves against it, which invariably led to criminal abuses. On 1 March 1978 it was revealed that Lloyds of London had paid out large sums of money in false insurance claims on fake kidnappings.

On 16 March 1978, during the Renato Curcio trial (which began on the 9th), Aldo Moro, leader of the Christian Democratic Party was kidnapped by members of the Red Brigades who ambushed his automobile in a Rome street, killing his five bodyguards. Moro had been premier of Italy five times and was expected to be nominated as the next president of his country. The Red Brigades issued a series of communiqués stating that he was to be tried by a "people's court," and then that he had been "condemned to death." The terrorists demanded the release of Renato Curcio and those on trial with him, as well as others in detention, for his safe release. The Italian government refused this demand. Thousands of soldiers and extra police were moved into Rome to help in the search for Moro, but all their efforts proved to be fruitless. Despite further threats by the terrorists to kill Moro, the government retained its firm resolve. There was some alarm both in Italian political circles and in NATO that Moro might reveal embarrassing political or NATO secrets under torture that the left-wing terrorists could make use of in Italy, or pass on to the Soviet Union. A similar anxiety had been felt, needlessly, in 1974, when Mario Sossi, who had been a foreign minister, was kidnapped and held prisoner by terrorists for thirty-five days.

The Curcio trial continued. Eventually, on 9 May, Moro's body was discovered in a parked automobile in the center of Rome, then swamped with 50,000 troops and police, near the headquarters of the Christian Democratic Party. Considerable criticism was directed towards the security forces for their failure. The authorities were of the opinion that both West German and South American terrorists had collaborated with the Red Brigades in the Moro kidnapping. The extreme terrorist groups, chiefly the Red Brigades and the NAP, continued with their course of violence for the remainder of 1978: assassinations and *azzoppamentis* of government officials, industrialists, and police officers; bomb attacks on industrial targets such as the offices of the multinationals and their showrooms in the cities; and kidnapping.

Turning to West Germany, during 1976 interest was focused on the trial of Andreas Baader, Ulrike Meinhof, Jan-Carl Raspe, and Gudrun Ensslin, the four leading members of the Red Army Faction. These four defendants were still detained in the specially constructed top-security prison at Stammheim, Stuttgart. They were charged with five murders, fifty-four attempted murders (of people injured in explosions they had caused), bank robberies, and other allied offenses. Evidence revealed, among other things, that the Baader-Meinhof Gang had planned to kidnap the three Allied commanders in West Berlin. The trial itself was a dramatically long-drawn-out affair, with defense lawyers employing every delaying tactic they could devise.

On 9 May 1976 Ulrike Meinhof hanged herself in her cell at Stammheim. Allegations were made by her defense lawyers that she had been driven to suicide by the authorities. There were street demonstrations and disturbances by sympathizers, and a rash of firebombs were thrown. A crowd estimated at over 4,000 attended her funeral, many of them masked to avoid identification. The trial of the other three defendants continued, and eventually judgment was given on 28 April 1977, when the three were found guilty on most charges, and each sentenced to life imprisonment. The trial, which had been in progress for almost two years, cost over $10 million and consisted of 192 sessions in which over 400 witnesses had been examined.

Almost a month previously, on 1 April, the Swedish authorities announced they had uncovered a Red Army Faction plot to kidnap Anna-Greta Leijon, a former minister who had authorized the extradition of the five terrorists who had attacked the West German embassy in Stockholm, including the badly injured Siegfried Hausner, who had died a few days after being deported against the medical advice of Swedish doctors. About fourteen people of several nationalities, but mainly West German, were arrested, and either deported or released later because of lack of evidence. Explosives, false passports, and gas masks were found at a flat in Stockholm occupied by one of the arrested terrorists, Norbert Krocher.

A few days later, on 7 April, Siegfried Buback, the federal chief prosecutor who had been involved in the Baader-Meinhof trial, was killed in Karlsruhe, shot from the back of a moving motorcycle by a person identified as Gunther Sonnenberg. Sonnenberg was later arrested after a shoot-out with the police in which he was wounded. The Ulrike Meinhof Commando claimed responsibility. On the 27th of the same month, in Wiesbadan, Jurgen Ponto, chairman of the Dresdner Bank, was killed by terrorists, the Red Morning Commando claiming responsibility. Ponto was the first financier and industrialist to fall victim to RAF terrorists.

The Federal Bureau of Criminal Investigation spokesman stated that the Buback and Ponto assassinations were connected with each other and blamed the small terrorist group that had been organized by Siegfried Haag, one of the defense lawyers at the Baader-Meinhof trial. Haag, who was accused of taking messages from the defendants to terrorists outside the prison and suspected of smuggling items into Stammheim, went underground in May 1975 to organize his own terrorist group. He was arrested in November 1976, but later released, to escape to France in July 1977, where he made an inflamatory speech over the radio that resulted in his being deported back to West Germany to stand trial. Members of the Red Army Faction tended to drift aimlessly and became disorganized and disoriented when they were divorced from the original imprisoned leadership. Many were organized into small "commandos" by enterprising individuals. Yet another defense lawyer at the Baader-Meinhof trial was Kurt Groenwold, who later (on 10 July 1978) was given a suspended prison sentence for running an information network that enabled the three principal defendants on trial to communicate with their underground organizations.

Four female terrorists staged a dramatic escape from the Moabit prison in West Berlin on 7 July 1977. One was Monika Berberich, who was serving a sentence for bank robberies with the Baader-Meinhof Gang, while the other three were Gabriele Rollnik, Inge Viett, and Juliane Plambeck, who were in detention awaiting trial on charges of kidnapping Peter Lorenz, a West Berlin politician. Plambeck was additionally charged with the murder of Judge Drenkmann, killed in West Berlin in November 1974. Armed with a pistol and metal piping, they overpowered their warders, climbed through a skylight, and escaped down a rope made of sheets. They had external assistance, and the roadway outside the prison was scattered with crows' claws (small steel spikes) to hamper any following vehicles. On 20 July the four surviving terrorists of the Holger Meins Commando, who had attacked the West German embassy in Stockholm, were sentenced to life imprisonment by a Dusseldorf Court, after a long-drawn-out fourteen-month trial.

On 26 August 1977 a forty-two-tube rocket-battery device, which came to be called a Stalin Organ by the press, was discovered in a flat overlooking the Federal High Court at Karlsruhe. It was aimed at the office of the new federal chief prosecutor, Kurt Rebmann. It was found and defused only about an hour before it was scheduled to be activated. This incident coincided with a hunger strike, already seventeen days old on this date, of thirty-four urban terrorists, including the three surviving Baader-Meinhof Gang leaders held in West German prisons. They all demanded to be in the same prison and allowed to mix with each other instead of being rigidly separated.

On 5 September Hans-Martin Schleyer, chairman of the Employers Federation and a prominent West German industrialist, was ambushed by terrorists in his car near Cologne. His three bodyguards and driver were killed, and he was kidnapped. The responsibility was claimed by the Siegfried Hausner Commando, which demanded the release of eleven named terrorists from West German jails, including the three Baader-Meinhof Gang leaders, in exchange for his safety. Negotiations began, with Denis Payot, a Swiss lawyer and human rights leader, acting as the go-between. The authorities clamped a news blackout on the incident and all matters relating to it. For over a month there was official silence. It was disclosed afterwards that Schleyer was held for most of this time in a flat in a Cologne suburb.

Suddenly, on 13 October, four Palestinian terrorists hijacked a Lufthansa Boeing airliner with ninety-one people on board soon after it had taken off from Las Palmas, Majorca, bound for Frankfort. The hijack team was led by Zuhair Yusef Akache, who called himself Captain Mahmoud. He had killed three Yemenis in London on 10 April 1976. The other man was named as Wabil Harb. The other two members were women, Hind Alameh and Suhaila Sayed. The leader declared the hijack was being carried out by the Struggle Against World Imperialism Organization and the Red Army Faction. At first it was not clear what their demands were, but they eventually emerged as being the release of eleven terrorists—the same individuals the kidnappers of Schleyer were demanding—and two other Palestinian terrorists held in a Turkish prison after they had attacked an El Al plane. Each was to be given DM100,000, and an additional ransom of $15.5 million was to be paid in exchange for the safety of the aircraft and all on board. The released prisoners, together with the money, were to be flown to South Yemen, Vietnam, or Somalia.

Then followed a five-day terrorist saga as the hijacked plane moved jerkily from Rome to Cyprus, Baghdad, Bahrein, Dubai, and Aden, to end up at Mogadishu, Somalia. Other Middle Eastern airports refused to accept the aircraft, and indeed at Aden the runway was deliberately blocked with vehicles, the aircraft having to make a forced landing in the sand alongside it. At Aden, Captain Mahmoud shot and killed the West German pilot, Jurgen Schumann. On the 17th the copilot flew the plane towards Kuwait, but as it was refused permission to land there it turned and made for Mogadishu.

Meanwhile, the West German government was organizing a rescue operation with its GSG-9, an antiterrorist force formed for just such an emergency. Another aircraft, carrying sixty-three members of the GSG-9 squad, shadowed the hijacked plane for much of its Middle Eastern odyssey. The West German government asked the international media not to mention this fact so as not to alert the terrorists. Most of the media complied with this request, but there were exceptions. The GSG-9 squad was about to go into action at Dubai, where the hijacked plane stayed for two days, but it suddenly flew off again before a local difference was settled. The Dubai authorities wanted to take part in the rescue operation too, which the GSG-9 commander resisted, as they could not be integrated with his men, who had been specially trained for instant coordinated high speed action. The GSG-9 aircraft followed the hijacked one to Mogadishu, and on the morning of the 18th the antiterrorist squad launched its rescue operation. Three of the terrorists were killed—the two men and Hind Alameh. The other woman, Suhaila Sayed, was wounded and captured, and held by

268 / Language of Violence

the Somalia authorities.* Two British Special Air Service (SAS) soldiers had been involved in the action, and the British stun grenade was used for the first time. Ten passengers, one air hostess, and one soldier were slightly wounded. The rescue operation was an outstanding success.

The rescue of hostages at Mogadishu had taken place at about 0550 hours on 18 October, and sometime during that morning, at Stammheim prison, the three Baader-Meinhof Gang leaders committed suicide, and another female terrorist attempted to kill herself. Andreas Baader was found shot dead in his cell, Jan-Carl Raspe was also found shot in his cell and died on the way to hospital, and Gudrun Ensslin had hanged herself. The other woman, Irmgard Moeller, who had stabbed herself, survived. News of the failure of the Mogadishu hijack had been received by the terrorists on their illicit radios in their cells. The body of Hans-Martin Schleyer was found the following day, the 19th, in the trunk of a car at Mulhouse, just across the border in France.

There were now about forty terrorists on the West German "top wanted list," but they remained elusive. However, on 20 December 1977, two of them were involved in a shoot-out with customs officers at the Swiss border and were captured. One was Gabriele Kroecher-Tiedeman, who had been released in exchange for Peter Lorenz. She had taken part in the OPEC raid in Vienna. The other was named as Christian Moeller. Both were put on trial in Switzerland.

Apart from their own terrorists, the West German authorities at times had the problem of coping with foreign ones who used their territory as a battleground amongst themselves, or for targets of their own choosing. The Croatians were particularly notable for causing explosions at Yugoslav diplomatic and other premises. On 18 and 19 August 1978 the IRA also appeared on the West German scene in its fight against the British government. During those two days eight explosions occurred near British military installations in Minden, Bielefeld, Dusseldorf, and Munchon Gladbach.

The West German government announced in 1976 that 20 submachine guns and 15 automatic rifles had been stolen from NATO forces stationed in the Federal Republic, as well as half a ton of explosives, 304 mortar bombs, 225 grenades, and 15 U.S. rockets, of which the majority went underground to political dissi-

*She was held in Somalia, brought to trial, and on 26 April 1978, under her real name of Soraya Ansari, was sentenced to twenty years' imprisonment.

dent and criminal organizations. It also revealed that of the 3,000 British sten guns officially scrapped by the Canadian NATO contingent in West Germany when it was reequipped with more modern replacements, according to the police, 41 were later used in murders and crimes of violence. There was no shortage of weapons in West Germany for terrorists or ciminals. If they could not be stolen they could be bought. Just across the border, in Czechoslovakia, was a government armaments factory known as Omnipol, which supplied arms to anyone in the West willing to pay for them. From Omnipol a steady stream of illicit arms, ammunition, and explosives moved westward into Western Europe.

Interesting sets of figures were released by Chancellor Helmut Schmidt on 20 April 1977 when he said that during the previous ten years 123 terrorists had been sentenced to terms of imprisonment, another 60 were in prison awaiting confirmation of their sentences, and charges were pending against 85; while 240 suspected terrorists were in "investigative detention" and arrest warrants had been issued for another 35 suspects. He stated that during the same period 10 terrorists had been killed in battles with the police and 88 wounded, while 13 hostages had been seized.

Nearly three months later, on 12 July 1977, the Bureau, which had its headquarters at Wiesbaden, stated that West Germany had become the main European arms smuggling and trading center, and that during 1976, 3,145 firearms and 186,631 rounds of ammunition had been stolen in the Federal Republic.* The weapons included not only pistols and automatic rifles, but also machine guns and rockets. It added that these were only the reported losses, saying that the number of firearms legally registered was just under 750,000. It was thought there were about twenty times that number in existence, which would total more than was possessed by the Bundeswehr.

Holland had a South Moluccan problem that erupted from time to time. When the Dutch ruled the Dutch East Indies, now Indonesia, the South Moluccans had provided a greater part of the Dutch colonial armed forces for those islands. They had also fought with the Dutch in the bitter civil war that preceded independence. When Indonesia emerged as a sovereign state, the South

*According to *Stern* magazine.

Moluccans were not reconciled to becoming part of the new nation and wanted the South Moluccan group of islands to have its own independent government. Some 40,000 of them opted to leave and settle in Holland, where mainly they were clustered together in camps. Their political case was a hopeless one, as the Dutch government no longer had any power to do anything for them. The Indonesian government rejected them and the UN would not take up their cause.

On 2 December 1975 South Moluccan terrorists hijacked a train near Belien, in Holland, taking forty-six hostages and killing one person in the process. A few passengers managed to escape. Eventually, on the 14th, the terrorists gave themselves up and were sentenced to terms of imprisonment. While this exploit had been in progress, another six South Moluccan terrorists seized the Indonesian consulate in Amsterdam on 4 December. They took hostages, one of whom died from injuries received in the initial assault. Eventually, on the 17th, they too surrendered and were imprisoned.

The next major incident of this nature began on 23 May 1977 when a group of nine Moluccan terrorists hijacked a train near Glimmen and held about fifty-six passengers hostage. At the same time another three terrorists seized a school at Bovenmilde, some fifteen miles from the hijacked train, and held three teachers and 106 children hostage. They demanded the release of the imprisoned South Moluccan terrorists. The two sieges lasted for nineteen days, until Dutch troops, supported by combat aircraft, mounted a rescue assault at dawn on 11 June. Within fifteen minutes it was all over. Six of the nine terrorists (one a woman) were killed and two of the survivors wounded; but two of the hostages had been killed as well, and seven injured. Dutch troops made a simultaneous assault on the school, where they quickly captured the three terrorists and rescued the three teachers. The children had all been released a few days previously.

The next South Moluccan exploit began on 13 March 1978, when three terrorists entered and took over the local government offices at Assen, in north Holland. Firing their automatic weapons as they entered the building, they killed one person and took seventy-one others hostage. The dead person's body was thrown from a window, and the terrorists fired on police and bystanders. Their demands were outlined in a letter received that morning by the minister of justice at The Hague: the release of twenty-one

South Moluccans in detention and an aircraft to fly them out of the country. The deadline was set at 1300 hours on the 14th. Early on the 14th, the terrorists called in two South Moluccan mediators, making an additional demand for a ransom of $13 million. They released one female hostage. The Dutch government firmly refused. When the deadline was reached and nothing had happened, the terrorists said they would kill two hostages every half hour, commencing at 1400 hours. A few minutes before 1400 hours, a detachment of Dutch marines stormed the building successfully, capturing the three terrorists and rescuing the hostages just in time. Two hostages had just been picked out and were only three minutes away from death when the Dutch marines burst in to save them.

The French also had their terrorist problems, and during 1977 there were 549 explosions in their country due to terrorist activities. Many of these were caused by small groups, as much a gesture of defiance, and to register their presence, as to bring down governments. France also had a few separatist movements, some with terrorist military arms, of which the Corsicans and the Bretons were the most active. The small French island of Corsica, with a population of only about 273,000, had vainly voiced its demand for independence and had resorted to terrorism to achieve its aim. In August 1975 Edmond Simeoni, leader of the Action for Corsican Renaissance (ACN), was arrested and his organization shattered by arrests and banned. He was released in January 1977, but by this time terrorist activities had been taken over by a rival group, the Front de Liberation National de Corse (FLNC). The FLNC launched a campaign of explosions on 5 May 1977. There were 16 that day in Corsica alone, and by the end of the year they totaled 342. On 12 August the terrorists blew up the television transmitter, which remained out of action for months, because they did not want French propaganda to reach Corsica. They also caused explosions in France, including one at a railway station near Paris in November. This campaign was continued in 1978, averaging one explosion a day at least.

The FLNC suffered a setback in June 1978 when over thirty of its members were arrested, but it soon struck back, and there were, for example, thirty-three explosions on the night of 4 July.

On 11 August the terrorists blew up the Chateau de Formali, in Bastia, Corsica, a luxury holiday home. As they wanted publicity, they took two journalists along with them on this exploit.

The other active terrorist group was the terrorist arm of the Breton Liberation Front, known as the Breton Revolutionary Army. The Front wanted severance from France and the right to use its own language. The Breton terrorists first began their activities in 1966, confining them to small explosions at government buildings, mainly in Brittany. In 1977 they made thirty-four attacks of this type. By the end of June 1978 this group claimed to have made 206 attacks, including one at the main radio transmitter at Finnisterre. The most spectacular exploit in 1978 occurred on 26 June when an explosion wrecked several rooms at the Palace of Versailles, Paris, and damaged many priceless paintings. The leader of the Breton Revolutionary Army, Serge Rojinsky, and seven other members, were captured and brought to trial. They were sentenced to terms of imprisonment on 25 July. This terrorist group still has a number of activists in Brittany and exiles in Ireland.

Paris occasionally became a stamping ground for foreign terrorists. For example, on 17 April 1977 two members of the Action Front for the Liberation of Baltic Countries threw two bombs at the office of the French-Soviet Movement building, and another at the Soviet embassy. On 16 June 1977 an explosion wrecked the office of *France-USSR* magazine and another caused some damage to the Soviet Commercial Bank of Europe, while bombs were discovered, and defused in time, at the Paris offices of *Tass* and Aeroflot.

The French still experienced an occasional hijack situation. On 30 September 1977 a Caravelle with 107 people on board was hijacked by Jacques Robert and brought back to Orly airport. When an air hostess tried to intervene, she was shot in the arm by the hijacker. Robert was regarded as a political fanatic. He had been sentenced to imprisonment for killing his father and had held a technician hostage at the Radio Luxembourg studios in Paris in 1974 while he made a political speech. Seven people were allowed to leave the aircraft and another escaped. Jacques Robert, who was armed with a pistol and grenades, ordered the aircraft to be refueled, and then demanded that a long political message be broadcast over Europe Number One, a Paris commercial radio station, and also over Radio Monte Carlo. A radio personality went to the airport control tower and engaged the hijacker in conversation. The deadline, 1400 hours, passed without any hostages being shot, but shortly afterwards French security forces made a rescue assault on the aircraft. Robert exploded a grenade as they entered the plane, injuring five people, one of whom later died. The French police were condemned for their hasty action and the French Pilots' Union spokesman said the casualties "showed the absurdity of a hasty, ill-timed, and unsuitable operation." He also said the security at Orly airport was "insufficient."

On 11 May 1976 the Bolivian ambassador to France was assassinated in Paris and the responsibility was claimed by the Che Guevara International Brigade. On 7 July 1977, also in Paris, the Mauretanian ambassador to France was shot and wounded. Responsibility was claimed by the Mohammed al-Wal Said International Brigade, a tiny terrorist group named after a Polisario Front leader who had been killed the previous year.

When General Franco, dictator of Spain for thirty-six years, died in November 1975, his country took its first painful steps towards becoming a parliamentary democracy with a constitutional monarchy. Even before his death political discontent that bred terrorism seethed under a seemingly placid surface of law and order. After his death its momentum increased, as both left- and right-wing groups became active. During the years 1976–78 political murder, kidnappings, explosions, and acts of arson became commonplace in Spain.

One prominent left-wing terrorist organization became known as GRAPO, the initial letters for the Spanish phrase translated as "October First Anti-Fascist Revolutionary Resistance Group." This designation referred to an incident, probably the group's first major one, on 1 October 1975, in which they claimed responsibility for killing four policemen. On 11 December 1976 GRAPO kidnapped Antonio Oriel, one of Spain's most influential politicians. A few days later it also kidnapped General Villascua, president of the Supreme Council of Military Justice, demanding the freedom of certain political prisoners in return for their safe release. Both were eventually released on 11 February 1977 during a massive police search.

GRAPO terrorist exploits continued during 1977. On the evening of 24 January a small group of its members surprised a private meeting of lawyers in Madrid. Firing their automatic weapons at them, they killed five and injured four. On 12 July GRAPO caused an explosion in the French embassy in Madrid in protest against the "monopolistic government of France," while on the 18th (the forty-first anniversary of the commencement of the civil war) four members of GRAPO burst into Madrid's commercial radio station and forced the technicians to broadcast a revolutionary message. On 17 August a time bomb was discovered in an underpass in Majorca shortly before King Juan Carlos was due to travel along that route. It was identified by the police, who took the bomb away to explode.

The year 1978 was much the same, and on 22 March Jesus Haddad, governor of a Madrid prison, was assassinated by GRAPO members as he was leaving home. On 17 May GRAPO caused an explosion in the U.S. Cultural Center in Madrid that injured two people and did considerable damage. It coincided with a visit by Vice President Mondale. On 4 August Hierro Chamoun, the GRAPO leader, was arrested and charged with nine assassinations and a series of kidnappings. In January 1979 GRAPO murdered a high court judge in Madrid.

Right-wing terrorist organizations were also active in Spain. One known as the Warriors of Christ the King specialized in explosions. On 23 February 1977 Mariano Sanchez Covisa, the leader of this group, was arrested in a flat in Madrid. Also in the flat were eight Italians and one French woman, and equipment sufficient to produce fifty automatic weapons a month. Another right-wing organization which developed a notorious reputation was known as the Apostolic Anti-Communist Alliance (AAA).

Apart from terrorists striving to impose their political persuasion on their country, separatist groups also existed in Spain. The most virulent and active was the ETA, which killed the Spanish premier in Madrid in December 1973. The ETA carried out a series of terrorist exploits with the object of pressuring the central government into giving the Basques independence. On 9 May 1977 the ETA kidnapped Jose Marques, an industrialist, and an explosive device with a timing switch was taped to his chest. The terrorists demanded a huge ransom, but allowed Marques to go free, warning him not to touch the explosive device. The victim became a walking human time bomb. He returned home, but was killed when the bomb exploded while he was attempting to remove it.

On the 18th of the same month two ETA members killed two policemen in San Sebastian, and the following day attacked others in Pamplona. On the 20th the ETA kidnapped Javier Ybarra, a Bilbao industrialist, who was taken from his home by four men and a woman dressed as medical orderlies. A large ransom was demanded, and when it had not been paid by the time the terrorists' deadline expired, he was killed. His body was discovered on 22 June. At the end of 1977 the ETA managed to stock up with explosives when members hijacked a truckload of 2,000 pounds of them on 28 December, and another of 600 pounds on the 29th.

On 29 June 1978 the ETA killed a journalist, and on 22 July killed General Sanchez Ramos and Colonel Juan Perez Rodriguez outside an army headquarters in Madrid. GRAPO originally claimed responsibility for the murder of the army officers, but so did the ETA. The ETA claim was at first doubted because it had not carried out any assassinations outside the Basque region since December 1974. On 25 September 1978 the ETA killed another two policemen in northern Spain in its thirty-fourth attack that year, bringing the total number of policemen assassinated to fifteen in the declared ETA "permanent armed offensive against the police."

Another small group wanting independence from Spanish central rule was the Movement for Self-Determination and Independence of the Canary Archipelago, which in retaliation for the alleged killing of one of its members by the police a week previously caused an explosion at the Las Palmas airport on 27 March 1977. This small terrorist incident was the inadvertent cause of the world's worst air disaster. Because of damage at Las Palmas airport, air traffic had to be diverted to other airports and airfields. Two airliners were diverted to Tenerife airport; one was a KLM Boeing 747 and the other a Pan American 747. They collided on the runway, and 582 people were killed.

Turkey, a country beset by problems of inflation with some three million unemployed, had a continuing terrorist problem during the years 1977–78. The most active terrorist group remained the Turkish People's Liberation Army (TPLA), a left-wing organization which was given considerable assistance by the PFLP. One of the TPLA's bomb factories was revealed on 24 March 1977 when there was an explosion in a building in an Ankara suburb. Two women working in it were injured. The police stated the TPLA had been responsible for at least ten recent explosions in Turkey.

However, the TPLA was not the only terrorist group operating in Turkey or against the Turkish government overseas. There were also a number of smaller ones, of both left- and right-wing persuasion, some of which used violence against each other as much as they did against the government or society at large. One of these organizations was Armenian, known generally as the Armenian Liberation Front, and was seeking the restoration of an Armenian homeland in Turkey, where about one-third of some 1.5 million Armenians living in Turkey in World War I had been massacred and another third had been deported. The Front and its splinters operated under various code names, including the May 28th Organization, Justice for Genocide in Armenia, and the New Armenian Resistance.

One of its first overseas exploits was to assassinate two Turkish employees of the Turkish consulate in Los Angeles in 1973. Two years later, in October 1975, the Armenian Liberation Front claimed responsibility for killing both the Turkish ambassador to Austria and the Turkish ambassador to France within three days of each other. At the time it was suspected that the Front was operating from New York. This was followed by the killing of a Turkish diplomat in Lebanon, and in June 1977 it claimed responsibility for assassinating the Turkish ambassadors to the Vatican and Belgium. On 3 January 1978 the Front stated it had caused explosions in London and Brussels at the Turkish embassies, a Turkish bank, and other Turkish property. On 12 March an exploding bomb damaged three Turkish embassy automobiles in Athens, injuring four people. In Madrid, on 2 June, three members of the Justice for Genocide in Armenia stopped an automobile in a street in which the wife of the Turkish ambassador to Spain, her brother (mistaken by them for the ambassador), and a driver were traveling. All three were shot and killed at point-blank range.

Another small group that operated internally in Turkey was the Youth Section of the Neo-Fascist National Action Party, led by Colonel Alpasian Turkes, which became known as the Grey Wolves. The Grey Wolves terrorized university campuses and high schools and had succeeded in driving left-wing activists underground in many places. On May Day 1977 unidentified gunmen fired into a large crowd of demonstrating left-wing students, killing thirty-four and wounding many more. The police blamed a rival Maoist terrorist group, but generally unspoken suspicion rested on the Grey Wolves. These casualties brought the totals due to terrorist violence in the preceding two years to over two hundred killed and over four thousand injured.

Yet another small Turkish terrorist group was known as the Secret Liberation Army. It claimed responsibility for an explosion at Istanbul airport on 29 May 1977 that injured five people, and for another four explosions at the offices of right-wing political organizations. During the first four months of 1978, 213 people in Turkey died as the result of terrorist activities.

Iran continued to be troubled by terrorism, and on 18 May 1976 it was officially announced that in gun battles with the police at three separate places ten terrorists, including three women, were killed, which brought the number killed or executed so far that year to fifty-one. It was estimated that over three thousand political prisoners were held in Iranian prisons. A section of the National Iranian Front, also known as the Islamic Marxists, had launched a terrorist campaign aimed at eradicating all foreign, and especially Western, influence from the country. The Shah was trying to modernize and industrialize his country, but some felt he was moving too fast to carry the traditionalists with him. Religious leaders especially saw their entrenched authority slipping away from them.

As far back as 1970, the minority left-wing elements coined the title "Islamic Marxists," hoping to harness and then gain control of the Islamic masses for their cause. While both wanted to remove the Shah, they each wanted him to be replaced with ideologically opposite types of government, one being Islamic and the other Marxist. In 1972 the two opposing elements fell out, and since have conducted a spasmodic terrorist campaign against each other as much as against the Shah's government. The left-wing terrorist groups have retained the designation of Islamic Marxists, but they are now almost wholly secular and Marxist.

One of the first exploits of the Islamic Marxists occurred on 21 May 1975 when two American officers were killed in an ambush. The three terrorists responsible were arrested, tried, and executed. During 1976 the Islamic Marxists were alleged to have been responsible for over forty assassinations in Teheran alone, a number that included five senior police officers. The Iranian government accused both Libya and Cuba of training terrorists to operate in Iran, claiming that the Islamic Marxists were financed by a foreign power, but did not go so far as to mention the Soviet Union in this respect. On 29 August 1976 three American civilians installing a sophisticated radar surveillance system at Teheran international airport were ambushed while driving to work and killed. The Islamic Marxists responsible were eventually arrested, tried, and executed. It was alleged that the Islamic Marxists were collaborating with Soviet espionage agents on Project Ibis, a Soviet intelligence operation aimed at obtaining Western electronic secrets.

Of the many terrorist incidents, perhaps two should be singled out. On the night of 13 August 1978 an exploding bomb in a restaurant in Teheran killed one person and injured forty, ten of whom were Americans. The Islamic Marxists were continuing their terrorist campaign against foreigners associated with the Shah's modernization program. A week later, on the 21st, a cinema full of people in Abadan was set on fire by a terrorist incendiary device. In the blaze 377 people died and another 23 were injured.

Led and encouraged by the exiled Ayatollah Khomeini, Islamic agitation and discontent in Iran rose to a crescendo against the Shah, forcing him to quit the country on 15 January 1979. Shortly afterwards Ayatollah Khomeini arrived in Iran to an hysterical and enthusiastic welcome. Arms were taken by, or distributed to the mobs. The country teetered on the brink of civil war for a few days, but the pro-Shah armed forces backed away. The future in Iran is uncertain, but it is obvious that the terrorist groups, Marxist and Muslim, now have ample weapons in their possession.

The fanatical Japanese Red Army made an occasional spectacular appearance. One exploit began on 28 September 1977 when a Japanese airliner on a flight from Paris to Tokyo with 156 people on board was hijacked after leaving Bombay by five JRA terrorists. They forced the pilot to land the plane at Dacca, Bangladesh, where they demanded the release of nine of their members from Japanese prisons and a ransom of $6 million in hundred-dollar bills. Air Marshal Abdul Gafur Mahmoud, head of the Bangladesh Air Force, took charge of the negotiations. The hijackers claimed to be the Hidaka Commando. (Toshihiko Hidaka was a JRA member who had died in mysterious circumstances in Jordan in 1976.)

The next day, the 29th, the Japanese government agreed to the demands and the terrorists released five hostages. But it required time to assemble the demanded terrorists, one of whom was in prison in Okinawa, and also to obtain the money in cash. Indeed, $4 million had to be specially flown from New York to Tokyo on 30 September. When the Japanese aircraft arrived at Dacca on 1 October with six released prisoners (three had refused to leave their prisons to rejoin their old comrades) and the money, the hostages began to be released in batches.

The Japanese government now came up against a problem. It had asked twenty countries to accept the aircraft so the hostages could be freed safely, but all refused. Eventually, the Algerian government agreed to accept the plane on "humanitarian grounds." The exchange of hostages and released prisoners was going well when, in the early hours of 2 October, there was an attempted coup in Bangladesh. Fighting occurred at Dacca airport in which eleven air force officers and seventeen civilians were killed and over two hundred others wounded. The Air Marshal was wounded and another official took his place as the negotiator. He ordered the Japanese aircraft to take off immediately as he wished to impose a curfew on the airport. Only about one hundred hostages had been released before the plane flew off with thirty-six hostages on board, including seven crew, to arrive at Algiers and safety on 3 October. Enroute, ten hostages were released in exchange for fuel at Damascus, and another seven at Kuwait for the same reason.

The ease with which this exploit had been successfully carried out was a setback in the fight against terrorism, and the Bangladesh government was criticized for allowing the hijacked aircraft to take off at all. A JRA statement in English thanked the Algerian government, adding, "Now we, the Japanese Red Army, are going to tie arms with the revolutionary soldiers who were liberated from jail; and are going to return to the battle front. . . . Our Hidaka unit has completed its duty and achieved the aim of the operation, to liberate our comrades and revolutionary friends." The Japanese police stated that the JRA was down to about one hundred members still at large, of whom only about twelve were activists. An ironic footnote to this hijacking was that, unknown to the hijackers, diamonds worth almost $2 million were in a case lying on an aircraft seat throughout the whole six days of the exploit.

The volume of terrorism in the United States was also heavy, and FBI figures for 1975, for example, listed 2,074 bombings in which 69 people were killed and 326 injured. In 1976 there were 45 people killed and 206 injured in 1,564 terrorist incidents. The FBI also stated that during the period 1968–75, 82 U.S. diplomats abroad had been subjected to terrorist attacks in which 18 of them had been killed.

Another notable terrorist incident in the United States occurred in March 1977 when twelve Muslim fanatics held 134 people hostage in three buildings in Washington, D.C. for thirty-six hours, threatening to behead them. It was an act of revenge by Hams Abdul Khalis, the leader of the group, because Black Muslims had allegedly killed four of his children and three of his followers. Intervention by the ambassadors of Pakistan, Egypt, and Iran brought about his surrender to the police without anyone being injured.

The Soviet Union has not been without its terrorist problems either, despite a rigid censorship that forbids all mention in the media of such activities. It was announced on 2 May 1976 that in the Soviet Republic of Georgia, which has a population of about 4.7 million people and lies adjacent to Turkey, there had been a series of bombings and acts of arson at public buildings during the previous two years, the culprits claiming to belong to the Bearers of the Voices of the Past. Some individual terrorist exploits could not be completely hidden and in January 1977 several people were killed and many injured (the Soviet authorities never revealed exactly how many) in Moscow by a terrorist explosion in the Metro underground railway system. On 30 January 1979 the Soviet authorities announced the execution of three Soviet Armenians for causing this explosion. Only one person was named: Stepan Zadikyan who had previously been imprisoned for demanding independence for the Soviet Republic of Armenia. On 11 June there was another terrorist explosion in Moscow just outside the Hotel Sovietskaya, used to accommodate high-ranking foreign diplomats and visitors.

On 26 May 1977 a Soviet aircraft carrying twenty-three people on an internal flight was hijacked by a Russian, Vasily Sosnovosky, and diverted to Stockholm, Sweden. The hijacker was granted political asylum, but was sentenced to a term of imprisonment as well. The only previous two internal hijackings admitted by the Soviet authorities had both occurred in 1970. In one, two Russian students hijacked an aircraft and flew it to Turkey, but were handed back to the Soviet Union. In the other, a Lithuanian father and son hijacked a Soviet plane to Turkey, but were not extradited.

On 10 July 1977 two Russians hijacked a Soviet airliner on an internal flight with sixty-four people on board and demanded to be flown to Sweden. However, the plane did not have enough fuel and had to put down at Helsinki, Finland, instead. On the 11th the hijackers released thirty-one women and eight children, and six men escaped through a rear door. The remaining hostages were either released or escaped the following day, and on the 13th the hijackers surrendered. Having a bilateral agreement with Finland, the Soviet government demanded their extradition and the two hijackers were returned to the Soviet Union to face trial.

East European countries are not without their terrorist problems either. On 10 June 1977 a Bulgarian, Tsanko Dimitrov, hijacked a Bulgarian aircraft on an internal flight with forty-nine people on board. He ordered the pilot to fly to Munich or London, but the Bulgarian authorities ensured that their aircraft had only sufficient fuel for a particular journey. It had to put down at Belgrade, Yugoslavia, where the hijacker was overpowered. A letter bomb addressed to the Bulgarian embassy in Athens exploded in the hands of a postman, and responsibility was claimed by the anticommunist Greek National Socialist terrorist group. The same terrorist group sent a parcel bomb to the Greek Defense Ministry that injured an army officer on 2 March 1977 when he opened it.

There had been a few instances of Czech aircraft being hijacked to the West, mainly by political refugees. In March 1977 there was another when a Czech hijacked a Yak-40 with twenty-seven people on board to Munich, West Germany. The next exploit was on 11 October 1977, when two Czechs, a man and a woman, hijacked a small aircraft with twenty-eight people on board. Wearing the uniform of the Czech airlines and armed with pistols, they ordered the pilot to fly them to Munich, where they surrendered after some negotiation. They declared they had gone to West Germany for political reasons.

Neither did Poland escape the attentions of terrorists. On 25 April 1977 a Polish soldier hijacked a TU-134 of the Polish State airlines (LOT) at Krakow airport. It was on a charter flight carrying West German tourists. He shot and wounded one man and then demaded to be flown to Africa. Shortly afterwards Polish paratroops disguised as airport staff stormed the plane and captured the hijacker, an army deserter.

On 30 August 1978 a Polish airliner with seventy-one people on board, on a flight from Warsaw to East Berlin, was hijacked by a Pole named as Detlef Alexander Tiede, who was accompanied by his wife and child. Armed with a pistol, he forced the pilot to fly to the U.S. airfield in West Berlin, where he surrendered, asking for political asylum. Seven of the East Germans on the plane, in an impromptu fashion, also decided to remain in the West.

The other communist country with a terrorist problem that seemed to spread itself across Europe to America, and even to Australia, was Yugoslavia, itself a union of several East European peoples. It had an active separatist movement known as the Young Croatian Army (sometimes translated as the Free Croatian Movement), which wanted independence from Yugoslavia. Its first major terrorist exploit occurred on 11 August 1976 when five of its members hijacked an American Boeing 727 on an internal flight in the United States and ordered the pilot to fly to Europe. The aircraft stopped to refuel at Montreal, where Free Croatian propaganda leaflets were handed out, and then at Gander, Newfoundland, where a number of hostages were allowed to leave the plane on condition they took leaflets with them to distribute in New York and Chicago. The hijackers said that copies of their manifesto were to be found in a locker in Grand Central Station, New York City, and must be published in certain newspapers. At the same time three bombs were discovered in New York that had been planted by the Young Croatian Army. One exploded, killing a policeman who was trying to defuse it.

The next stop for the hijacked plane was Keflavik, Iceland, where more leaflets were handed out. Then the aircraft, still with twenty-six hostages on board, crossed the Atlantic Ocean and landed at De Gaulle airport, Paris, after being refused permission to put down at London airport. On landing, the plane was surrounded by French security forces, and marksmen punctured the tires by shooting at them. The French gave the terrorists the hard choice of either shooting it out with the security forces or surrendering to be instantly deported to either Yugoslavia or America. They surrendered and opted to return to America, where in May 1977 they were sentenced to terms of imprisonment.

On 14 June 1977 three members of the Young Croatian Army attacked the Yugoslav mission at the UN in New York and wounded one security guard. They intended to kidnap the Yugoslav ambassador. Yugoslav diplomatic personnel were held hostage for about three hours before the terrorists could be persuaded to surrender. A few days later, on the 19th, explosions occurred on the Dortmund-Athens train just after it entered Yugoslavia, killing one person and injuring others. The Young Croatian Army had put itself on the terrorist map.

Even religious politics and strife occasionally took on a terrorist tinge. For example, on 24 August 1977, in Cyprus, an island no stranger to terrorism in the past, there was an abortive bomb attack on the palace of the bishop of Limasol, who was a candidate in the impending election for a successor to Archbishop Makarios as head of the Cypriot Church. Some thirty-two sticks of dynamite with primed detonators attached were detected and defused in time. They were identified as part of a 4,900-pound consignment of explosives stolen by the now moribund EOKA-B terrorist organization from a mine in 1972.

The following day, the 25th, an explosion occurred at Lourdes, France, blowing a large hole in the dome of the underground basilica. On this occasion the usual national Roman Catholic pilgrimage to Lourdes coincided with a rival pilgrimage organized by the traditionalists who supported the rebel Archbishop Lefebvre. In Christian Malta, on Christmas Day in 1977, a letter bomb had killed a fifteen-year-old girl and injured two other people.

This chapter has included but a few of the countless incidents of terrorism to illustrate its volume and scope. It is only when the problem is examined in detail, and in breadth, that its immensity and ubiquitousness can be appreciated. The totals of terrorist activities for 1978 are expected to show an increase over 1977. In short, the volume of worldwide terrorism is tremendous, of almost epidemic proportion.

16 Fedayeen Infighting

*The Iraqi security guard wanted to kill the terrorist at all costs,
even if it meant taking the lives of French policemen.*
French police chief, Paris, 31 July 1978

MEANWHILE, IN THE Middle East, Fedayeen terrorist activities continued, with Israel as the main target, of course, but factions were formed that quarreled amongst themselves.

Since the 1973 War there had been a gradual shifting and realignment of Middle East terrorist groups, and by 1976 the new Fedayeen lineup had begun to crystalize. The PLO, still with Arafat as its chairman, and with a seat on the Arab League, was officially receiving money from certain Arab states. It had eight terrorist groups owing allegiance, nominal or otherwise, to it. They were Fatah, Arafat's own organization, still the largest numerically; the PLA, also directly under Arafat's control; Hawatmeh's DPF; the Syrian Saiqa; the Iraqi ALF; the Jabril Front (the PFLP–General Command); Abu Nidal's Fatah Revolutionary Council; and Hassan Abu Abbas' PLF. As George Habash had withdrawn his PFLP from the Central Committee in 1974, it was regarded as being outside the PLO. Wadia Hadad's group, which came to be known as the PFLP–Special Operations, was independent of the PLO, as well as of the PFLP.

Among these terrorists groups the two main factions were supported by the governments of Syria and Iraq, traditional enemies. These groups fought each other on behalf of their sponsors. Added to this, they both became hostile to Arafat. The struggle between the Fedayeen groups became a deadly three-sided internal contest. The four groups sponsored by the Iraqi government or allowed to operate from Iraqi soil were the ALF, the Jabril Front, the Fatah Revolutionary Council, and the PLF; while the two groups that worked for, and from, Syria were the Saiqa and the DPF, both somewhat pro-Soviet in outlook. Attempts were actually made to oust Arafat from the chairmanship of the PLO.

285

The civil war that erupted in Lebanon in April 1975 became a complicated factional struggle in which Christians, Muslims, Druse, and Palestinians became involved. An official cease-fire was enforced in November 1976, although it did not bring the war to an end, since cease-fires were regularly broken. In June 1976 Syrian armed forces had moved into Lebanon and prevented Palestinian guerrillas from eliminating certain Christian strongholds. This action was sharply criticized by the Iraqi government, and seemed to cause its hostile feelings towards Syria to escalate into a terrorist war. Abu Nidal formed an active terrorist group to take action against both the Syrian regime and the Jordanians. It was estimated that Abu Nidal had about 1,500 members of his Fatah Revolutionary Council training in Iraqi camps. From them he began selectively recruiting commandos into what became known as the Black June movement, named after the month in which Syrian armed forces invaded Lebanon.

The first time the name Black June came to general notice was on 26 September 1976, when five of its members took over the Semiramis Hotel in the center of Damascus in the early hours of the morning. Some ninety guests and hotel employees were held hostage. They demanded the release of a number of Iraqi political prisoners from Syrian jails. Syrian security forces immediately attacked the hotel, and a three-hour battle ensued. One terrorist was killed, as were four hostages, three of whom were women, while another thirty-four people were injured. The other four terrorists were captured, interrogated, tried, and condemned to death. The following morning at dawn they were hanged in public in the main city square outside the Semiramis Hotel, where their bodies, with details of their crimes written on posters wrapped around them, remained in full view for several hours. This was the first the world at large knew of Abu Nidal's Black June movement, but it had already been in operation for some weeks. Probably its first exploit was the murder of Ahmed al-Azzawi, a senior member of the Syrian Baath Party, on 11 July 1976. He was killed by an explosion in Damascus.

Some Black June exploits were not carried out in the Middle East. On 11 October 1976 two such incidents occurred. One was in Rome, when three Black June members attacked the Syrian embassy with grenades and automatic weapons, wounding a Syrian diplomat. The terrorists seized three hostages and demanded to see the ambassador. For a while they defied the police, but eventually were persuaded to surrender. The other was in faraway Islamabad, capital of Pakistan. Three members of the Black June movement entered the compound of the Syrian embassy, firing their automatic weapons and throwing grenades. This developed into a battle with the police, who had quickly arrived on the scene, in which one terrorist and one policeman were killed, and several other people were injured. The two other terrorists were captured, but soon deported. The Pakistani government did not want to become involved in the inter-Arab subterranean warfare. In both instances the terrorists claimed that their mission was to "avenge the massacres in Lebanon."

The attention of the Black June movement was also directed towards Jordanian targets, and on 17 November 1976 four of its members took possession of the Intercontinental Hotel in Amman at dawn. Jordanian security forces quickly moved in for the assault, and a one-hour battle developed in which three of the terrorists were killed and the other captured. Two Jordanian soldiers and two civilians were also killed. The surviving Black June member, named as Khairy Ibrahim Omar, even though seriously wounded, was executed on 19 December. The Syrian foreign minister, Abdul Halim Khaddam, became a Black June target, and he was slightly wounded on 1 December by a terrorist riding on a motorcycle. The Syrians held Abu Nidal responsible for this exploit.

By the beginning of 1977 the Syrian government realized that the Iraqi government was waging a terrorist war against it, and decided to retaliate with its Saiqa. The first blow was struck on 14 January when a suitcase bomb exploded at Baghdad airport, wrecking part of the building and causing part of the roof to collapse. Three people were killed and at least ten others seriously injured. The suitcase bomb had been put on an Egyptian airliner at a stopover at Damascus. No organization claimed responsibility for this outrage, but the fingers of suspicion pointed to Zuhair Mohsin's Syrian Saiqa organization. It showed that no single group had a monopoly on terrorism. On 9 February a suitcase bomb was discovered in a mosque at Karbala, Iraq, and defused in time, the blame being placed on an "agent of the Syrian regime." Again, on 5 June 1977, a bomb in a Baghdad street injured thirty-five people. This time the government accused the Syrian Saiqa.

The Black June movement continued to be active, and on 19 June 1977 Syrian Brigadier Abdul Hamid Razouk was shot and killed. Abu Nidal was blamed. The Syrian foreign minister, Abdul

Halim Khaddam, remained a priority target, and on 25 October a Black June terrorist, Saleh Mohammed Khalid, attempted to shoot him when he was visiting Abu Dabai. Khalid missed Khaddam and instead fatally wounded the foreign minister of the United Arab Emirates, Said al-Ghobesh. This terrorist seized seven hostages, but soon surrendered to the security forces. Khalid, who was in possession of Iraqi travel documents, was tried by a Shia (religious) court, found guilty, and executed by a firing squad on 16 November.

When President Sadat of Egypt made his historic journey to Jerusalem, he aroused the fury of the rejection states and caused Egyptians to become targets for terrorist groups. The Syrians were extremely bitter against Sadat and used their Saiqa to demonstrate their dislike. For example, two Syrians were killed in a London street on 31 December 1977 when a bomb in their automobile exploded. They were named as Jawdat Awad, who was listed as a medical attaché at the Syrian embassy in London, and Fayez Shibili, a Syrian driver. It was suspected that they were about to plant the bomb in the nearby Egyptian Tourist Office. On 2 January 1978 a bomb was discovered at the Egyptian embassy in Bonn, but was defused in time. On 21 December 1977 Lebanese security forces foiled an attack with rockets and time bombs on the Egyptian embassy in Beirut for the third time in three days.

During 1977 responsibility for a number of terrorist incidents was claimed by the Black June and September movement, which was puzzling, as the original Black September Organization, which had in any case been part of Fatah, had become defunct after the Khartoum Massacre of March 1973. The explanation seems to be that former BSO members, now in Abu Nidal's breakaway Fatah Revolutionary Council, still favored that title, which had gained such a tremendous reputation in the Arab world and indeed in the world at large.

During 1978 a conflict developed between the Iraqi-sponsored terrorist groups such as Abu Nidal's Fatah Revolutionary Council and Hassan Abu Abbas' Palestine Liberation Front on the one hand, and the PLO headquarters organization, backed by Fatah, on the other. Assassinations of Fatah leaders caused Abu Iyad, who had raised and operated the Black September Organization, to reassemble a killer squad to strike back. The ensuing underground struggle, which spread to the streets of Paris and London, was fought with such vindictiveness and ferocity that in comparison the Mossad-BSO campaign of twilight warfare in 1972–73 paled into insignificance. The Fedayeen movement was tearing itself to pieces. Eventually, it was the Soviet government, in pursuit of influence in the Middle East, that firmly stepped in to halt the suicidal internecine contest. The Soviets were anxious to try to marshal a united Fedayeen effort against Israel and Egypt to counter the Sadat-Begin agreement of Camp David, which excluded Soviet participation.

The first major Fatah exploit of 1978 occurred in March. It was a great success from their point of view and temporarily united the Arabs. On 11 March thirteen Fatah terrorists of the Kamal Adwan Commando (named after the Fatah leader who was killed in the Israeli raid on Beirut in April 1973) sailed in a small fishing vessel from the tiny Lebanese port of Dabour, just south of Tyre, southwards through choppy seas. The Kamal Adwan Commando was part of the Deir Yasin Unit, named after the Israeli terrorist massacre of Arab villagers at Deir Yasin (since renamed Beit Shaul) near Jerusalem in April 1948. The leader of the Kamal Adwan Commando was a woman who spoke Hebrew, named as Dalal (or Dalida) al-Maghrabi, who had been expelled from Israel in 1969.

In the afternoon of the 11th, believing they were about fifty miles due west of Tel Aviv, the commandos embarked in three small French-made Zodiac assault boats. One capsized and two commandos were drowned, but the other two boats set off eastwards, and the commandos in them landed on the Israeli coast at about 1600 hours near the kibbutz of Malagan Michael, about thirty-six miles north of Tel Aviv. The terrorists' mission had been to land at Bat Yam, which was just south of Tel Aviv, seize one of the hotels there, take hostages, and demand the release of five specifically named prisoners from Israeli jails. On stepping ashore on the beach, the terrorists encountered a young woman whom they killed after questioning her to find out exactly where they were.

They then moved on to the adjacent main Haifa–Tel Aviv coastal road, where they stopped a taxi, into which they loaded their weapons and ammunition. They had Kalishnikov automatic rifles, RPGs (rocket propelled grenades), and 52mm mortars and grenades, all of Soviet manufacture. They also had leaflets, printed in Hebrew, outlining their demands. Their intention was to travel by taxi through Tel Aviv to their original destination. Realizing the taxi was not large enough, the terrorists ambushed and stopped a bus. By this time they were firing their weapons indiscriminately. Having loaded their weaponry and themselves on the two vehicles, with the passengers as hostages, the terrorists set off southward towards Tel Aviv. They overtook another bus, a larger one, fired into it, and brought it to a halt. Then all moved into the second bus — terrorists, drivers, and passengers, except that a few Israelis managed to escape in the changeover. Those Israelis already wounded were left by the roadside. A Soviet-made antitank weapon was left in the taxi. The bus sped southwards, with the terrorists firing their automatic weapons and throwing grenades at passing vehicles, shouting Fatah slogans and singing Fedayeen songs.

Having arrived at the wrong jumping-off spot, there was now some argument among the terrorists as to what to do and where to go. Some wanted to make for Lod airport to seize a plane and demand a safe-conduct out of Israel. The leader was a strong-minded woman, and her decision was that they carry on to Tel Aviv, take over a hotel on the northern outskirts, and demand the release of the five prisoners.

By this time the alarm had been sounded in Israel, and police and troops moved into action stations. An ambush site was selected just north of Tel Aviv, near Hertzlia, in open country, where a roadblock was set up. Just as it was getting dark, after a wild rampage that lasted forty-five minutes, the bus was halted. A ten-minute gun battle followed in which the bus was set on fire. Inside the vehicle one of the passengers was able to seize a weapon from a terrorist and kill three Fatah commandos.

The battle died down, and dead and injured people were dragged from the burning bus. It was not certain at that moment exactly how many terrorists there were or whether any had escaped in the darkness, so some 300,000 Israelis were confined to their homes in an eighteen-hour curfew, while a twenty-mile sector of the coastal area was searched. In fact, nine of the eleven terrorists, including the woman leader, had been killed, and the other two, one of whom was wounded, were captured. In all thirty-five Israelis were killed, including one senior police officer, and eighty-two were injured. Fatah claimed responsibility, saying that it was in response to Sadat's peace initiative. The two survivors admitted they had been briefed personally by Abu Iyad. Fatah was once again carrying out terrorist exploits inside Israel. This incident showed the Israelis how vulnerable their coastline was to infiltration from the sea, despite aerial and naval patrols and shore-based radar defenses.

This Fatah exploit temporarily united the Arabs. At first Egypt was silent, but after some hesitation President Sadat condemned it, urging the Israelis not to retaliate. President Amin, of Entebbe fame, sent a message of condolence to the Israelis. Now all waited in suspense to see what reprisals the Israelis would make on Palestinian refugee camps in Lebanon, their usual form of retribution. Prime Minister Begin postponed his scheduled trip to Washington. For a couple of days nothing happened, but this was due to bad weather that made flying almost impossible. Then suddenly, about midnight on 13 March the Israelis crossed the border into southern Lebanon on a wide front, in six land columns supported by artillery, armor, aircraft, naval guns, and missiles. Forcing their way northwards against mainly Palestinian resistance, they eventually reached, and remained at, the lateral Litani River.

The next major planned Fatah exploit against Israel failed. On 30 September 1978 an Israeli naval patrol boat in the Gulf of Akaba intercepted a Greek freighter, the *Agaeus Dimitrius,* steaming northwards off Dahab some seventy-seven miles south of Eilat, the southern Israeli port, during the afternoon. The Israelis ordered it to stop to be identified, but this was ignored, causing them to fire shots into the air as a warning. The Greek ship suddenly changed course and made for the Saudi Arabian shore. The patrol boat then fired directly at the vessel, which caused an explosion on board, and the ship began to sink. Six of the seven-man crew, jumped overboard to be picked up by the patrol boat. The seventh terrorist was captured on the sinking ship, which was discovered to have a cargo of forty-two long-range 122mm rockets and a large quantity of explosives.

The Fatah crew had intended to sail the ship to Eilat, bombard the hotels on the seafront with rockets, then drive the ship onto the beach in front of the hotels and explode it. The terrorists anticipated escaping swiftly at the last moment by dinghy to the adjacent Jordanian port of Akaba, a couple of miles away. Had the terrorists succeeded in their exploit the carnage and destruction in Eilat would have been tremendous, as the hotels were packed full of holidaying Israelis who had arrived there to celebrate the Jewish New Year the following day.

A number of other terrorist incidents, some allegedly committed by Abu Nidal's organization, some by the Syrian Saiqa, and others by Wadia Hadad's PFLP–Special Operations, occurred in Britain during 1978. For example, in January Ali Shafik, an Iraqi who was a former friend of President Nasser living in exile, was killed at his London apartment. The following month an attempt was made to kill Ayad Alawi, a former president of the Iraqi Students' Union, who had come to live in Britain after being expelled from the Baath Party.

On 9 July Abdul Razzak al-Nauf, a former premier of the Yemeni Republic (North Yemen), was shot outside his London hotel and died a few hours later. Two men were arrested and charged with his murder. They were Salem Hassan and Saadi Abdul Rahman al-Skukri. One had been caught immediately after the shooting by a member of the hotel staff, and the other had been arrested at London airport as he was about to flee the country. The responsibility was ascribed to the PFLP Special Operations.

On 21 August there was a terrorist attack on a bus carrying an El Al air crew and passengers from the London airport to a London hotel by two members of the PFLP Special Operations who fired automatic weapons and threw grenades at the vehicle as the people were dismounting from it. One air hostess was killed, as was a terrorist when his grenade exploded in his hand; nine other people were injured. The surviving terrorist, Fahad Mihyi, was caught by a passerby. This was probably the first exploit of the PFLP Special Operations under its new leader, Saleh Saleh, an Iraqi and a former member of the ALF. The Jabril Front also claimed responsibility for this act.

Something of an end to a terrorist era came early in 1978 when Wadia Hadad entered a sanatorium in East Germany, where he died of cancer on 28 April 1978. His funeral took place in Baghdad. Hadad was indeed a terrorist mastermind, and had organized the majority of the larger spectacular exploits for a decade.

Said Hammami's death in London in January 1978 made Arafat realize that the Iraq-based terrorist groups were working to decimate or even eliminate the PLO leadership. This caused him to tighten up the security arrangements for senior PLO personnel and offices. He also decided to hit back hard. This latter task he gave to Abu Iyad, who had led and organized the BSO from 1970 until 1973. He began to assemble a vengeance team known as Squad 17.

Arafat's other main problem was retaining his leadership of the PLO, the two chief challengers being Abu Iyad, his Fatah deputy, a militant, and Khalid Fahoum, chairman of the PNC, a moderate. Other Fatah leaders objected to certain aspects of his policies. However, the politically astute Arafat weathered this storm of discontent, dampening the opposition and then stamping out dissidence and adventurism with a ruthless hand. Two Fatah leaders who were alleged to have organized an unsuccessful attempt to kill him were executed, an extreme punishment rarely meted out by the PLO. In April 1978, when Abu Daoud, a former BSO leader who had several hundred Fatah guerrillas under his command in southern Lebanon, wanted to ignore Arafat and continue fighting the Israelis and the UN forces, Abu Iyad, politically reconciled to Arafat and his PLO policies, loyally attacked Abu Daoud's group, killing three, wounding several, and capturing almost one hundred guerrillas. Abu Daoud was thus brought to heel. In June several DPF leaders in Lebanon were kidnapped by Abu Iyad's vengeance squad and executed.

The dissident groups opposing Arafat were headed by Hawatmeh's DPF and four Iraqi-based groups. No compromise was found. Arafat remained determined to impose his authority whenever possible, especially in Lebanon. On 15 July a unit of PLF guerrillas led by Hassan Abu Abbas seized fifty-one UN soldiers manning roadblocks. The following day a PLO unit descended upon El Buss, the village where the UN men were being held. In the fighting at least seven PLF members were killed, and many wounded. The UN soldiers were released. On 16 July a grenade was thrown through the window of the offices of the ALF near Beirut, killing two of its members and wounding six. It was Abu Iyad's Squad 17 swinging into action. At a full meeting of the Central Committee of the PLO held in Damascus on 17 and 18 July, differing opinions were aired, but no compromise solutions were found.

Meanwhile, in London, after the killing of Abdul Razzak al-Nauf, the former Yemeni premier, on 9 July, the British government deported eleven Iraqis—five diplomats, including the military attaché, and six employees of Iraqi concerns. In retaliation twelve British diplomatic and other personnel were ejected from Iraq. The British authorities had been reluctant to take such an extreme step, which broke up the Iraqi intelligence and terrorist rings in London. They had been content to let them think they were safely underground, while the British knew exactly where to lay their hands on any particular terrorist whenever that might be necessary. Pressure had been brought to bear by certain Arab states, including Saudi Arabia, on the British government to take this step.

Because of the tense situation in London caused by terrorist acts in the capital, the Tripartite Talks due to be held at the Churchill Hotel in July 1978, were suddenly switched to Leeds Castle in Kent, a medieval castle surrounded by a moat, and more suitable for tight security measures. These talks were attended by U.S. Secretary of State Cyrus Vance, Egyptian Foreign Minister Mohammed Ibrahim Kamel, and Israeli Foreign Minister Moshe Dayan. Dayan's caustic remarks about the necessity for the sudden change of venue and the strict security precautions were hardly deserved, as subsequent events showed.

On 16 July Fatah issued pamphlets calling Iraqi Foreign Minister Saddam Hussein Takriti, thought by Arafat to be the guiding hand behind the underground campaign against him, a "professional killer" and comparing him to Menachem Begin and his IZL terrorist organization of British Mandate times. Fatah threatened to retaliate in kind and moved into action the following day, the 17th, when rockets were fired at the Iraqi embassy in Beirut. Other incidents followed, and on the 24th a bomb exploded outside the Iraqi embassy in Brussels. In London, on the 28th, a bomb exploded under the automobile of the Iraqi ambassador, and two people were injured. A Fatah woman named as Khloud al-Maghrabi was caught by a passerby, and later another Arab, named as Abu Naama Mahmoud, was arrested in connection with this exploit.

Paris suddenly became a terrorist battleground when on 31 July 1978 two PLO terrorists walked into the Iraqi embassy about 1000 hours. One asked for the office of the military attaché and walked upstairs to it. The Iraqi ambassador was absent, officially saying farewell at the Elysée Palace, as his tour of duty in France was ending. The other terrorist remained in the entrance hall, and after a few seconds fired a burst from his automatic weapon. He then dashed from the building to escape into the Metro underground system. The first terrorist took eight people hostage and barricaded himself on the first floor of the embassy. Police cordoned off the area, and negotiations began. The terrorist demanded the release of Khloud al-Maghrabi, the Fatah woman arrested in London, an aircraft to pick her up, and a safe-conduct for both. He set a deadline at 1600 hours, after which he threatened he would shoot the hostages if the demands were not met. The Iraqi ambassador returned and was joined by other Arab ambassadors while senior Arab diplomats met in the Paris Arab League office.

The terrorist agreed to surrender at about 1800 hours, and as he was being taken from the embassy by the police shots were deliberately fired at him by Iraqi security guards. One shot missed the target and killed the policeman next to him. A shoot-out flared up in which one Iraqi security guard was killed and three others arrested.Until that moment the Iraqi embassy staff had been fully cooperating with the French police. The police chief in charge at the scene said, "It is clear we fell into an ambush. The Iraqi security guard wanted to kill the terrorist at all costs, even if it meant taking the lives of French policemen." The three arrested Iraqis, who all had diplomatic immunity, were simply deported.

Reaction to this Abu Iyad–organized exploit came swiftly, and at about 1030 hours on 3 August 1978 two Black June terrorists forced their way into the Paris PLO office. The two French policemen on duty at the entrance did not notice anything unusual and let them pass. That day many Paris policemen were attending the funeral of their colleague, who had been killed on 31 July. The two terrorists went to the third floor of the building and ordered the people they found in a waiting room to go into another room as hostages. They then entered the office of Ezzedine Kalak, the PLO representative who had been in charge in Paris since 1973, when Mohammed Hamshari was killed by the Israeli Mossad, and shot him dead. At least one grenade was exploded, fatally wounding Hamad Abdan, an Iraqi consul general. One of the terrorists tried to get away, but was held by PLO security men, while the other escaped to an upper floor, where after a couple of hours he surrendered to the police. The captured men were named as Abdul Kader Hatem and Assad Kayed, both students. They admitted to belonging to Abu Nidal's Fatah Revolutionary Council — which, of course, produced the Black June movement.

There was still opposition to Arafat in Lebanon, and on 2 August, when he returned from visiting the World Youth Festival in Cuba, he ordered Abu Iyad to curb the dissident PLF elements that were cooperating with the PFLP in the Badawi refugee camp. On the 3rd, using mortars and automatic weapons, PLO units attacked the camp, and the PLF lost at least thirty-five killed and fifty wounded in the fighting.

This terrorist vendetta reached out to Pakistan, where on 2 August, in Karachi, two PLO gunmen on a motorcycle tried to follow an official automobile, in which they thought the Iraqi consul general was traveling, through the gates of the Iraqi consulate. When they were stopped by the policeman on duty, they fired at the automobile ineffectively, and also at the policeman, wounding him. The policeman then bayoneted one of the terrorists to death. The other terrorist was captured; his name was given as Toha Ahmed.

There was a quick reaction by the Iraqis, and on 5 August two Black June members attacked the PLO headquarters at Islamabad, killing three Palestinians and a policeman. The PLO representative accused the Iraqi government of organizing this exploit, saying that the weapons used had been supplied to the terrorists by the Iraqi embassy in Islamabad. On the 13th the Pakistani authorities arrested two suspects, and four more on the 16th. Responsibility was claimed by the Black June and September movement.

Back in Lebanon, on 13 August, the second anniversary of the fall of the Palestinian-held Tel Zaatar refugee camp in Beirut, there was a terrific explosion that completely demolished a nine-story building and killed over one hundred people. It occurred only one hour after the end of a three-day meeting of the Central Committee of the PLF in the building, which also housed a small element of Fatah. Fatah blamed the Israeli Mossad, but others thought it was the Jabril Front.

The vendetta continued, and on 17 August an employee at the Iraqi embassy in Libya, Hussain Mohammed Ali, was killed by a member of Abu Nidal's group. When this happened, Colonel Gaddafi came down heavily on all Fedayeen elements in his country. Tired of their perpetual squabbling, he forced them all, regardless of which organization they belonged to, to merge together under close Libyan surveillance. All terrorists had to account for their movements, arms, and ammunition, and instructions could only be given to them through the Libyan-controlled secretariat. No other external communication was allowed, not even with their own group headquarters. For the time being this smothered the underground Fedayeen struggle in Libya.

However, Abu Nidal was beginning to appreciate what a wasps' nest he had aroused by his vindictive vendetta against Arafat. He had now become the hunted instead of the hunter, so through the medium of the Algerian ambassador to Lebanon he held out an olive branch to Arafat. This was coldly ignored, so Abu Iyad's Squad 17 continued with its deadly work. On 27 August shots were fired at night at the house of a senior Iraqi diplomat in London. An interesting facet came to light on 24 August in London, when two men, a father and son, were remanded in police custody, accused of attempting to kidnap a former Libyan ambassador.

They were also charged with possessing a "clinical lance, adapted to discharge noxious gas." It looked as though a new extension of terrorism was being tried out.

Concurrently with this twilight war there was a spasmodic campaign of letter bombs in which both factions were involved. Beginning in January 1978, the French police intercepted some that had been posted in Strasbourg and were addressed to the Egyptian and Syrian embassies in Paris. There were others at irregular intervals. For example, on 11 September 1978 one letter bomb was received at the Iraqi embassy in London, but was detected in time and defused. It was said to be the third such bomb received at that embassy in two months. A few days later, another letter bomb was received at the Iraqi embassy in Bonn.

There was also another campaign of assassination in progress in Syria at the same time, in which dissident elements of the large Shia community assassinated leaders and prominent personalities drawn from the smaller (15 percent of the population) Alawites, a sect that held a very high proportion of top jobs. In February 1978 an attempt had been made on the life of Rafat Assad, the president's brother, and in March, when the body of a prominent Alawite was discovered in the northern military region, it was admitted that within the space of a month over twenty Alawites had been killed. The Shia terrorists objected to the presence of Soviet advisers, technicians, and military personnel in Syria, mainly on religious grounds. A number (perhaps almost a dozen) of senior Soviet military officers also had died in unusual circumstances, such as road accidents, within the space of twelve months.

The Soviet government saw that the Fedayeen movement was tearing itself to pieces and felt that if it became too badly shattered it would disintegrate and disappear from the Middle Eastern scene. If the Fedayeen disappeared, so also might the Palestine problem. Accordingly, the Soviet government stepped in, both to save the Fedayeen and to make it into an effective Soviet instrument to counter U.S. influence in that region.

Yasir Arafat and other Fatah leaders were summoned to Moscow in August 1978, and the leaders of the Rejection Front groups went to Cuba, where Premier Castro was cooperating with the Soviets on this project. The Fedayeen leaders of all persuasions were told that Soviet pressure would be heavily brought to bear unless they all agreed to unite and stay united. They were told that the Soviet government would help them reorganize all their military elements into the Army and Armed Forces of the Palestine Revolution, which was to come under the direct control of the Central Committee of the PLO. Arafat, as chairman of the PLO, would retain his power and his title of Commander-in-Chief, of which he was so proud, and he would be strongly backed by the Soviet government.

Arafat, Habash, and Hawatmeh, the three key leaders, agreed to the Soviet proposals, and Arafat and Habash issued a joint statement to that effect. It was their first joint statement for four years. The Central Committee of the PLO was to be enlarged to 290 members, of which about one-third would be from Fatah and about one-third from the other Fedayeen groups, and about one-third were to be nominated Palestinian personalities. Arafat still hopes he will be able to establish a Palestinian government on the West Bank one day through talks with the Israelis, and perhaps the Soviet government might like to be involved in this project. But talks are peaceful means, and the rejection states are still firmly against such a course. The problem for the Soviets will be to persuade them to agree and unite.

17 The Terrorist Profile

To be a successful terrorist a university degree is almost mandatory.

THE SUCCESSFUL MODERN terrorist is no ordinary person. He possesses special motivation, characteristics, and qualities. First of all he must have a political belief or cause—otherwise, if he uses terrorism for personal material gain, he is simply a common criminal. Political causes a would-be terrorist could adopt, or be converted to, broadly fall into three categories. The first is to work for world revolution, to destroy the existing framework of governments, law, and order, and to impose a certain political philosophy on one and all, eliminating or forcibly converting those who resist.

The second category consists of those who wish to force their own extreme political philosophy, be it of the left or the right, on their own country. It includes the Red Brigades and the NAP in Italy, the Baader-Meinhof Gang in West Germany, GRAPO and FRAP in Spain, the Tupermaros in Uruguay, and the Montoneros in Argentina.

The third category can be broadly described as liberation movements—countries, races, or groups of people struggling to free themselves from unwelcome and unwanted governments.

A variation on these three categories is an ideological clash over some material fact such as territory. When one side is militarily weak, it may resort to terrorism to gain its end. This is the root of the Palestine problem, where a militarily strong Israel has occupied and is firmly ensconced in territory which the Palestinians believe is their homeland and from which they were ejected by military force.

Another variation is the clash of rival ideologies, usually between those of right-wing and those of left-wing persuasions, as is the case in Spain, Italy, and Argentina. Yet another motivation for terrorism is the splintering of political groups, usually over obscure

299

points of doctrine, such as the Baath Party in the Middle East, which, supported by the Iraqi government and the Saiqa organization, overthrew Abu Nidal's Fatah Revolutionary Council, supported by the Syrian government.

Once dedicated to his particular cause, the terrorist must become active in its service, to the extent of risking, and even giving, his life, if required. He must become a Fedayeen, a Man of Sacrifice. Many terrorists, keyed up with martyrlike fervor, have deliberately set out with the intention of dying gloriously in a terrorist exploit. To be successful, a terrorist cannot be a casual or part-time mercenary, willing only to operate when it suits his convenience or his pocket. The terrorist mounts a tiger and cannot dismount. Dedication also implies absolute obedience to the leader of the political movement.

The would-be terrorist must have a high degree of personal bravery, as he has to face the risk of death, injury, imprisonment, or even torture if captured. A few terrorists become kamikaze-conditioned, like those in the JRA, even to the extent of taking an explosive device onto an aircraft to explode it, causing a crash that kills all on board, including themselves. However, not all terrorists fall into that elite category, and many are of lesser, more average caliber. It has been estimated that about 80 percent of all terrorist acts involve explosions: throwing bombs, firing rockets, setting booby-traps, or igniting explosives by electronic remote control or a timing device. Such explosions produce fear, even panic, in victims and bystanders, while at the same time ensuring the maximum security for the perpetrator.

The would-be terrorist must be devoid of the human emotions of pity and remorse, as so few of us are, since his victims will include innocent men, women, and children. He must have the "killer instinct," not only able to kill, but able to shoot a person at a certain time and place, or on the receipt of a signal or code word, without hesitation or squeamishness. Many can kill in the heat of anger or battle, but few can do so in cold blood.

The would-be terrorist must have a fairly high standard of intelligence, as he has to collect, collate, and assess information, devise and put into operation complicated plans, and always keep one step ahead of the police, security forces, rival groups, and hostile intelligence services. He must also have a fairly high degree of sophistication, no matter what his race or nationality, so as to be able to travel first class on airliners, stay at first-class hotels, and be able to mix with the international executive set without seeming out of place. If he becomes conspicuous, he automatically becomes suspect.

The would-be terrorist must be reasonably well educated, and possess a fair share of general knowledge. He should be able to speak English, which is almost an international language for the educated, and one other major language, so as to be able to mix generally and make himself understood. He must also be able to understand what others are saying—perhaps about him. To be a successful terrorist, a university degree is almost mandatory.

All terrorists do not measure up to these high standards, but the leaders, planners, couriers, liaison officers, and activists must, if they wish to operate successfully and still retain their precarious freedom. There is, of course, a place in terrorism for the less well educated and the less urbane, but it is a minor one. In short, there is no place in a successful terrorist organization for the old-time gunman or mindless thug. Organizations that recruit such types are soon decimated by the security forces, are eliminated by their rivals, or just disintegrate.

Pointedly, perhaps, in these days of recognition of the equality of women, the terrorist need not be a man. In fact, many female terrorists are more determined and deadly than their male colleagues. For example, twelve out of the original twenty-two founder-members of the Baader-Meinhof Gang were women, as were about up to 50 percent of the JRA members. In most of the small terrorist teams that have committed exploits during the last decade, frequently at least one member was a woman, who was sometimes the leader. Gabriele Kroecher-Tiedeman, for example, killed two people in the raid on the OPEC headquarters in December 1975 and was arrested in a shoot-out with Swiss customs officials in August 1978. Another was Ulrike Meinhof, who led a raid that released Andreas Baader from German detention. Margarita Cargol led a raid that released her husband, Renato Curcio, leader of the Red Brigades, from Italian police custody, and was herself later killed in a shoot-out with the police.

Juliene Plambeck was alleged to have been involved in the murder of Judge Drenkmann. Monika Berberich carried out bank robberies for the Baader-Meinhof Gang that brought in about $100,000 within a very few months. In June 1977 two teenage female members of the Red Brigades ambushed and shot a university professor on the steps of his flat in Rome. The two female companions of Antonio Lo Musico, leader of the NAP, took pistols from their handbags and joined in the fight with the police in Rome who killed him in a gun battle. And remember Leila Khalid, the Arab woman who achieved notoriety for unsuccessfully leading a PFLP hijacking team and was arrested and held in London for a while. Because they were successful, other Arab women who led terrorist exploits remain unnamed. There can be no doubt the female terrorist can be as resolute, ruthless, and efficient as any male.

Additionally, certain assets and conditions must be favorable to allow the terrorist to operate successfully. The four most important of these are money, sanctuary, support, and publicity. With money the terrorist can usually buy all his material requirements, such as weapons, ammunition, explosives, informants, safehouses, agents, clothing, food, and transportation. Also, he can obtain silence, cooperation, or noncooperation by bribery. If he has money in sufficient amounts, there are few things he cannot buy. Terrorists generally subscribe to the theory that all men have their price and all material objects their market value.

Terrorists do not care how they obtain money. Their methods tend to fall into three categories: intimidation, kidnapping hostages for ransom money, and plain bank robbery. All these are criminal offenses, but the terrorist does not regard himself as a common criminal by committing them, believing that the end is more important than the means. Many terrorist organizations use all three methods, or variations of them, as the opportunity arises.

Terrorist organizations may obtain money by intimidation, or persuading unwilling victims to make contributions and gifts. The group that has excelled in this method is Fatah, the largest associated with the Palestinians. The three million Palestinian refugees were captive donors in the sense that the majority of them had little mobility and could not escape from the insistent demands of the Fatah fund raisers. They gave their mite reluctantly and fearfully whenever Fatah agents took their collecting boxes into refugee camps and villages. Palestinians of more substance, such as merchants, farmers, and shopkeepers, were intimidated into giving more generously. This method, a sort of political protection racket, funded Fatah in its early years and was its financial mainstay during 1969 and 1970, until it developed other means of obtaining money.

During those two years, Fatah military and political fortunes fell, and with them their financial standing. Certain sums of money were deliberately withheld in the hope of bringing the Fedayeen groups to heel or pointing their terrorism in a certain direction. All in all, the donations from Arab states were unreliable, uncertain, and politically loaded. In July 1971 the PNC bitterly complained that of the $30 million promised by the Arab states to the PLO, only $120,000 had been received (from Qatar) during the previous twelve months. However, PLO fortunes perked up in 1972 and 1973.

As early as 20 January 1973, an unidentified Arab appeared on West German television to state that the BSO was annually receiving a total of about $80 million, the main contributors being Libya ($30 million), Saudi Arabia ($15 million), the Gulf states ($15 million), and Algeria ($5 million); there were other smaller contributors. The unknown Arab spokesman also said that Colonel Gaddafi gave the BSO $5 million for the Munich Massacre.

Arafat had the intimidation aspect of fund raising down to a fine art, and he organized it further. About 300,000 Palestinians worked in adjacent Arab states as engineers, doctors, teachers, scientists, technicians, and semiskilled laborers, many in booming oilfields such as Kuwait's. Arafat managed to persuade these Arab governments to deduct 5 percent of their salaries at the source and hand it over to him, which brought the PLO over $10 million annually for several years, considerably helping his PLO umbrella organization to survive a lean period of financial difficulty.

Having experienced a period of poverty, Arafat appreciated the need for money to give him freedom to pursue his political activities, and Fatah, his own organization, began to develop business ventures, many of which became profitable, such as chicken farming in Syria. Sometime in the mid-1970s Fatah also began to dabble in drug growing and drug smuggling into Europe. The drugs such as hashish, were grown on Fatah farms in Turkey and northern Lebanon. The drug trade brought several million dollars annually into Fatah coffers.

After the October War of 1973, Arafat became "respectable and responsible" and was supported financially by Arab states to a greater extent, especially by the conservative nations. It was an open secret that the total amount received from them in 1977 exceeded $70 million. *Time* magazine alleged in July 1977 that the PLO was "probably the richest, best financed revolutionary-terrorist organization in history" and had at least $60 million invested in U.S. business concerns, the assets being held either in numbered accounts or under false names to prevent discovery by the Mossad to avoid Israeli depredations. A Christian Lebanese newspaper printed in Beirut, *Al Ahrar,* gave an extremely high estimate of the wealth of Fatah on 24 June 1977, stating it was in the region of $4,400 million, the greater part in British securities or banks. This estimate was perhaps too high, but there was no doubt that Fatah finances were in an extremely healthy state. These sound Fatah assets enabled the PLO to care for the some four thousand Fedayeen disabled in action, to pay for staff for its offices in about one hundred countries, and to finance the Fedayeen war effort in the War in the Lebanon of 1975–78.

Despite a lax accounting system, as most of the PLO leaders and their followers led a simple, ascetic life, there was little evidence of theft, misappropriation, or fraud from within. When such incidents were detected, usually of a comparatively minor nature, the culprits were harshly punished by detention in PLO prison camps. In this respect Fatah was more lenient than some guerrilla groups, which executed members caught misappropriating group funds.

The second method of raising money for terrorism is by kidnapping persons of substance and holding them for ransom. Strictly speaking this is a criminal act, as opposed to holding people hostage for the safe-conduct of terrorists or the release of political prisoners held by governments; but in terrorist philosophy it is a political expediency. This practice has become common in several South American and European countries. Indeed, in Italy, kidnappings for ransom have averaged over one a week, bringing almost $2 million to the terrorists annually. Although the sums paid for the safe return of a kidnapped person have not always been large, some have been outstandingly high. The record for Italy stands at $15 million, while $3 million was demanded for the ransom of a wealthy duke, and $1 million for the president of the law faculty of Rome University. In Italy, not only have people been kidnapped for ransom, but this practice has on occasions been extended to include valuable works of art, a race horse, an Afghan hound, and even corpses. It also seems that business can be business in the world of terrorism as well as in the market place. In November 1976, when a Florentine industrialist was kidnapped, his captors released him on partial payment of the ransom demanded; the remainder was to be paid in installments.

Governments are not immune from paying out ransom. In February 1972, when the PFLP hijacked a Lufthansa airliner and flew it to Aden to hold the aircraft and crew for ransom, the West German government authorized the chairman of Lufthansa to pay the $5 million demanded. In September 1974 the Dutch government paid $300,000 for the safety of its nationals, although this was recovered. In the OPEC kidnapping incident of December 1975, the governments of Saudi Arabia and Iran each paid out $25 million for the safe release of their oil ministers. Of this reputed sum, $20 million went to the PLO and $5 million to Carlos, the international mercenary employed by the PFLP. It would be of interest to know how much he was allowed to keep for himself and how much he had to hand over to the PFLP.

Terrorist groups in South America rely to a large extent upon ransom for their financial stability, and indeed the Montoneros of Argentina hold the record. In September 1974 they kidnapped Juan and Jorge Born, two owner-executives of one of Argentina's largest business corporations. The Born ransom was estimated to be $60 million, plus another million dollars for food for the poor. In Argentina, Charles Lockwood, a British industrialist, was kidnapped twice, paying total ransom for his freedom estimated to be in the region of $10 million.

Perhaps the most common method of obtaining cash, especially by the smaller terrorist groups, has been that of simply robbing a bank. Some have specialized in this method, such as the Baader-Meinhof Gang in West Germany. In Argentina, the Montoneros have obtained large sums of money both from kidnapping and bank robberies. Other notorious groups have obtained money by mugging, as well as from blackmail. In Argentina a scandal known as the Graiver Affair blew up when it was alleged that David Graiver, an Argentinian financier, faked his own death in August 1974 by causing a plane in which he was supposed to be traveling to crash into a mountainside near Mexico City. One of the bodies found in the wreckage was supposedly identified as being his. This scandal brought to light allegations that large sums of money, obtained by the Montoneros and other Argentinian organizations by kidnappings and bank robberies, had been invested in banks, businesses, government bonds, industry, and real estate, and that several prominent bankers and financiers had handled this money, with Graiver acting as the middleman, all knowing it to be "hot."

306 / Language of Violence

Occasionally, a paymaster extraordinary appears who is prepared to buy political violence. Such a man is Colonel Gaddafi of Libya, who is dedicated to the destruction of Israel. As his military means are too puny even to contemplate achieving his objective by war, he has hired terrorists for the purpose. The Israelis allege that for some time Gaddafi has been paying selected terrorists organizations a total of $73 million annually. Additionally, he gives bonus payments for successful terrorist exploits, such as the $5 million he gave to the BSO for its Munich Massacre exploit. Gaddafi obviously believes in rewarding terrorist productivity.

Gaddafi has tried to persuade the active Palestinian terrorist organizations to act according to his wishes, but found that although they were willing to take his money and accept any facilities he offered them, they have minds of their own and go their own way. This led Gaddafi, in mid-1974, to form his own terrorist group, NAY, into which he tried to entice the best international terrorists by offering them large sums of money. He has only had moderate success. Even in terrorism money cannot buy everything.

The other essential a successful terrorist must have is sanctuary, even if only occasionally; a place where he can rest, recoup, plan, train, and from which he can operate. Otherwise he is forever on the run, always looking over his shoulder. Without a sanctuary he perpetually risks identification and arrest, even years after an exploit. For example, Astrid Proll, of the Baader-Meinhof Gang, who had disappeared from sight for over four years, was caught and arrested in England in September 1978 and extradited for trial to West Germany. Psychologically, this tension plays on the nerves of a terrorist. Everyone, including dedicated top-class terrorists, has a breaking point, and many terrorists commit suicide—perhaps far more than is realized, as some simply disappear and are never heard of again. This is a factor perhaps not sufficiently appreciated by governments and their security forces. This tension snapping was demonstrated by the Israeli Mossad killers who were turned loose to hunt down and kill the BSO members involved in the Munich Massacre. Despite their fine qualities and dedication, the Israeli killers began to crack up after about six months in the field and had to be replaced by other operators. The terrorist groups are not able to replace their members as easily.

Few countries can exist in complete isolation, and because they have diplomatic, trade, and other relations with other countries, almost all are unwilling to give terrorists sanctuary. A few states have gained a dubious reputation for harboring terrorists, particularly in the Middle East—for example, Libya, Syria, Kuwait, and the Yemens—but a closer examination of each known case shows that this facility was selectively and often grudgingly given. The South Yemen government has allowed a few terrorist groups of its own Marxist persuasion to occupy camps openly, in which the terrorists can rest, plan, and train in complete security from retribution, but this is the exception that proves the rule.

Many countries give political asylum to exiles if their governments are hostile to the exile's regime. For example, Kenya and Uganda harbor each other's political discontents, as do Ethiopia and the Sudan, Libya and Egypt, Syria and Iraq, America and Cuba, and so on. Although political asylum is given in such circumstances fairly frequently, the harbored exiles have to conform to the host government's conditions, which usually involve remaining politically inactive. Otherwise they risk detention and deportation. Very few states in the world today allow their territory to be used as a terrorist base, and those that do blandly and officially deny the fact.

Terrorist groups have extreme difficulty existing without some popular support from either a country or a section of a population that sympathizes with their political ideals and aims sufficiently to help, or at least not to hinder, their activities. At one stage it was estimated by the West German police that the Baader-Meinhof Gang had about ten thousand passive supporters in West Germany who, doubtless within limits, were willing to provide money, safehouses, and information. The ideal for a terrorist group is to find a host country that will give vocal support to its aims, as is the case with the Republic of Ireland and the IRA.

The Palestinian terrorist groups are fortunate in this respect, as they shelter under the wide umbrella of Fedayeen ideals, which are hostile to Israel, the declared enemy of the Arabs. All Arab governments must give verbal and moral support to all anti-Israeli terrorists, and even though some governments mildly condemn the atrocity itself, they praise the ideal behind it. In the first excited flush of the Fedayeen movement, Arab countries were only too willing to allow Arab hijackers to land at their airports, and then quietly be allowed to go free. More recently, national interest has obtruded, and one by one this facility has been refused. Even Libya and Kuwait, favorite places for hijacked planes to land at one time, now refuse to accept them and will switch off all navigation and landing lights and even block the runways with vehicles to prevent such landings. Terrorists can soon wear out their welcome in any country, even an Arab one.

A terrorist especially needs publicity to generate and spread his terror, and he needs the media to help him do this. He uses and exploits the media to the fullest. If his deeds are unknown, unspoken, and unrecorded, no one knows about them, and accordingly no one will be intimidated. The terrorists need the media to transmit and disseminate fear and apprehension. If the media writes up their exploits, dramatically emphasizing the gruesome aspects, causing the public to shudder in horror or distaste, the terrorists are smugly satisfied. Without publicity their effectiveness decreases rapidly. Knowing this, the small terrorist groups usually try to carry out newsworthy exploits to put themselves firmly on the world terrorist map. With the PFLP it was the mass hijacking to Revolution Airfield, with the BSO it was the Munich Massacre, with the JRA it was the Lod Massacre, and so on.

In repressive regimes where there is a controlled press, such as the Soviet Union, China, and some of the iron curtain countries, deprived of the advantage of a free press always looking for something exciting to titillate its readers, the terrorist is far less successful. Terrorism occurs in communist countries, but its sting is largely smothered by censorship.

18 The Nuclear Question

Anyone could have done it.
American student who designed a viable nuclear device
in 1975

A ND NOW A few uneasy words on the nuclear question. Will terrorists one day be able to make a
nuclear device, steal one, or take over a nuclear
establishment and threaten a whole city with destruction? In short,
will governments soon have to face up to nuclear blackmail? So far
terrorists have used familiar, conventional weapons such as pistols,
grenades, and explosives for causing death and destruction and
propagating fear. Faced with shortages of natural fuel in the years
ahead, nations that have developed an insatiable appetite for energy to improve or maintain their standards of living, such as France,
are moving quickly into a plutonium economy, which will depend
upon a host of nuclear reactors to provide the required energy.

The world has lived under the dark shadow of a potential
nuclear war for so many years that people have become ostrichlike
about it. Since it has not happened, they have tended to push the
unpleasant possibility to the backs of their minds. Like people who
live near the edge of a dormant volcano, they have forgotten its
terrible potential as time obliterates their awareness of danger.
Others think that only a madman would press the nuclear button
that would destroy whole nations and countries. They are bol-
stered by the belief that sanity must prevail, instead of international suicide. The possibility of a nuclear war seems to have
become less inevitable because of its wholesale destructiveness and
the fact that nations basically want to survive. Some even feel that
a major conventional war itself is less of a possibility nowadays
than ever before because of the possibility of escalation to nuclear
proportions. Accordingly, we are left with selective warfare or
terrorism.

Whenever the question of nuclear terrorism has been raised,
until recently authorities soothingly gave the impression that the

309

odds were firmly against it, as the sophisticated techniques and apparatus required were beyond the capability of all but a few specially trained, high-level scientists. It was claimed that nuclear security was far too good to be breached, and that a terrorist could not simply pick up a nuclear bomb, tuck it under his arm, and walk away with it.

As long as the military were responsible for the nuclear program, strict security was maintained. Each nuclear nation was fearful and jealous lest the slightest scrap of information of any advantage to another nation leak out. The nuclear club was determined to keep its membership select and small. As long as that situation obtained, the possibility of terrorist blackmail was remote.

In broad lay terms, the basic material for a nuclear bomb is uranium, which by itself in its natural state cannot be used to cause an explosion. Raw uranium, sometimes known as Yellowcake, is concentrated uranium oxide. Nuclear reactors process uranium to produce plutonium, which is a by-product of the fission that takes place. Enriched uranium or plutonium is used to cause nuclear explosions. Almost parallel with the development of huge military nuclear arsenals came the spread of nuclear power for peaceful purposes. Nuclear reactors are fueled by non-weapon-grade material—that is, low-grade uranium. A certain amount of nuclear waste is produced and left over, of which about 96 percent is uranium and up to 1 percent plutonium, the remainder being a mixture of highly radioactive isotopes produced by the nuclear fission reaction.

Plutonium, used with the correct proportion of uranium, can reproduce itself rather like baker's yeast. Thus it can not only perpetuate itself continually, but can increase in quantity. The next progression was the fast-breeder reactors, which can be fueled on the separated and reprocessed nuclear waste from nuclear reactors in an endless circle. As there are limits to natural uranium resources in the world, the fast-breeders have become popular from a practical point of view, and have been increasingly adopted by countries looking to nuclear energy to fill the anticipated energy gap as oil reserves run dry. France, for example, which has no natural oil reserves, is planning to become virtually dependent upon nuclear power by 1990.

The spread of nuclear reactors meant that a large number of people were employed in the civilian nuclear industry, bringing an additional security problem. This did not cause much alarm, as it was believed that the plutonium used in, and produced from, nuclear reactors under civilian control was not suitable for use in the manufacture of nuclear bombs. This illusion was shattered on 6 September 1977 when it was revealed that the United States had exploded a nuclear device using low-grade plutonium. It was officially admitted that civilian nuclear reactors could produce the material required to make a nuclear warhead in the range of the 1- to 20-kiloton yield; India had done just that. The essential apparatus was a separating and reprocessing plant.

By mid-1978 there were over one hundred nuclear reactors in some fifteen countries and plans were in hand to introduce them into another sixteen within the next few years. This would mean that within a decade over thirty countries could have a military nuclear potential, provided they additionally possessed, or had the use of, separation and reprocessing plants. Some countries had agreements with other countries for this purpose, such as Japan, which did not have the essential plant, and Britain, which did.

To make a nuclear bomb, terrorists would require the technical knowledge, the material, and the apparatus. The deliberate shroud of mystery and complexity that initially encased the manufacturing of nuclear weapons and the classified technology was gradually penetrated by outsiders. The first real civilian breakthrough in this respect was in 1975, when John Phillips, a physics undergraduate at Princeton University, New Jersey, designed a crude but viable 125-pound nuclear bomb as a summer project, about one-third the yield of those dropped on Japan. It would have required only seven kilograms of plutonium to activate it.

He had gained all his information from unclassified scientific papers, and his explanation was, "It took me about four months to get all the information together, but it was no sweat. When I didn't know something I phoned up the government people, and they told me. Anyone could have done it." There was no doubt that scientific nuclear literature had become prolific and comprehensive. Just previously, in March 1975, another young student, from the Massachusetts Institute of Technology, was seen on television assembling a nuclear device over a five-week period.

The London *Daily Express,* in its issues of 17 and 18 May 1977, told its readers in some detail how to manufacture a nuclear bomb, listing all the essential unclassified literature. It showed a photograph of the nuclear device its researchers had constructed. One of the people involved in producing this feature later told me that only two or three minor details had been altered or omitted, but that otherwise it was an accurate description that could be followed and applied easily by anyone with some scientific knowledge. In view of the spread of scientific nuclear information in unclassified journals, it can no longer be assumed that the techniques of design and manufacture are beyond the comprehension of terrorists, especially those with a university background.

Academic knowledge is one thing, but obtaining the essential fissionable materials—the plutonium or the enriched uranium—is another. Soon over thirty countries will possess the means for the manufacture of a nuclear bomb. With so many countries involved, it is inevitable that the state of security of nuclear establishments will vary from very good, to good, down to indifferent. Many people are (and in the future more will be) employed in the nuclear industry. For example, in 1978 the U.S. Atomic Energy Commission had over twenty-one thousand employees working for six civilian firms at seven nuclear weapon manufacturing sites. Although they will automatically be cleared for security and for general reliability, the uncertain human factor may intrude. Pressure on individual workers by terrorists cannot be ruled out, and some workers may develop extreme political opinions that can be played upon. Some may even become sympathetic to terrorist ideals. A situation could arise when someone on the inside of a nuclear establishment, under some kind of terrorist influence might assist the terrorist to obtain what he wants—plutonium or enriched uranium.

A general impression has been given, and never contradicted officially by authorities until recently, that nuclear materials of all types are extremely dangerous to handle and have to be kept in thick lead containers because of radiation hazards. The fact is that plutonium, although one of the most toxic substances known to man if it enters the human body, can be handled safely with rubber gloves, and its radioactive emissions are only slight. In other words, with simple precautions, plutonium can be easily and safely handled, stored, and transported.

The next disturbing fact is that it is not possible to measure the exact amounts of plutonium or uranium held in a nuclear establishment, as the measuring instruments in use have an error of between 2 and 4 percent. This means there can be no way of knowing for certain at any given moment whether or not any is missing. James Liverman, assistant administrator of environment and safety for the U.S. Energy Research and Development Association, said in July 1977 that "there may be sixty miles of piping in a uranium processing plant, and there could be a lot of material stuck in those pipes." Plutonium rubs off from gloves and garments, there is wastage in drilling processes, and there are plutonium chippings and dust. In fact, there are tiny bits of it everywhere inside a plant.

By 1984 the nonmilitary nuclear reactors in nearly thirty countries are expected to have an annual plutonium output of over thirty thousand kilograms. Think of 2 to 4 percent of that amount being unaccountable, when it takes only thirteen kilograms to produce a 20-kiloton bomb—the same size as that dropped at Hiroshima. In May 1977 the U.S. General Accounting Office told Congress that commercial nuclear facilities in the United States were "not able to account for thousands of pounds of highly enriched plutonium."

The London *Daily Express* of 18 May 1977 reported that "more than 10,000 kilograms of plutonium [are] in circulation in the United States which are not behind the walls of military or police establishments, but in ordinary *private* [the newspaper's italics] industrial premises." Several instances of shortfalls in accounting have been spotlighted and admitted, but so far no nuclear authority has confirmed that any nuclear material has ever been stolen. Small particles of plutonium and enriched uranium inside nuclear reactor plants could conceivably be collected secretly and taken out.

Assuming a terrorist possessed the necessary knowledge and had somehow obtained plutonium or enriched uranium, would he be able to assemble a nuclear bomb? Nuclear plants are usually of gigantic size, sheltered behind high walls or metal fences, and guarded by security personnel. This gives the impression that a nuclear bomb could not be assembled in a small shed. There is considerable misconception over this. Professor John Fremlin, giving evidence before the British Windscale Inquiry on 30 September 1977, said, "If terrorists want plutonium to make bombs with, all they need to do is to build a small, much cheaper reactor specifically for that purpose. It isn't difficult. Enrico Fermi did it in a squash court in Chicago in 1942, when he built the world's first nuclear reactor."

A report of the American government's Office of Technology to Congress stated that "a less than sophisticated group of terrorists could build a crude nuclear device with only modest machine shop facilities." He added, "A small group without access to classified literature could design and build a nuclear device." In short, the terrorist's finished product, which he could assemble in a small workshop or garage, might be about the size of a tea chest, weigh a half ton, and could be transported on a small truck. Therefore, it is possible for terrorists to manufacture a crude but workable nuclear device. However, there is a caution from an expert, Professor Jo Rotblat, who worked on the original Manhattan Project and was the only scientist to pull out on moral grounds before the first atomic bomb was exploded. Giving evidence before the British Windscale Inquiry, he said, "It would take a very brave and skilled terrorist to make a bomb from stolen plutonium. The chances that he would survive to explode the bomb, when and where he wanted, would be about 50 percent. If a terrorist really wanted a nuclear bomb, he would be better advised to steal a ready-made one." If that is so, what are his chances of doing just that?

On 16 October 1973 the U.S. Department of Defense admitted to possessing 7,042 strategic multimegaton nuclear warheads and bombs. While the locations in which they were stockpiled remained secret, it was common knowledge they were scattered across Europe, the Pacific, and Southeast Asia. However, the terrorist would no doubt ignore such monsters as being too heavy, cumbersome, and complicated to trigger off, but would be much more interested in the smaller nuclear weapons, such as shells and land mines, which the United States possesses in quantity, and which are easier to transport.

Nuclear weapons would be at their most vulnerable while being transported from one place to another. American methods of transporting nuclear weapons, and their routes, are reputed to be randomly chosen by computer to preserve secrecy until the last moment. Obviously, at certain points they might be open to hijacking or ambush tactics. Also vulnerable while in transit are the large quantities of nuclear waste on their way from the reactors to the separation and reprocessing plants, and likewise on their return journey as plutonium and enriched uranium.

The London *Daily Express* of 18 May 1977 suggested an ideal site for such an ambush: a deserted road between Inverness and Thurso in Scotland, two miles from the nearest village and only ten miles from a small, little–used harbor. Nuclear material might be seized in transit to and from the Scottish fast-breeder reactor complex at Dounreay.

With terrorists being able to intimidate, bribe, or threaten nuclear employees to help them, we cannot say it will not be possible for a nuclear weapon to be stolen. Even if a terrorist does not have a nuclear device, he can say he has one, and with such poor accountability one could not be sure whether he did or not.

Obviously countermeasures have to be considered to prevent nuclear terrorism, and they tend to hinge on security restrictions and surveillance of personnel employed at nuclear establishments. Clearly, as such staff are susceptible to terrorist blackmail, it would mean that not only would they have to be carefully selected initially and screened for their political views, but that they would have to be kept under surveillance continually. This would include opening private mail, telephone tapping, checking on private bank accounts, and the use of informers. One of the objects of terrorism is to make the state so repressive that it will be regarded as fascist and dictatorial, and thus cause its citizens to turn against their regime. The restrictions on the plutonium economy may be the path to a police state.

Bad though the nuclear terrorist scene may seem, there may be worse in store if terrorists explore other means. Professor Jo Rotblat said, "I can think of several ways in which a terrorist in Britain could kill 1,000 people, but I am not going to tell you what they are." Let us optimistically hope terrorists will never acquire Professor Rotblat's knowledge, which presumably embraces bacteriological and chemical warfare, which, if selectively applied, could be even more devastating than nuclear terrorism.

19 Thoughts on Countermeasures

One man's terrorist is another man's freedom fighter.

IN 1603 GUY FAWKES required thirty-six barrels of gunpowder for his project, which was to blow up the British Houses of Parliament. One can imagine his problem in those horse-and-cart days in getting that number of cumbersome barrels secretly by night into the cellars below the building. It is no wonder he was detected in time and arrested. It is not like that any more. Since those far-off days science has come to the aid of the terrorist, who can travel light, carrying small, easily concealed automatic weapons, malleable plastic explosive material with detonators as small as match sticks and batteries as small as shirt buttons, and a whole array of James Bond-like gadgets of death and destruction. If he does not want to travel at all, he can send letter bombs by post. The better educated and more intelligent terrorist has been quick to add science and sophistication to his armory.

Governments and their security forces, especially those of the Western democracies, have been slow to grasp and grapple with the problem of terrorism, and in particular they have been slow to recognize political terrorism for what it is and to devise counters for it. Political terrorism, especially international terrorism is a form of selective warfare mounted against a government, and as in any wartime situation, concentrated and combined efforts are required to contain and defeat it. Governments and their security forces are still halfheartedly fumbling in the dark, many hoping that procrastination will cause the specter of terror to vanish.

So far countermeasures seem to fall into three broad categories, which can be classified as personal security, intelligence, and punishment. Personal security includes visible and obvious precautions taken against probable terrorist attacks, their open thoroughness being a deterrent. Perhaps the most familiar to most

317

people today is the search they undergo at international airports before they are allowed to travel by air. Prior to 1970, apart from customs examinations at airports, which only lightly touched the majority of travelers, thorough searching of passengers and their luggage en masse was the exception rather than the general rule. After the two explosions that occurred in the luggage compartment of two aircraft in flight on 21 February 1970, the Israelis took the hint and affixed armor plating inside their aircraft luggage compartments and also in the pilot's cabin. The weight of the armor plating meant a compensating loss of payload, but this was accepted in the interests of safety. A number of international airports purchased equipment to X-ray luggage, but they were slow to bring it into use, and lax in its employment. The PFLP hijackers of the four airliners on Skyjack Sunday, 6 September 1970, had all managed to board their aircraft with their weapons and grenades after passing through only perfunctory customs examinations.

As terrorist activity increased rather than declined, more sophisticated electronic detection apparatus was introduced. The searchers still tended to concentrate upon the person and the hand luggage, the heavier luggage being largely ignored. As late as 28 May 1972, in fact, the PFLP sent a woman decoy with two pistols concealed in her clothing through the newly installed detector screen at Rome airport to test it. She was detected and arrested. This told the PFLP exactly what it wanted to know. Two days later the JRA killers on their way to commit the Lod Massacre, passed through the same detector screens "clean," indicating they had no weapons on them. Instead, they had placed their weapons, ammunition, and grenades in their heavy luggage, which was taken from them and put on the aircraft without being examined.

There is no doubt that searching passengers' hand luggage, and their heavy luggage also, proved to be a very effective countermeasure. One problem was that the thoroughness of the search tended to vary from country to country, and even from time to time within a country, and in lulls between terrorist activity they tended to be less painstaking.

In the eary 1970s, for example, the airport at Beirut was considered by airline pilots to be a black spot. It was alleged there were many terrorist sympathizers on the airport staff. Several terrorists admitted that arms and explosives had been placed on board an aircraft for them before they boarded while they themselves passed through the security searches without exciting suspicion.

Unusual or unexpected occurrences sometimes cause laxity in security, and on 27 June 1976 the four terrorists who were to hijack the French Airbus and divert it to Entebbe stopped over at Athens airport for several hours to change aircraft. As there happened to be a strike of airport staff at the time, the terrorists were able to move freely from one plane to another, together with their weapons and explosives, without being searched or detected. It was the constant complaint by some airlines whose own countries conducted rigorous searches of passengers and their luggage that passengers who boarded aircraft at stopovers were not always subjected to the same strict procedure. After the Entebbe hijack, on 2 July, the El Al manager at Athens airport claimed that his was the only airline at the airport that searched both passengers and their luggage. Indeed, Athens was one of those airports that had a poor reputation with airline pilots.

As terrorist incidents continued, security staffs were increased and control of personnel at airports became more strict. Everyone who came onto airport premises, including staff, had to be identified. Even pilots and air crews were searched before being allowed through barriers. Airport buildings and aircraft were periodically searched by security staff, and any article of unattended luggage was regarded with deep suspicion. A loophole was created by passengers who claimed diplomatic immunity, which meant that they and their luggage were immune from search. There were constant allegations that the diplomatic bags of certain countries, also immune from customs and other examination, were used to transport weapons and explosives for terrorist use. Hans-Joachim Klein, who was wounded in the raid led by Carlos on the OPEC headquarters in Vienna in December 1975, said in an interview printed in the West German periodical *Der Spiegel* on 6 August 1978 that "I picked up a very large diplomatic bag stuffed with weapons, which an ambassador had hauled through Rome customs, at the ambassador's private residence in Vienna."

Security at airports was a matter of extreme interest to terrorists, who obviously selected airports where poor security measures were in force. They would often spend days or even weeks monitoring security arrangements at the airports they intended to use. On 28 September 1977 five JRA terrorists used Bombay airport to board a Japanese Airlines DC-8, which they hijacked to Dacca, Bangladesh. The allegation was that they had boarded the aircraft with their weapons without being properly searched, and although this was indignantly denied by the Indian authorities, it was later revealed that members of the JRA had kept Bombay airport under close surveillance for over three weeks beforehand.

After the hijacking of a Lufthansa airliner to Somalia in October 1977, the West German government insisted upon sending members of its GSG-9 antiterrorist force to thirteen international airports considered to have lax security arrangements. The men were unarmed, wore Lufthansa uniforms, and worked in the Lufthansa area of the airports in Accra, Algiers, Baghdad, Barcelona, Bombay, Dakar, Istanbul, Jeddah, Karachi, Lagos, Las Palmas, Tripoli, and Tunis. These countries were forced to accept the security guards under threat of withdrawal of airline facilities by the West Germans. The Spanish government protested that this infringed upon national sovereignty, which brought the sharp answer that all flights of German aircraft to and from Spain would be immediately canceled. Spain, which relied heavily upon the German tourist trade, withdrew its protest. Even Algeria and Libya, after protesting, had to agree to this West German measure.

The Americans introduced strict security measures early at their airports, employing large numbers of security personnel for searching passengers, inspecting hand luggage, and operating electronic detection screens. The U.S. Federal Aviation Administration was convinced that the place to stop hijackers "is on the ground and not at 30,000 feet."

The Israeli El Al airline was the first one to carry armed security guards openly as a precaution against hijacking. The failure of Leila Khalid to hijack the El Al airliner in September 1970 was due to the presence of an armed security guard on board. Despite frequent hijackings, this practice was only hesitantly followed by a few other national airlines, such as Soviet Aeroflot, the Iraqi, Jordanian, Rumanian, and South African airways, and later by Pan American. Many national airlines refused to resort to this measure, mainly because of possible danger to the aircraft if there were a gunfight on board, when bullets might puncture the fuselage with disastrous results. The British were always firmly against carrying armed security guards. In July 1976, after the Entebbe hijacking, a spokesman for the British Airline Pilots Association said, "We think it is better to go along with the skyjacking and hope it will sort itself out later, rather than risk a gun battle in the cabin." After the terrorist attack in London on a bus carrying El Al crew and passengers to their hotel on 20 August 1978, in which one air hostess was killed and another injured, the Israelis applied to the British government for permission for their security guards to carry weapons all the time they were in Britain. This request was firmly rejected by the British government, and the arms of the Israeli security personnel began searching passengers (and their at London airport.

Additionally, on El Al aircraft the pilot's cabin was locked on takeoff so that no hijacker could enter it while in flight. Also, Israeli security personnel began searching passengers (and their luggage) who boarded at intermediate stops. Many aircraft have a safety device in the pilot's cabin that makes it possible to dial "We have been hijacked" as a code number on the transponder (the radio transmitter), which instantly indicates what has happened to every radar screen on the ground within range. This is something the pilot or copilot could do easily without being detected in the act by the hijackers.

Another visible means of personal security were the squads of heavily armed riot police frequently in evidence in Italy, Germany, Argentina, and other countries with serious terrorist problems. Such security forces have their limitations, and are only able to afford general protection. Individuals and nongovernmental establishments, feeling they require round-the-clock protection, tend to hire private bodyguards and security forces. Some large commercial organizations recruit and maintain what is virtually a private police force. In Italy, for example, in mid-1978 there were estimated to be 483 private police forces with over 100,000 privately hired security personnel. These private police outnumber the 82,000-strong national police force. In Germany, after the murders of Judge Drenkmann, Siegfried Buback, and Jurgen Ponto and the kidnapping and murder of Hans-Martin Schleyer, private bodyguards were in great demand.

Selective terrorism has caused potential target buildings to be given special protection, which has meant the employment of extra security staff whose task is to check the identity and business of all callers. Other visible protective measures have included the erection of blast-walls, steel shutters, burglar alarms, bulletproof glass, exterior arc lights, wire fencing, and patrols with guard dogs. In August 1978 bulletproof glass screens were erected in the area of the El Al desks in the transit sector at London airport because it was feared the personnel might be attacked by Arab terrorists. We may be entering an age of siege-mentality architecture, when buildings and factories, and indeed homes for the wealthy, those active in politics, or those engaged in the administration or enforcement of justice may be designed and constructed with protection from terrorist attacks in mind.

A great deal of money is now being spent by some nations on antiterrorist measures. El Al admitted that it spent over $14 million on security in 1974. The West German government launched a $400-million campaign against terrorism in 1977, in which the security forces were strengthened, the number of riot police increased, and five thousand more agents recruited on the federal level. Additionally, $18 million was made available to establish a permanent working group to study terrorism. In August that year the Swiss government stated it was planning to form a new security body of some three hundred specially trained men for antiterrorist duties, to avoid having to use soldiers except in extreme circumstances.

Only a very few countries, such as America, Britain, France, Holland, and Japan, have small forces specially trained to deal with a hijack or terrorist siege situation. Indeed, few others have the serious capability to cope with professional terrorists. A suggestion occasionally put forward was that the UN should recruit and train a special antiterrorist force, which could be ready to handle any terrorist hijack situation worldwide. However, as this would transgress national sovereignty, it was never really initiated. The other suggestion was that countries without the capability to deal with a hard terrorist incident could call on the services of a friendly country; but again national pride and political suspicion seemed to be the drawbacks.

Cooperation between nations on dealing with terrorists has always been touchy and difficult, but during the last two days of May 1977 senior officials of certain European countries deeply concerned by terrorist activities, and the threat of them, met in London. They made an almost secret agreement that each of the governments represented would quietly train and maintain an antiterrorist force. Additionally, they agreed to exchange information about international terrorists and antiterrorist techniques, and also to send and accept observers whenever they were faced with a terrorist situation, who would both gain experience and offer advice. In Britain, the Special Air Service Regiment (SAS) was given this role, although no official announcement was ever made to this effect. On 31 May 1977 SAS personnel went to the scene of the terrorist train siege in Holland. They offered the Dutch authorities their new British stun grenades, as yet untried. This grenade had a plastic sleeve that prevented fragments from flying outward and exploded with a blinding flash and an especially loud noise. It was designed to stun people for five or six seconds, vital ones enabling antiterrorist personnel to take action. But these were rejected by the Dutch on the grounds they might have made some of the hostages permanently deaf.

There was an exception made to the general rule of sovereign dignity in October 1977, when the Somalia authorities allowed the West German GSG-9 squad to operate at Mogadishu, where the new British stun grenades were used for the first time with great success. This was a severe blow against international terrorism. A Muslim, Marxist government had collaborated with a European democratic one, enabling it to kill or capture terrorists, who, like those at Entebbe, thought they were beyond the reach of any Western retribution. However, this surprising West German–Somalia cooperation was prompted, it was admitted, by pressure that had been brought to bear by both West Germany and Britain. Somalia was then engaged in a war with Ethiopia, and the Soviet Union had, just previously, suddenly withdrawn its military support and supplies. One can perhaps deduce that the price tag on this cooperation was the promise of Western arms and other aid to fill the void. King Khalid of Saudi Arabia, supported by President Sadat of Egypt, also brought pressure to bear on the Somalia government to cooperate. The West German government had wanted its special troops to assault the hijackers at Dubai, where the plane stayed for almost two days, but there was hesitation because the Dubai government insisted that its own soldiers should also be involved in the projected rescue. Before this difficulty had been resolved the hijacked plane had flown off to Mogadishu.

The West German antiterrorist squad was formed after the Munich Massacre of 1972 from volunteers in the Federal Frontier Force, a paramilitary organization controlled by the federal minister of the interior. In West Germany the individual states were responsible for their own internal police matters. Known as the Grennz-schutz-Gruppe Nein, or GSG-9, it was about two hundred strong. Its members were specially trained, and well-equipped with helicopters, armored vehicles, automobiles, precision weapons,

image intensifiers for night operations, radios, and the latest paratroop equipment. About sixty GSG-9 men took part in the Mogadishu rescue operation.

"There is nothing new" is the old adage of Sun Tsu, the Chinese
philosopher, who wrote his classic *Art of War* about 200 B.C. He
said, "Know your enemy and you can fight a hundred battles."
This maxim leads to the second major countermeasure against
terrorism: intelligence. This means collecting and evaluating all
possible information about terrorists, their methods, habits, contacts, colleagues, safe-houses, aims, and ambitions, just as national
police forces do about hard-core criminals. But information as
such has no value unless it is put to some good use, which in the
case of the fight against terrorism, must go beyond normal police
surveillance and detection practices.

Countries with a terrorist problem should feed all this information into a separate central computer, a computer surveillance
bank, which would enable instant information to be passed to
police at airports, ports, police stations, and other key centers
whenever required. Photographs, fingerprints, and all other details
can be flashed onto a local terminal screen within seconds. Such
an idea is slow to be adopted in Western democracies. There are
objections to so much intimate information being collected and
stored about people who need not necessarily have been convicted
of any crime. A computer surveillance bank would be a powerful
weapon if unauthorized access to it could be gained and the information used for blackmail, political or otherwise.

In West Germany the Federal Bureau of Criminal Investigation
already had a computer at Wiesbaden to help trace stolen vehicles.
This was expanded to include major criminal activities. Terrorism
in West Germany in 1975–77 resulted in permission being given to
the Bureau to compile a special bank of information about the terrorists. This computer bank is referred to as the PIOS — Personen,
Institutionen, Objekte, Sachen (meaning "persons, institutions,
movable and immovable objects"). The information now covers
over ten million pages and is catalogued and cross-referenced for
instant recall, which means there is immediate access to data that
would otherwise take days or even weeks to research.

After the Schleyer incident in 1977, this Federal Bureau initiated a new system of Target Searches, whereby small teams of detectives each concentrated upon tracing and arresting one wanted terrorist. The first real success was the arrest of Stefan Wisniewski in Paris in May 1978, and this was followed by the arrest of four others in Yugoslavia in the same month.

A computer surveillance bank to combat terrorism has been in use by the police and the British army in Northern Ireland for some time, collecting and storing information about terrorists and suspects, their background, relatives, acquaintances, homes, careers, employment, political persuasion, and general activities. This has enabled the security forces to keep close surveillance on known terrorists and suspects, and also to check instantly on unfamiliar faces that appear in any location. This has proved to be an extremely valuable aid in fighting terrorism in Northern Ireland, but it is an extremely sensitive subject to the British government, which tries to play it down as much as possible.

Furthermore, a study of terrorist information collected may allow the identification of potential victims so that they too could be warned beforehand and briefed on how to avoid capture or attack, and if captured, how to survive. Men are creatures of habit and tend to do the same things in the same way at the same time every day. For example, most men invariably leave home in the morning for the factory or office at the same time, travel by the same means by the same route, and return in the evening in the same habitual manner. It has been estimated that over 80 percent of planned terrorist attacks on individuals occur either in the morning when they are going to work or in the evening when they are returning home.

A briefing on how to avoid terrorist attacks on individuals would include advice such as to be unpredictable; to vary the route and timings; not to travel on foot alone, even from the door of the house or office to the automobile; and to have a vehicle with bulletproof windows, an earsplitting siren in case of emergency, and several rear mirrors to see any vehicle or person who appears to be following it. Also, the automobile should always have plenty of fuel so as not to have to call at a gas station unexpectedly. If a road accident is encountered, the potential victim should not pause, as it may be a deliberate fake to get him to stop.

The potential victim should have only a limited number of

trusted employees around him in the office, factory, or home, as it is from employees that terrorists obtain the vital information needed to plan an attack of kidnap. All outsiders, especially strangers, should be carefully screened, and their reasons for calling investigated. Children are frequently victims of kidnapping, so similar precautions should apply to them. They especially should be escorted to and from school and wherever else they may go.

Hostage survival briefing includes such advice as to avoid a fight in the initial attack as the victim may be injured unnecessarily; not to antagonize the terrorists, but to enter into conversation with them if possible, to try to establish some form of relationship no matter how shallow, and to collect as much information as possible. Captain Schumann, the pilot of the Lufthansa aircraft hijacked on 13 October 1977, by leaving the aircraft at Dubai, arguing with the terrorists, and refusing to carry out their instructions, obviously provoked the hijackers to kill him. Hostages have frequently identified with their captors to some degree and have even become sympathetic to their cause. The hostages should listen carefully for external sounds such as the noise of trains, traffic or aircraft, or church bells, and should memorize all details of the terrorists, as well as eavesdropping on all their conversations. The victim has to call upon all his resources of fortitude and endurance; it is the extreme test of survival.

For those unfortunate enough to be captured by terrorists, the situation need not be thought of as entirely hopeless. In fact, RAND studies over a period of years have showed that 86 percent of the victims in a kidnap or hostage situation survived, as did all the over four hundred hostages taken in the multiple hijackings to Revolution Airfield, Jordan, in September 1970. Terrorists will sometimes kill at the outset of an attack to show their capability and determination and to demonstrate their powers of destruction, but in general they seek to influence people by terror and obtain some material advantage, such as ransom money or the release of prisoners, and do not usually kill in a wholesale manner. There have, of course, been notable exceptions, such as the Lod Massacre.

One of the best counters to terrorism would be to make it unprofitable by the arrest, trial, and punishment of all involved in terrorist activities. An ideal measure would be to have a United Nations agreement, ratified by all member nations, enabling a terrorist to be arrested wherever found, regardless of where the alleged offense may have been committed, and either tried and punished by the country in which he is detained, or extradited to any state that wanted him for trial. This is a splendid idea in theory, but unfortunately it does not work in practice. America tried to instigate such a measure in the UN in 1972, but only a handful of states could be persuaded to support it.

Since 1972 several further attempts have been made to instigate a common UN agreement to combat terrorism. In 1974 the UN secretary general said that the UN could not be a mute spectator to acts of terrorism, but each time the issue was brought forward it was negated, or tabled. A UN committee has been working since 1976 on a West German proposal to outlaw terrorism, but it has not yet arrived at any satisfactory, generally acceptable solution. Many nations insisted on including special clauses. One that frequently crops up is that when arrested, terrorists should be granted Geneva Convention prisoner-of-war status, like soldiers captured in battle, regardless of what crimes they have committed.

The Hague Convention of 1970 and the Montreal Convention of 1971 obliged countries to either prosecute or return hijackers to the country in which they had committed their alleged offense. Less than half the 130-odd member countries of the International Civil Aviation Organization (ICAO) have ratified these agreements. To make them effective, all must do so.

In March 1977 yet another attempt in the UN to produce a mutually acceptable antiterrorist agreement failed after two weeks of discussions that seemed merely to emphasize the differences that divided nations on this subject. The Afro-Arab states in the UN consistently blocked measures for arresting terrorists and punishing them as criminals, insisting that terrorism should be excused if it was carried out in the name of a national liberation movement. Another drawback was that some recently independent countries feared losing their revolutionary reputation if they either supported such motions in the UN or took action against terrorists on their own soil.

Outside the UN, the most comprehensive attempt to deal with terrorism was made by the Council of Europe, which produced a Repression of Terrorism Convention, signed at Strasbourg in January 1977 by seventeen out of the nineteen member countries, Ireland and Malta abstaining. Its main object was to declare acts of terrorism to be criminal offenses and their perpetrators subject to extradition. Other countries had reservations, four (Italy, Norway, Portugal, and Sweden) declared they would not extradite for political offenses, and another five (Belgium, Denmark, France, West Germany, and Holland) said their own laws would not permit the extradition of their own nationals to a foreign country. It was to come into effect when three or more signatories had ratified it, but ratification has been slow. The nine member countries of the European Economic Community had already made an agreement among themselves to return terrorists to other countries within the Community that wanted to prosecute them. A number of terrorists have been extradited under this agreement, particularly from France and Holland to West Germany.

In April 1978, at a conference in Vienna, representatives from Austria, Italy, West Germany, and Switzerland agreed that their senior law enforcement officers should be able to exchange terrorist information rapidly by computer. They hoped to be able to expand this project to include Belgium, France, and Holland, and eventually other West European countries. This is a solid start, but many difficulties relating to differing legal systems, problems of extradition, and the varying national political climates remain.

In the continuing absence of an all-embracing UN agreement to combat international terrorism, the next best course would be to make bilateral treaties between countries that have terrorist problems and common interests in security. The one made between America and Cuba in 1969 is a good example. It drastically curtailed the incidents of hijacking of ships and aircraft from one country to the other. It fell short of what was desirable, as terrorists were granted political asylum. Another example of a bilateral treaty was one concluded in 1974 between the Soviet Union and Finland. It was put to the test in July 1977 when two Russians hijacked a Soviet aircraft and flew it to Helsinki, where they asked for political asylum. They apparently did not know of the agreement, and neither did the majority of the Soviet citizens, as it was not publicized internally by the Soviet authorities. The two Russian hijackers were returned to the Soviet Union to stand trial. More bilateral treaties of this nature should be made to work.

There can sometimes be forces within a country that hold contrary views on dealing with terrorism, especially in states that have more than one security force. In January 1977 the French DST arrested Abu Daoud, the Black September leader, in Paris, where he had secretly arrived to attend the funeral of the French PLO representative, who had been killed a few days previously. He was under the impression that the French government was deliberately turning a blind eye to his presence. Immediately both Israel and West Germany demanded his extradition. At that moment the French government was negotiating a very large arms deal with Arab states. Had Abu Daoud been handed over to the Israelis, it would have caused acute friction to develop between the French and the Arabs, which would have imperiled the arms deal. Despite Israeli and West German protests, Abu Daoud was quickly deported to Algeria and freedom. The Yugoslav government has frequently accused the West German government of deliberately turning a blind eye to the presence and activities of Croatian terrorists on German soil.

At the time of the Schleyer incident in 1977, the West German chancellor stated that there were ninety-one convicted terrorists, of whom many were serving life sentences, in prison. This brought an outcry from those in favor of capital punishment, who claimed that if these convicted terrorists had been executed there would be no terrorist problem in West Germany.

The anti-capital-punishment lobby insists that judicial execution does not cure or deter terrorism. It points to such countries as Iran, which executes a number of terrorists each year, and yet still has one of the biggest terrorist problems in the Middle East. Countries such as Iraq, Egypt, and others retain and use capital punishment for terrorism and allied offenses, as does Syria, one of the few remaining countries in the world today to carry out executions in public—but all still have terrorist problems. The Soviet Union executes criminals and also terrorists, but it still has not eliminated crime and terrorism. Such facts are used by advocates who insist that capital punishment is not the answer to terrorism, and that more humane methods must be employed, and efforts made at rehabilitation.

Israel, which has retained the death penalty only for the crimes of treason and genocide, has not yet executed a convicted terrorist, although it is admitted that several thousands are detained, some of whom have been sentenced to death. Israel's reason for not executing convicted terrorists is that it does not wish to create Palestinian martyrs, which would make good propaganda on world forums. The counterargument is that if only a handful were executed this might be the case, but as there are so many who have been convicted of capital crimes, the currency of political martyr-dom would be debased if they were executed.

A suggested solution of some interest involving capital punish-ment was put forward by Gideon Paglin, who was appointed anti-terrorist adviser to the prime minister of Israel in September 1977. Paglin suggested that a number of convicted terrorists held by the Israelis be placed in a death row cell, and whenever any Israelis were seized by terrorists anywhere in the world and were killed or died of their injuries, as happened at the Munich Massacre, an equal number of condemned terrorists would be taken from the death row cell and executed. The world waits with interest to see what effect such a measure would have.

The appointment of Paglin was an unusual one, even poetic, on the lines of the old saying, "Set a thief to catch a thief," modified to "Set a terrorist to catch a terrorist," and his remedy was novel. Paglin was a former member of the IZL, its chief of operations during the days of the Mandate, when it was led by Menachem Begin. In an interview printed in the Israeli newspaper *Yediot Aharonot* on 25 September 1977, Paglin boasted that he had planned and led over two hundred terrorist operations while in the IZL, including the explosion at the King David Hotel in ʾ lem in 1946. Paglin modestly said, "Mr. Begin had spe when he appointed me to my present position last week

Another ploy used by governments, a quite legal or to take full advantage of the slow, cumbersome pr justice during which accused persons were detained. example, it could be up to three years from the time to sentencing, and as long in Germany, or even longe case in the Baader-Meinhof trial.

The Israelis take full advantage of their laws that tion without trial and holding people incommunica pected that they carry this further than is consider the international sense. The Nairobi Five were virtually abducted to Israel, and all knowledge of them officially denied for many months. One wonders precisely where the three terrorists officially unaccounted for at the Entebbe rescue are now. Rumors are that they are also in Israeli silent detention, which causes speculation as to who else may have also disappeared into an Israeli prison. An Israeli prison official once told me that if all the Israeli prisons were opened up to neutral inspection they would be found to con-

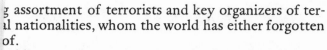

ɟ assortment of terrorists and key organizers of ter-
ıl nationalities, whom the world has either forgotten
of.

ıolding a prisoner incommunicado, especially one
:t been convicted, is obnoxious to those who believe
ɔf the individual, apprehension caused by terrorism
ı liberal and democratic governments to introduce
ive measures. The government of West Germany
iterrorist law to prevent communication between
rists and others which came into force on 2 October
ıe invoked whenever it is thought to be necessary for
y, or freedom of a person in danger." It allows those
detained to be kept in absolute isolation for up to thirty days and
to be deprived during that period of newspapers, radio, television,
visitors, and even defense lawyers. On the day this law, which was
widely criticized for its basic infringements of human rights, came
into force, eighty-nine hard-core terrorists in West German prisons
were placed in isolation cells. This severe measure had been caused
by the behavior of the denfense lawyers at the long-drawn-out
Baader-Meinhof trial, who were accused by the government of
transmitting messages and instructions from the imprisoned leadership to members of the Red Army Faction at large.

A sanctuary is almost an essential to a hijacker or his exploit becomes sterile. Although initially the Palestinian terrorists usually
had little difficulty finding airports to accept them, gradually Arab
countries began refusing to allow hijacked aircraft to land on their
territory. While this was a good sign in the struggle against terrorism
generally, it had the disadvantage of leaving some countries that had
formerly given refuge to terrorists open to terrorist reprisals. Often
diplomats from such countries were vulnerable to attack. Terrorists
branded governments that changed their policy in this respect as
traitors to whatever cause it was they had previously supported.

In September 1977, when a Japanese airliner was hijacked by
five JRA terrorists and flown to Dacca, Bangladesh, they demanded
the release of nine of their comrades from Japanese prisons and a
ransom of $6 million. The Japanese government agreed to all their
demands, which was regarded as a setback in the fight against international terrorism. Then came the problem. The hijackers had

nowhere to fly to. The Japanese government contacted twenty countries, asking them to accept the aircraft and all on board so that the hostages could be released safely. All refused. National interest reared its head; none wanted to become involved in some other country's terrorist problems. Eventually, the Japanese premier had to make a special arrangement with the Algerian government and agree that if Algeria accepted the plane and released the hostages the Japanese government would not ask for the terrorists to be extradited or for the ransom money back. The Algerian government, for its part, was not enthusiastic, as it had initially refused to become involved. It only changed its mind to avoid an open rupture with the terrorists, which might invite assassinations of Algerian diplomats abroad.

When suddenly faced with a terrorist situation—a kidnapping, an aircraft hijacking, or hostages held in a building—all too often local security forces are uncertain what tactics or techniques to employ. National methods vary considerably, depending on the attitude of the government and the capability of its security forces. West Germany, for example, has evolved a high-level crisis staff composed of ministers and security chiefs, usually headed by the chancellor, which assembles whenever a terrorist situation develops. This crisis staff has considerable powers of negotiation and decision. Israel also has the equivalent of a crisis staff. Other countries are not so well prepared, and when caught by surprise have to improvise as best they can.

National attitudes towards terrorist blackmail vary. In the multiple hijackings of September 1970, the governments of Britain, France, and Switzerland released terrorists they held in exchange for hostages. In December 1972 the Thai government allowed four terrorists a safe-conduct to Cairo for the same purpose, while in February 1974 the Singapore government gave a safe-conduct to four JRA terrorists. In Austria, in September 1973, when terrorists demanded the closure of Schonau Castle transit camp and a safe-conduct for themselves, the government agreed, despite widespread Zionist and Israeli protest. A year later the French government released Yoshiaki Yamada, the JRA terrorist, in exchange for hostages held in the French embassy at The Hague. In February 1975 the West German government released five terrorists in exchange for the safety of Peter Lorenz, and in December that year the Austrian government quickly provided an aircraft to take away the terrorists involved in the raid on OPEC headquarters and their hostages. There are many other instances when governments have tamely surrendered to terrorist blackmail in this way.

At the other extreme, certain governments, although not consistently, when faced with terrorist situations, whenever possible have taken the hard line of no compromise, putting the principle of resisting terrorist blackmail before the sanctity of individual human lives.

Dependent upon circumstances, other governments faced with terrorist situations have tried various measures that fall somewhere in between these two extremes. One method that has achieved some success was developed by the British and has been copied by other nations. It is to make the terrorist situation a long-drawn-out test of stamina, nerve, and patience, by making and keeping contact with the terrorists to begin a dialogue without alarming them or promising anything, until through sheer exhaustion and despair they surrender. Examples are the five-day Spaghetti House Siege in London in September-October 1975 and the Balcon Street Siege, also in London, in December of that year, which were both concluded successfully. Another example was the case of Tiede Herrema, a Dutch industrialist working in the Republic of Ireland, who was kidnapped on 3 October 1975. The release of three members of the Provisional IRA was demanded in exchange for his safety. The siege was brought to a successful termination by the exercise of patience on 7 November.

The attitude of the Americans, who are bedeviled by hostage situations, is officially one of no negotiation with terrorists, but with modifying variations that allow discussions, and even intercession by private individuals. Their method is very flexible and experimental.

The French authorities tend towards taking speedy action in terrorist situations, and seem determined that once a hijacked aircraft touches down on French soil, it will never depart until the problem is resolved. In the case of the Croatian hijack of August 1976, as soon as the aircraft landed at the Paris airport, French security forces immobilized it by deflating the tires with rifle shots. They then gave the hijackers the choice of either shooting it out with them or surrendering. Again, in September 1977, when a French plane on an internal flight was hijacked and brought back into Orly airport, the French security forces were quick to storm it when the hijacker showed no signs of surrendering. He was captured, but five other people were injured in the rescue, one of whom later died.

Nations have not yet found the blueprint for successfully coping with all terrorist situations, and their security forces are still at the trial and error stage. A wide and wild variety of suggestions have been put forward, many of them impractical. One of the most frequently mentioned is that gas of some type should be introduced into the aircraft or building to put the terrorists to sleep. The drawback to this suggestion is that it would take a few seconds to work, and as soon as the terrorists realized what was happening they would have time either to kill their hostages or blow up the plane or building before they became unconscious. It is considered that this method would merely drive the terrorists to desperation. Again, the amount of gas required to put a healthy terrorist to sleep might kill a child or an elderly or infirm person.

As in all things, exceptions often prove the rule. At Lahore, Pakistan, on 12 September 1976, hijackers held an aircraft with eighty-four hostages on board. When they asked for food and drink they were given drugged water, which put them to sleep and enabled the security forces to capture them without loss of life or injury. Yet another unusual counter was used on 2 March 1977 at Rome airport, when the pilot of a Spanish plane sprayed a would-be hijacker with fire-fighting foam, which made it possible to overpower him.

There is one aspect of the fight against terrorism that I feel has not been fully appreciated, and if it has, it has not been fully exploited, and that is to help a terrorist opt out of terrorism. A terrorist may have a genuine change of heart or see the error of his philosophy, but there is little he can do to take a different path, as the least sign of waning enthusiasm will be regarded with deep suspicion. Kangaroo courts mete out swift and salutary punishment to backsliders. Youthful revolutionary zeal tends to fade with marriage and middle age, and to evaporate with the futility of always being at odds with authority and forever on the run. If he leaves or attempts to leave his group, he is regarded as a traitor and his lot is certain death. He knows too much, and his group cannot allow him to fade into innocent retirement to write his memoirs (Hans-Joachim Klein may yet be the exception) like the senior government servants he hates so much.

Perhaps governments could exploit this aspect and selectively do more to help terrorists who genuinely wish to opt out of terrorism. Indeed some terrorists seem to prefer to remain in prison to serve their sentences rather than be released to return to active terrorism. There have been a number of examples. In the case of the kidnapping of Peter Lorenz, two of the six named terrorists whose freedom was demanded, Gabriele Kroecher-Tiedeman and Horst Mahler (the latter the founder of the Red Army Faction), both refused to "leave Germany in this way." However, Gabriele Kroecher-Tiedeman changed her mind, and one wonders what pressures were put on her to persuade her to stick to the thorny path of terrorism. In the JRA terrorist situations in Malaysia, in August 1975, of the seven terrorists whose release was demanded and agreed to by the Japanese government, two refused to rejoin their terrorist comrades; and again, in September 1977, three of the nine JRA terrorists refused to leave their prisons.

A revealing incident occurred in May 1976 when Hans-Joachim Klein, the terrorist who was badly wounded in the Carlos raid on the OPEC headquarters in Vienna, wrote to the West German magazine *Stern* saying that he had decided to quit terrorism when he recovered from his wound and retire to a secret hideout. But he added that he was "under great pressure to remain active." This sums up the probable desire of many terrorists the world over. The deduction must be that he who rides the tiger of terrorism cannot dismount and live. Klein may prove to be the exception to this rule too.

Finally, a few conclusions. International terrorism is still a great threat to world democracy, and its virus lurks just beneath the surface, often inactive or dormant, but still alive and festering. An epidemic may suddenly break out at any time, whenever opportunities present themselves and circumstances are favorable. In the future terrorists will be better educated and more sophisticated and technically qualified, and thus will be able to harness modern scientific aids and attempt exploits that require technological expertise. The success or otherwise of future terrorist activities will depend upon preventative measures. Incidents of terrorism have made governments aware of the problem, even though some do little or nothing about it. Generally, it has made them more security conscious, causing security to become a growth industry in democratic countries, both in the public and private sector.

The main weapon in the fight against international terrorism will be the strength of will of governments to resist blackmail. Cooperation between governments in this field is also essential, and every single opportunity should be taken to improve it, so that individual terrorists can be detected, arrested, and brought to trial. Lack of this type of cooperation only plays into the hands of the international terrorist.

The executive instrument in the fight against terrorism is the country's security and police forces, and there is considerable scope for increased efficiency in some of them. They must be equipped with all modern aids available, such as computers and electronic devices of all types, and personnel must be taught to use them to their maximum potential, and acquire the skills and techniques of intelligence gathering and assessment. Greater priority should be given to their recruitment and training, and also to compensation for their exacting task. Security forces must be kept firmly under democratic control, perhaps by an all-political-party committee, to prevent them falling into exclusive hands, or the information stored in computers being used for political advantage, blackmail, personal gain, commercial profit, or any other form of exploitation. They must be openly answerable for all their actions. Because of their vulnerable nature, some professions, appointments, and jobs, such as security forces personnel and those who work in nuclear or sensitive establishments, will have to accept certain restrictions of normal liberties and intrusions into privacy. They must accept them willingly before appointment, but they should be compensated by material or other rewards.

Governments should carefully study and apply crisis management, and should establish, perhaps as part of the crisis staff, an inspecting body or committee to monitor safeguards, essential security regulations, and contingency plans. Governments must not overreact to terrorist incidents, as they must keep public opinion on their side. Essential repressive measures should be fully explained, and not retained a moment longer than necessary. Governments must be careful not to alienate human rights or restrict freedoms, liberties, and privacy normally enjoyed.

A free press is an essential part of democracy, but all countries have some curbs to protect against libel and obscenity and to aid national security. It would be ideal if the national press could form its own representative committee, which could decide whether or not to publish details of a terrorist situation while it was in progress. Failing that, it would seem to be reasonable for democratic governments to apply *sub judice* rules similar to those in force in criminal cases. In the diplomatic field governments must work for better international cooperation, and implement agreements such as the Council of Europe's Suppression of Terrorism Convention. Detection and punishment of terrorists are two great deterrents.

How well international terrorism in future will be countered, curbed, or contained will depend mainly upon government policy, the effectiveness of security forces, and the degree of international cooperation.

Bibliography

Bar-Zohar, Michael. *Armed Prophet.* London: Davis and Poynton, 1966.

Bar-Zohar, Michael. *Spies in the Promised Land.* London: Davis and Poynton, 1972.

Becker, Jillian. *Hitler's Children: The Story of the Baader-Meinhof Gang.* London: Michael Joseph, 1977.

Ben-Hanan, Eli. *Our Man in Damascus: Eli Cohen.* New York: Steinmatsky-World Wide, 1976.

Dayan, Moshe. *The Story of My Life.* London: Weidenfeld and Nicolson, 1976.

Dobson, Christopher, and Payne, Ronald. *The Carlos Complex.* London: Hodder and Stoughton, 1977.

Forsyth, Frederick. *Day of the Jackal.* London: Hutchinson, 1971.

Guardian Newspapers. *Windscale: A Summary of the Evidence and the Argument.* London: Guardian Newspapers, 1977.

Harel, Isser. *The House on Garibaldi Street.* London: Andre Deutsch, 1975.

Hirst, David. *The Gun and the Olive Branch.* London: Faber and Faber, 1977.

Institute for the Study of Conflict. "Power and Conflict." *Annuals for the years 1974-75, 1975-76,* and *1976-77.* London: Institute for the Study of Conflict.

Khalid, Leila. *My People Shall Live.* London: Hodder and Stoughton, 1973.

Kiernan, Thomas. *Yasir Arafat.* London: Abacus Books, 1976.

Koch, Peter, and Hermann, Kai. *Assault at Mogadishu.* London: Corgi Books, 1977.

Laqueur, Walter. *Terrorism.* London: Weidenfeld and Nicolson, 1977.

Meir, Golda. *My Life.* London: Weidenfeld and Nicolson, 1975.

Ofer, Yehuda. *Operation Thunderbolt: The Entebbe Raid.* London: Penguin Books, 1976.

Phillips, David. *Skyjack: The Story of Air Piracy*. London: Harrap, 1973.

Schleifer, Abdullah. *The Fall of Jerusalem*. New York: Monthly Review Press, 1972.

Shukairy, Ahmed. *Dialogues and Secrets with Kings*. (In Arabic) Beirut, 1971.

Smith, Colin. *Carlos: Portrait of a Terrorist*. London: Sphere Books, 1976.

Stevenson, William. *90 Minutes at Entebbe*. New York: Bantam Books, 1976.

Tinnin, David B. *Hit Team*. London: Weidenfeld and Nicolson, 1976.

U.S. Central Intelligence Agency. *International and Transnational Terrorism: Diagnosis and Prognosis*. Langley, Va.: U.S. Central Intelligence Agency, 1977.

U.S. Senate Proceedings. *Terrorist Activity: Hostage Defense Measures*. Washington: July 1975.

Wilkinson, Paul. *Terrorism and the Liberal State*. London: Macmillan, 1977.

Abbreviations

AAA	Apostolic Anticommunist Alliance (Spanish)
ALF	Arab Liberation Front
ANM	Arab Nationalist Movement
AGLP	Action Group for the Liberation of Palestine
BSO	Black September Organization
BOAC	British Overseas Aircraft Corporation
CIA	U.S. Central Intelligence Agency
DPF	Democratic Popular Front (for the Liberation of Palestine)
DPA	Deutsche Presse Agentur (German)
DST	Direction de la Surveillance du Territoire (French)
FBI	U.S. Federal Bureau of Investigation
FFI	Fighters for the Freedom of Israel (Stern Gang)
FLN	Front de Liberation Nationale (Algerian)
FPS	Front for the Popular Struggle (Jabril Front)
FLOSY	Front for the Liberation of the Occupied South Yemen
GUPS	General Union of Palestinian Students
GUPW	General Union of Palestinian Workers
GRAPO	A Spanish terrorist group
GSG-9	Grennzschutzgruppe-9 (German antiterrorist force)
IATF	International Air Transport Federation
IRC	International Red Cross
IFALPA	International Federation of Airline Pilots Association

IZL	Irgun Zvai Leumi (Jewish terrorist organization)
IRA	Irish Republican Army
JRA	Japanese Red Army
KGB	Soviet secret service
MENA	Middle East News Agency
NAP	Nucleus of Armed Proletariat (Italy)
NAY	National Arab Youth (Libyan terrorist group)
NIF	National Iranian Front
NATO	North Atlantic Treaty Organization
OPEC	Organization of Petroleum Exporting Countries
PASC	Palestine Armed Struggle Command
PLA	Palestine Liberation Army
PLF	Palestine Liberation Front
PLO	Palestine Liberation Organization
PNC	Palestine National Council
PNF	Palestine National Front
PSU	Palestinian Students Union
PFLOAG	Popular Front for the Liberation of the Arab Gulf
PFLP	Popular Front for the Liberation of Palestine
PFLP–General Command	The Jabril Front—a breakaway group
RAF	Red Army Faction (German terrorist group)
R–PFLP	Revolutionary–PFLP (A breakaway group)
SAMs	Surface-to-air missiles
SAS	Special Air Service (British)
TAL	Trans-Alpine Oil Pipe Line
TAP	Trans-Arab Pipeline
TDF	Telediffusion de France (French broadcasting corporation)
TPLA	Turkish Peoples Liberation Army
UN	United Nations
UNWRA	UN Works and Relief Agency
WAFA	Palestinian News Agency

Appendix

At its fourth session, held 10 to 17 July 1968, at Cairo, the Palestinian National Council amended the National Covenant it had issued in May 1964. The following is the basis of the new one:

Article 1   Palestine is the homeland of the Arab Palestinian people; it is an indivisible part of the Arab homeland, and the Palestinian people are an integral part of the Arab nation.

Article 2   Palestine, with the boundaries it had during the British Mandate, is an indivisible territorial unit.

Article 3   The Palestinian Arab people possess the legal right to their homeland and have the right to determine their destiny after achieving the liberation of their country in accordance with their wishes and entirely of their own accord and will.

Article 4   The Palestinian identity is a genuine, essential and inherent characteristic, transmitted from parents to children. The Zionist occupation and the dispersal of the Palestinian Arab people, through the disasters which befell them, do not make them lose their Palestinian identity and their membership in the Palestinian community, nor do they negate them.

Article 5   The Palestinians are those Arab nationals who, until 1947, normally resided in Palestine regardless of whether they were evicted from it or have stayed there. Anyone born after that date, of a Palestinian father — whether inside Palestine or outside it — is also a Palestinian.

Article 6   The Jews who had normally resided in Palestine until the beginning of the Zionist invasion will be considered Palestinians.

Article 7   That there is a Palestinian community and that it has material, spiritual and historical connections with Palestine are indisputable facts. It is a national duty to bring up individual Palestinians in an Arab revolutionary manner. All means of information and education must be adopted in order to acquaint the Palestinian with his country in the most profound manner, both spiritual and material, that is possible. He must be prepared to sacrifice his wealth and his life in order to win back his homeland and bring about its liberation.

Article 8 The phase in their history which the Palestinian people are now living, is that of national struggle for the liberation of Palestine. Thus the conflicts among the Palestinian national forces are secondary, and should be ended for the sake of the basic conflict that exists between the forces of Zionism and of imperialism on the one hand, and the Palestinian Arab people on the other. On this basis the Palestinian masses, regardless of whether they are residing in the national homeland or in a diaspora, constitute — both their organizations and the individuals — the one national front working for the retrieval of Palestine and its liberation through armed struggle.

Article 9 Armed struggle is the only way to liberate Palestine. Thus it is the overall strategy, not merely a tactical phase. The Palestinian Arab people assert their absolute determination and firm resolution to continue their armed struggle and to work for an armed popular revolution for the liberation of their country and their return to it. They also assert their right to normal life in Palestine and to exercise their right to self-determination and sovereignty over it.

Article 10 Commando action constitutes the nucleus of the Palestinian popular liberation war. This requires its escalation comprehensiveness and the mobilization of all Palestinian popular and educational efforts and their organization and involvement in the armed Palestinian revolution. It also requires the achieving of unity for the national struggle among the different groupings of the Palestinian people, and between the Palestinian people and the Arab masses so as to secure the continuation of the revolution, its escalation and victory.

Article 11 The Palestinians will have three mottoes: national unity, national mobilization and liberation.

Article 12 The Palestinian people believe in Arab unity. In order to contribute their share towards the attainment of that objective, however, they must, at the present stage of their struggle, safeguard their Palestinian identity and develop their consciousness of that identity, and oppose any plan that may dissolve or impair it.

Article 13   Arab unity and the liberation of Palestine are two complementary objectives, the attainment of either of which facilitates the attainment of the other. Thus, Arab unity leads to the liberation of Palestine: the liberation of Palestine leads to Arab unity: and work towards the realization of one objective proceeds side by side with work towards the realization of the other.

Article 14   The destiny of the Arab nation, and indeed Arab existence itself, depends upon the destiny of the Palestine cause. From this interdependence springs the Arab nation's pursuit of, and striving for, the liberation of Palestine. The people of Palestine play the role of the vanguard in the realization of this sacred national goal.

Article 15   The liberation of Palestine, from an Arab viewpoint, is a national duty and it attempts to repel the Zionist and imperialist aggression against the Arab homeland, and aims at the elimination of Zionism in Palestine. Absolute responsibility for this falls on the Arab nation—peoples and governments—with the Arab people of Palestine in the vanguard.

Accordingly the Arab nation must mobilize all its military, human, and moral and spiritual capabilities to participate actively with the Palestinian people in the liberation of Palestine. It must, particularly in the phase of the armed Palestinian revolution, offer and furnish the Palestinian people with all possible help, and material and human support, and make available to them the means and opportunities that will enable them to continue to carry out their leading role in the armed revolution, until they liberate their homeland.

Article 16   The liberation of Palestine, from a spiritual point of view, will provide the Holy Land with an atmosphere of safety and tranquility, which in turn will safeguard the country's religious sanctuaries and guarantee freedom of worship and of visit to all, without discrimination of race, color, language, or religion. Accordingly, the people of Palestine look to all spiritual forces in the world for support.

Article 17   The liberation of Palestine, from a human point of view, will restore to the Palestinian individual his dignity, pride and freedom. Accordingly the Palestinian Arab people look forward to the support of all those who believe in the dignity of man and his freedom in the world.

Article 18   The liberation of Palestine, from an international point of view, is a defensive action necessitated by the demands of self-defense. Accordingly, the Palestinian people, desirous as they are of the friendship of all people, look to freedom-loving, justice-loving and peace-loving states for support in order to restore their legitimate rights in Palestine, to reestablish peace and security in the country, and to enable its people to exercise national sovereignty and freedom.

Article 19   The partition of Palestine in 1947 and the establishment of the state of Israel are entirely illegal, regardless of the passage of time, because they were contrary to the will of the Palestinian people and to their natural right in their homeland, and inconsistent with the principle embodied in the Charter of the United Nations, particularly the right to self-determination.

Article 20   The Balfour Declaration, the mandate for Palestine and everything that has been based on them, are deemed null and void. Claims of historical or religious ties of Jews with Palestine are incompatible with the facts of history and the true conception of what constitutes statehood. Judaism, being a religion, is not an independent nationality. Nor do Jews constitute a single nation with an identity of its own: they are citizens of the states to which they belong.

Article 21   The Arab Palestinian people, expressing themselves by the armed Palestinian revolution, reject all solutions which are substitutes for the total liberation of Palestine and reject all proposals aiming at the liquidation of the Palestinian problem, or its internationalization.

Article 22   Zionism is a political movement organically associated with international imperialism and antagonistic to all action for liberation and to progressive movements in the world. It is racist and fanatic in its nature, aggressive, expansionist and colonial in its aims, and fascist in its methods. Israel is the instrument of the Zionist movement, and a geographic base for world imperialism placed strategically in the midst of the Arab homeland to combat the hopes of the Arab nation for liberation, unity and progress.

Israel is a constant source of threat vis-à-vis peace in the Middle East and the whole world. Since the liberation of Palestine will destroy the Zionist and imperialist presence and will contribute to the establishment of peace in the Middle East, the Palestinian people look for the support of all the progressive and peaceful forces and urge them all, irrespective of their affiliations and beliefs, to offer the Palestinian people all aid and support in their just struggle for the liberation of their homeland.

Article 23   The demands of security and peace, as well as the demands of right and justice, require all states to consider Zionism an illegitimate movement, to outlaw its existence, and to ban its operations, in order that friendly relations among peoples may be preserved, and the loyalty of citizens to their respective homelands safeguarded.

Article 24   The Palestinian people believe in the principles of justice, freedom, sovereignty, self-determination, human dignity, and in the right of all peoples to exercise them.

Article 25   For the realization of the goals of this Charter and its principles, the Palestine Liberation Organization will perform its role in the liberation of Palestine in accordance with the constitution of this Organization.

Article 26   The Palestine Liberation Organization, representative of the Palestinian revolutionary forces, is responsible for the Palestinian Arab people's movement in its struggle — to retrieve its homeland, liberate and return to it and exercise the right to self-determination in it — all military, political and financial fields and also for whatever may be required by the Palestine case on the inter-Arab and international levels.

Article 27   The Palestine Liberation Organization shall cooperate with all Arab states, each according to its potentialities: and will adopt a neutral policy among them in the light of the requirements of the war of liberation; on this basis it shall not interfere in the internal affairs of any Arab state.

Article 28　The Palestinian Arab people assert the genuineness and independence of their national revolution and reject all forms of intervention, trusteeship and subordination.

Article 29　The Palestinian people possess the fundamental and genuine legal right to liberate and retrieve their homeland. The Palestinian people determine their attitude towards all states and forces on the basis of the stands they adopt vis-à-vis the Palestinian case and the extent of the support they offer to the Palestinian revolution to fulfill the aims of the Palestinian people.

Article 30　Fighters and carriers of arms in the war of liberation are the nucleus of the popular army which will be the protective force for the gains of the Palestinian Arab people.

Article 31　The Organization shall have a flag, an oath of allegiance and an anthem. All this shall be decided upon accordance with a special regulation.

Article 32　Regulations, which shall be known as the Constitution of the Palestine Liberation Organization, shall be annexed to this Charter. It shall lay down the manner in which the Organization and its organs and institutions shall be constituted; the respective competence of each; and the requirements of its obligations under the Charter.

Article 33　This Charter shall not be amended save by (vote of) a majority of two-thirds of the total membership of the National Congress of the Palestine Liberation Organization (taken) at a special session convened for the purpose.

Note:　The acceptance of this Covenant is a formal requirement of all members of the PLO.

Index

The words Arab(s), Israel(i)(s), Palestin(e)(ian)(s), Terror(ism)(ist)(s) are not included in this index as they are mentioned on a majority of the pages.

Abdullah, King (Hajez), 17
Abdullah, King (Jordan), 8, 17
Abedian, 82
Abu Amar (Yasir Arafat), 50, 55
Abu Daoud (Mohammed Daoud Odeh), 182-83, 190-91, 196-98, 293, 328-29
Abu Hassan (Ali Hassan Salameh), 96, 107, 178-79
Abu Iyad (Salah Khalif), 53, 144, 212, 228-29, 237, 288, 290, 292, 295-96
Abu Jihad (Khalid al-Wazir), 53, 227
Abu Khalil, 168
Abu Nidal, 196, 209, 212-13, 222, 226, 285-88, 295-96, 300
Abu Rubbah, 232, 234
Abu Sami, (Ali Ahmed Abdul Khaim), 174
Abu Yusef (Mohammed Yusef Najjar), 110, 112-13, 107-8, 175, 191, 237
Accra, Ghana, 326
Acre, Israel, 111
Action for Corsican Renaissance, 270
Action Front for the Liberation of Baltic Countries, 273

Action Group for the Liberation of Palestine (AGLP), 65, 78
Adan, General Yekutiel, 253-54
Aden, 60, 103, 135, 145, 159, 162, 164, 201, 206, 267, 305
Aden Protectorate, 164
Adwan, Kamal, 174, 177, 289
"Al Eqab," 196-97
Aeroflot (Soviet airlines), 273, 320
Afghan, 304
Aflak, Michael, 60
Africa(n)(s), 281
Agha Khan, 5
Ahmed, General al-Bagaara, 191
Ahmed, Imam (Yemen), 9
Airbus (A.300B), 319
Air France (airlines), 70, 202, 213, 244-47
Akaba, Jordan, 102
Alamut Valley, 3, 5
Aleph (squad), 172-75, 178, 225
Alexandria, 7, 32, 49, 80
Algeria(n)(s), 38, 51-53, 68-69, 91, 108, 110, 131, 133, 167, 172-73, 178, 182, 196, 199, 209, 213, 216-18, 226, 279, 296, 303, 320, 329, 332
Algiers, 68-69, 91, 168, 218, 223, 320
Al Goumbariya (Egyptian newspaper), 188
Al Hadaf (PFLP newspaper), 140, 145
Aliya, Jordanian airline, 105-6
Allenby, Bridge, 228

349

Allenby, General, 16
Allie(d)(s), 6, 17, 39
Aman (Agaf Modiin), 31, 34, 172, 230
Amelia Hotel, Athens, 195
Amersfoort, Holland, 25-26
Amin, President Idi, 124, 241-43, 245-52, 290
Amir, Rehaven, 187
Amman, Jordan, 8, 59-61, 66, 73, 80, 84, 87-89, 90, 98-99, 106, 109, 117, 165, 191
Amoozegar, Jamshid, 218
Amsterdam, 72-73, 85-86, 156, 165 167, 209, 225, 270
Anderson, Rolf, 74
Andreotti, Italian Premier, 262
Ankara, Turkey, 141, 276
Anotov (aircraft), 80
Apostolic Anti-Communist Alliance, AAA, 274
Arab Higher Committee, 19
Arab-Israeli War (1948), 7
Arab League, 244, 247, 285, 294
Arab Liberation Front, ALF, 189, 222, 237-38, 285, 292-93
Arab Nationalist Movement, ANM, 60, 75-76, 105
Arab Socialist Union (Egyptian), 82
Arafat, Yasir, 47, 50-51, 53, 55-61, 63-67, 82-83, 90, 96-100, 106-7, 110, 142, 168, 173, 175, 182, 191-92, 201, 205, 209, 211, 221-22, 226, 285, 292, 303
Arafat Trail, 95-96
ARAMCO, 101
Aref, President (Iraq), 60
Argentina(n)(s), 135, 138, 321
Arguello, Patrick, 85-86, 88, 136
Arjam, Jail Naji al, 246
Arkia (airline), 194-95
Arkoub, Lebanon, 94-96
Armenian(s), 16, 45, 275, 280
Arm of the Arab Revolution, 216-17

Ashem, Adnam Mohammed, 132
Asia(n)(s), 242, 259
Asifa (Kuwat al-Asifa), 67, 96
Assad, President Hafez al, 196, 198
"assassins," 2, 4
Assawi, Salim, 74-76
Assayed, Ali, 86
Aswan Dam, Egypt, 47
Atassi, President Nureddim, 61
Athens, 70-72, 77, 80-82, 195, 201, 244, 281, 283, 319
Atomic Energy Commission (U.S.), 312
Atrassi, Abdul Aziz, 111, 112, 188
Australia(n)(s), 282
Austria(n)(s), 40, 195, 198-99, 200-2, 215-18, 224, 236, 276, 328, 332
Austrian Airlines, 79
Avagur, Shaul, 30
Avimor, Shimon, 187
Azzawi, Riyafh al, 216, 286
"Azzoppanento," 11

Baader, Andreas, 116, 138-39, 264, 268, 301
Baader-Meinhof (Gang), 137, 139, 145, 190, 206, 214, 264-65, 268, 299, 301, 305-7, 330-31, 333
Baalbeck, Lebanon, 152
Baath(ist)(s) (Party), 54, 60, 286, 292, 300
Bab El Mendab Straits, 102-3
Badawi (refugee camp), 144, 184
Badran, Fuad Mahmoud, 108-9
Badran, Ibrahim Masoud, 123
Baghdad, 2, 5, 60, 73, 97, 170, 177, 201, 203, 213, 222-23, 267, 287, 292, 320
Baghdadi, Ahmed Zaidi Ben, 132
Baghdadi, Jawad Khalil, 108-9
Bahrein, 201, 267
Balfour Declaration, 17-18, 210-11
Banna, Hassan, 5-7

"Baraka," 184
Barges, Evelyne, 130
Barka, Ben, 174
Bar-Lev, Colonel Baruch, 247
Bar-Lev, General Haim, 247
Barnawi, Fatima, 188, 247
Bar-Zohar, Michael, 28
Basle, Switzerland, 15, 41
Batzak, Ahmed, 83
Begin, Menachem, 27, 208, 330
Beirut, 8, 51, 60, 68, 70-72, 74-77,
    79, 81, 83-84, 89, 90-92, 97-98,
    100, 103-4, 106, 109-10, 117,
    125, 129-30, 150-52, 156-57,
    162-63, 166, 168-69, 173-74,
    176-79, 180, 184-85, 189, 191,
    200, 202-3, 208, 210-11, 213-14,
    221, 224, 229-33, 237, 239, 244,
    256, 288, 293-94, 296, 318
Beit Shaul, Israel (formerly Dier
    Yassin), 26, 289
Belaziz, Ali, 91
Belg(ium)(ian), 77, 110, 113, 180,
    190-91, 276, 328
Belgrade, 164, 168, 281
Belien, Holland, 270
Ben-Gal, Joseph, 40-41
Benghazi, 156, 196
Ben Gurion, David, 22, 27, 28-31,
    33-43, 69, 74, 169, 173
Bennett, Max, 32
Berberich, Monika, 265, 301
Berim, Israel, 118
Bernadotte, Count Folke, 27-28
Berne Committee, 88-89
Bethlehem, 16,111
Bevin, Ernest, 25
Bilboa, Spain, 275
Biltmore Program, 23
Black June (Movement), 286-88,
    295-96
Black Muslim, 247, 280
Black September Organization, BSO,
    96-97, 107-11, 114-19, 122,

124-27,137,145,154,165-66,169,
    172-75, 177-83, 185, 187-98, 201,
    205, 209-10, 212, 222-28, 236-38,
    288, 293, 296, 303, 306-7, 328
Blood Oath League (Japanese), 50
Bombay, 5, 89, 168-69, 210, 319-20
Bonn, 40, 43, 77, 120, 166-67, 182,
    288, 297
Born, Jorge, 305
Born, Juan, 305
Bose, Ernst Wilfred, 137, 244-45,
    253
Bouchiki, Ahmed, 179-80
Boudia, Mohammed (Cell)(Com-
    mando), 133, 137, 139, 160-62,
    178, 183, 188-89, 206-8, 212,
    223-25, 244-45
Boumedienne, President, 133,
    218-20
Bouvier, Antonia Dages, 245-46,
    254, 257
Brandt, Chancellor, 117, 119
Brazil(ian)(s), 131, 139
Breguet, Bruno, 91, 130
Breton Liberation Front, 139, 272
Bretons, 139, 271
Briancon, France, 225
"Bricha," 29-30
Brit(ain)(ish), 5-6, 11, 17, 20-21,
    23-27, 37, 47, 71, 84, 86-89, 110,
    143, 155, 162, 164-65, 179-80,
    189, 207-11, 239, 241-43, 245,
    254, 268, 293-94, 305, 311, 313,
    317, 320-23, 325, 332
British Airline Pilots Association,
    BAPA, 320
British Overseas Air Corporation,
    BOAC, 89
Brussels, 77, 110, 136, 164, 180,
    226, 276, 294
Buback, Seigfried, 265, 321
Bucharest, 233
Budeiry, Brigadier Mahdat, 98
Buenos Aires, 165

Bukom, Singapore, 157
Bulgaria(n), 144, 281
Bundeswehr, 269
Burej, al-, Lebanon (refugee camp), 50

Cagliari, Sardinia, 199
Cagol, Margarita, 261
Cairo, 2-3, 5, 22, 32, 40-41, 43, 48, 50, 53-54, 63, 65, 79-80, 82, 108-9, 112, 160, 177, 188-89, 191, 195-96, 201, 210-11, 246, 250, 255, 332
Cairo Agreement (Jordanian), 96
Cairo Agreement (Lebanese), 196
California(n), 86
Cambodia(n)(s), 187
Cambridge, Godfrey, 258
Campbell, Diana (See Diane LeFebvre), 225
Canad(a)(ian)(s), 143, 169, 269
Capucci, Archbishop, 227-28, 236-37, 247
Caravelle (aircraft), 106, 196-97, 272
"Carlos" (Ilich Ramirez Sanchez), 156, 206-8, 212-20, 305, 319, 335
Casablanca, 53
Castro, President, 67, 136
Castro, Raul, 67
Central Africa, 239, 242
Cessna (aircraft), 199
Chandley, Peter, 254
Chatti, Habid, 211
Che Guevara cell, 244
Che Guevara Commando unit, 74
Che Guevara Intelligence Brigade, 273
Chicago, 282, 313
Chin(a)(ese), 56, 62-63, 136, 147, 308, 324
Chir, Hussein Abad al-, 173-74, 181
"Chopin Express," 198
Christian(s), 3-4, 16, 60-61, 64, 95, 111, 118, 154, 177, 184, 228, 239, 268, 283, 286, 304
Christian Democrats (Italian), 263
Chukaka (Japanese group), 159
Churchill, Winston, 17, 22
Civil Guard (Israeli), 35-36
Cohen, Baruch, 180-81
Cohen, Justice Haim, 34
Colmann, Herbert, 126
Cologne, 104, 180, 266
Colombia(n)(s), 214
"Column Six," 67
Commun(ism)(ist)(s), 145, 150, 260, 263
Como, (Italy), 224
Copenhagen, Denmark, 74, 169, 173
Coral Sea (ship), 102
Cordello, Ludovico, 133
Corsica(n)(s), 139, 271-72
Cripps, Sir Stafford, 25
Crisis Staff (German), 115-18
Croat(ian)(s), 133, 268, 329, 333
Crusade(r)(s), 3-4, 16
Cuba(n)(s), 67, 214, 278, 328
Cyprus (Cypriot)(s), 23, 84, 91, 125, 174, 181, 194-95, 201, 223, 233, 267, 283
Czechoslovakia(n)(s), 153, 165, 183, 198-99, 269, 281-82

Dacca, Bangladesh, 278-79, 319, 331
Daily Express (British), 311-12, 314
Daisuke Namba (Kozo Okamoto), 153
Dakar, 320
Damascus, 8, 54, 59, 61, 88, 75-76, 94, 100, 106, 125, 156, 162, 167-68, 176-77, 179, 184, 188, 196, 200, 203, 213, 223, 232-34, 237, 279, 286, 293

Damascus Gate (Jerusalem), 16
Dar el-Beida airport, Algeria, 68
Dassa, Robert, 32
David, King (Biblical), 5, 17
Dawson, Air Marshal Sir William, 85
Dawson's Field (see Revolution Airfield), 85
Dayan, Moshe, 20, 33, 35-36, 58, 78, 98, 112-14, 120, 171-72, 183, 199, 230-34, 294
De Gaulle, President, 38
De Gaulle airport, Paris, 282
Deir Yassin (now Beit Shaul), 26, 289
Delhi (New), India, 103, 168
"Delia," 132
Democratic Popular Front (for the Liberation of Palestine), DPF, 65-66, 80, 99, 176, 201, 222, 231-34, 236, 238, 285
Denmark, 74, 169, 328
Diaspora, 48
Dimitrov, Tsanko, 281
Dimona, Israel, 38
Direction de la Surveillance du Territoire, DST, 207-8, 225-26, 244, 328
Doumidi, Issam, 77
Draper, Morris, 99
Drenkmann, Judge Gunter von, 139, 266, 301, 324
Dresdner Bank, Germany, 265
Dreyfus (Affair) (Case), 30, 35
Druse, 95, 111
Dubai, 10, 156, 201, 210-11, 267, 323, 326
Dubrovnik, Yugoslavia, 199
Dueschike, Rudi, 138
Dusseldorf, 166, 266, 268
Dutch, 131-32, 165, 167, 200-1, 209-10, 225-26, 228, 269-71, 322, 333

"Eagles of the Palestinian Revolution," 198
East Africa(n)(s), 21, 243
East African Airways, 242
East Berlin, 118, 138, 214, 282
"Easter Commando," 130
East Europe(e)(ean)(s), 273
East Germany, 165, 282
East Indies, 269
East Jerusalem, 227
Eban, Abba, 126
Ecuador(an)(s), 156, 216, 218
Egypt(ian)(s), 2, 5-7, 15, 22, 33, 36-43, 45-47, 50, 55, 66, 74-76, 80, 82-83, 87, 94, 98, 101, 105, 108-9, 134, 168, 188-89, 192, 195-200, 211, 213-14, 237, 242, 247, 251-52, 255, 280, 287-90, 294, 297, 307, 329
Eichmann, Adolf, 37
Eid, Guy, 190-91
Eilat, 102
Ein Gev, 235
Eire, 25
El Al (airline), 68-70, 77, 80, 85-86, 126-27, 132-33, 153, 181-82, 185, 195, 197, 212-13, 224, 239, 256, 292, 319-22
Elazar, General, 176
Embaksi airport, Nairobi, 253
Eng(land)(lish), 33, 104, 115, 132, 156, 207, 225, 245, 277, 301, 306
Enotria, 130
Ensslin, Gudrun, 138, 264, 268
Entebbe (Raid), Uganda, 241, 243, 245-50, 254, 256-59, 262, 291
EOKA (Cypriot terrorist organization), 283
Erhard, Chancellor, 42
Eshkol, Levi, 36-37
Essawy, Mustafa el-, 188

Ethiopia(n)(s), 102-3, 142, 192-93, 239, 242-43, 251, 307, 323
European Command (U.S.), 138
European Community, 328
European Convention on the Repression of Terrorism, 327, 337
Euzkadi Ta Askatasuna, ETA, (Basque terrorist organization), 139, 274-75, 305
"Extra Parliamentary Opposition," 138
Eytan, Brigadier Rafael, 71

Farah, Hashi Abdullah, 249
Fascist(s), 6
Fatah (newspaper), 100
Fatah, al, 51-55, 57, 59, 61, 63-65, 68, 78, 81-82, 89, 93-95, 97-101, 103, 106-8, 110-11, 125-27, 130, 134-35, 137, 139-40, 142, 144, 164, 167-68, 173, 175, 177, 182-84, 189, 191-93, 195, 197-98, 201, 203, 222, 227-28, 237, 285, 288-92, 294, 296-97, 300
Fatahland (Arkoub), 95, 100
Fawkes, Guy, 317
Federal Aviation Administration (U.S.), 320
Federal Border Guards (German), 127
Federal Bureau of Criminal Investigation (German), 265, 324
Federal Bureau of Investigation (U.S.), FBI, 86, 181, 280
Federal Frontier Force (German), 127, 323
Fedayeen, 4-5, 8, 46-47, 49, 51-54, 56-61, 62-64, 66, 68, 70-71, 76-78, 80, 82-84, 89, 91-92, 93-94, 96-101, 103, 105, 114, 125-27, 129, 131, 133-36, 141, 144, 150, 163-64,

168-69, 174-75, 177-78, 180, 182-85, 189-90, 197, 199, 201-2, 209, 221-23, 229-31, 233-34, 236-37, 242, 256, 285, 289, 296-98, 300, 304, 307
Feinstein, Dennis, 167
Feisal, King (Saudi Arabia), 9-10, 190
Feisal II, King, 101
Fermi, Enrico, 313
Fighters for the Freedom of Israel, FFI (Stern Gang), 21
Finch, Peter, 258
Finland, 281
Firmenich, Edvardo, 137
First Israeli Bank, 181
Ford, President (U.S.), 255
France (French), 32, 38, 47, 50-51, 70, 72, 84, 110, 129-31, 133, 152, 160-62, 166, 169, 188, 173-74, 189, 196, 207-8, 212-14, 217, 224-26, 232, 235-36, 239, 244-49, 252, 256, 265, 268, 271-74, 283, 289, 294-95, 297, 309-11, 319, 322, 328-29, 332-33
France-USSR (magazine), 273
Franco, General, 273
Frankfurt, 79, 84, 103, 111, 138-39, 152, 208, 241, 261
FRAP (Spanish terrorist group), 299
Free Croats, 282
Front de Liberation Nationale (Algerian)FLN, 51
Front de Liberation Nationale de Corse, 271
Front for the Liberation of the Azores, 271
Front for the Liberation of the Occupied South Yemen, FLOSY, 134, 164
Front for the Popular Struggle (Jabril Front), FPS, 65
Furstenfeldbruck airfield (Germany), 121

Gabon, 216, 218
Gaddafi, Colonel Maummar, 82-83,
    104, 106, 109, 118, 120, 123,
    135, 189, 201, 212, 215, 219-20,
    222, 241-43, 254, 296, 303, 306
Galilee, Israel, 227, 231, 235
Galili, Israel, 172, 249
Gaza (Strip), 37, 45-50, 55, 64, 74
Gazit, General Shlomo, 230
Gazit, Mordecai, 247
Geneva, Switzerland, 68, 110, 118,
    165, 168, 195, 216-17
Geneva Conference, 202-3
Geneva Convention, 327
Genghis Khan, 5
Genscher, Dietrich, 117, 121, 124
German(s)(y) (Federal) (West), 6,
    17-18, 20, 21, 29, 32, 38-43, 50-51,
    77, 79, 82, 84-85, 87-88, 91, 103-5,
    110, 115-27, 130, 133, 137-39,
    166, 169, 171, 180, 190, 208,
    210-13, 215, 239-41, 244, 253,
    255, 264-66, 267, 269, 271, 299,
    303, 305, 306-7, 319-24, 327-32,
    335
Ghosen Brothers, 222
Gibli, Colonel Benyamin, 33-35
Gilzer, Simia, 181
Goercke, Fraulein, 40-41
Golan (Heights) (Plateau), 55, 95,
    100-1, 168, 235
GRAPO (Spanish terrorist group),
    273-75, 299
Gravier, David, 305
Gravier Affair, 305
Greater Syria, 54
Greece, 178, 195, 201-2, 223
Greek(s), 70, 81, 115, 130, 178,
    196, 227, 281, 291
Grennzschutzgruppe-9, GSG-9,
    267, 320, 334
Grey Wolves (Turkish terrorist
    group), 276
Gulf of Akaba, 291
Gulf States, 303

Gur, General, 232, 234, 250-51,
    254-55

Haag, Seigfried, 265
Haas, Monika, 241
Habash, George, 60-61, 63, 66-67,
    98, 101, 104-5, 135, 145, 150,
    155, 184, 206, 243-44, 246, 285,
    298
Hadad, Wadia, 60, 83-85, 87, 90, 98,
    101, 145, 150-51, 155, 206-7,
    214-15, 239, 243-45, 247, 255-56,
    285, 291-92
Hadassah (organization), 166
Hafez, Colonel Mustafa, 37
Haganah (Jewish Defense organiza-
    tion), 19-21, 23, 26, 29-30
Hague, Holland, 77, 160-61, 270,
    332
Hague Convention, 327
Haifa, 21, 22, 75, 224, 231, 244,
    289
Haile Selassie, 192-93, 243
Hakim, Eliahu, 22
Hakim, Jamil Abdul, 225
Halash, Therese, 111, 114-15, 188
Halla, 116
Hamburg, 110, 138
Hammad, Omar Hassan, 81
Ha-Mossad La Aliya (See Mossad),
    29
Hamouda, Yahya, 61, 63
Hamshari, Mohammed, 173-74
Haram al-Sharíf, Jerusalem, 17
Harel, Isser, 28, 30, 33-34, 37-39, 41
Hari-kari, 148
Hashomer (Watchman), 19
"Hassan," 92
Hassan, Abdul Mohsin, 73
Hassan, Ali Ahmed, 231
Hassan, Khalid, 222
Hassan, Mohammed Abu, 156
Hausner, Seigfried, 264
Hawatmeh, Nayef, 64-65, 99, 233,
    285, 298

Hawker-Siddeley (aircraft), 126
Hebron, 189, 246
Helsinki, Finland, 281, 328
Hercules (aircraft), 251, 254, 257
Heroes of the Return, 246
Hertzl, Theodore, 15
Herut (Freedom Party), 28
Herzog, Chaim, 245
Hillel, Shlomo, 230
Hindawi, Colonel Rafah, 198
Hirohito, Emperor of Japan, 153
Hiroshima, Japan, 311, 313
Histradhut (Israeli organization),
    34, 36
Hitler, Adolf, 18, 20, 23, 247
Ho Chi Minh, 76-77
Hofi, General Yitzhak, 230
Holger Meins Commando, 266
Holland, 160-61, 200, 209-10, 225,
    269-70, 322-23, 328
Holy Land, 130
Homan, Peter, 139
Hong Kong, 103, 115
Horev, General, 234
"Hundred Hours War," 48
Hussein, King of Jordan, 47, 49,
    58-59, 73, 96, 99, 105-7, 109, 124,
    188, 191, 197-98, 222, 228-29
Hussein, Talaat, 195, 202
Husseini, family, 18, 50

Idris, King of Libya, 9, 83
Ikrit, Israel, 18
India(n)(s), 5, 52, 103, 166, 210
Indonesia(n), 216, 218, 269-70
Intercontinental Hotel, Amman,
    287
International Civil Aviation Organi-
    zation, ICAO, 185, 327
International Federation of Airline
    Pilots Association, IFALPA, 76,
    114
Iran(ian)(s), 2, 3, 8, 83, 102, 115,

132, 137, 140, 216, 218-20, 223,
    244, 250, 277-78, 280, 329
Iran Liberation Movement, 140
Iraqi(i)(s), 8, 27, 55, 60-61, 63, 89,
    92, 94, 97, 103, 144, 156, 182,
    192, 195-96, 209, 211, 212-16,
    219, 222-23, 237, 247, 285-87,
    291-97, 307, 320, 329
Irbid, Jordan, 96
Ireland (Republic), 272, 307, 327,
    333
Irgun Zvai Leumi (National Mili-
    tary Organization), IZL, 20-24,
    26-28, 218, 330
Irish Republican Army, IRA, 25,
    139, 145, 268, 307
Ishikawa, Ryoko, 158
Ishmaili(s), 2-5, 7
Islam(ic), 2, 16, 93, 157
Islamabad, Pakistan, 287, 296
Islamic-Marxists, 277-78
Istanbul, 106, 142-43, 277
Ital(y)(ian)(s), 11, 115, 130, 132-33,
    172, 185, 197, 202, 223-27,
    259-63, 299, 304, 321, 328, 330
Iyad, 98-99, 107, 109

Jaber, Fayes Rahman, 246
Jabotinsky, Vladimir, Captain, 20
Jabril, Ahmed, 54, 63
Jabril Front (PFLP-General Com-
    mand), 65, 79-80, 105, 132, 135,
    222-23, 231, 238, 285, 292, 296
"Jackal" (See Carlos), 206, 220
Jadid, General Salah, 54
Jaffa, 18, 22
Jaloul, Jamor Khatib, 91
Japan(ese), 11, 147-60, 200, 235,
    278-79, 322
Japanese Airlines, 148, 156, 319
Japanese Red Army, JRA, 135,
    145, 147-51, 154-62, 179, 206,
    247, 278-79, 300-1, 308, 318-20,
    331-32, 335

"Jaru," 152-53
Jawari, Khaled Dahham al-, 182
Jebel Sheikh (Mount Hermon), 94-95
Jedda, 71, 110, 320
Jerusalem (New), 8-9, 15-19, 21, 24-27, 33-34, 45, 47-49, 57-60, 66, 76, 188, 227-28, 231, 233, 238, 247, 258, 330, 349
"Jetti," 132
Jew(s)(ish), 15-27, 29-30, 33, 37, 42, 48, 166-67, 169, 198-200, 206, 224-26, 232, 247, 249-50, 252, 291
Jewish Agency, 19-23, 181
Jewish Brigade, 22-23
Jewish Legion, 21
Jewish Settlement Police, 19-20
Johannesburg, 239
Joklik, Doctor Otto, 40-42
Jordan(ian)(s), 37, 45, 47, 49, 53-54, 56-59, 70, 77, 82-85, 87, 89, 90-91, 93-94, 95-102, 105, 107-8, 110, 115, 123, 134, 139, 144, 165, 173, 177, 180, 182, 189-90, 197-98, 222, 224-25, 228, 235, 247, 279, 320, 326
Jordan River (Valley), 48, 55, 57, 96, 99
Juan Carlos, King of Spain, 274
Judenstaat, 15, 17-18

Kakamara (Japanese Revolutionary Marxists), 159
Kalishnikov (automatic rifle), 118, 174, 239, 253, 289
Kamikaze, 148
Kampala, Uganda, 242, 247, 250, 256-57, 264
Kanafani, Ghassam, 87, 90, 145
"Kangaroo justice," 334
Kannou, Khodr, 225
Kantara, Egypt, 189
Karachi, Pakistan, 295, 320
Karameh, 57-60, 63

Karlsruhe, Germany, 265
Katanga, Congo, 69
Katiuzawa, Japan, 149
Katusha (rocket), 228, 236
Kennedy, Joseph, 103
Kennedy, Senator Robert, 9, 103, 190
Kennedy airport, New York, 181
Kenya(n)(s), 239-40, 242, 247, 251-52, 254, 256-57, 307
Kenyatta, President, 240, 242, 257
KGB (Soviet Secret Service), 133, 173-74, 178, 206-7, 209
"Khalid," 218-19
Khalid, King of Saudi Arabia, 231, 323
Khalid, Leila, 74-76, 83-89, 91-92, 116, 302, 320
Khalif, Saleh (Abu Iyad), 50-51, 53, 175, 178
Khalifa, Muntzer, 108-9
Khartoum, Sudan, 56, 189-93, 210, 251
Khartoum Conference (1967), 216, 288
"Khartoum Eight," 210-11
Khatib, Yusef, 103
King David Hotel, Jerusalem, 23-24, 228, 330
Kiryat Shimona, 167, 230-31
Kissinger, U.S. Secretary of State, 202, 228
Klein, Hans-Joachim, 215, 217-19, 319, 334-35
Kleinwachter, Doctor Hans, 40, 41
KLM (Dutch airline), 200, 225
"Knee-capping," 11
Knesset (Israeli Parliament), 35, 40-41, 171, 177
Kol Israel (Voice of Israel), 23
Krackow, Poland, 282
Kreisky, Chancellor Otto, 199, 217, 219-20

Krocher, Norbut, 215, 265
Kuala Lumpur, 167
Kuhlmann, Brigitte, 244-45, 253
Kurd(s)(ish), 141, 189, 218-19, 223
Kuwait(s), 50-51, 158-59, 177,
    195-97, 201, 203, 210, 214, 216,
    244, 261, 279, 303, 306
Kuwait, Emir of, 183
Kyoto University, Japan, 151
Labor Party (Israeli), 29
Laird, U.S. Defense Secretary, 168
Laju (ferryboat), 58
Lake Victoria, 242
Latif, Abed el-, 246
L'Aurore (French newspaper), 207
Lavon, Pinhas, 32-37
Lavon Affair, 32, 33, 37
League of Nations, 6, 17-18
Lebanese Air Lines, 184
Leban(on)(ese), 8, 25, 27, 45, 54,
    59-60, 71-72, 75, 82, 84, 91, 93-97,
    100, 114, 125, 128, 129, 134,
    145, 152, 175-77, 184, 189,
    197-99, 213, 217, 224-25, 227-29,
    233, 235-36, 276, 286-87, 289-90,
    293, 295-96, 303, 304
Leber, George, 104
Le Bourget airport, France, 196
Le Febvre, Diane, 133, 225
Le Monde (French newspaper), 212
Levi, Pinhas, 187
Levy, Captain Reginald, 111
Libya(n)(s), 83, 104, 106, 109,
    115, 118, 120, 124, 126, 133-35,
    157, 168, 172, 180, 182, 189,
    191-92, 195-97, 199, 200-1, 209,
    211-12, 214, 216, 219, 241, 243,
    245, 247, 254, 278, 296, 303,
    307, 320
Lillehammar, Norway, 179-80, 226
"Lillehammar Six," 226
Lockwood, Charles, 305
Lod, Israel, 68, 72, 74-76, 79, 93,
    110, 112-13, 130-32, 152, 155,
    188-89, 193, 229

Lod Massacre, 155, 157, 161, 170,
    229, 318
London, England, 72, 77, 86, 89,
    92, 110, 164, 168, 179, 206, 208,
    210, 217, 226-45, 266, 281, 288,
    291-94, 296-97, 311, 320-21, 333
Lorenz, Peter, 265, 268, 332, 335
Lorrach, Germany, 40
Lufthansa (airline), 103-4, 121-22,
    125-26, 135, 202-3, 266, 305, 320,
    326
Luk, Mordecai, 43

Maalot (Massacre), 31-34
MacArthur Plan, 39
Madrid, Spain, 180-81, 274, 276
Mafia, 262
Maghrabi, Dalal al, 289, 294
Mahir, Premier Ahmed, 6
Mahler, Horst, 138, 335
Mahmoud, Ahmed, 230
Majorca, 266, 274
Makarios, President (Archbishop),
    194, 283
Malabi, Mohammed, 27
Malay(a)(sia), 166-67
Malhouk, Sheikh Abdullah al-,
    190-91
Malki, Colonel Adnan, 8
Malta, 190, 201, 283, 327
Mandate of Palestine (Government),
    11, 330
Manhattan Project, 311, 314
Mansour, Mohammed Ben, 131
Mao Tse-tung, 56-57
Mapai (Party), 36
Mapam (Party), 35
Marques, Jose, 274
Marx(ist)(s), 133, 135, 139, 150,
    172, 206, 277-78, 307, 323
Marxist-Leninist, 140-41, 144, 206
Masada, Israel, 12
Masalhad, Mohammed, 115-18,
    120-23
Mauretania, 273

Mauritius, 21, 249, 251, 255
Mediterranean Sea, 156, 250
Meinhof, Ulrike, 116, 138, 264, 301
Meins, Holger, 139
Meir, Premier Golda, 30, 33, 37, 124, 171-72, 177, 181, 184, 199, 229-30, 233-34
Merk, Bruno, 117, 121
Messalia (ship), 223
Metulla, Israel, 237
Mexico City, 305
MiG(s) (Soviet aircraft), 250, 252, 254
Milan, Italy, 224, 260, 262
Mishima, Yokio, 148
Mitsukoshi Gift Shop, Paris, 151, 160
Mobutu, President (Zaire), 69
Moeller, Irmgard, 268
Mogadishu, Somalia, 244, 246, 267-68, 323-24
Mohammed, Jihad, 195, 202
Mohammed, Mahmoud, 70
"Mohammed al-Wal Said International Brigade," 273
"Molotov cocktails," 148
Molou, Uri (*See also* Cohen, Baruch), 180
Moluccans (South), 269-71
Mombassa, Kenya, 243, 256
Mondane (French/Italian frontier), 226
Montoneros, 135, 137, 299, 305
Montreal, Canada, 165
Montreal Convention, 327
Moore, George, 190-91
Mordecai, Narkis, 232
Moreau, Christopher, 130
Morocco(n)(s), 43, 66, 79-80, 202, 228-29, 237
Moscow, 198, 225, 280-81, 297
Mossad (Israeli), 30-34, 37, 39-43, 74, 86, 119, 122, 124-29, 163-65, 167-69, 171-72, 174, 178, 185, 194,

214, 221, 224-27, 229-30, 239-40, 251, 288, 295-96, 304, 306
Mosul, Iraq, 223
Mount Herman (Jebel Sheikh), 235
Movimiento de Libracion National (Uruguay), 137
Moyne, Lord, 22
Mufti (of Jerusalem), 8, 18-19, 45
Munich, Germany (Massacre), 40, 115-16, 118-21, 122, 124-25, 127, 130, 137-38, 171, 180, 182, 185, 188, 196, 281-82, 306, 308, 323, 330
Murad, Mansour, 77, 82
Muscio, Antonio, 260, 302
Muslim(s), 2-3, 139, 177, 241, 242, 278, 280, 286, 323
Muslim Brotherhood, 5-7, 37, 50-51

Nahariya, Israel, 235
Nahas, Mustafa, 6
Nahr el-Bared (refugee camp), Lebanon, 18, 189-90
Nairobi, Kenya, 239-41, 243, 250, 252, 254-55
"Nairobi Five," 241, 247, 256-57, 330
Nashashibi(s), 18-19
Nasser, Kamal, 93, 98, 175
Nasser, (President) Gamal Abdul, 7, 37-38, 46-49, 51-53, 55-56, 63, 65, 84, 92, 94-97, 104, 117, 124, 250, 291
Natason, Phillip, 32
Nathan, Abbie, 250
National Arab Youth, NAY, 194, 200-1, 208, 210-11, 222, 228, 306
National Democratic Front for the Liberation of Oman and Persian Gulf, 145
National Guard (Jordanian), 49
National Iranian Front, NIF, 135, 140, 277

National Liberation Front (Aden Party), 134
NATO, 121, 123, 143, 263, 268-69
Nazareth, 19
Nazi(s), 6, 21, 29, 37, 42
Negev, Israel, 48, 169, 250
New York, 23, 74, 84-86, 65-66, 181, 195, 212, 276, 279, 282
Nicaragua(n)(s), 86
Nicosia, Cyprus, 194
Nigeria, 216, 218
Nixon, President (U.S.), 168, 235
Northern Ireland, 11, 307, 325
North Korea(n)(s), 148, 158
Norway, 91, 179, 226, 328
Nosseiry, Mohammed, 7
Nucleus of the Armed Proletariat, NAP, 260-62, 264
Numeiry, President (Sudan), 190-91, 193, 210, 241, 251

Occupied Territories (Palestinian), 67, 101, 106, 177-78, 201, 227
October War (1973), 183, 198-99, 201, 205, 207, 222, 229-30, 258, 303
Odeh, Mohammed Daoud (Abu Daoud), 107
Office of Technology (U.S.), 313
Okamoto, Kozo, 116, 124, 152, 153-57, 188, 229, 247
Okudaira, Takeski, 151, 153, 160
Old Man of the Mountains, 3
Olympic Airlines, 81-82
Olympic Games, 115-17, 119, 127
Olympic Hotel, Nicosia, Cyprus, 174
Olympic Village, 115-16, 124
Oman(i)(s), 135, 144
Omar, Khairy Tewfik Khalid Ibrahim, 287
Omnipol (Czech arms factory), 269
Onassis, Aristotle, 81

Operation Arguello, 152
Operation Tariq, 192
Operation Thunderbolt, 251
Organization of African Unity, OAU, 242, 249, 251, 257
Organization of Petroleum Exporting Countries, OPEC, 215-17, 219, 248, 301, 305, 319, 333, 335
Oriel, Antonio, 273
Orly airport, Paris, 160, 212, 223, 239, 245, 272-73, 333
Osaka, Japan, 148
Osmanli Turks, 16
Ottoman Empire (Government) (Sultan), 16-17
Ouzai (Beirut), Lebanon, 176

Pacific Theatre (U.S.), 314
Pakistan(i)(s), 5, 11, 280, 287, 296, 334
Palestine Arab Party, 19
Palestine Armed Struggle Command, PASC, 66, 83, 97, 107
Palestine Liberation Army, PLA, 49, 60, 66, 74, 97, 285
Palestine Liberation Front, PLF, 54-55, 285, 293, 295-96
Palestine Liberation Organization, PLO, 49, 53, 55, 61, 63-67, 68, 80, 82, 90-91, 96-98, 100-102, 107, 109, 159, 164, 168, 173-75, 185, 191-92, 195, 197, 203, 209-13, 216, 221-23, 226, 236, 242, 246-48, 303-5, 329
Palestine National Council, PNC, 64-65, 93, 98, 222, 292, 303
Palestine National Covenant, 64
Palestinian National Front, PNF, 65
Palestinian Students Union, PSU, 50
Pan American (airline), Pan-Am, 86-87, 202, 228, 275, 320
Paris, France, 70, 72, 129, 133,

137, 139, 151, 156, 160, 164, 173, 178, 180, 196-97, 206-8, 213-14, 223, 225, 235-36, 244-45, 247-48, 271-73, 288, 292, 294, 325, 328, 333
Parti Populaire Syrienne, 8
Passover, Jewish Feast, 230
Patrice Lumumba University, Moscow, 206-7
Peaceful co-existence, 297
Peking, China, 63, 136
Peled, General (Israeli Air Force Commander), 253-54
Penang, Malaya, 166-67
Pension Scalighera, Rome, 152
Peres, Shimon, 3-4, 165, 249-50
Peru(vian), 67, 131, 137, 156
Petah Tikva, Israel, 57
Phantom (aircraft), 70
Phillips, John, 311
Piazza Barberini, Rome, 225
Pilz, Professor Wolfgang, 39, 42
Plambeck, Juliene, 265-66, 301
Pohle, Rolf, 137
Pol(and)(ish), 77, 282
Polisaro Front, 273
Pollock, Manfried, 218
Ponto, Jurgen, 265, 321
Popular Front for the Liberation of Palestine, PFLP, 60-61, 63-66, 67-89, 91-92, 93, 99, 101-3, 105, 111, 130-33, 135, 137, 139, 140-45, 147, 150-52, 154-60, 173-79, 184, 194, 201, 205-8, 213, 221-22, 239-41, 243-46, 256, 275, 285, 291-92, 302, 305, 308, 318
Popular Front for the Liberation of the Arab Gulf, PFLOAG, 135, 144
Port Said, Egypt, 50, 250
Portugal, 328
Powiatowski, Michel, 161, 213
Prague, Czechoslovakia, 50
Provisional Irish Republican Army, 11, 333

Qatar, 216, 303
Quatermaine, Alan, 207

Rabah, Izzat Ahmed, 108-9
Rabat (Conference), 228-29
Rabin, Yitzhak, 229-30, 234, 249, 251, 253, 255
Rachman, Mordecai, 73
Radio Beruit, 73
RAF (Royal Air Force), 84, 91, 111
Ramallah, 37
RAND Corporation (Research and Development), 326
RASD (Jehad al-), 53, 255
Raspe, Jan-Carl, 139, 264, 268
Rauf, Ahmed, 83
Raziel, David, 20
Red Army Faction, RAF (German), 135, 138-39, 264-65, 267, 331, 335
Red Brigades, 11, 260-64, 299, 301
Red Front (Israeli), 232
Red Morning Commando, 265
"Red Queen," 151
Red Sea, 102-3, 251-52
Rejection (Front) (States), 218, 297
Renard, Pierre, 215, 247
Revolution Airfield (Jordan), 87-89, 90, 96, 115, 308, 326
Revolutionary Command Council (Libyan), 83, 118
Revolutionary Council (Egyptian), 7
Revolutionary Court (PLO), 222-23
Revolutionary-PFLP, R-PFLP, 105
Reuter, Thomas, 239-40
Reuters News Agency, 110, 212, 244
Revisionist Party, 20
Rhodesia(n)(s), 133, 166, 225
"Roberto," 131
Roche, Andre, 82, 88

Rocket Projected Grenade, RPG, 89
Rogers, William, 76, 97, 168
Roman Catholic, 260, 283
Rom(e)(an), 43, 72, 74, 76, 129, 131-32, 152, 166, 172, 181, 185, 197, 201-2, 210, 225-28, 261-63, 267, 286, 301-2, 319, 334
"Rome Five," 210
Rome University, 261-62, 304
Rotblatt, Professor Jo, 314-15
Rothschild (Lord), 17
Rumania(n)(s), 232-33, 235, 320

Sabbah, Hassan ben, 3-5
Sabena (airline), 110, 113
Sadat, President (Egypt), 105, 109, 119, 197-98, 251-52, 288-90, 323
Safad, 60, 231
Saiqa (Jordanian), 224
Saiqa (Syrian), 65, 107, 185, 287
Saladin, 4
Salamah, Ali Hassan (Abu Hassan), 107
Samaria, 27
Samir, Abdullah, 123-24
SAMs (surface-to-air missiles), 197, 201, 224, 239, 241
Samuel, Sir Herbert, 18
"Samurai Nine," 148, 155
San Dorligo, Trieste, 133
Sarafand (Lebanon), 235
Sardinia, 199
SAS (Special Air Service)British, 322
Saudi, Arabia(n)(s), 9-10, 71, 101, 167, 189, 197-200, 202-3, 210, 214, 216, 218-20, 291, 293, 303, 305, 335
Saut al-Asifa, 53, 178
Saut al-Falastin, 53, 183
Savoy Hotel, Tel Aviv, 237

Scanair (airline), 153
Schiphol airport, Amsterdam, 167
Schleyer, Hans-Martin, 266-68, 321, 325, 329
Schmidt, Helmut, 255, 269
Schmuker, Ulrich, 138
Schonau Castle, Austria, 199-200, 224, 332
Schreiber, Manfred, 116, 121
Schumann, Captain Jurgen, 268, 326
Schwochat airport, Vienna, 199
Second June Movement, 135, 145, 137-39, 215
Secret Liberation Army (Turkish), 277
Seljuk (Turks), 5
Semiramis Hotel (Damascus), 286
Shaabi, President, Qahtan al-, 134
Shachori, Ami, 164
Shah of Iran, 137, 219, 277
Shalom (ship), 250
Shalom-Salaam (aircraft), 250
Shamir, Israel, 235
Sharrett, Moshe, 32
Shavit II (rocket), 38
Shemeli, Fuad, 107, 118-19, 145
Sherif, Bassam Abu, 150
Shia sect, 5, 288, 297
Shigenobu, Fusaka, 149-52, 162
Shin Beit, 31
Shiomi, Takoyu, 147-48
Shukairy, Ahmed, 49, 55, 61, 109
Sicily, 199, 261, 263
Sidon, Lebanon, 72, 101, 174, 194, 235, 237
Sinai, 47-48
Singapore, 157-59, 166, 169, 241, 332
Singapore Airlines, 244
Sirhan, Sirhan Bishara, 9, 103, 190
"Snow Murders," 149

Society of the Shield, 148
Sofia, Bulgaria, 144
Somalia, 244, 246, 248-49, 267-68, 320, 323
"Sons of the Occupied Territories," 156-57, 159
South Africa, 225
South African Airways, 320
South America(n)(s), 136, 138, 145, 152, 166, 228, 245, 259, 264, 304-5
South Moluccan (*See* Moluccan), 269-71
South Yemen, 102-4, 134, 267
"Skyjack Sunday," 318
Soviet (Union), 39, 43, 47, 52, 62-63, 82, 124, 130, 133, 136, 147, 173-74, 178, 189, 197-200, 202-3, 206, 226, 239, 241-43, 250, 254-55, 263, 272, 278, 280, 289-90, 297-98, 320, 333, 338-39
Soviet Commercial Bank of Europe, 273
Spaghetti House Siege (London), 333
Span(ish)(iards), 40, 139, 180, 273, 276, 299, 320, 334
Spears, General Sir Edward, 25
Spitfire (aircraft), 84
Spitz, Mark, 117
Springer Group (German), 138
"Squad 101" (Wrath of God), 172, 178-79, 183, 185
"Stalin organ," 266
Sterling (submachine gun), 180
Stern, Abraham, 20, 21
Stern Gang, 21-23, 25-27
Stockholm, Sweden, 74, 169, 179, 264-66, 281
Strachey, John, 25
Strasbourg, Germany, 297, 327
Streuber (factory), 110
Struma, 21

Stuttgart, Germany, 50, 264
Stuttgart-Stammheim, 264-65
Sudan(ese), 189-93, 210-11, 241-42, 251-52, 307
Suez (Canal)(Zone), 6, 33, 76-77, 84, 189, 216
Sufan, Omar, 169
Sunni sect, 4-5
Sun Tsu, 324
Supreme Council of Military Justice (Spanish), 273
Sweden (Swedes), 74, 141, 264-81, 323
Swiss, 72-74, 79-80, 82, 84-85, 87-88, 91-92, 130
Switzerland, 15, 142, 169, 247, 266, 268, 322, 328, 332
Syria(n)(s), 3-4, 8, 17, 25, 27, 45, 49, 52, 54-57, 60-61, 63, 66-68, 83, 94-95, 100, 111, 123, 134, 144, 162, 165, 192, 197-98, 200, 214, 216, 225, 233-34, 237, 247, 285-88, 297, 300, 303, 307, 329
Syrian Nationalist Party, 54

Taha, Ali Shafik Ahmed, 67, 188
Taketomo, Takahashi, 151, 160
TAL (Trans-Alpine Oil Pipeline), 133
Tal, Wasfi, 98, 100, 108-10, 177
Tannous, Rima Aissa, 111-12, 114-15, 189
Tanzania(n)(s), 242
TAP (Trans-Arab Pipeline), 101, 194
Tass (Soviet News Agency), 273
Teheran, Iran, 8, 23, 277
Tel Aviv, Israel, 21-22, 24, 84-85, 88, 132, 156, 169, 213, 221, 236-37, 239, 244, 248, 255, 289-90
Tel Zaata (Israel), 296
Tenerife, Canary Islands, 275
"Terrorist Olympiad," 129

Thailand (Thais), 187-88
Tiedeman, Gabrielle-Krocher, 268, 301, 335
Tokyo, Japan, 11, 103, 148, 151-52, 159, 279
"Toni," 116, 120, 123
Tore, Mahit, 147
Trieste, 132-33, 225
Tripartite Declaration, 47, 293
Tripoli, Lebanon, 72, 105, 144, 184, 189
Tripoli, Libya, 126, 189, 191, 218, 320
Trotsky(ist)(s), 135-36
Tschombe, Moise, 69
Tunis(ian)(s), 117, 119, 199, 210-11, 320
Tupac Amaru, 137
Tupermaros, 135, 137, 299
Turin, 261
Turin Lawyers Association, 261
Turk(ey)(s)(ish), 16-17, 19, 21, 81, 129, 141-44, 169, 189, 226, 267, 275-77, 280-81
Turkish Peoples Liberation Army, TPLA, 135, 141-45, 206, 226, 275-76
TWA (Trans World Airlines) U.S., 74, 77, 84-85, 90, 129, 195, 208
Tyre, Lebanon, 72, 234-35, 289

Uganda(n)(s), 124, 239, 241-43, 245-5, 307
Ulrike Meinhof Commando, 265
Umari, Fakhi al-, 107, 118
UN (United Nations), 25, 27-28, 45-46, 62, 74, 120, 199, 211, 222, 233, 236-37, 245, 255, 258, 282, 293, 322, 326-27
UN Emergency Force, 3
United Arab Emirates, 10, 156, 216, 224, 288
United Arab Front, 48

United Red Army (Japanese), 149
UN Security Council, 72, 76, 185, 231, 255
UNWRA (UN Works and Relief Agency), 51
Uruguay(an)(s), 115, 137, 299
U.S. 6th Fleet, 89

Vatican, 276, 278
VC-10 (aircraft), 89-90, 210
VE Day (Victory in Europe), 3
Venezuelan, 206, 216-18
Vengeance of Youth, 60
"Victory at Entebbe" (film), 258
Vienna, Austria, 110-11, 164-65, 198-99, 215-16, 219, 224, 319, 328, 335
Viet Cong, 236
Vietnam(ese) 56, 137, 267
Villascua, General, 273
Viscount (aircraft), 194-95

Wadi, Saad ad-Din (See Abu Daoud), 182
WAFA (Palestinian News Agency), 133, 157, 203
Wahdat (refugee camp), Jordan, 90-91
Waldheim, Kurt, 120, 255
Warner Brothers, 258
Warriors of Christ the King, 274
Warsaw, 282
Wazir, Khalid al- (Abu Jihad), 50-53, 107
Wehrmacht, 39
Weinrich, Johannes, 212
Weisbaden, Germany, 265, 269
Weizmann, Chaim, 22
West Banks (River Jordan), 49, 55-56, 198, 235, 298
West Berlin, 137-38, 265-66
Western Wall (Wailing Wall), 16
Westwind (aircraft), 241

Windscale Enquiry (British), 313-14
Wingate, Major Orde, 19
Winterhur, Germany, 73
World Bank, 47
World War I, 45, 276
World War II, 6, 29, 111, 147, 155
"Wrath of God" (Israeli), 172, 183, 185

Yafi, Abdulla al-, 72
Yahya, Brigadier Abdul, 97-98
Yahya, Imam of the Yemen, 9, 13
Yamami, Sheikh Ahmed Zaki, 218-19
Yamamoto, Mariko, 151, 160
Yariv, General Aharon, 86, 171, 174, 178-79, 183, 185, 229, 236
Yarmuk, Battle of, 16
Yassin, Kawaz, 191-92
Yasuda, Yasoyuki, 151, 153-54
Yediot, Aharonot (Israeli newspaper), 330
"Yellowcake" (uranium), 310
Yemen(i)(s), 2, 19, 60, 206, 266, 292-93, 307
Young Croatian Army, 282-83
Yugoslavia(n)(s), 115, 125, 132,

199, 212, 268, 281-83
"Yusef," 218
Yusef, Bisham Lutfi, 224

Zadok, Haim, 249
Zadok, Ophir, 180
Zafir al- (Egyptian rocket), 39
Zagreb, Yugoslavia, 125-26, 164
Zahrur, Fadil, 54, 65, 78
Zaire, 69
Zamir, General Zwi, 119, 125, 171, 229
Zeevi, General Rehavan, 154, 229
Zeid, Mustafa Awadh Abu, 168, 178
Zeina, Queen (Jordan), 105
Zerka, Jordan, 99
Zion(ism)(ist)(s), 15, 23-26, 29, 32, 103, 133, 166, 188, 173, 199, 208, 216-17, 230-45, 258
Zionist Congress, 15
Zionist Federation (British), 16
Zionist Movement, 15
Zurich, Switzerland, 73, 80, 84, 91
Zwaiter, Abdul, 172, 226